Kyoto

Mason Florence

Kyoto

1st edition

Published by
   Lonely Planet Publications
   Head Office: PO Box 617, Hawthorn, Vic 3122, Australia
   Branches: 150 Linden Street, Oakland, CA 94607, USA
                      10a Spring Place, London NW5 3BH, UK
                      1 rue du Dahomey, 75011 Paris, France

Printed by
   SNP Printing Pte Ltd, Singapore

Photographs by
   Mason Florence
   Martin Moos
   Chris Taylor
   Anthony Weersing
   Tony Wheeler

   Front cover: Yellow umbrellas by door, Fushimi-Inari Taisha Shrine (Carlos Navajas, The Image Bank)

First Published
   January 1999

**Although the authors and publisher have tried to make the information as
accurate as possible, they accept no responsibility for any loss, injury or
inconvenience sustained by any person using this book.**

National Library of Australia Cataloguing in Publication Data

   Florence, Mason.
   Kyoto.

   Includes index.
   ISBN 0 86442 564 3.

   1. Kyoto (Japan) – Description and travel. 2. Kyoto (Japan) – Guidebooks.
   I. Title.

915.218640449

Mason Florence

Since graduating in 1990 from the University of Colorado, Mason has been a photojournalist based in Kyoto, and a regular contributor to the *Japan Times*. When not in Kyoto, or traipsing through the Japanese countryside seeking remnants of traditional life, he disappears into South-East Asia where he explores and documents the indigenous peoples and cultures of the region.

As well as writing this 1st edition of *Kyoto*, Mason has worked on Lonely Planet's *Japan*, *Vietnam* and *South-East Asia* travel guides, and his photographs and stories have appeared in numerous books, newspapers and magazines worldwide.

From the Author

First and foremost my heartfelt thanks go to Mrs Akiko Tara, who has been a tireless companion and invaluable helping hand. I would also like to extend special thanks to Alex Kerr, Chris Rowthorn, Yasuyoshi Morimoto, Ed Gutierrez, Justin Giffin, Dominic Al-Badri, Junji Sugita, Peter Lau, Mark P Keane, Kazuhiko Miyazaki, Alexander and John, Tom Daniell, Matthias Ley, Eric Johnston, Ian Ropke and Hal Gold.

Last but not least, on behalf of the thousands of lost gaijin longing for 'old' Kyoto, a deep bow to both the Japan National Tourist Organization (JNTO) and the ever-helpful staff at the Kyoto Tourist Information Center (TIC).

This Book

Parts of this book were based on Lonely Planet's *Japan* guide, which was written by Chris Taylor, Nicko Goncharoff, Mason Florence and Chris Rowthorn.

From the Publisher

This 1st edition of *Kyoto* was coordinated and edited in Melbourne by Anne Mulvaney. It was proofed by Russell Kerr, Darren Elder and Katrina Browning.

Rachael Scott coordinated design and drew the maps, traipsing through many a backstreet and secluded temple of old Kyoto along the way. She was assisted by Anna Judd, Lyndell Taylor, Sarah Sloane and Trudi Canavan. Rachael also laid out the book.

The illustrations were drawn by several people, namely Ann Jeffrey, Trudi, Joelene Kowalski and Jenny Bowman. The cover was designed by Margie Jung. Also thanks to the Kyoto National Museum and the Tokyo National Museum.

For photographs, we are indebted to our prolific author Mason Florence, as well as Anthony Weersing, Martin Moos and Tony Wheeler.

A special thanks goes to Megan Fraser for her input on the finer points of the Japanese language and the Kyoto rail and bus systems. Thanks also to Quentin Frayne for his language expertise, and to Kristin Odijk, Pete Cruttenden and Tim Fitzgerald for their last-minute assistance.

Warning & Request

Things change – prices go up, good places go bad and bad places go bankrupt – nothing stays the same. So, if you find things better or worse, recently opened or long since closed, please tell us and help make the next edition even more accurate and useful.

We value all of the feedback we receive from travellers. Julie Young coordinates a small team who read and acknowledge every letter, postcard and email, and ensure that every morsel of information finds its way to the appropriate authors, editors and publishers. Everyone who writes to us will find their name in the next edition of the appropriate guide and will also receive a free subscription to our quarterly newsletter, *Planet Talk*. The very best contributions will be rewarded with a free Lonely Planet guide.

Excerpts from your correspondence may appear in new editions of this guide; in our newsletter, *Planet Talk*; or in updates on our Web site – so please let us know if you don't want your letter published or your name acknowledged.

Contents

Introduction

Kyoto is Japan's cultural treasure house. With an astonishing 1600 Buddhist temples, 400 Shintō shrines, a trio of palaces, and dozens of gardens and museums, Kyoto ranks as one of the most culturally rich cities on the planet. Also, more than any other city in Japan, Kyoto thrives on its ancient heritage. This is where the sought-after enchantment of old Japan can be found.

Kyoto's 40 million annual visitors come to absorb the architectural, religious and artistic heritage nestled in the foothills of the mountains that surround the city on three sides, and in the labyrinth of its narrow backstreets. The city's cultural pedigree is world renowned. In a country steeped in history and art, Kyoto houses some 20% of Japan's National Treasures; 17 of its ancient structures and gardens have been designated UNESCO World Heritage Sites.

But there is far more to this 1200-year-old city than the sights proudly paraded in the tourist brochures. Spared the onslaught of the American firebombs which annihilated Tokyo and nearby Osaka during WWII, postwar Kyoto ironically suffers from deep cultural and aesthetic wounds that have been largely self-inflicted. During the past few decades much of the city's facade has been swept away in a euphoric rush to modernise. As Kyoto struggles to reconcile development with historical preservation, this living museum seems to face the threat of extinction.

Yet appearances can also be deceiving. A cursory glance at the city centre suggests the absence of traditional architecture. It is merely out of sight, tucked away behind tall buildings and flashy storefronts. Ancient teahouses sit sandwiched between high-rise apartment buildings, sacred shrines are tucked neatly into modern shopping arcades and exquisite *kaiseki* restaurants compete for customers with a growing legion of McDonald's and pasta joints.

Filled with 'old Japan' anticipation, many flinch at their first sights of Kyoto – the ultramodern 16 storey train station complex and the jarring appearance of Kyoto Tower, the city's dominant landmark. Yet hidden in the shadow of these stark eyesores is the monumental Higashi Hongan-ji Temple, and only streets away are rows of quaint wooden houses. There is an enigmatic quality to the city born of this juxtaposition of old and new – perfectly demonstrated by the shuffling step of a latter-day geisha chattering away on a mobile phone while in pursuit of a taxi. Whether you prefer the traditional or ultramodern, this unresolved tension is undeniably part of Kyoto's allure.

Perhaps also there is hope for the city's survival in the special place Kyoto holds in the hearts of Japanese themselves. The city embodies the refined spirit of things Japanese, reflected in its 1.5 million inhabitants' immersion in the city's changing seasons – spring and autumn are the high points of celebration, when the cherry blossom and maple leaf seasons take hold of Kyotoites' imaginations.

You could spend months exploring Kyoto and still turn up new surprises. The ancient city remains elusive, and as such can be reinvented by each new visitor. Perhaps now, more than ever, is the time to visit Kyoto. Modern Kyoto presents a chequerboard of ancient and high-tech spaces, where a high-stakes game is at a critical moment. Along with the city, you will find yourself standing at a crossroads – looking back to Japan's elusive past and glimpsing what may lie ahead.

Facts about Kyoto

HISTORY
Early History

Though the origins of the Japanese race remain unclear, anthropologists believe humans first arrived on the islands via the land bridges that once connected Japan to Siberia and Korea, and by sea from the islands of the South Pacific. The first recorded evidence of civilisation in Japan is pottery fragments with cord marks *(jōmon)* produced in the Neolithic period, about 10,000 BC. During this Jōmon period, people lived a primitive existence as independent fishers, hunters and food-gatherers.

This stone age period was gradually superseded by the Yayoi era, dating roughly from 300 BC. The Yayoi people are considered to have had a strong connection with Korea and their most important developments were the wet cultivation of rice and the use of bronze and iron implements. The Yayoi period witnessed the progressive development of communities represented in more than 100 independent family clusters dotting the archipelago.

As more and more of these settlements banded together to defend their land, regional groups became larger and by 300 AD, the Yamato kingdom had emerged in the region of present-day Nara. Forces were loosely united around the imperial clan of the Yamato court, whose leaders claimed descent from the sun goddess, Amaterasu, and who introduced the title of emperor *(tennō)*. The Yamato kingdom established Japan's first fixed capital in Nara, eventually unifying the regional groups into a single state. By the end of the 4th century, official relations with the Korean peninsula were initiated and Japan steadily began to introduce arts and industries such as shipbuilding, leather-tanning, weaving and metalwork.

The Yamato period is also referred to as the Kofun period by archaeologists, who discovered thousands of ancient burial mounds *(kofun)*, mainly in western Japan.

These massive tombs contained various artefacts including tools, weapons and *haniwa*, clay figurines of people and animals which had been ceremonially buried with people of nobility. With the arrival of Buddhism, this labour-intensive custom was abandoned in favour of cremation.

Historical Periods

Historical Periods	Date
Palaeolithic	pre-10,000 BC
Jōmon	10,000-300 BC
Yayoi	300 BC-300 AD
Yamoto (Kofun)	300-710
Nara	710-94
Heian	794-1185
Kamakura	1185-1333
Muromachi	1333-1568
Azuchi-Momoyama	1568-1600
Edo (Tokugawa)	1600-1868
Meiji	1868-1912
Taishō	1912-26
Shōwa	1926-89
Heisei	1989 to present

Buddhism & Early Chinese Influence

When Buddhism drifted onto the shores of Japan, Kyoto was barely more than a vast, fertile valley. First introduced from China in 538 via the Korean kingdom of Paekche, Buddhism was pivotal in the evolution of the Japanese nation. It brought with it a flood of culture, in literature, arts, architecture, and a distinctive system of writing in Chinese characters, *kanji*. Buddhism eventually received the endorsement of the nobility and emperors, who authorised widespread temple construction and in 588, as recorded in the 8th century *Chronicle of Japan* (Nihon Shoki), Japan's first great temple complex, Asukadera, was completed.

Gradually the wealth and power of the temples began to pose a threat to the governing Yamato court, prompting reforms from

Prince Shōtoku (574-622), regent for first Empress Suiko. He set up the Constitution of 17 Articles and laid the guidelines for a centralised state headed by a single ruler. He also instituted Buddhism as a state religion and ordered the construction of more temples, including Nara's eminent Hōryū-ji Temple, the world's oldest surviving wooden structure.

Despite family feuds and coups d'état, subsequent rulers continued to reform the country's administration and laws. Previously, it had been the custom to avoid the pollution of imperial death by changing the site of the capital for each successive emperor, but in 710 this custom was altered and the capital, known as Heijō-kyō, was shifted to Nara Prefecture, where it remained for 74 years.

The prosperous Nara period (710-94) saw further propagation of Buddhism, and by the end of the 8th century the Buddhist clergy had become so meddlesome that Emperor Kammu decided to sever the ties between Buddhism and government by moving the capital. The first move occurred in 784, to Nagaoka (a suburb of Kyoto), and a decade later the capital was shifted to present-day Kyoto, where it remained until 1868.

Establishment of Heian-kyō

The Kyoto basin was first settled in the 7th century when the region was known as Yamashiro-no-kuni. The original inhabitants were immigrants from Korea, the Hata clan, who established Koryū-ji in 603 as their family temple in what is today the Uzumasa District. A major reason for Emperor Kammu proclaiming Heian-kyō as the new capital of Japan was his realisation that the city lay within a strategic natural fortress created by the rivers and mountains which surround it on three sides.

As with the previous capital in Nara, the city was laid out in accordance with Chinese geomancy in a grid pattern adopted from the Tang dynasty (618-907) capital, Chang'an (present-day Xi'an). The rectangle-shaped precincts were established west of where the Kamo-gawa River flows today. Originally

measuring 4.5km east to west and 5.3km north to south, the city was about one-third the size of its Chinese prototype. Running through the centre was Suzaku-ōji, an 85m-wide, willow-lined thoroughfare dividing the eastern (Sakyō-ku) part of the city from the west (Ukyō-ku). The northern tip of the promenade was the site of the ornate Imperial Palace and to the far south stood the 23m-high, two storey Rajō-mon Gate, over 35m wide and 10m deep.

Literally, capital of peace *(hei)* and tranquillity *(an)*, the ensuing Heian period (794-1185) effectively lived up to its name. Over four centuries, the city went beyond its post as a political hub to become the country's commercial and cultural centre. Toward the end of the 9th century contact with China became increasingly sporadic, providing an opportunity for Japan to cultivate its native culture. This produced a great flowering in literature, the arts and religious thinking, as the Japanese adapted ideas and institutions imported from China.

The development of *hiragana* (Japanese native characters) led to a popular literary trend best recalled by Murasaki Shikibu's legendary saga, *The Tale of Genji* (Genji Monogatari). This period in Kyoto's history conjures up romantic visions of riverside moon gazing parties where literati drew calligraphy and composed poetry while the aristocracy frolicked in their self-imposed seclusion.

Rivalry between Buddhism and Shintō, the traditional religion of Japan, was reduced by presenting Shintō deities as manifestations of Buddha. Religion was separated from politics, and Japanese monks returning from China established two new sects, Tendai and Shingon, that became the mainstays of Japanese Buddhism. Soon other sects were springing up and temples were being enthusiastically built.

The Heian period is considered the apogee of Japanese courtly elegance, but in the provinces a new power was on the rise – the *samurai* or warrior class, which built up its armed forces to defend its autonomy. Samurai families moved into Kyoto, where they muscled in on the court, and subsequent conflicts between rival military clans led to civil wars and strife. This was the beginning of a long period of feudal rule by successive samurai families *(shōgunates)*. This feudal system effectively lingered on for seven centuries until imperial power was restored in 1868.

From Aristocracy to Military Rule

Although Kyoto served as home to the Japanese imperial family from 794 to 1868, it was not always the focus of Japanese political power. During the Kamakura period (1185-1333), Kamakura (near present-day Tokyo) was the national capital, and again during the Edo period (1600-1868) the Tokugawa Shōgunate ruled Japan from Edo (present-day Tokyo). Still, despite the decline in influence of the imperial court, commercially the city flourished as townspeople continued manufacturing age-old traditions.

By the 12th century the imperial family had become increasingly isolated from the mechanics of political power. By the time the corrupt Fujiwara Shōgunate was eclipsed by the Taira clan, who ruled briefly before being ousted by the Minamoto family (also known as the Genji) in the epic battle of Dannoura (Shimonoseki) in 1185, the name 'Kyoto' had emerged as the common title of the city.

Minamoto Yoritomo set up his headquarters in Kamakura in 1192, while the emperor remained nominal ruler in Kyoto. Yoritomo purged members of his own family who stood in his way, but after his death in 1199 (he fell from his horse), his wife's family (the Hōjō) eliminated all of Yoritomo's potential successors and in 1213 became the true wielders of power behind the figureheads of shōguns and warrior lords.

During this era, the popularity of Buddhism spread to all levels of society. From the late 12th century, Japanese monks returning from China introduced a new sect, Zen, the austerity of which appealed particularly to the samurai class.

Meanwhile, as the spiritual fervour grew,

Japanese merchants prospered in increased trade dealings with China.

Forces beyond the sea undermined the stability of the Kamakura regime. The Mongols, under Kublai Khan, reached Korea in 1259 and sent envoys to Japan seeking Japanese submission. The envoys were expelled and the Mongols sent an invasion fleet which arrived near present-day Fukuoka in 1274. This first attack was only barely repulsed, with the aid of a typhoon, and further envoys were beheaded as a sign that the government of Japan was not interested in paying homage to the Mongols.

In 1281, the Mongols dispatched an army of over 100,000 soldiers to Japan. After an initial success, the Mongol fleet was almost completely destroyed by yet another typhoon. Ever since, this lucky typhoon has been known to the Japanese as *kamikaze* (divine wind) – a name later given to the suicide pilots of WWII.

Although the Kamakura government emerged victorious, it was unable to pay its soldiers and lost the support of the warrior class. Emperor Go-Daigo led an unsuccessful rebellion against the government and was exiled to the Oki Islands near Matsue. A year later, he toppled the government, ushering in a return of political authority to Kyoto.

Country at War

After completing his takeover, Emperor Go-Daigo had refused to reward his warriors, favouring the aristocracy and priesthood instead. In the early fourteenth century this led to a revolt by the warrior, Ashikaga Takauji, who had previously supported Go-Daigo. Ashikaga defeated the emperor in Kyoto, then installed a new emperor and appointed himself shōgun, initiating the Muromachi period (1333-1568). Go-Daigo escaped to set up a rival court at Yoshino in a mountainous region near Nara. Rivalry between the two courts continued for 60 years until the Ashikaga made a promise (which was not kept) that the imperial lines would alternate.

Kyoto gradually recovered its position of political significance, and within the sanctuary of the art-loving Ashikaga enjoyed an epoch of cultural and artistic fruition. Talents now considered typically Japanese flourished, including such arts as landscape painting, classical nō drama, flower arranging *(ikebana)* and tea ceremony *(chanoyu).*

Many of Kyoto's famous gardens date from this period, as do such monuments as Kinkaku-ji Temple (Golden Pavilion) and Ginkaku-ji Temple (Silver Temple). Eventually formal trade relations were reopened with Ming China and Korea, although Japanese

Samurai

However difficult to envision today, legendary samurai warriors once waged bloody battles on Kyoto's streets. In the Museum of Kyoto you can see painted scrolls *(e-maki)* depicting courageous sword fights and bands of costumed crusaders proudly parading along Sanjō-dōri displaying the freshly severed heads of traitors for all to heed.

The prime duty of a samurai was to give faithful service to his feudal lord. In fact, the origin of the term samurai is closely linked to a word meaning 'to serve', and this can be seen in the *kanji* (Chinese script) character for the word. Over the centuries, the samurai established a code of conduct which came to be known as *bushidō* (the way of the warrior). This code was drawn from Confucianism, Shintō and Buddhism.

Confucianism required the samurai to show absolute loyalty to his lord; toward the oppressed he was expected to show benevolence and exercise justice. Subterfuge was to be despised, as were all commercial and financial transactions. A real samurai had endless endurance, exhibited total self-control, spoke only the truth and displayed no emotion. Since his honour was his life, disgrace and shame were to be avoided above all else and all insults were to be avenged.

From Buddhism, the samurai learnt the lesson that life is impermanent, enabling him to face death with serenity. Shintō provided the samurai with patriotic beliefs in the divine status both of the emperor and of Japan, the abode of the gods.

Ritual suicide *(seppuku)* or *(harakiri)*, to which Japanese Buddhism conveniently turned a blind eye, was an accepted means of avoiding dishonour. This grisly procedure required the samurai to ritually disembowel himself before a helpful aide, who then drew his sword and lopped off the samurai's head. One reason for this ritual was the requirement that a samurai should never surrender but always go down fighting. Since surrender was considered a disgrace, prisoners received scant mercy. During WWII this attitude was reflected in Japanese treatment of prisoners of war – still a source of bitter memories for those involved.

The samurai's standard battle dress or armour (usually made of leather or lacquered steel) consisted of a breastplate, a similar covering for his back, a steel helmet with a visor, and more body armour for his shoulders and lower body. Samurai weaponry – his pride and joy – included a bow and arrows (in a quiver), swords and a dagger, and he wasn't complete without his trusty steed.

Before entering the fray, a samurai would be freshly washed and groomed, with even a dash of perfume added! The classic samurai battle took the form of duelling between individuals rather than the clashing of massed armies. In slack moments when he wasn't fighting, the samurai dressed simply but was easily recognisable by his triangular *eboshi*, a hat made from rigid black cloth.

Not all samurai were good warriors adhering to their code of conduct: portrayals of samurai indulging in double-crossing, subterfuge or outright cowardice became popular themes in Japanese theatre. ■

Unquestioning loyalty to his lord was the primary duty of the *samurai*, seen here in standard battle dress.

piracy remained a bone of contention with both.

The Ashikaga ruled, however, with diminishing effectiveness in a land slipping steadily into civil war and chaos. By the 15th century Kyoto had become increasingly divided as *daimyō* (domain lords) and local barons fought for power in bitter territorial disputes that were to last for a century. In 1467, the matter of succession to the shōgun between two feudal lords, Yamana and Hosokawa, ignited the most devastating battle in Kyoto's history. With Yamana's army of 90,000 camped in the south-west and Hosokawa's force of 100,000 quartered in the north of the city, Kyoto became a battlefield. The resulting Ōnin War (Ōnin-no-ran ;1467-77) wreaked untold havoc on the city; the Imperial Palace and most of the city was destroyed in fighting and subsequent fires and the populace left in ruin.

The war marked the rapid decline of the Ashikaga family and the beginning of the Warring Sates period (Sengoku-jidai) which lasted until the start of the Momoyama period in 1568.

Return to Unity

In 1568 Oda Nobunaga, the son of a daimyō, seized power from the imperial court in Kyoto and used his military genius to initiate a process of pacification and unification in central Japan. This manoeuvre marked the start of the short-lived Azuchi-Momoyama period (1568-1600). In 1582, Nobunaga's efforts were cut short when he was betrayed by his own general, Akechi Mitsuhide. Under attack from Mitsuhide and seeing all was lost, Nobunaga disembowelled himself in Kyoto's Honnō-ji Temple.

Nobunaga was succeeded by his ablest commander, Toyotomi Hideyoshi, who was reputedly the son of a farmer, although his origins are not clear. His diminutive size and pop-eyed features earned him the nickname Saru-san (Mr Monkey). Hideyoshi worked on extending unification so that by 1590 the whole country was under his rule and he developed grandiose schemes to invade China and Korea. The first invasion was

repulsed in 1593 and the second was aborted on Hideyoshi's death in 1598.

By the late 16th century, Kyoto's population had swelled to 500,000 and Hideyoshi was fascinated with redesigning and rebuilding the city. He transformed Kyoto into a castle town and greatly altered the cityscape by ordering major construction projects including bridges, gates and the Odoi, a phenomenal earthen rampart designed to isolate and fortify the perimeter of the city, and to provide a measure of flood control.

The rebuilding of Kyoto is usually credited to the influence of the city's merchant class, which led a citizens' revival that gradually shifted power back into the hands of the townspeople. Centred in Shimogyō, the commercial and industrial district, these enterprising people founded a self-governing body *(machi-shū)*, which contributed greatly to temple reconstruction. Over time, temples of different sects were consolidated in one quarter of the city, creating the miniature 'city of temples' *(tera-machi)*, a part of Kyoto which still exists.

The Momoyama period has been referred to as the 'Japanese Renaissance' as the arts further flourished. Artisans of the era are noted for boisterous use of colour and goldleaf embellishment, while Zen-influenced tea ceremony was developed to perfection under Master Sen no Rikyū. The performing arts also matured, along with skill in ceramics, lacquerware and fabric-dyeing. There was also a vogue for building castles and palaces on a flamboyant scale; the most impressive examples were Osaka-jō Castle, which reputedly required three years of labour by up to 100,000 men, and the extraordinary Ninomaru Palace in Kyoto's Nijō-jō Castle.

Peace & Seclusion

The supporters of Hideyoshi's young heir, Toyotomi Hideyori, were defeated in 1600 by his former ally, Tokugawa Ieyasu, at the battle of Sekigahara. Ieyasu set up his field headquarters *(bakufu)* at Edo, marking the start of the Edo (Tokugawa) period (1600-1868).

Meanwhile the emperor and court exercised purely nominal authority in Kyoto.

The Tokugawa family retained large estates and took control of major cities, ports and mines; the remainder of the country was allocated to autonomous daimyō. Tokugawa society was strictly hierarchical. In descending order of importance were the nobility, who had nominal power; the daimyō and their warriors (samurai); farmers; and, at the bottom, artisans and merchants. Mobility from one class to another was blocked; social standing was determined by birth.

To ensure political security, the daimyō were required to make ceremonial visits to Edo every alternate year, and their wives and children were kept in permanent residence in Edo as virtual hostages of the government. At the lower end of society, farmers were subject to a severe system of rules which dictated in minutest detail their food, clothing and housing.

There emerged a pressing fear of religious intrusion (seen as a siphoning of loyalty to the shōgun) and Ieyasu set out to stabilise society and the national economy. Japan entered a period of national seclusion *(sakoku)* during which Japanese were forbidden on pain of death to travel to (or return from) overseas, or to trade abroad. As efforts to 'expel the barbarians and protect the throne' spread, only Dutch, Chinese and Koreans were allowed to remain and they were placed under strict supervision.

One effect of this strict rule was to create an atmosphere of relative peace and isolation in which the native arts excelled. There were great advances in *haiku* poetry, *bunraku* puppet plays and *kabuki* theatre. Crafts such as wood-block printing, weaving, pottery, ceramics and lacquerware became famous for their refined quality. Furthermore, the rigid emphasis of these times on submitting unquestioningly to rules of obedience and loyalty has lasted to the present day.

By the turn of the 19th century, the Tokugawa government was facing stagnation and corruption. Famines and poverty among the peasants and samurai further weakened the system. Foreign ships started to probe Japan's isolation with increasing insistence and the Japanese soon realised that their outmoded defences were ineffectual. Russian contacts in the north were followed by British and American visits. In 1853, Commodore Matthew Perry of the US Navy arrived with a squadron of 'black ships' to demand the opening of Japan to trade. Other countries also moved in with similar demands.

Despite being far inland, Kyoto felt the foreign pressure, which helped bring to a head the growing power struggle between the shōgun an emperor, eventually pushing Japan back into a state of internal conflict. A surge of antigovernment feeling among the Japanese followed and Kyoto became a hotbed of controversy. The Tokugawa government was accused of failing to defend Japan against foreigners, and of neglecting the national reconstruction necessary for Japan to meet the west on equal terms. In 1867 the ruling shōgun, Keiki, resigned and Emperor Meiji resumed control of state affairs.

Under Emperor Meiji, Kyoto experienced a renewed, but short-lived, period as the centre of political power.

Emergence from Isolation

Prior to the Meiji era (1868-1912) Kyoto was under the jurisdiction of the prefectural government. With the Meiji Restoration in 1868, political power was again restored in Kyoto, but the following year the capital was transferred to Edo along with the imperial court. Political power now resided in Edo and many great merchants and scholars of the era followed the emperor. After more than a millennium as capital, the sudden changes came as a major blow to Kyoto as the population dropped dramatically and the city entered a state of bitter depression.

Kyoto quickly set its sights on revival, taking steps to secure self-autonomy and rebuild its infrastructure. It again flourished as a cultural, religious and economic centre, with progressive industrial development. By the late 1800s Kyoto led the country in education reforms by establishing Japan's first kindergarten, elementary and junior high schools and public library. In the same period the city introduced Japan's first electricity system, water system and fully functioning transportation network. In 1885, work began on the monumental Lake Biwa Canal, which in just five years made Kyoto the first Japanese city to harness hydroelectric power.

A city government system was finally formed in 1889, a factor which further strengthened Kyoto's industrial dominance. As traditional industry pushed on, research developed in the sciences, in particular physics and chemistry. Modern industries like precision machinery also grew, as did the introduction of foreign technologies like the automated weaving loom; western architectural techniques too are reflected in many of the city's Meiji-era brick and stonework buildings. In 1895, to celebrate the 1100th anniversary of the city's founding, Kyoto hosted the 4th National Industrial Exhibition Fair and established the country's first streetcar system (fuelled by the Keage Hydroelectric Plant). The same year saw the construction of the Heian-jingū Shrine (actually a five-to-eight scale replica of Daigokuden, the emperor's Great Hall of State), and the birth of the Jidai Matsuri (Festival of the Ages).

The initial stages of this restoration were resisted in a state of virtual civil war. The abolition of the shōgunate was followed by the surrender of the daimyō, whose lands were divided into the prefectures that exist today. With the transfer of the capital to Edo, now renamed Tokyo (Eastern Capital), the government was recentralised and western-style ministries were appointed for specific tasks. A series of revolts by the samurai against the erosion of their status culminated in the Saigō Uprising, when they were finally beaten and stripped of their power.

Despite nationalist support for the emperor under the slogan of *sonnō-jōi* (revere the emperor, repel the barbarians), the new government soon realised it would have to meet the west on its own terms. Promising *fukoku kyōhei* (rich country, strong military), the economy underwent a crash course in westernisation and industrialisation. An influx of western experts was encouraged to provide assistance, and Japanese students were sent abroad to acquire expertise in modern technologies. In 1889, Japan created a western-style constitution.

By the 1890s, government leaders were concerned at the spread of liberal western ideas and encouraged a swing back to nationalism and traditional values. Japan's growing confidence was demonstrated by the abolition of foreign treaty rights and by the ease with which it trounced China in the Sino-Japanese War (1894-95). The subsequent treaty nominally recognised Korean independence from China's sphere of influence and ceded Taiwan to Japan. Friction with Russia led to the Russo-Japanese War (1904-05), in which the Japanese navy stunned the Russians by inflicting a crushing defeat on their Baltic fleet at the battle of Tsu-shima Island. For the first time, the Japanese commanded the respect of the western powers.

The Pursuit of Empire

On his death in 1912, Emperor Meiji was succeeded by his son, Yoshihito, whose period of rule was named the Taishō era. When WWI broke out, Japan sided against Germany but did not become deeply involved in the conflict. While the Allies were occupied with war, the Japanese took the opportunity to expand their economy at top speed.

The Shōwa period commenced when Emperor Hirohito ascended to the throne in 1926. A rising tide of nationalism was quickened by the world economic depression that began in 1930. Popular unrest was marked by political assassinations and plots to overthrow the government. This led to a significant increase in the power of the militarists, who approved the invasion of Manchuria in 1931 and the installation of a Japanese puppet regime, Manchukuo. In 1933, Japan withdrew from the League of Nations and in 1937 entered into full-scale hostilities against China.

As the leader of a new order for Asia,

Japan signed a tripartite pact with Germany and Italy in 1940. The Japanese military leaders saw their main opponents as the USA. When diplomatic attempts to gain US neutrality failed, the Japanese drew the USA into WWII with a surprise attack on Pearl Harbor on 7 December 1941.

At first, Japan scored rapid successes, pushing its battle fronts across to India, down to the fringes of Australia and out into the mid-Pacific. But eventually the Battle of Midway turned the tide of the war against Japan. Exhausted by submarine blockades and aerial bombing, by 1945 Japan had been driven back on all fronts. In August, the declaration of war by the Soviet Union and the atomic bombs dropped by the USA on Hiroshima and Nagasaki were the final straws: Emperor Hirohito announced unconditional surrender.

Despite avoiding air raids, Kyoto suffered a great drain of people and resources during

What Really Saved Kyoto?

Kyoto's good fortune in escaping US bombing during WWII is a well publicised fact. Still, while it may provide patriotic colour for some Americans to hear that the city was consciously spared out of US goodwill and reverence for Kyoto's cultural heritage, not everyone agrees with the prevailing story.

The common belief is that Kyoto was rescued through the efforts of American scholar Langdon Warner (1881-1955). Warner sat on a committee during the latter half of the war which endeavoured to save artistic and historical treasures in war-torn regions. Now, more than a half-century later, Warner is a household name in Japan and is still alluded to in discussions on the future preservation of Kyoto. He is said to have gotten a desperate plea through to top US military authorities to spare the cities of Kyoto, Nara, Kamakura and Kanazawa.

Despite this popular account, other theories have surfaced, along with documentation pointing to an elaborate *X-Files*-style conspiracy aimed at quelling anti-American sentiment in occupied Japan. The evidence has fuelled a debate as to whether or not it was in fact a well planned public relations stunt scripted by US intelligence officials to gain the trust of a nation that had been taught to fear and hate the American enemy.

Some historians have suggested that in fact both Kyoto and Nara were on a list of some 180 cities earmarked for air raids. Kyoto, with a population of over one million people, was a prime target (along with Hiroshima and Nagasaki) for atomic annihilation and many avow the choice could easily have been Kyoto. Nara, it has been suggested, escaped merely due to having a population under 60,000, which kept it far down enough on the list not to be reached before the unconditional surrender of Japan in September 1945.

Whether the preservation of Kyoto was an act of philanthropy or a simple twist of fate, the efforts of Warner and his intellectual contemporaries are etched into the pages of history and even taught in Japanese schools. Disbelievers avow that the 'rumour' was sealed as fact for good after Warner was posthumously honoured by the Japanese government, who bestowed upon him the esteemed Order of the Sacred Treasure in recognition of his invaluable contribution to the Japanese nation. There is a symbolic tombstone placed as a memorial to Warner in the precincts of Nara's Hōryū-ji Temple. ■

the war. To prevent the spread of fires, hundreds of magnificent wooden shops and houses were torn down, and even great temple bells and statues were melted down into artillery, but thankfully most of its cultural treasures survived.

Postwar Reconstruction & Revival

Japan was occupied by Allied forces until 1952 under the command of General Douglas MacArthur. The chief aim was a thorough reform of Japanese government through demilitarisation, the trial of war criminals and the weeding out of militarists and ultranationalists from the government. A new constitution was introduced which dismantled the political power of the emperor, who completely stunned his subjects by publicly renouncing any claim to divine origins. This left him with the status of being a mere figurehead.

At the end of the war, the Japanese economy was in ruins and inflation was running rampant. A program of recovery provided loans, restricted imports and encouraged capital investment and personal saving. In 1945, the Kyoto Revival Plan was drafted and again, as had been done repeatedly in its history, Kyoto was set for rebuilding. By 1949 Kyoto University had already produced its first in a long line of Nobel Prize winners and the city went on to become a primary educational centre.

By the late 50s, trade was flourishing and the Japanese economy continued to experience rapid growth. From textiles and the manufacture of labour-intensive goods such as cameras, the Japanese 'economic miracle' had branched out into virtually every sector of society and Kyoto increasingly became an international hub of business and culture.

In 1956 Japan's first public orchestra was founded in Kyoto and two years later the city established its first sister-city relationship, with Paris. Japan was now looking seriously toward tourism as a source of income and foreign visitors were steadily arriving on tours of both business and pleasure. By this time Kyoto had further developed as a major university centre and during the 'Woodstock

era' of the late 60s, anti-war movements and Japanese flower power mirrored that of the west and brought student activism out into the streets.

In the 1970s, Japan faced an economic recession, inflation surfacing in 1974 and again in 1980, mostly as a result of steep price hikes for imported oil, on which Japan is still gravely dependent. By the early 80s, however, Japan had fully emerged as an economic superpower and Kyoto's high-tech companies were among those dominating fields such as electronics, robotics and computer technology. The notorious 'bubble economy' which followed led to an unprecedented era of free spending by Japan's 'nouveau-riche'. Shortly after the 1989 death of Emperor Shōwa and the start of the Heisei period (with the accession of the current emperor, Akihito) the miracle bubble burst, launching Japan into a critical economic downfall from which many contend it may never fully recover.

Kyoto Today & Tomorrow

The battles in Kyoto today are being fought not with swords, but with pens, as preservationists desperately struggle to save the city from local government forces which continue to ravage the natural environment and steer the skyline upward. While there

Kyoto's Sister Cities (Shimai Toshi)

City	Chronological Order of Affiliation
Paris, France	1958
Boston, USA	1959
Cologne, Germany	1963
Florence, Italy	1965
Kiev, Ukraine	1971
Xi'an, China	1974
Guadalajara, Mexico	1980
Zagreb, Croatia	1981
Prague, Czech Republic	1996

The official sister 'province' of Kyoto Prefecture is Oklahoma State, USA.

A and B: Participants in the July Gion Matsuri, Kyoto's most renowned festival. C, G and H: Celebrants at the Mifune Matsuri Festival, held on the Oi-gawa River, Arashiyama. D: *Maiko* (apprentice geisha) at Gion Matsuri. E: Preparing for the Momiji Matsuri. F: Geisha making her traditional greeting rounds in the Gion District. I: Young child out late for the Kurama-no-Hi Matsuri fire festival, Kurama.

A	B
C	D
E	F

A: Old-style transport carrying woven baskets. B: An old man in kimono waits at a bus stop. C: Selling sweets at a traditional stall in Gion. D: Relaxing outside a wooden shop, Arashiyama. E: An elderly couple strolls toward the *torii* (entrance gate) of Shimogamo-jinja Shrine, north-eastern Kyòto. F: Buddhist pilgrims at Mii-dera Temple, in the Òtsu area of Lake Biwa-ko.

UNESCO World Heritage Sites in Kyoto

In 1994, 13 of Kyoto's Buddhist temples, three Shintō shrines and one castle met the criteria to be designated World Heritage Sites by the United Nations. Each of the 17 sites has buildings or gardens of immeasurable historical value and all are open for public viewing.

Kamigamo-jinja Shrine
Shimogamo-jinja Shrine
Ujigami-jinja Shrine
Tō-ji Temple
Kiyomizu-dera Temple
Enryaku-ji Temple
Daigo-ji Temple
Ninna-ji Temple
Byōdō-in Temple
Kōzan-ji Temple
Saihō-ji Temple
Tenryū-ji Temple
Kinkaku-ji Temple
Ginkaku-ji Temple
Ryōan-ji Temple
Nishi Hongan-ji Temple
Nijō-jō Castle

have been a handful of tenuous victories in the efforts to protect Kyoto's surviving cultural heritage, such triumphs are few and far between.

Marking the 1200th anniversary of the founding of Kyoto, 1994 was a monumental year. Developers capitalised on this proud milestone by further exploiting the city. Controversy swelled over the blatant bending of city construction ordinances which allowed projects such as the Kyoto Hotel and new Kyoto station to be built higher than legal limits, setting a frightful precedent for the future.

The survival of Kyoto's true cultural substance has become a grave concern. Still, the city remains an important cultural and educational centre. Today over 60 museums and 37 universities and colleges are scattered throughout the city, and it houses more than 200 of Japan's National Treasures and nearly 1700 important Cultural Properties. Architecturally, for now, the religious structures seem out of danger. And there have been positive signs, including the notable rise in grassroots citizens movements expressing a growing appreciation for the city's remaining wooden townhouses *(kyō-machiya)*.

There is still enough existing for Kyotoites to discover worthier ways to develop their city. Other cities have already proven that with enough money anyone can construct a bland metropolis; the real challenge for Kyoto now is finding ways to cultivate a modern tradition without letting go of its roots.

GEOGRAPHY

Landlocked and surrounded by mountains to the north, east and west, the city of Kyoto sits in the south-east of Kyoto Prefecture at 135° east longitude and 35° north latitude. About 370km west of Tokyo and 45km north-east of Osaka, present-day Kyoto occupies what was once a massive lake bed. Originally the city had a total area of just 30 sq km, which in the course of the following century sprawled outward, incorporating several surrounding towns and villages. Today it covers more than 600 sq km and is divided into 11 wards. At its extremities, the total city acreage extends some 50km north to south and 25km east to west.

Though the land slopes gradually up toward the north and several small hills crop up throughout the city, the basin itself is relatively level. Kyoto has two major rivers flowing north to south, the Kamo-gawa and Katsura-gawa. Traditionally these rivers and their tributaries played a crucial role in the lives of the people, both as a means of transportation and a vital source of daily survival. The purity of the water too was highly praised for the production of Fushimi *sake* and also for use in traditional fabric-dyeing. In times of heavy rains, however, the rivers frequently wreaked havoc when major floods struck the city. Today the problem has been solved primarily by concrete reinforcement of the river banks and improved drainage.

CLIMATE

Japan is renowned for its changing scenery through four distinct seasons, and perhaps in no place else on the archipelago are the cycles of nature more clearly expressed than in Kyoto. References to Kyoto's fickle weather, caused by its valley location, have appeared in countless poems and works of literature, and consequently provide material for a large share of the daily conversation of Kyoto residents.

While this changeability is reflected in the awe-inspiring beauty of spring and autumn, Kyoto's summers and winters are severe. The humid summers can reach over 40°C while in winter the temperature frequently falls below 0°C and snow blankets the city. Kyoto even has a special local saying, 'kyo no sokobie', to convey the bone-chilling winter cold.

Even within Kyoto itself, weather patterns can vary greatly. Locals site the fork in the Kamo-gawa River at Imadegawa-dōri as a barrier which locks in a notably bitter winter climate in the north of the city. In contrast, people flock to the north when the lack of summer breezes makes the city centre unbearable. The average yearly rainfall is around 140cm, much of which arrives during the rainy season in June and brings some relief before the scorching heat of late summer sets in.

Traditional architecture has surely played a role in the attitudes of people toward the weather, as life in a wooden house with paper windows does tend to make people one with the elements. Throughout the city, this has played a conspicuous role in the transition from traditional-style homes to newer residential architecture.

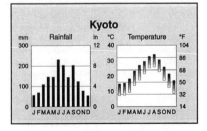

ECOLOGY & ENVIRONMENT
In the ecologically conscious 'green' 1990s Japan is frequently cast as an international vandal, slaughtering whales and dolphins, hacking down rainforests and polluting the ocean and atmosphere, all in the name of the rising yen. There is a low level of concern in Japan about environmental issues, particularly when it comes to Japanese activities which do not have an effect on life within Japan itself.

One example of this lack of environmental concern (which every visitor will soon be aware of) is the Japanese penchant for over-packaging. At a time when most western nations are trying to cut back on packaging, in Japan it's full speed ahead to wrap things in the largest possible number of layers of paper, plastic and cardboard, all tied together with string and bows. Likewise, Japan's vast number of restaurants almost all provide their customers with disposable chopsticks (waribashi).

Recycling is two-sided in Japan. On one hand, many household disposables, such as glass bottles, are efficiently recycled. On the other, Japan is the throwaway society par excellence. The severe shaken vehicle inspection system encourages car owners to constantly update their vehicles; cars more than a few years old are a rare sight on Japanese roads. There's little demand for second-hand goods and appliances, and consumer equipment is quickly replaced by the latest model. Stories abound of resident foreigners completely furnishing their homes from Japanese throwaways. Around almost any big city railway station there will be tangled heaps of perfectly good, but abandoned, bicycles.

In recent years there has been a steadily growing environmental awareness, even bordering on 'chic' among some young Japanese. Kyoto has a long history of grassroots activism and the large student population helps make it one of the country's eco-centres. Even the city government has jumped on the bandwagon, hosting an international summit on global warming in 1997 and passing a law to curb widespread littering. Still, the law

What Goes Up Must Come Down

Japan likes to burn things. It is estimated that 70% of the world's incinerators are located in this country and indeed the smokestacks seem to be everywhere: running up the sides of university buildings, on the playgrounds of schools, behind hospitals, towering over the outskirts of cities.

Trash is burned rather than buried because most of Japan is ridged with mountains. There have been attempts to dump garbage onto artificial islands near port cities such as Kōbe and Yokohama, but these sites are of limited capacity. Despite a decreasing population and scientific warnings of the potential dangers of toxic emissions from large-scale incinerators, Japan continues to burn.

In 1997 city officials in Kyoto decided to construct a supermodern incinerator in the northern mountain outskirts. Though Kyoto already has five large-scale, ageing incinerators, they claimed a new one was needed to fill the gap when the old ones were shut down for repairs.

Local residents argued that a new incinerator would not be needed if recycling efforts were boosted. They found fault with the city's environmental assessment surveys for the area and even conducted their own weather balloon tests to back up their claim that gases from the proposed incinerator could become dangerously trapped in the valley. Despite an agreement with local residents to proceed only after mutual, step-by-step consensus, the city broke its promise and began construction of the incinerator in the middle of the night.

Locals have continued to protest fiercely (while the rest of the population has remained blissfully complacent), but the plant is scheduled to be completed in five years. City officials say it will meet the strictest of European engineering and emission standards and, as a tradeoff, have promised villagers in the northern mountains new recreational facilities and cable TV that will run off the power generated by the incinerator at reduced prices – perhaps a high price to pay for better reception.

Some positive moves as far as recycling goes include a 1997 national container law to put more pressure on industry to recycle PET plastic bottles and packaging materials. And Kyoto, with a recycling rate far behind Tokyo and Nagoya, is finally planning to build a second recycling plant in 1999. ■

only applies to certain 'beautification enforcement areas' in the city, mostly around major sightseeing venues, and enforcement – imposing the ¥30,000 (maximum) fine – is still under scrutiny.

Kyoto's environmental organisations have made great efforts to focus attention on items like recycling, reducing construction of incinerators in residential areas, and the country's nuclear future (Japan's greatest concentration of nuclear power plants runs along the Sea of Japan coast north of Kyoto). Another controversial issue is urban construction, which can be environmentally unsound and obstruct views of the surrounding mountains. The 'stop idling' campaign is targeting the nationwide problem of people sleeping in parked cars, engines purring away, all in the name of providing a climate controlled environment in which to catch a bit of shuteye.

Though it is Kyoto's residents who ultimately need to own up to environmental responsibility, even short-term visitors can have an impact. Shoppers willing to do without fancy wrapping can use the simple phrase *'fukuro wa iranai desu'* to decline a bag. Carrying your own chopsticks is also a good way to save a tree and let others get the idea (you can buy a very nice pair of chopsticks with their own case for around ¥500). Anyone planning to make an extended stay should pick up a copy of the eco-friendly *Kyoto Green Map* (see the Maps section in the Facts for the Visitor chapter). Several local groups organise events like river cleanups and regular hikes in and around Kyoto, great ways to meet local residents and find your way into nature (see The Great Outdoors boxed text in the Things to See & Do chapter).

One of the best organisations to contact is the Japan Environmental Exchange (JEE), a Kyoto-based, multicultural citizens' group with representation in Tokyo and the USA. The group's office is in an old Japanese home at Kurodani-chō 25, Sakyō-ku, Kyoto 606 (near Heian-jingū; Map 10). Call or fax on ☎ 751-5404, or visit JEE's Internet home page (web.kyoto-inet.or.jp/org/s-world/jee/index.html).

Kyō-machiya

Topping the list of Kyoto's endangered species are its priceless *kyō-machiya* (wooden townhouses), with their delicate lattice-work exteriors, exquisite inner gardens and deep living traditions.

Since the end of WWII, it is estimated that some 40,000 of these irreplaceable treasures have been razed. Perhaps even more dreadful, though, is the sea of mundane concrete slabs and parking lots that has replaced them. Tragically, the Kyoto cityscape continues to slip into a uniform facade matching most other Japanese cities. Stay in Kyoto just a short time, and you will no doubt see demolition crews at work and trucks hauling loads of history away down the narrow streets.

The causes of the destruction are complex. It is partly to do with ghastly tax inheritance laws that make it cheaper to tear down an old building and replace it with an office or apartment building than to pass it on to descendants. There is also the general desire to live in less cramped, brighter spaces and widespread apathy among home owners.

Despite the losses, however, more and more people realise how much has disappeared and are starting to take action. In recent years the number of citizens' groups fighting to preserve what's left of traditional Kyoto has increased exponentially. One of the most recent battles has been over the city's controversial plan to construct a replica of Paris' Pont des Arts bridge between the Shijō and Sanjō bridges. While an overwhelming majority of Kyotoites feel this frivolous scheme is the last thing their city needs, the city government claims the project is receiving strong support.

At the forefront of the preservation movement is the International Society to Save Kyoto (ISSK), an organisation working to promote ways for the city to integrate its rich cultural heritage with development. Among its recent projects is an intriguing program called 'Art in Machiya', which urges kyō-machiya owners to open their homes for art installations and related events, helping to foster a growing appreciation for these buildings.

To learn more about ISSK, and how you can help, write to ISSK, Floor 5, Kotobuki Building, Kawaramachi Shijō-sagaru, Shimogyō-ku, Kyoto 600, or call ☎/fax 352-7225. ■

A pressing conservation issue in Kyoto is the destruction of many of the city's *kyō-machiya* (wooden townhouses), which despite increased public awareness are disappearing at an alarming rate. (Illustration courtesy of Mark P Keane.)

FLORA & FAUNA
Flora

Kyoto's valley locale, ample water supply and extreme temperature differences make it an area of diverse vegetation. The city boasts an abundance of foliage throughout the year, particularly on the fringes, in the Imperial Palace Park and at the superb Kyoto Botanical Gardens. Camellias *(tsubaki)* in winter, spring cherry blossoms *(sakura)* and lotuses *(hasu)* in summer, plus kōyō – the changing colours of the autumn maples *(momiji)* – are just a few of the hundreds of species of plant life which flourish around the city.

When Kyoto was originally being developed, the locations for temples and shrines were thoughtfully picked according to a specific place in nature which considered the existing foliage, proximity to streams and waterfalls and the potential for autumn moon viewing. These sacred places best highlight the changing of the seasons and offer endless spots to take in Kyoto's extensive array of flora.

What you see today as you travel around Kyoto is typically not what Japanese saw hundreds of years ago. Japan's natural landscape has succumbed to modern urban culture, and much of its flora is not indigenous. It is thought that some 200 to 500 plant species have been introduced to Japan since the Meiji period, mainly from Europe but with the USA becoming a major source in recent years. In Kyoto, however, many of the gardens were laid out in the Edo period or earlier and represent a great opportunity to see native Japanese flora.

Much of the region was once heavily forested and modern Kyoto is still a world of magnificent trees. Small forests surround many temples and shrines, great bamboo groves shade the walking paths of the Sagano area, and exhaustively cultivated forests of cedar (*sugi*) blanket the northern hills.

There are also several places to see fantastic old-growth trees like the 800-year-old camphors at Shōren-in Temple, gigantic pines in the precincts of Nanzen-ji and Shōkoku-ji temples, and in the Tadasu-no-mori Forest leading into Shimogamo-jinja Shrine. For anyone willing to embark on a substantial hiking route, the immense protected forest reserve in Ashyū, Miyama-chō, about an hour's drive north of Kyoto city, provides an excellent area to explore virgin forest terrain (see the Miyama-chō section in the Excursions chapter).

Fauna

Japan's one-time conjunction with the Asian continent led to a sizable migration of animals from Korea and China, and its fauna has much in common with these regions. Japan also has a number of indigenous species and Kyoto's proximity to the mountains ensures that wildlife is never far away. The hills surrounding the city are home to a large population of deer (*shika*), monkeys (*saru*) and Japan's beloved raccoon dog (*tanuki*), all of which can be spotted, especially in the north.

Perhaps the region's most popular animal is the Japanese macaque (*nihon-zaru*), a

Flower Viewing in Kyoto

Flower	Japanese	Season in bloom	Places
Azaleas	*tsutsuji*	late April to late June	Shōren-in Temple, Manshu-in Temple, Shōden-ji Temple, Chishaku-in Temple, Shisen-dō Temple, banks of Hozu-gawa River
Hydrangeas	*ajisai*	late May to mid-July	Sanzen-in Temple, Fujinomori-jinja Shrine, Tō-ji Temple, Shisen-dō Temple, Jakkō-in Temple, Nison-in Temple
Water lilies	*suiren*	early June to early July	Ryōan-ji Temple, Kanshū-ji Temple, Heian-jingū Shrine, Ōharano-jinja Shrine, Tōfuku-ji Temple
Wisteria and irises	*fuji* and *ayame* or *shōbu*	late May to mid-June	Heian-jingū Shrine, Byōdō-in Temple, Umemiya-taisha Shrine, Hokongo-in Temple, Shisen-dō Temple
Lotuses	*hasu*	mid-July	Hokongo-in Temple, Heian-jingū Shrine, Kajū-ji Temple
Bush clover	*hagi*	mid to late September	Nanzen-ji Temple, Heian-jingū Shrine, Nashinoki-jinja Shrine
Chrysanthemum	*kiku*	October and November	Kyoto Botanical Gardens, Arashiyama area, Daikaku-ji Temple, Fushimi Momoyama-jō Castle

Three Beloved Trees

The Japanese affinity for 'viewing nature' comes in many forms. Probably the most prevalent form involves reflecting on the changing beauty of the trees which fortify the Japanese islands from the elements. For anyone visiting during seasonal blossom times, the ritual of viewing the metamorphosis is not to be missed. In keeping with the Japanese custom of categorising attractions into 'threes', here is a brief rundown on Kyoto's most adored trees: plum, cherry and maple. Dispersed throughout the city, from jam-packed temples to secluded mountain paths, Kyoto offers some of the best spots in Japan to join the seasonal spectacle.

Japanese Plum The arrival in late February of the fragrant pink flowers on Kyoto's plum trees *(ume)* is one of nature's eloquent signs that spring is trying to find its way through the tail end of winter. Plum trees are believed to have arrived from China in the 8th century and were warmly adopted in Japan as protective charms against evil. As with other forms of 'shrubbery talismans' *(o-momori)*, these trees are typically found near the north-east corner of gardens, from where evil spirits are believed to enter peoples' lives. Another daily preventative measure for disabling misfortune involves eating the super-sour pickled version of the Japanese plum *(ume-boshi)* with breakfast (if you can survive the biting, tart flavour, you should be able to endure anything!).

One of the best days of the year to see plum trees in bloom is during the 25 February Baika-sai Festival at Kitano-Tenman-gū Shrine (see the Festivals boxed text in the Facts for the Visitor chapter). Other popular viewing spots are the Imperial Palace Park, Zuishin-in Temple, Nijō-jō Castle and Seiryō-ji Temple.

Cherry Tree With the beginning of April comes cherry blossom *(sakura)* season, when the telltale pink and white flowers of Japan's indigenous cherry trees bloom throughout the city. Triumphant messengers of spring, the blossoms celebrate their coming by preparing bean-filled *sakura-mochi*, exquisite pink-coloured rice cakes carefully wrapped in the leaves from neighbourhood cherry trees.

Thousands flock daily to stare in awe at the tremendous branches of Kyoto's most beloved cherry tree, the Gion shidare-zakura, in Maruyama-kōen Park, the site of the city's largest cherry blossom viewing *(hanami)* parties.

Groves of sakura can also be viewed in the Imperial Palace Park, along the Tetsugaku-no-michi (Path of Philosophy), the banks of the Kamo-gawa River, at Nijō-jō, the Arashiyama area, Heian-jingū Shrine, and Ninna-ji, Kiyomizu-dera, Daikaku-ji and Daigo-ji temples.

Japanese Maple Chances are most westerners have never tasted a tempura-fried red maple leaf, but autumn visitors with a yen for culinary adventure should not pass up the prospect. When the first frigid breezes of late autumn sweep down into the valley from the north, *kōyō* (the changing of the autumn foliage) transforms Kyoto's countless Japanese maples *(momiji)* into a breathtaking spectrum of vibrant colour.

Momiji season is an ideal time for walking the mountain trails of Kyoto, as nearly every place you reach will be teeming with maples. Popular kōyō viewing spots include the Arashiyama/Sagano district, the Kurama/Kibune area, Ōhara, and Mt Yoshida-yama, as well as Kiyomizu-dera, Eikan-dō, Nanzen-ji and Tōfuku-ji temples. ■

MARTIN MOOS

In eastern Kyoto, Maruyama-kōen Park is a favourite location of locals and tourists alike for viewing the riotous colour of the cherry blossoms in spring.

medium-sized monkey inhabiting Honshū, Shikoku and Kyūshū. It averages around 60cm in length and has a short tail. If you don't have the time to spend romping the hills in search of the wily critters, you can see their antics at the Iwatayama Monkey Park (see the Arashiyama-Sagano District section in the Things to See & Do chapter).

Other wildlife roaming the Kyoto hills includes rabbits *(usagi)*, foxes *(kitsune)*, weasels *(itachi)* and serow *(kamoshika)*, Japan's indigenous mountain goat. Hunting season for several regional species lasts from mid-November to mid-February, and hikers venturing beyond well travelled trails should take caution not to be mistaken for possible game, eg wear bright-coloured clothing, although the actual danger of being fired upon or attacked by any animal is slim.

Deep into Kyoto's northern mountains is a large populace of wild boar *(inoshishi)*, and on occasion they have even found their way into the city. Boar meat is widely enjoyed in winter stew *(botan-nabe)*, but the hunter faces a risky occupation; the rounded tusks

on these ferocious beasts can inflict fatal damage. Though sightings are relatively infrequent, if you do come across a boar in the forest, try not to face it from a downhill slope – you are far less vulnerable if positioned above the creature.

An equally dangerous, but ever rarer, sight are bears. Hunting and rural development have contributed to their dwindling numbers. According to a recent study conducted by Kyoto Prefecture, there are approximately 400 brown bears living in the mountain region between Kyoto and the Sea of Japan. Smaller than Hokkaidō's *higuma* (brown bear), the *tsuki-no-wa-guma* (Asiatic brown bear) on Honshū is named for its white collar breast-mane resembling the moon. They average a height of 1.4m and weight of 200kg, and getting off on the wrong foot with these creatures could be perilous. On the remote chance you should end up face to face with one, it is advisable *not* to run away, but to stand your ground and even create noise to try and frighten it away.

Kyoto is a prime locale for birdwatching,

Animal Welfare in Kansai
Compared to most 'developed' nations, Japan scores low marks for its treatment of both wild and domesticated animals. While the UK passed its first statute concerning animal protection in 1822 and today enforces more than 70 such laws, Japan has but one piece of similar legislation, the 1973 Animal Control Law. Though this law is supposed to protect the welfare of animals, critics maintain it is so riddled with vague language and loopholes that it's nearly impossible to enforce.

This general lack of governmental and public concern has produced a disturbingly high number of stray cats and dogs. Even many full-breed canines like huskies and golden retrievers become abandoned as a result of short-lived fads for owning large dogs (just one of Japan's 'bigger is better' status trends). In a country where the police label stray dogs *wasuremono* (lost objects), such creatures stand little chance of being saved.

Luckily for the ever-growing legion of helpless animals in the Kansai area, there is Animal Refuge Kansai (ARK), a charity organisation which since 1990 has taken in, nurtured and found homes for countless abandoned and abused animals. Like a modern-day Noah's Ark, the group's facilities on the outskirts of Osaka, south-west of Kyoto, act as a refuge for a vast hodgepodge of animals, including hundreds of dogs and cats, goats, a rabbit, a pig, a pony and even a silver fox.

ARK's British founder, long-term Japan-hand Elizabeth Oliver, has dedicated her life to the plight of stray animals and operates the organisation solely through the generosity of animal-loving people. All of the animals at ARK are neutered, vaccinated and receive regular health check-ups. Far from the paltry conditions at many of Japan's animal centres, ARK has spacious enclosures.

For anyone interested in volunteering, ARK is always in need of helping hands. Visiting ARK is a great way to see another side of Japan and spend some time in the lovely (yet not-so-distant) rural areas. You can contact Animal Refuge Kansai (☎ 0727-37-0712/1885; fax 0727-37-1645; email arkbark@wombat.or.jp) at Noam Ohara 595, Nose-chō, Toyono-gun, Osaka 563-01. ARK publishes the quarterly bilingual newsletter *A Voice for Animals.* ∎

especially from late spring to early autumn. Japan's vital position on the trans-Asian and trans-Pacific flyways means feathered friends swoop in from as far south as Tasmania, west from South-East Asia and north from Siberia, Alaska and the Arctic tundra. More than 100 species of birds are found in the Kyoto region including pheasant, flycatchers, kingfishers and owls. Some of the best areas to spot birds are the bird sanctuary at Midori-ga-ike Pond (Map 4) in the far north-east of Kyoto, the Arashiyama area, the Imperial Palace Park, Kyoto Botanical Gardens and the many small forests surrounding temples and shrines. The rivers flowing into Kyoto are home to a variety of fish such as the Japanese river trout *(ayu)* and a stroll along the banks of the Oi-gawa or Kamo-gawa rivers often provides the chance to see graceful egret *(sagi)* bathing and hunting for fish.

Some of the most popular creatures in Japan are insects *(mushi)*, and bug-lovers in Kyoto can encounter a wide array of beetles *(kabuto-mushi)*, butterflies *(cho-cho)* and dragonflies *(tonbo)*. During summer people relish the chance to be serenaded by orchestras of cicada *(semi)*, whose high-pitched chirping fills the air.

GOVERNMENT & POLITICS

The Kyoto city government is made up of 72 council members elected by majority vote. Council members serve a four year term, and elections are held every two years. Despite its post as prefectural capital, the city assembly is completely autonomous from the Kyoto prefectural assembly, which is set up like a state government with an elected governor.

The Liberal Democratic Party (LDP), a misnomer if there ever was one, is the majority party. The conservative LDP has strong ties to Osaka-based construction and utility companies, through which much of the money for electing Kyoto LDP members is funnelled.

Kyoto is also well known as a stronghold of the Japan Communist Party (JCP). As the second largest party in the city council, it has

the ability to check the LDP's power and initiatives. The JCP is known for its straight-talking politicians, an emphasis on social welfare programs and a lack of scandals and corruption. The JCP has a long history in Kyoto and many young people still see it as the best alternative to the LDP.

The Kyoto government does not have the clout to challenge the central government on certain issues, such as inheritance taxes. These draconian taxes are one reason for the destruction of so many of Kyoto's traditional wooden homes, and most people who inherit traditional homes opt for replacing them with cheaper, modern houses or, with land prices so high, for more lucrative parking lots, apartment complexes or office buildings.

Voter concern at the destruction of traditional aspects of Kyoto, and anger at the failure of either the LDP or the JCP to turn the economy around, has forced leadership changes. In 1996, Masumoto Yorikane, an independent candidate, upset the LDP old guard by winning the mayoral race, promising to halt wasteful construction projects and revitalise the city's economy.

ECONOMY

Because of Kyoto's role as the historical and cultural centre of Japan, much of the city's economy is dependent on tourism. Its tourism and related retail and service industries employ about 65% of the workforce, down from about 70% in 1988. A large number of tourists continue to pass through Kyoto, but the strong yen has hurt international tourism and the number of overseas visitors has dropped by half in the last 15 years. Many visitors now come as businesspeople. With the construction of the enormous Kyoto International Conference Hall (Map 4) in the far north-east of the city, Kyoto has had great success in drawing international conventions and continues to enthusiastically promote itself as 'Conference City Kyoto'.

Recent economic trends show Kyoto is continuing to lose business to Osaka, especially in low-tech industries. In manufacturing, the Kyoto economy is heavily dependent on the textile and clothing, and machinery

The Current Emperor

For over 1000 years, Kyoto was home to the emperor and imperial family. With the opening up of Japan, the decline of the *shōgun* and the restoration to national prominence of the Meiji emperor in 1868, the imperial family relocated to Edo (now Tokyo). Although the clan will not be returning to Kyoto any time soon, there are local citizens' groups who still occasionally issue public calls for bringing back the throne.

The current emperor, Akihito, is the great-grandson of the Meiji emperor. Akihito formally ascended the throne in 1990, about 18 months after the death of his father, Emperor Hirohito (known posthumously as the Emperor Shōwa). Hirohito's reign is known as the Shōwa era, while Akihito's is called the Heisei era. Born on 23 December 1933, Akihito is the first emperor to ascend the Chrysanthemum Throne under Japan's postwar, American-drafted constitution.

Unlike his father, whom Japanese were taught was a living god, Akihito's functions are purely ceremonial. He bestows formal authority on a newly chosen prime minister, as well as on the chief judge of the Supreme Court. Newly appointed ambassadors present their credentials to him, and he receives formal visitors of state, occasionally at one of the imperial properties in Kyoto. The constitution also provides him with the role of convening the Diet, dissolving the House of Representatives, and attesting to the appointment and dismissal of government ministers. All of this is done with the advice and approval of the Cabinet.

In Kyoto, the Imperial Household Agency (a collection of descendants of aristocrats whose functions are extremely secretive) owns and maintains four properties: the Imperial Palace (Gosho), the Sentō Gosho within the palace grounds, and the Katsura Rikyū and Shūgaku-in Rikyū imperial villas. It is interesting to note that when the emperor or other members of his family visit Kyoto, they do not stay at any of these ancient properties, but opt for the modern amenities of one of Kyoto's finer hotels.

Akihito is head of an imperial family which includes Empress Michiko, Crown Prince Naruhito and Crown Princess Masako (a former diplomat), second son Prince Akishinomiya and his wife Princess Kiko (and their two daughters Mako and Kako), and Princess Sayako, the emperor's youngest daughter. Crown Prince Naruhito is to ascend the throne upon the death of his father.

The comings and goings of the imperial family are tightly controlled by the Imperial Household Agency. The Japanese media treats the family very carefully, censoring stories at the request of the agency, out of fear of violent attacks from right-wing thugs, and to avoid the displeasure of those senior business and political leaders who support the current system. In fact, this fear of offending the wrong people led to a major embarrassment in 1993, when the Japanese press promised the agency it would not publish news of Naruhito's engagement to Owada Masako until the 'proper time'. The news, however, leaked to a Tokyo correspondent for the *Washington Post* and the story broke first in the USA.

Today's Japanese have differing opinions about the imperial system. Akihito is not nearly as controversial as his father, who led Japan to war and later renounced his divine status in defeat. Newspaper polls show many Japanese simply don't care about the imperial family, and there is no serious debate about whether the family should modernise along the lines of Europe's monarchies. Some feminists have been disappointed with Princess Masako's virtual silence since tying the knot and her complete lack of initiative to open up the system. Meanwhile, the media wonders when Masako will produce a male heir to the throne. Although empresses occasionally ruled Japan in its early history, men have commanded the throne for over a millennium. ■

industries, which account for almost half its wholesale industry. In 1992, the total export volume of Kyoto companies was 1.04 trillion yen, with total import volume about 136 billion yen.

While many of Kyoto's traditional industries such as silk weaving, fabric dyeing and cabinet making have been in steady decline, several of its high-tech companies are thriving, including international camera giant Kyocera and video game trailblazer Nintendo.

With origins as a playing card manufacturer, Nintendo gets little respect, some say, from the Kyocera-dominated Kyoto Chamber of Commerce & Industry.

Kyoto's business and civic leaders today face a dilemma: how to keep tourism and the traditional industries an integral part of the economy while modernising to remain competitive. Some effort is under way to preserve parts of traditional Kyoto (perhaps those most profitable to tourism) and as part of its plan to boost local infrastructure, the city has invested heavily in both creating world-class science facilities and in joint private-public ventures, such as Kyoto Research Park, Kyoto Science City, and Kansai Science City on the border of Kyoto and Nara prefectures.

POPULATION & PEOPLE

Kyoto has a population of about 1.46 million people, making it the fifth largest city in Japan behind Tokyo, Yokohama, Osaka and Nagoya. Over the past 50 years, the city's birth rate and population have declined by about 20%. Although Kyoto is home to one of the largest concentrations of colleges and universities in Japan, the majority of students leave after graduation for the bigger economic centres of Tokyo and nearby Osaka. Consequently, many traditional industries are dying out for lack of younger apprentices, who are unwilling to undergo years of training and hard work for relatively little pay.

Kyoto is famous for its aesthetic beauty and refined culture, but not for the kindness of its people, who often are said to be cold, unnecessarily formal and snobbish to outsiders. While short-term tourists are made to feel welcome, many who live long-term in the city receive a very different reception – one of strained patience.

The Kyoto language itself can be extremely vague, allowing people to mask their true feelings behind a smokescreen of veiled smiles and nebulous wording. Needless to say this *tatemae* mode of communication can easily confuse the visitor. Perhaps the best example of this is the expression for guests, *'Ochazuke demo dō desu ka?'*, literally 'Won't you have a cup of tea?' (actually, tea poured over rice), which is in fact a signal that the guest's visiting time is up.

Such manners and phrases are often not understood even by other Japanese, and Tokyo and Osaka businesspeople agree that Kyotoites are the most difficult to do business with, being notoriously ambiguous. Kyoto people are also known for their finicky sense of style. An old Japanese proverb says

an Osaka merchant will spend time and money on eating, whereas a Kyotoite will spend time and money on nice clothes. In general, Kyoto people prefer small and refined over large and voluminous. Many exhibit a passion for the culture and fashions of Paris and Italy and see these two cultures as the epitome of civility.

While held in contempt by other Japanese, Kyotoites are, at the same time, admired for their struggle to retain their city's traditional values. Many younger Japanese tourists who visit Kyoto see it as a kind of vast amusement park, full of temples and other peculiar attractions not seen in everyday life. Kyoto also offers a sense of comfort to many older Japanese, who find remnants of a prewar Japan.

But Kyoto is not all Japanese. A large number of Japanese-Koreans have made their homes here, especially in the neighbourhoods south of Kyoto station. Many are second or third generation Koreans of parents or grandparents forced to come to Japan as slave labourers following Japan's annexation of Korea in 1905.

Though born and raised in Japan, these Japanese-Koreans must carry Korean passports and cannot vote. They face severe job discrimination, especially when applying to public universities or for civil service positions. 'Prestigious' Japanese companies often refuse to hire them. While working-class Japanese are more accepting, middle and upper-middle class Kyotoites are known to hire detectives from special agencies to ensure that potential marriage partners are neither of Korean heritage nor of the *burakumin* class (Japanese whose ancestors worked in trades such as leather tanning, grave digging, or other professions deemed 'unclean'). Many burakumin also reside in south Kyoto and, although their situation has vastly improved over the last 20 years, they still face conspicuous discrimination, from schools to the workplace.

Kyoto is also home to a large number of foreign artists, musicians, teachers, scholars, writers and people 'just passing through'. A large percentage of these, including some

The Mausoleum of Tokimune Hojo

The Mausoleum in which the mortuary tablet of Tokimune Hojo is enshrined is built on his own grave. Here we can see a tablet with the Empress Dowager shoken's poem dedicated to him. The meaning of the poem is this:

Noisy waves of foreign forces do not come surging again upon this country because of the god-sent storm originating from the seughing winds among the pine trees of Mt. Kamakura.

Now, this mausoleum belongs to the Butsunichi-an, one of the branch temples of the Enkakuji. In former days, Butsunichi-an was

were enshrined in respective mausoleums previous to that time and brought together in one mausoleum in the Edo period. There was a time when Butsunichi-an was falling into decay. However, it has been a most important branch temple of Enkakuji since Rev. Kakuin Shuon, who was a member of the Gohojo family, did everything in his power to revive the temple.

The present wooden image of Tokimune Hojo was possibly made about 1700 by Rev. Gikai Shosen and repaired by Rev. Shizan Bonshun, who was once head priest of the Butsunichi-an, in 1811 when the 500th annual ceremony was held in memory of Sadatoki Hojo. The present mausoleum was built in the same year, too. In the garden of this temple, there are three hermitages called Ensoku-ken, Fuko-an, and Hoko-den.

The first one was built by Rev. Kakuin and the second by Daiyu Kokushi, noted priest of this temple. This temple has been holding a tea ceremony on the fourth of every month since Jan. 4th, 1934.

This was begun by Rev. Bisan Takahatake, previous head priest of the temple, in memory of the virtue of Tokimune who had saved a national crisis seven hundred years before.

former hippies who came over in the 1960s and never left, live in old wooden houses that most Japanese don't want to live in today. A bohemian atmosphere is still found among many of Kyoto's resident foreigners and many former Japanese student activists now run offbeat coffee shops, restaurants, bars and other establishments.

SOCIETY & CONDUCT
Traditional Culture

The Japanese live in a society where subtle behaviour patterns and a battery of manners greatly dictate their daily lives. Deeply rooted within these 'Japanese ways' is a complex set of unwritten rules that even many Japanese can't fully comprehend in a lifetime.

Japanese notoriously view themselves as being utterly distinctive from the rest of the world, yet even within Japan there are great societal and geographical variations unknown to most foreign visitors. Still, more than any place else in Japan, Kyoto has developed a breed of conservatism that takes the rigours of Japanese protocol to uncontested heights.

Likewise, as Japan has abandoned much of its age-old traditions, Kyoto is where often the flame still burns. One classic custom, for example, still practised religiously today in Kyoto is the morning ritual of *kadohaki* (sweeping) and *mizumaki* (spreading water). Like clockwork, every morning a large majority of home and business owners purify the ground in front of their house or shop with a sweeping up and splashing of water.

The complex mythology of uniqueness which has accrued around the Japanese is difficult to ascertain and the effects of modern customs (notably the impact of foreigners and imported culture) on local traditions have complicated this enigma further. In view of all of the stereotypes and preconceived notions of the Japanese, one of the greatest challenges of discovering Japan for yourself is setting the myths straight.

The Group

One of the most common ideas about the Japanese is that the group forever takes precedence over the individual. The image of loyal company workers bellowing out the company anthem and attending collective exercise sessions is synonymous with the cliché of Japan Inc.

It's easy to fall into the spirit of such images and to start seeing Japan's business-suited crowds as members of a collectivised society that rigorously suppresses individual tendencies. It's useful to remember that the Japanese are no less individual than their western counterparts – they experience the same frustrations and joys, complain about their work conditions, the way their boss treats them and so on, as westerners do. The difference is, that while these individual concerns have a place, they are less likely to be seen in Japan as defining.

The tension between group and individual interest has been a rich source of inspiration for Japanese art. Traditional values see conflict between *honne*, the individual's personal views, and *tatemae*, the views that are demanded by the individual's position in the group. The same difference is expressed in the terms *ninjō* – human feelings – and *giri* – social obligations. Salaried workers who spend long hours at the office away from the families they love are giving priority to giri over ninjō.

At this point the argument tends to disintegrate into psychobabble. But one thing is certain – the Japanese are great joiners: clubs and associations are hugely popular, and the responsibilities that come with a job or a position are taken very seriously indeed.

Men & Women

The stereotypical view of Japanese women as submissive homebodies holds little water these days. As with everything else in contemporary Japan, women's roles are in flux and they are marrying later (or choosing not to), working more and assuming more prominent roles in public life.

Traditional Japanese society circumscribed the woman's role to the home, where as housekeeper she wielded considerable power, collecting her husband's pay and allocating it to various domestic needs. Even

Nihonjinron

While everyone is ethnocentric to a degree, in Japan the 'uniqueness of being Japanese' *(nihonjinron)* concept is not just a cultural trait but also a profitable industry. As a centre of history and traditional culture, Kyoto is a magnet for many converts to nihonjinron. Disillusioned with modern 'westernised' Japan, these people seek simple answers to what it means to be Japanese in today's complex world.

Advocates of Japanese uniqueness share several traits. First is a deeply rooted suspicion, often fear, of western teachings which emphasise universal values and the moral rights of the individual. Such ideas are seen as a threat to both the existing political arrangements (from which many of the nihonjinron proponents benefit) and rapidly retreating traditional values. A second common thread is a belief that such 'unique' Japanese values (harmony in the workplace, shyness in dealing with outsiders, groupism etc) are inherited cultural traits rather than learned social norms. Third is a belief that it is impossible for non-Japanese to understand (and here 'understand' largely means 'agree with') Japanese values.

While many Japanese find aspects of nihonjinron dubious, the basic claim that because Japan's historical development occurred in relative isolation, the Japanese are a unique (which can cross the line into 'superior') race receives a good deal of support. Japanese who have lived abroad often enthusiastically embrace this position, possibly as a reaction to inferior and alienated feelings toward foreign culture.

In Kyoto, nihonjinron is supported by academics, housewives, businessmen and others who bemoan the city's lost aristocracy and the advent of an educational system that they feel fails to instil in students any sort of pride in the Japanese nation.

Curiously, nihonjinron's defenders often stress a Japanese connection with aspects of foreign cultures, not just separateness. Since the foreign elements chosen are ones mythologised in the west, these identity claims may be evidence of a Japanese 'cultural cringe'.

Two interesting variations on 'the essence of Japaneseness' are the proclamations of some pseudo-scholars that the Japanese are actually the Lost Tribe of Israel (the logic being that both races value education and hard work, and are often feared by others). Then there are the speculations by several professors in the Kyoto area that the ancient Japanese were a Celtic tribe that migrated east (they cite as evidence similarities between Celtic and early Japanese artwork).

At least no-one has yet suggested that the Japanese are the descendants of the inhabitants of Atlantis, Lilliput or Shangri-La. ∎

in the early Meiji period, however, the ideal was rarely matched by reality: labour shortfalls often resulted in women taking on factory work even though legally they were relegated to the same category as the 'deformed and mentally incompetent'.

The contemporary situation, as might be expected, is complex. There are those who stick to established roles. They tend to opt for shorter college courses, often at women's colleges, and see education as an asset in the marriage market; once married they leave bread-earning to their husbands.

While in the 1990s such women are becoming a minority, the stereotypes are still alive and kicking. Switch on a Japanese TV and you will soon see the traditional male-female dynamic. The male host invariably has a female shadow whose job it is to agree with everything he says, make astonishing gasps at his erudition and to giggle politely behind a raised hand at his off-the-cuff witty remarks. These *'sō desu'* girls, as they're known, are a common feature of countless aspects of Japanese life. All companies employ a bevy of nubile OLs, or 'office ladies', whose tasks include chiming a chorus of falsetto 'welcomes' to visitors, making cups of tea and generally adding a personal touch to an otherwise stolid male atmosphere.

Perhaps most disturbing for westerners visiting Japan is the way in which women feature so much in comic strips, magazines and movies, as brutalised, passive victims in bizarre, sadomasochistic rites. While these fantasies are disturbing, it is possible to take refuge in the thought that they *are* real fantasies, and women are in fact a great deal safer in Japan than they are in many other parts of the world. Harassment, when it does occur, is usually furtive, occurring in crowded areas such as trains; with direct confrontation, almost all Japanese men will be shamed into withdrawing the groping hand.

Japanese & Gaijin

As a foreign visitor to Japan, you are a *gaijin*, literally, an outside person. Away from the big cities it's not unusual to hear whispered exclamations of *'Gaijin da!'* ('It's a foreigner!') and many school children, even *in* the cities, are unable to resist erupting into giggles at the sight of a foreign face.

Long-term visitors to Japan are prone to an ongoing love-hate relationship which frequently shifts sides. After being initially overwhelmed by Japanese courtesy, many foreigners end up feeling they have been in Japan long enough to deserve more intimate treatment; they often come to the conclusion that Japanese politeness and helpfulness mask a morbid ethnocentricity. Fortunately for the short-term visitor, the polite and friendly nature of most Japanese is likely to be the main and lasting impression.

The best advice to the visitor is to enjoy Japanese courtesy; most visitors come away with miracle stories of Japanese indulgence: the hitchhikers who are treated to lunch and taken kilometres off their host's original route to be deposited at their destination; the traveller who arrives too late at the bank to change money and, standing miserably outside the closed doors, is offered a loan by a passer-by.

Etiquette

One of the most enduring western notions about Japan is that of Japanese courtesy and rigid social etiquette. With a little sensitivity, however, there is little chance of mortally offending anyone with your lack of social grace.

To be sure, many things are different: the Japanese bow and indulge in a ritualised exchange of *meishi* (business cards) when they meet; they exchange their shoes for uncomfortable plastic slippers before entering the home; and social occasions involve sitting on the floor in positions that will put the legs of an ill-bred foreigner to sleep within five minutes. But, overall, most of the really complex aspects of Japanese social interaction are functions of the language and only pose problems for the advanced student who's trying to get as close to the culture as possible.

Sitting

When socialising with the Japanese or visiting them in their homes, sitting on the floor for extended periods of time can be a real nightmare for many foreigners. Sit with your legs beneath you for as long as possible and then, if you *must* stretch your legs out, do so discreetly without pointing them in anyone's direction. Pointing your feet (literally and figuratively, the lowest part of the body) at people, even inadvertently, is bad form throughout Asia.

Bowing When you meet Japanese, it's polite to bow slightly from the waist and incline your head. Actually, the rule is that the deepness of a Japanese bow depends on the status (relative to oneself) of the person to whom one is bowing. When A has higher status than B, it is important that B's bow is deeper than A's. As the bows take place simultaneously, it is often incumbent on B to give a quick, surreptitious glance in the direction of A's exalted presence to determine that his or her bow is indeed lower than A's. Fortunately, no one expects foreigners to carry on like this, and nowadays, many Japanese have taken to shaking hands, though the bow is still the most important mark of respect.

Business Cards If you're going to be working in Japan, have some business cards made up: without them, you'll be a nobody. All introductions and meetings in Japan involve an exchange of business cards – handing out yours to the right people can make things happen; not having a card will definitely look very bad. Cards should be handed over, and accepted, with some ceremony, studied carefully and referred to often. It's polite to accept a card with two hands. Do not simply stuff a proffered card into your pocket. Also, never write anything on a card you are given.

Gift Giving The exchange of gifts and the return of a kindness are important parts of Japanese daily life. If you visit somebody at their home, you should bring them a gift such as chocolates or flowers – much the same as you would give in the west. Ideally, it is nice to bring something from your own country. Gifts used for cementing friendships and for

Omiyage

Gifts are the grease that keeps the wheels of Japanese society turning. A gift can serve as a token of appreciation, a sign of respect, a guarantee of continued favour or even a bribe (especially in politics).

Perhaps the most troublesome and time-consuming gift of all is the *omiyage* – a souvenir given to friends, family and co-workers upon return from travel. In most Japanese companies, leaving for a vacation naturally entails a sense of shame, of letting down the team. To make up for this betrayal, an armful of omiyage is required. Of course, shopping for all these gifts can eat up an entire vacation (particularly a Japanese vacation, which usually lasts only a few days anyway).

Ever resourceful, the Japanese have come up with a solution to this problem – the train station's regional speciality store. These stores are in the passageways around big-city train stations, and anyone riding the *shinkansen* (bullet train) into Kyoto station will have the chance to participate in a nationwide shopping spree. In the space of a few hundred metres you can pick up crab from Hokkaidō, dolls from Kyūshū and pickled vegetables from Shikoku. Recently these stores have sprung up in airports, selling goods from favourite international destinations: Hawaii, Disneyworld and Paris. Even if everybody knows that their souvenir was picked up locally, the obligation is fulfilled and everybody is happy.

Apparently, these gifts are also commonly used as alibis – after a weekend spent at the local love hotel with a secretary, a gift purchased at a regional speciality store is proof that a wayward boss was actually on a business trip. ∎

you must dole out for your new home. For many westerners, this all seems like so much bribery; for the Japanese, these rituals operate to show respect, to give face and to ensure smooth interpersonal relations.

Flattery What passes for flattery in the west is often perceived as quite natural in Japan. The Japanese recognise the importance of a bit of ego-stroking and generally will never pass up the opportunity to praise each other in company. The foreigner who has made an effort to learn a few sentences of Japanese or to get by with chopsticks is likely to be regularly regaled with gasps of astonishment and unctuous praise. Don't feel anxious about this, as it's genuinely meant to make you feel good.

The correct response to praise is to decline it, eg to exclamations of 'How skilful you are!', smile and say something like 'Not at all'. Importantly, don't forget to return a few compliments here and there – there's no need to force yourself if it doesn't come naturally.

Directness One major difference between the Japanese and westerners is that the Japanese do not make a virtue of being direct. Indeed, directness is seen as vulgar; the Japanese prefer to resort to vaguer strategies and to feel their way through a situation when dealing with others. The Japanese have a term for this that translates as 'stomach talk' – where both sides tentatively edge around an issue, feeling out the other's point of view until it is clear which direction negotiations can go. This can often result in what seems is an interminable toing and froing that only ever yields ambiguous results. But don't be deceived: the Japanese can usually read the situation just as clearly as if both sides were clearly stating their interests.

Basically, when you're dealing with the Japanese, avoid direct statements that are likely to be perceived as confrontational. If someone ventures an opinion, however stupid it may seem, try not to crush it with a 'No, I disagree completely'.

Calls of Nature It's not unusual to find

paying off small obligations are usually small and unostentatious. Where money is given it is presented in an envelope.

As a foreigner, it's quite likely that people will sometimes want to give you gifts 'for your travels'. You may not be able to reciprocate in these situations. The polite thing to do is to refuse a couple of times when the gift is offered.

Gift giving is so important in Japan that it has become institutionalised in many aspects of Japanese social life. If, for example, you are invited to a wedding, you are expected to bring a 'gift' of at least ¥20,000. One of the most notorious 'gifts', among foreign residents at least, is 'key money', the two months rent

Japanese men urinating in crowded streets, and public toilets are occasionally unsegregated, but public use of a handkerchief for blowing your nose is definitely frowned upon. The polite thing to do if you have a cold is to keep sniffing (an admirable sign of self-restraint in Japanese eyes) until you can get to a private place to do your business.

Dos & Don'ts

Avoiding Offence Japanese are remarkably tolerant when it comes to the curious ways of foreigners and there's little chance of committing any grave faux pas. There are certain situations, however, where it is important to follow Japanese example. Shoes should almost always be removed when entering a home or entering a tatami room of any kind. When you remove your shoes in the *genkan* (entryway) to someone's home, it is considered courteous to arrange them neatly by turning them facing out to from where you entered.

When paying a visit the proper form is to arrive announced, rather than dropping in unexpectedly. Likewise, cold-calling on business is a definite way to have the door politely slammed in your face. Always call

Urban Anthropology

Visitors to Japan expecting to find a nation of suit-wearing conformists are often shocked at the sheer variety they discover. Certainly in a 'traditional' centre like Kyoto one still can spot graceful, kimono-clad women among other remnants of 'old Japan'; notwithstanding, ordinary city-centre traffic on a weekend night approaches a gaudy street theatre rivalling places like Tokyo's Shibuya. People-watching in areas like Shijō-Kawaramachi and Kiyamachi-dōri is often half the fun of being there. The following guide delineates some of the more usual human types.

Salarymen Just what you'd expect: businessmen, always clad in suits, right down to the matching company lapel pins. Observe the metamorphosis after they've kicked back a few *mizu-wari* (whisky and water).

Office Ladies Also known as OLs, these women may be secretaries, but may equally be women who do the same work as their male bosses for half the pay. OLs usually travel in small groups wearing matching uniforms of skirt, white blouse and vest.

Ojō-sans These are young women, usually college students or graduates, middle-class and headed for marriage to young salarymen. Ojō-sans dress conservatively, with the exception of the occasional miniskirt.

Yanquis Pronounced 'yankees', these men prefer brown or blond hair, sport flashy clothes and have a cellular phone permanently glued to their ear. Yanquis often work in the construction industry, where their taste for loud clothes is expressed in brightly coloured *nikka-bokka* pants (from the English word knickerbocker).

Chimpiras These are often yanquis who've taken rebellion a step further. They hope to attract the attention of *yakuza* (mafia) gangsters and be asked to join the gang, becoming another type – junior yakuza.

Bosozoku These motorcycle gangs offer more dyed hair and flashy clothes. A typical night is spent loudly revving motorcycle engines and speeding off tailed by the police, who never catch them. Like chimpira, some of the wilder bosozoku go on to become yakuza.

Yakuza This is the real thing. They used to stand out, with tight 'punch-perms' and loud suits, but modern yakuza are hardly noticeable, except perhaps for the swagger and black Mercedes with tinted windows.

Ike-Ike Onna Literally, go-go girl; these young women fancy day-glo miniskirts, dyed brown hair, dark suntans and expensive handbags. Sometimes referred to as *o-mizu*, as in 'mizu-shōbai', the so-called water trade (many ike-ike onna work in hostess bars, massage parlours and the like).

Ko Gāru The name derives from *kōko*, the Japanese word for high school, and *gāru*, from the English word 'girl': a high school girl who dresses like an ike-ike onna, often seen talking on a cellular phone.

Chanelah A young woman who leans strongly toward Chanel goods, particularly expensive handbags with gold chains – perhaps the world's most dedicated shoppers. ■

first. Incidentally, be on time; most Japanese view punctuality as a virtue.

Bathing in Japan also conforms to fairly strict rules and you should follow them. Whether it's a Japanese-style bath or an *onsen* (hot-spring bath), remember the actual washing takes place before entering the water, and baths are for soaking in after you have washed.

As in other parts of Asia, the respectful way to indicate for someone to approach you is by waving your fingers with the palm downwards – not beckoning with the fingers upwards, as we do in the west. As a westerner you can offer your hand when you meet someone for the first time, though if you want to add a Japanese touch to the proceedings you can make a slight bow.

Japanese generally don't eat food in the street unless there are seats provided to do so. Ice creams are an exception to this rule. It's up to you whether you want to abide by this custom: no one's going to be particularly upset if they see you wandering down the street munching on a Big Mac, but they might feel it's a little uncivilised. There are worse eating faux pas, such as the passing of food from chopsticks to chopsticks (a practice dreadfully reminiscent of a Buddhist funeral ceremony).

Finally, the cardinal rule of dealing with people is: stay cool, don't express anger and keep smiling. When things aren't going your way, try a different tack and don't force anyone into a situation they can't back down from without a loss of face.

Meeting the Japanese One of the best ways to meet Kyotoites is by checking the listings for local events in *Kansai Time Out*. On the last Saturday of each month, for example, there is a bohemian local gathering dubbed the Kyoto Connection which anyone with the chance to go shouldn't miss (see the Activities section in the Things to See & Do chapter). You can also read about events organised by groups like JEE, a local environmental organisation (see the earlier Ecology & Environment section in this chapter).

The Kyoto International Community House (KICH) sponsors a noteworthy home-visit program where, with a day's notice, you can arrange to visit the home of a local Kyoto family. Bringing a small gift, especially from home, is always appreciated. You can apply over the phone by calling ☎752-3511. There is also a message board at KICH which can provide some interesting leads on meeting people (for more information on KICH see the Useful Organisations section in the Facts for the Visitor chapter).

Being such a large college town, universities also provide places for meeting people. All schools have a variety of clubs from English Speaking Society (ESS) networks to ecogroups and an ample number of computer nerds (see the Campuses section in the Facts for the Visitor chapter). Some universities even have clubs which provide free tour-guide services for foreign visitors, and the TIC should be able to give you leads on how to contact them.

Last, but surely not least, is Kyoto's vast assortment of 'something for everyone' watering holes. Like it or not, these bars are practically a fail-safe facility for finding conversation, and alcohol does have a tendency to shave away the shyness (see the Entertainment chapter for a sample).

Shyness Perhaps the most difficult aspect of getting to meet the Japanese is their almost chronic shyness. Young Japanese generally have been discouraged from taking individual initiative and consequently, visitors are perhaps more likely to be surrounded by a gaggle of giggling school children chorusing 'Haro!' than having an interesting conversation with a Japanese. Some young Japanese will simply freeze in embarrassed silence if directly addressed by a foreigner. Unfortunately, the same applies to many adults if they have had little experience talking to non-Japanese.

Much of this shyness stems from fear of making a mistake and somehow causing offence. If you need to make casual contact with a Japanese, say, to ask directions, try to appear calm and relaxed and smile as you talk.

continued on page 47

Arts

ANTHONY WEERSING

MASON FLORENCE

Top: Example of prized Nishijin-ori weaving, found in temples around Kyoto.
Bottom: Painted screen door (fusuma-e) depicting a peacock in mating season.

ANTHONY WEERSING

ARTS

Until the last century, the main influences on Japanese art came from China and Korea, which had passed Buddhism on from India in the 6th century AD. These outside influences notwithstanding, the Japanese add something of their own to their art. There is a fascination with the ephemeral, the unadorned and with forms that echo the randomness of nature. A gift for caricature is also present, from early Zen ink paintings right up to contemporary *manga* (comics). An interest in the grotesque or the bizarre is also often visible, from Buddhist scrolls depicting the horrors of hell to the highly stylised depictions of body parts in *ukiyo-e* wood-block prints of the Edo period.

When asked to define their aesthetic principles, Japanese reach for words like *wabi*, *sabi* and *shibui* (see the Wabi-Sabi boxed text below). Such ideals are by no means the final say on a long and vibrant artistic tradition that continues to seek new inspirations and produce new forms.

Wabi-Sabi

The Japanese have long been known for their astute ability to recognise and appreciate things of beauty. Even in modern Japan, where eyesores are *never* out of sight, the Japanese continually extol the radiance of even the smallest pocket of allure. This prowess for detecting beauty, even in the face of ugliness, may have its roots in the simple, heartfelt concepts of *wabi* and *sabi*. A related concept is *shibui*, which is in fact more a feeling or atmosphere than a descriptive term, but which could be described as 'restrained elegance'.

Two of the most convenient terms in the Japanese vocabulary, wabi and sabi coexist like happy siblings. Equally difficult to define, they both embody simplicity and serenity. Kyoto is the wabi-sabi capital of Japan, and these concepts can be found in everything from traditional architecture to the tea ceremony *(chanoyu)*. Yet, while there are perhaps no two terms more truly 'Japanese', they are more easy to 'feel' than to explain.

Wabi can be likened to an aesthetic or moral principle of tranquillity and austerity. Wabi's roots stem from the civil strife that tore Japan apart in the warring Kamakura and Muromachi periods. With devastation all around them, people began looking for virtue in the face of destitution. Filtered through Zen philosophy, the idea of simplicity gradually took on a positive value, and its attributes were celebrated in poems and literature, such as in Kamo no Chomei's *Hojoki* (An Account of My Hut) and praised by 16th century tea masters, most notably Sen no Rikyū (1522-91).

Sabi, though frequently used synonymously with wabi, is closer to a poetic ideal. In striking contrast to the elaborate taste and flamboyant perfectionism of the Heian period (when sabi is said to have first been employed), it reveals joy and beauty through loneliness and imperfection. Whether in a faded, cracked tea bowl, a fallen, moss-covered tree or a desolate old person, sabi is the virtue of not seeing things as flawed, 'broken' or 'dead', but rather finding pleasure in and recognising a refined elegance. ■

Below: An earthenware figure (haniwa) *from the ancient Yayoi period.*

Art Periods

MASON FLORENCE

The Jōmon period (10,000-300 BC) takes its name from the decorative 'coiled rope' pottery produced by early hunters and gatherers. Similarly, the Yayoi period (300 BC-300 AD), which saw the introduction of wet-rice farming and bronze and iron use, has left many examples of simple earthenware and clay figurines. The Kofun period (300-710 AD) is named after the keyhole-shaped burial mounds of the earliest emperors. *Haniwa* (clay ring) earthenware cylinders and sculptures, some as tall as 1.5m, surrounded these burial mounds.

The Asuka (552-645) and Hakuhō (645-710) periods mark an important turning point. The arrival of Mahayana (Greater Vehicle) Buddhism introduced religious themes that would inspire Japanese art for over five hundred years. The earliest works of sculpture were produced by Korean artisans – notable examples can be seen at Kōryū-ji Temple in Kyoto and Hōryū-ji in Nara – but by the Nara period (710-94) a golden age of Japanese sculpture had arrived, producing such masterpieces as the Yakushi Nyorai (Healing Buddha) at Shin-Yakushi-ji Temple in southern Nara.

By the early Heian period (794-1185), as Japan distanced itself from China, a truly native culture began to emerge. The imperial capital moved from Nara to Heian-kyō (modern-day Kyoto), and the break with Chinese tradition can be seen in the development of the 31 syllable *waka* poem, precursor to the 17 syllable *haiku*, and in narrative epics like *Genji Monogatari* (The Tale of Genji) by Murasaki Shikibu. In the visual arts, *yamato-e* (Japanese painting) broke with Chinese landscape tradition by depicting court scenes on folding panels. The graceful lines of Uji's Byōdō-in Temple south of Kyoto are testament to the beauty of Heian architecture.

The early art of the Kamakura period (1185-1333), when power moved away from Kyoto, was filled with a wild energy, later becoming more subdued under the influence of a military government. During this period, Zen became popular in Japan. Its disavowal of Buddha images gave rise to a new tradition of human portraits and statues, and marked the beginning of a secularisation of art.

In 1336 the centre of power moved back to Kyoto. During the Muromachi period (1333-1568), Zen had an enormous impact on the arts, exemplified by the ink paintings of Sesshū, the tea ceremony of Sen no Rikyū and the garden at Kyoto's Ginkaku-ji Temple. However, in 1467, the Ōnin War broke out, which essentially destroyed Kyoto. This 'brush with the void' left a deep impact on Japan, and the idea of wabi, or stark simplicity, was born (see the earlier Wabi-Sabi boxed text).

Eventually the powerful shōgun Toyotomi Hideyoshi took control and the new elite encouraged artists to produce elaborate works to decorate their palaces. This Momoyama period (1568-1600) was typified by huge gardens, gilded screen paintings and brilliant textile work. The first westerners arrived, bringing with them technology and treasures unlike anything seen before in Japan.

During the Edo period (1600-1868), Japan shut itself off from the world and its arts coalesced into the forms they are known by today. With the rise of the merchant class, art was no longer the province of emperors and nobles, and Japanese artists could now sell their work to a much wider audience. The most important development was the ukiyo-e wood-block print depicting the 'floating world' of Edo courtesans and *kabuki* actors.

Right: An ink painting by Sesshū showing a view of Ama-no-hashidate.

COURTESY OF KYOTO NATIONAL MUSEUM

From the Meiji Restoration, Japan's arts have been revolutionised by contact with the west, with Japanese artists moving swiftly from imitation to innovation.

Performing Arts

The two most famous Japanese theatrical traditions are kabuki and *nō*. Both forms work well as spectacle and some theatres have programs with an English synopsis, or even headphones for an English commentary.

Other forms of theatre include the comic drama of *kyōgen;* the puppet theatre known as *bunraku; rakugo,* which employs comic narrative; and *manzai,* a style of slapstick comedy.

Kabuki The origins of kabuki lie in the early 17th century when a maiden of a shrine led a troupe of women dancers to raise funds for the shrine. Soon prostitutes were performing the lead roles until the Tokugawa government banned women from the kabuki stage; they were replaced with attractive young men, and finally by older men. This had a profound effect on kabuki, as these older male actors required greater artistry to credibly perform their roles. Thus, while remaining a popular art form, kabuki also became a serious art form.

Kabuki employs opulent sets, a boom-crash orchestra and a ramp through the audience to allow important actors to get the most out of their melodramatic entrances and exits. For the most part kabuki deals with feudal tragedies, of the struggle between duty and inner feelings; the latter has produced a large body of work on the theme of love suicides.

Unlike the theatre of the west, the playwright is not the applauded champion of kabuki; the play is merely a vehicle for the genius of the actor.

Above: The head of a bunraku puppet.
Below: Nō masks: the horned hannya express-ing the violent anger of a woman whose love has been betrayed; and shikami, one of the demon masks.

Nō Nō is an older form of theatre, dating back some 600 years. It seems to have evolved as a cross-pollination between indigenous Shintō-related dance and mime traditions, and dance forms that originated elsewhere in Asia. It was adopted as a courtly performing art and underwent numerous refinements, becoming an essentially religious theatre whose aesthetic codes were defined by the minimalism of Zen. The power of nō lies in understatement. Its use of masks as a mode of expression and the bleak emptiness of its sets direct all attention to the performers.

Kyōgen Kyōgen is a comic drama that originally served as a light interlude within a nō play, but which is now more often performed separately between two different nō plays. Kyōgen draws on the real world for its subject matter and is acted in colloquial Japanese. The subjects of its satire are often samurai, depraved priests and faithless women – the performers are without masks and a chorus often accompanies.

A famous performance is held annually at Kyoto's Mibu-dera Temple (see the Festivals boxed text in the Facts for the Visitor chapter).

Bunraku Like kabuki, bunraku developed in the Edo period. It is Japan's professional puppet theatre, using puppets that are a half to two-thirds life-size and hand-held, controlled by three puppeteers dressed in black robes and usually hooded. On a raised dais near the stage, a narrator *(tayū)* tells the story and provides the voices for individual characters, while musical accompaniment is provided by the three stringed *shamisen.*

Rakugo Rakugo, the Chinese characters for which literally mean the dropped word, is an art of comic narrative thought to have emerged from the warlord practice of including comic storytellers in retinues for light amusement. It is delivered by a solitary kimono-clad performer, most commonly a middle-aged man, seated on a cushion in the centre of a propless stage. Performers are unaccompanied except for a brief musical flourish of shamisen, flute and drums which announces their entrance and exit. Vocal mimicry and facial contortions are used to comic and dramatic effect throughout the storytelling. The entertainers typically keep a traditional paper fan in the fold in their kimono which is repeatedly drawn and replaced during their routine.

Rakugo has a contemporary cousin called manzai, also highly popular in the Kansai region. This slapstick-style comedy routine is based on a call and response between the clever one *(tsukome)* and the fool *(boke)*. Manzai language reaches its peak of humour when neighbourly conversation turns quarrelsome. The largest manzai troupe is the Osaka-based Yoshimoto school, which produces countless comedy duos in its distinctive style.

There are frequent performances of rakugo and manzai, primarily in Osaka, and both regularly appear on TV (a cheaper bet for foreigners, as the racy dialogue is virtually impossible to understand).

Butō *Butō* is Japanese experimental/avant-garde dance which was born in the 1960s. Butō dancers perform nearly nude with loincloths and body paint. Movement is drawn-out and occasionally grotesque. The exaggerated expressions are intended to express the emotions of the dancers and choreographer in the most direct way possible, making it more accessible than other types of Japanese performance art.

Unfortunately for those interested in seeing butō performed, most troupes are small, underground affairs.

Music

Ancient Music *Gagaku* is the 'elegant' music of the Japanese imperial court which flourished between the 8th and 12th centuries, and became part of a revived interest in national traditions during the Meiji period.

The repertoire of an orchestra included *kangen* (instrumental) pieces and *bugaku* (dance) pieces. Nowadays, a gagaku ensemble usually consists of 16 players performing on drums and kettle drums, string instruments such

Right: Koto (plucked zither) players at a kabuki concert in Kyoto.

MASON FLORENCE

as the *biwa* (lute) and *koto* (plucked zither), and wind instruments such as the *hichiriki* (Japanese oboe) and various types of flute.

Traditional Instruments Several traditional instruments continue to play a part in Japanese life. The three stringed shamisen resembles a banjo with an extended neck. It was very popular during the Edo period and is still used as formal accompaniment in kabuki and bunraku. The ability to perform on the shamisen remains one of the essential skills of a geisha.

The koto is a type of plucked zither with 13 strings, adapted from a Chinese instrument before the 8th century. A bass koto, with 17 strings, has been created this century. The biwa, which resembles a lute, was also derived from a Chinese instrument. It was played by travelling musicians, often blind, to accompany recitations of Buddhist *sutras* (collections of dialogues and discourses). Most recently, the composer Takemitsu Tōru has found a niche for the biwa in the western orchestra.

The *shakuhachi* is a wind instrument that was popularised by wandering Komusō monks in the 16th and 17th centuries, who played it as a means to enlightenment.

Taiko refers to any of a number of large Japanese drums often played at festivals or in parades. The drummers train year-round to endure the rigours of playing these enormous drums.

Literature

Japan's first real literature, the *Kojiki* (Record of Ancient Matters) and *Nihon Shoki* (Chronicle of Japan), were written in the 8th century in emulation of Chinese historical accounts. Later, Japanese literature developed its own voice; interestingly, much of the early literature was written by women. One reason for this was that men wrote in imported Chinese characters, while women were relegated to writing in Japanese script *(hiragana)*. Thus, while the men were busy copying Chinese styles and texts, women were inadvertently producing the first authentic Japanese literature. Among these early female authors is Murasaki Shikibu, who wrote Japan's all-time classic *Genji Monogatari* (The Tale of Genji), documenting the intrigues and romances of early Japanese court life.

The Narrow Road to the Deep North is a travel classic by the revered Japanese poet Bashō Matsuo. *Kokoro*, by Sōseki Natsume, is a modern classic depicting the conflict between old and new Japan in the mind and heart of an aged scholar. The modern and the traditional also clash in the lives of two couples in *Some Prefer Nettles* by Tanizaki Junichirō. *The Makioka Sisters*, also by Tanizaki, is a family chronicle that has been likened to a modern-day *Monogatari*. Ibuse Masuji's *Black Rain* is a response to Japan's defeat in WWII.

Mishima Yukio's *The Golden Pavilion* reconstructs the life of a novice monk who burned down Kyoto's Kinkaku-ji in 1950. Mishima is probably the most controversial of Japan's modern writers and is considered unrepresentative of Japanese culture by many Japanese – his work makes for interesting reading.

Not all Japanese fiction can be classified as literature. Murakami Ryū's *Almost Transparent Blue* is strictly sex and drugs, and was a blockbuster in the 70s. Murakami has written another provocative bestseller for the 90s in *Coin Locker Babies*. Murakami Haruki is another bestselling author; novels available in English include *A Wild Sheep Chase* and *Dance, Dance, Dance* – both touch on sheep and Hokkaidō. Banana Yoshimoto has had unaccountable international success for her poorly translated novel *Kitchen*.

Ōe Kenzaburō is Japan's Nobel laureate. Look for *Pluck the Buds, Shoot the Kids* – which must rate alongside Mishima's *The Sailor Who Fell from Grace with the Sea* as one of the best titles in modern Japanese fiction – and his semi-autobiographical *A Personal Matter*, about how the birth of a brain-damaged child affects the father.

A Word Is Worth a Thousand Pictures

Bashō Matsuo, considered the father of haiku poetry (though the form originated in the 15th century), wielded the sword before picking up the pen. Born in Ueno, Mie Prefecture, in 1644 to a samurai family, the young Bashō studied the art of war in preparation for becoming a samurai. He swore loyalty to a local lord and would have gone on to become a regular fighting man, if not for two unforeseen events. First, the lord to whom Bashō had sworn loyalty was something of an aesthete who took to instructing his protege in the art of poetry. Second, the lord passed away while Bashō was only 22. Instead of finding another master, Bashō set out for Kyoto in search of culture and excitement.

After some time spent among the literati of the capital, Bashō moved to Edo (now Tokyo), where he refined his poetry and gained enough recognition to support himself as a teacher of haiku. In the fall of 1684, Bashō embarked on a voyage westward, hoping to quell an inner restlessness which had plagued him in the city. This was the first of the major voyages which would become the hallmark of his poetic life.

Back in Edo, Bashō studied Zen under a teacher by the name of Butchō. Zen philosophy had a deep impact on his work, and many comparisons have been made between his haiku and Zen *kōan* (short riddles intended to bring about a sudden flash of insight in the listener). Indeed, the best oi Bashō's haiku have the effect of a kōan on the listener – a rare case of a word being worth a thousand pictures.

Bashō was also influenced by the natural philosophy of the Chinese Taoist sage Chuangzi, from whom he learned a way of looking at nature uncritically – seeing the 'just-so-ness' of each object. Later, he developed his own poetic principle by drawing on the concept of *sabi*, usually translated as a kind of spare, lonely beauty. This lonely beauty is perhaps better experienced than explained, a good example being a haiku he wrote in Arano:

> on a withered branch
> a crow is perched
> an autumn evening

Bashō embarked on three more poetic pilgrimages in his life and was in the midst of a fourth when he fell sick and died in Osaka in 1694. His ceaseless peregrination certainly qualifies Bashō as the poet laureate of the traveller, to whom he addressed this haiku:

> traveller's heart
> never settled long in one place
> like a portable fire

After his death, Bashō's disciples went on to popularise the art of haiku, and today haiku is the best known of Japan's literary arts. For those who would like to delve deeper into Bashō's poetry, the most comprehensive books on the subject are *Bashō's Haiku, Volumes I and II* by Oseko Toshiharu. ■

Film

MASON FLORENCE

Motion pictures were first imported in 1896 and, in characteristic fashion, the Japanese were making their own by 1899. Until the advent of talkies, dialogue and general explanation of what was going on was provided by the *benshi*, a live commentator, who became as important a part of the cinematic experience as the film itself.

In the early 1900s, Kyoto became the centre of Japan's

motion picture industry, earning itself the designation of 'the Hollywood of Japan', having at one time 15 movie studios (only two remain). In the 1920s, a split developed between period films *(jidaigeki)* and new films *(gendaigeki)* which followed modern themes. The more realistic storylines of gendaigeki soon reflected on traditional films with the introduction of *shin jidaigeki*, or 'new period films'.

During this era, samurai themes became an enduring staple of Japanese cinema. After WWII, feudal films with their emphasis on blind loyalty and martial ability were banned by the Allied authorities, but cinematic energy soon turned to new pursuits, including animated films, monster movies and comedies.

The 50s are generally considered the golden age of Japanese cinema. Director Kurosawa Akira gained international success when his *Rashōmon* (1950) took the top prize at the 1951 Venice Film Festival. His *Shichinin-no-Samurai* (Seven Samurai; 1954) gained the ultimate accolade when it was shamelessly ripped off by the Hollywood blockbuster *The Magnificent Seven*. Other Kurosawa classics include *Yōjimbō* (1961), the tale of a masterless samurai who single-handedly cleans up a small town bedevilled by two warring gangs, and *Ran* (1985), an epic historical film.

In the 70s and 80s, Japanese cinema retreated before the onslaught of international movie-making, in part because of a failure to develop new independent film-making companies. Nonetheless, Itami Jūzō's *Tampopo* (1985) is a wonderful comedy weaving vignettes on the themes of food and sex into a story about a Japanese noodle restaurant. From the same director came *Marusa-no-Onna* (A Taxing Woman; 1988), an amusing insight into taxation, Japanese style. It was so popular in Japan that it spawned the equally amusing *A Taxing Woman 2*. Recently, there have been a number of independent Japanese films which have had some art-house success in the west, including Harada Masato's *Kamikaze Taxi* (1995).

Movies and TV shows are regularly made at Kyoto's Tōei Uzumasa Eiga Mura (Movie Village), now also a popular theme park, and the city is frequently used as a location for shooting both period and contemporary films.

Fine Arts

Painting By the end of the Heian period the emphasis on religious themes painted according to Chinese conventions gave way to a purely Japanese style, known as Yamato-e. Ink paintings *(suiboku-ga* or *sumi-e)* by Chinese Zen artists were introduced during the Muromachi period and copied by Japanese artists, who produced hanging pictures *(kakemono)*, scrolls *(e-maki)*, and decorated screens and sliding doors *(fusuma-e)*.

Below: An example of calligraphy by one of the great Zen masters Sengai Gibon (1750-1837).

During the Momoyama period, Japan's daimyō commissioned artists who painted in flamboyant colours and embellished with copious gold leaf.

Western techniques, including the use of oils, were introduced during the 16th century by the Jesuits, and the ensuing Edo period was marked by the enthusiastic patronage of a wide range of painting styles. The Kanō school was in demand for the depiction of subjects connected with Confucianism, mythical Chinese creatures or scenes from nature, while the Tosa school, whose members followed the Yamato-e style, were commissioned by the nobility to paint scenes from the classics of Japanese literature.

The Rimpa school not only absorbed the style of these other schools but progressed to produce a strikingly original decorative style. The works produced by Tawaraya Sōtatsu, Honami Kōetsu and Ogata Kōrin of this school rank among the finest of the period.

Calligraphy *Shodō* (the way of writing) is one of Japan's most valued arts, cultivated by nobles, priests and samurai alike, and studied by Japanese schoolchildren today as *shūji*. It was imported from China, but in the Heian period a more fluid and cursive style evolved called *wayō*. The Chinese style *(karayō)* remained popular in Japan even after the Heian period among Zen priests and the literati.

In both Chinese and Japanese shodō there are three important styles. Most common is *kaisho*, or block-style script. Due to its clarity, this style is favoured in the media and in applications where readability is a must. *Gyōsho*, or running hand, is semicursive, and often used in informal correspondence. *Sōsho*, or grass hand, is a truly cursive style. Sōsho abbreviates and links the characters together to create a flowing, graceful effect; it is popular for calligraphy.

Ukiyo-e

Ukiyo-e, or wood-block print, comes from the term *ukiyo*, a Buddhist metaphor for the transient world of fleeting pleasures. The subjects chosen by artists were from the 'floating world' of the entertainment quarters in Kyoto's Gion, of Osaka and Edo.

The floating world was an inversion of all the usual social hierarchies held in place by the power of the Tokugawa shōgunate. Here, money counted for more than rank, actors and artists were the arbiters of style, and prostitutes elevated their art to such a level that their social and artistic accomplishments matched those of the ladies of noble families.

Added to this was an element of spectacle. The vivid colours, novel composition and flowing lines of ukiyo-e caused great excitement in the west, sparking a vogue which a French art critic dubbed 'Japonisme'. Ukiyo-e became a key influence on impressionist (eg Toulouse-Lautrec, Manet and Degas) and postimpressionist artists. But among the Japanese, the prints were hardly given more than passing consideration – millions were produced annually in Edo. For many years, the Japanese were perplexed by the keen interest foreigners took in this art form, which they considered of ephemeral value.

The first prints of ukiyo-e were made in black and white in the early 17th century; the technique for colour printing was only developed in the middle of the 18th century. The first stage of production required the artist *(eshi)* to draw a design on transparent paper and indicate the colouring needed. The engraver *(horishi)* then pasted the design face down on a block of cherry wood and carved out the lines of the design in relief. The printer *(surishi)* inked the block and took a proof. Each colour required a separate block; it was up to the printer to obtain accurate alignment and subtle colour effects that depended on the colour mixture and pressure applied.

The reputed founder of ukiyo-e was Iwa Matabei. The genre was later

Right: This wood-block print (ukiyo-e) *depicts Japan's oldest surviving tea shop, Tsūen, in Uji. The tea shop has been in the Tsūen family for more than 830 years.*

COURTESY OF TSŪEN TEA SHOP

Top: Masked nō characters – the masks are so highly crafted that, when tilted at different angles under lights, they convey the mood of the characters. Centre left and right: Handcrafted kyō-ningyō dolls, elaborately dressed in fine brocade fabrics. Bottom: The large taiko drums which require year-round training to master.

Top: A walk along the moss-fringed, winding stone path of this shūyū (stroll style) garden varies with the changing seasons. Here, momiji-gari (autumn-colour viewing) is folded into the layout of the garden. Bottom: Ryōan-ji's famous karesansui (dry-landscaped) rock garden.

ALL PHOTOGRAPHS BY MASON FLORENCE

developed by Hishikawa Moronobu, whose wood-block prints of scenes from the entertainment district of Yoshiwara in Edo introduced the theme of *bijin-e* (paintings of beautiful women). Early themes also covered scenes from the theatre (including the actors) and erotic prints known as *shunga*. Kitagawa Utamaro is famed for his bijin-e which emphasise the erotic and sensual beauty of his subjects. All that is known about the painting prodigy Tōshūsai Sharaku is that he produced 145 superb portraits of kabuki actors between 1794 and 1795.

Toward the end of the Edo period, two painters produced outstanding works in this genre. Hokusai Katsushika was a prolific artist who observed his fellow Edo inhabitants with a keen sense of humour. His most famous works include manga, *Fugaku Sanjūrokkei* (Thirty-Six Views of Mt Fuji) and *Fugaku Hyakkei* (One Hundred Views of Mt Fuji).

Hiroshige Andō followed Hokusai, specialising in landscapes, although he also created splendid prints of plants and birds. His most celebrated works include *Tōkaidō Gojūsan-tsugi* (Fifty-Three Stations of the Tōkaidō) and *Omi Hakkei* (Eight Views of Omi) – Omi is now known as Lake Biwa-ko.

Crafts

Craftworkers in Japan have always enjoyed the same esteem accorded artists, and crafts are prized as highly as works of fine art. Since the 8th century, Kyoto's workshops have produced the full spectrum of Japanese crafts; there are still many craftspeople maintaining these traditions in Kyoto. For information on where to see craftspeople at work or how to make crafts yourself, see the Activities section in the Things to See & Do chapter.

Pottery & Ceramics Ceramic art *(tōjiki)* progressed greatly around the 13th century with the introduction of Chinese techniques and the founding of a kiln in 1242 at Seto in Aichi. One Japanese term for pottery and porcelain, *setomono* (literally, things from Seto), clearly derives from this still-thriving ceramics centre.

The popularity of tea ceremony in the 16th century stimulated developments in ceramics. The great tea masters, Furuta Oribe and Sen no Rikyū, promoted production of exquisite Oribe and Shino wares in Gifu. Toyotomi Hideyoshi encouraged the master potter Chōjiro to create works of art from clay found near his palace. Chōjiro was allowed to embellish the tea bowls he created with the character *raku* (enjoyment). This was the beginning of Kyoto's famous *raku-yaki* style of pottery. Tea bowls soon became highly prized; today's connoisseurs will pay as much as US$30,000 for just the right tea bowl.

Evidence of the first Kyoto wares *(kyō-yaki)* dates to the reign of Emperor Shōmu in the early 8th century. By the mid-1600s there were more than 10 different kilns active in and around the city; of these, only Kiyomizu-yaki remains today. This kiln first gained prominence through the workmanship of potter Nonomura Ninsei (1596-1660), who developed here an innovative method of applying enamel overglaze to porcelain. This technique was further cultivated by adding decorative features such as transparent glaze *(sometsuke)* and incorporating designs in red paint *(aka-e)* and celadon *(seiji)*. Kiyomizu-yaki is still actively produced in Kyoto and remains popular with devotees of tea ceremony.

During the Edo period, many daimyō encouraged the founding of kilns and the production of superbly designed ceramic articles. The climbing kiln *(noborigama)* was widely used, and a fine example can be seen at the home of famed Kyoto potter Kawai Kanjirō. Constructed on a slope, the climbing kiln had as many as 20 chambers and could reach temperatures as high as 1400˚C.

During the Meiji period, ceramics waned in popularity, but were later part of a general revival in *mingei-hin* (folk arts). This movement was led by Yanagi Sōetsu, who encouraged famous potters such as Kawai, Tomimoto Kenkichi and Hamada Shōji. The English potter Bernard Leach studied in

Top: A pottery kiln - the first kiln was founded in Japan in the mid-13th century.
Bottom: Fine pottery can be found throughout Kyoto, particularly in the Kiyomizu-zaka pottery village.

MASON FLORENCE

MASON FLORENCE

Japan under Hamada and contributed to the folk-art revival. On his return to England, Leach promoted the appreciation of Japanese ceramics in the west.

There are now over 100 pottery centres in Japan, with a large number of artisans producing everything from exclusive tea utensils to souvenir badges *(tanuki)*. Department stores regularly organise exhibitions of ceramics. The TIC's useful *Ceramic Art & Crafts in Japan* leaflet provides full details of kilns, pottery centres and pottery fairs in Japan.

Lacquerware The Japanese have been using lacquer to protect and enhance wood since the Jōmon period. In the Meiji era, lacquerware became very popular abroad and remains one of Japan's best known products. Today Kyoto lacquerware *(kyō-shikki)* is highly regarded for its elegance and sound construction.

Lacquerware *(shikki* or *nurimono)* is made using the sap from the lacquer tree *(urushi)*. Once lacquer hardens it becomes inert and extraordinarily durable. The most common colour of lacquer is an amber or brown, but additives are used to produce black, violet, blue, yellow and even white. In the better pieces, multiple layers of lacquer are painstakingly applied and left to dry, and finally polished to a luxurious shine.

Japanese artisans have devised various ways to further enhance the beauty of lacquer. The most common method is *maki-e*, which involves the sprinkling of silver and gold powders onto liquid lacquer to form a picture. After the lacquer dries, another coat seals the picture. The final effect is often dazzling and some of the better pieces of maki-e lacquerware are now National Treasures.

Textiles Textiles have always played an important role in Japanese society: the fabric used in a kimono was an indication of class status. Until the introduction of cotton in the 16th century, Japanese textiles were made mostly of bast fibres or silk. Of all Japanese textiles, intricately embroidered brocades have always been the most highly prized, but sumptuary laws imposed on the merchant class in the Edo period prohibited the wearing of such kimonos.

To circumvent these laws, new techniques of kimono decoration were devised, the most important being the elaborate and ingenious technique of *yūzen*. Yūzen is best represented by Kyoto's renowned *kyō-yūzen*, a method of silk-dyeing *(senshoku)* developed to perfection in the 17th century by fan painter Miyazaki Yūzen. Kyō-yūzen designs typically feature simple circular flowers *(maru-tsukushi)*, birds and landscapes, and stand out for their use of bright-coloured dyes. The technique demands great dexterity in tracing designs by hand *(tegaki)* before rice paste is applied to fabric like a stencil to prevent colours from bleeding into other areas of the fabric. By repeatedly changing the pattern of the rice paste, very complex designs can be achieved.

Traditionally, when the dyeing process was complete, the material was rinsed in the Kamo-gawa and Katsura-gawa rivers (believed to be particularly effective in fixing the colours) before being hung out to dry. Every year in mid-August this ritual is re-enacted and the fabrics flap in the wind like rows of vibrant banners.

Kyoto is also famed for techniques in stencil-dyeing *(kyō-komon)* and tie-dyeing *(kyō-kanoko shibori)*. Kyō-komon (komon means small crest) gained notoriety in the 16th and 17th centuries, particularly among warriors who ordered the adornment of both their armour and kimono, through the stencilling of highly geometric designs onto fine silk with vibrant colours. Typically the patterns incorporate flowers, leaves and other flora.

For those who thought tie-dyeing was invented by T-shirt touting Grateful Dead heads, think again. Kyoto's tie-dying is said to date as far back as the 6th century, and numerous allusions to its glamour appear in literature as early as the 17th century. By the early 18th century, tie-dyed kimono were at the height of fashion, sought after for the astonishing detail created out of thousands of tiny sections of cloth, each bit individually plucked to form a motif and tied tightly using silk thread. All tediously set by hand, it could

Below: Kyoto lacquerware (kyō-shikki) is highly regarded for its elegance and sound construction.

MASON FLORENCE

COURTESY OF KODAI YŪZEN

Left: Detail of a kimono. Such beautiful dress is still worn by many Kyoto-ites at important festivals.

take as long as six months just to complete enough fabric to produce one kimono, yet people still practise the craft and employ new techniques.

At the other end of the refined, courtly spectrum, *aizome* (the technique of dyeing fabrics in vats of fermented indigo plants) gave Japan one of its most distinctive colours. Used traditionally in making hardy work clothes for the fields, Japan's beautiful indigo-blue can still be seen in many modern-day textile goods.

Together with Kyoto-dyed fabrics *(kyō-zome)*, Nishijin weaving (Nishijin-ori) is internationally renowned and dates to the founding of the city. Nishijin techniques were originally developed to satisfy the demands of the nobility who favoured the quality of illustrious silk fabrics. Over time new methods were adopted by the Kyoto weavers and they began to experiment with materials such as gauze, brocade, damask, satin and crepe.

During the turbulent civil wars of the 15th century, Kyoto's weavers congregated into a textiles quarter near the Kitano-Tenman-gū Shrine called Nishijin (literally, Western Camp). The industry was revamped during the Edo period and the popularity of Nishijin workmanship endured through the Meiji Restoration. In 1915, the Orinasu-kan textile museum was established to display Nishijin's fine silk fabrics and embroidery.

The best known Nishijin style is the exquisite *tsuzure*, a tightly woven tapestry cloth produced with a hand loom *(tebata)*, on which detailed patterns are preset. Kyoto's weavers, however, have continually introduced new styles, such as Japanese brocade *nishiki* (woven on Jacquard looms first imported from France around the turn of the century). Even today, innovative methods are being employed, such as the utilisation of computers, both for creating new designs and to pilot automated looms.

Woodwork

If jade is the perfect medium for the expression of the Chinese artistic genius, then for the Japanese it is wood. Perhaps nowhere else in the world has the art of joinery been lifted to such levels, and the carpentry and woodwork of Kyoto *(kyō-sashimono)* is among the best in the country.

Once a variety of wood types has been carefully chosen, preparations to properly season them can take up to 10 years. Craftspeople work with superior woods, such as cedar *(sugi)*, cherry *(sakura)*, zelkova *(keyaki)*, mulberry *(kuwa)* and paulownia *(kiri)*. They also work with many types of finish, including oils, wax, lacquer and juices of fruits such as persimmon and lime.

Kyoto produces a plethora of wooden furniture and household goods.

MASON FLORENCE

Particularly admired by collectors of Japanese antiques are chests called *tansu*, and the most prized of these is the *kaidan dansu*, so-named because it doubles as a flight of stairs (kaidan means stairs). These are becoming increasingly difficult to find, and increasingly expensive, but determined hunting at flea markets and antique shops may still land the occasional good piece.

Another realm of Kyoto wood products is *sadō-sashimono*, props and utensils employed in tearooms *(cha-shitsu)* and used in tea ceremony. High-quality wooden trays, shelves and delicately shaped water containers are an important part of tea ceremony.

Kyoto is also famous for its superb bamboo crafts *(chikkōhin)*, in particular the tools used in tea ceremony like ladles and whisks (which make interesting souvenirs). Japanese bamboo baskets are among the finest in the world and are remarkable for their complexity and delicacy (as well as their price). Be careful when buying bamboo crafts in Japan, as many are cheap imitations imported from countries such as China and the Philippines.

Dolls Among the finest of Japan's handcrafted dolls *(ningyō)* are Kyoto's *kyō-ningyō*. Elaborate in detail and dressed in fine brocade fabrics, they date from the Heian period and their exquisite costumes reflect the taste and styles of that aristocratic time.

Today, dolls figure prominently in two Japanese festivals: the Hina Matsuri (Doll Festival) held on 3 March, when girls display rows of ornamental *hina-ningyō* on tiered platforms in their homes, and on Children's Day (5 May), when both boys and girls display these special dolls.

Some other common dolls are *daruma* dolls, which are based on the figure of Bodhidharma, the religious sage commonly considered to be the founder of Zen Buddhism; *gosho-ningyō*, chubby plaster dolls sometimes dressed as figures in nō dramas; *kiku-ningyō*, large dolls adorned with real chrysanthemum flowers; and *ishō-ningyō*, which is a general term for elaborately costumed dolls, sometimes based on kabuki characters.

MASON FLORENCE

Fans Easily recognisable, the folding fan *(sensu)* is one of the few remaining symbols of traditional Japan still commonly used (it is not unusual to see blue-suited businessmen fanning themselves on the train during the rush-hour heat of summer).

As with many of Japan's traditional crafts, fans were first made in Kyoto and continue to be prolifically produced here. *Kyō-sensu* first found popularity among the early aristocracy, but by the late 12th century had spread to the general populace. Though fans were originally a practical and fashionable tool to keep oneself cool in Japan's sweltering summers, they gradually took on more aesthetic purposes as Japan's arts flourished from the 15th century onwards, from plain fans used in tea ceremony and incense smelling, to elaborate ones used in nō drama and traditional dance. Fans are still commonly used as decorative items and for ceremonial purposes.

Originally made from the leaves of the cypress tree, fans are now primarily made with elaborately painted Japanese paper fixed onto a skeleton of delicate bamboo ribs. The paper can feature decorations from simple geometric designs to courtly scenes from the Heian period and are often sprinkled with gold or silver leaf powder. The meticulous, step-by-step process of making kyō-sensu is fascinating to watch at one of the Kyoto fan-making studios that is open to the public.

MASON FLORENCE

Above: Kyō-sensu *(fans) are delicate and meticulously constructed.*

Washi *Washi,* traditional Japanese handmade paper, was introduced from China in the 5th century and reached its golden age in the Heian era, when it was highly prized by members of the Kyoto court for their poetry and diaries. Washi continued to be made in large quantities until the introduction of western paper in the 1870s. After that time, the number of families involved in the craft plummeted. However, there are still a number of traditional papermakers active in Kyoto, as well as in the Yoshino area south of Nara city. Recently, washi has enjoyed something of a revival (there's even washi for computer printers!) and a large variety is available in several of Kyoto's speciality stores.

Flower Arrangement

MASON FLORENCE

Ikebana, the art of flower arranging, was developed in the 15th century and can be grouped into three main styles: *rikka* (standing flowers), *shōka* (living flowers), and freestyle techniques such as *nageire* (throwing-in) and *moribana* (heaped flowers). There are several thousand different schools, the top three being Ikenobō, Ōhara and Sōgetsu, but they share one aim: to arrange flowers to represent heaven, earth and humanity. Ikebana displays were originally used as part of tea ceremony, but can now be found in private homes – in the *tokonoma* (alcove for displays) – and even in large hotels.

Apart from its cultural associations, ikebana is also a lucrative business – its schools have millions of students, including many young women who view proficiency in the art as a means to improve their marriage prospects.

Gardens

MARTIN MOOS

For garden enthusiasts, look no further. Kyoto is *the* place, home to a vast collection of Japan's foremost gardens encompassing the entire spectrum of styles.

Unlike European gardens, you probably won't find flowers, water fountains and flowing streams in Japanese gardens, and grass rarely makes an appearance. No matter how random a Japanese garden looks – with its mossy rocks, gnarled roots, haphazard paving and meandering paths – it is meticulously planned, right down to the last pebble. In the best Japanese gardens there is an exquisite 'compositional' quality, and no component is without a nuance of meaning. Even features that lie outside the garden may influence the layout – *shakkei*, or borrowed scenery, may make use of distant hills or a river, even the cone of a volcano. One example of this is the garden at Shūgaku-in Rikyū Imperial Villa in northern Kyoto, which incorporates mountains 10km distant.

Japanese gardens fall into four basic types: *funa asobi* (pleasure boat style), *shūyū* (stroll style), *kanshō* (contemplative style) and *kaiyū* (many pleasure style).

The funa asobi garden is centred on a large pond used for pleasure boating. The best views are from the water. In the Heian period, such gardens were often built around noble mansions, the most outstanding remaining example being the garden which surrounds Byōdō-in in Uji.

The shūyū garden is intended to be viewed from a winding path, allowing the garden to unfold and reveal itself in stages and from different vantages. Popular during the Heian, Kamakura and Muromachi periods, shūyū gardens can be found around many noble mansions and temples from those eras. A celebrated example is at Kyoto's Ginkaku-ji.

The kanshō garden should be viewed from one place; Zen rock gardens, the rock and raked gravel spaces that are also known as *karesansui*, or dry mountain stream gardens, are an example of this sort. The kanshō garden is designed to facilitate contemplation: such a garden can be viewed over and over without yielding to any one 'interpretation' of its meaning. The most famous kanshō garden of all is at Ryōan-ji Temple in Kyoto.

Lastly, the kaiyū, or many pleasure garden, features many small gardens surrounding a central pond, often incorporating a teahouse. The structure of this garden, like the stroll garden, lends itself to being explored on foot, and provides the viewer with a variety of changing scenes, many built as miniature landscapes. The most famous kaiyū garden is at the Katsura Rikyū Imperial Villa.

Right: Winter drizzle accentuates the austere style of the dry landscaped rock garden (karesansui).

MASON FLORENCE

continued from page 32
RELIGION

Religion in Japan is a complex issue, intimately connected with the culture as a whole. Western commentators inevitably focus on the way the Japanese are able to reconcile being simultaneously Shintō and Buddhist. It is far from the contradiction it may seem: Shintō is not really a religion in the conventional sense. It is more like a cultural framework that defines the essence of Japanese culture. A Japanese cannot escape being Shintō any more than a foreigner would be able to convert to it.

The rituals of both Shintō and Buddhism are used depending on their appropriateness to a particular situation – Shintō tends to be used for joyful events (such as weddings) and Buddhism for more sombre ones (such as funerals). Many young Japanese choose also to have Christian wedding ceremonies.

Shintō

Shintō, the way of the gods, is the indigenous Japanese religion, based on respect and awe of natural phenomena. The most powerful of these – the sun, moon, weather, mountaintops, trees, rivers, even grains of rice – are considered to contain their own gods *(kami)*. Shrines are erected in areas considered particularly sacred.

It is difficult to trace the origins of Shintō, as it has no founder or creed. It encompasses myths of the origin of Japan and the Japanese people, beliefs and practices in local communities and the highly structured rituals associated with the imperial family. Until 1945, Shintō belief dictated that the emperor was a divine being. In fact, according to Shintō, the entire Japanese race is descended from the gods.

The concept of purification is central to Shintō. *Oharai* is the most common purification ritual, performed by a priest waving a *sakaki*, a small construction of wood, paper and leaves. Purification ceremonies are conducted for people, cars, wedding ceremonies – almost anything that requires divine assistance. Also central to Shintō are fertility rituals, and certain festivals use symbolic sex acts to pray for or celebrate a good harvest.

Shintō & Buddhism

Shintō received its name in the 6th century in order to distinguish it from Buddhism. The Japanese rationalised the coexistence of both by considering Buddha to be a deity from China. In the 8th century, Shintō gods were enshrined in Buddhist temples as protectors of the Buddha. It was believed that kami, like human beings, were subject to the suffering of rebirth and similarly in need of Buddhist intercession to achieve liberation. Buddhist temples were built close to Shintō shrines and Buddhist sutras (collections of dialogues and discourses) were recited for the kami.

As Buddhism came to dominate, kami were considered to be incarnations of Bodhisattvas (Buddhas who delay liberation to help others). Buddhist statues were included on Shintō altars and statues of kami were made representing Buddhist priests.

State Shintō

There was a revival of interest in Shintō during the Edo period, particularly among neo-Confucian scholars. Their writings called for a return to imperial rule with Shintō as a state religion. Nationalist fervour during the Meiji period resulted in 'State Shintō' becoming the official religion. Buddhism was severely restricted and most religious sites containing both Buddhist and Shintō elements were separated. Shintō doctrines were taught in school and became central to the national ideology. After Japan's WWII defeat, the Allied forces dismantled the mechanisms of State Shintō and forced the emperor to refute his divine status.

Shugendō

This somewhat offbeat Buddhist school incorporates ancient shamanistic rites, Shintō beliefs and ascetic Buddhist traditions. The founder was En-no-Gyōja, to whom legendary powers of exorcism and magic are ascribed. He is credited with the enlightenment of kami, converting them to *gongen* (manifestations of Buddhas). Practitioners of Shugendō, called *yamabushi* (mountain priests), train both body and spirit with arduous exercises in the mountains. During the Meiji era, Shugendō was barred as being culturally debased, and today yamabushi are more common in tourist brochures and popular fiction than in the flesh. Shugendō survives, however, on mountains such as Dewa Sanzan and Ōmine-san in Nara Prefecture.

Buddhism

The founder of Buddhism was Siddhartha Gautama, the son of King Suddhodana and Queen Mahamaya of the Sakya clan. He was born around 563 BC at Lumbini on the border of present-day Nepal and India. In his 20s, Prince Siddhartha left his wife and newborn son to follow the path of an ascetic. When this didn't work out, Siddhartha tried meditation. During the night of the full moon in May, at the age of 35, he became 'the enlightened' or 'awakened one' – the Buddha (Nyorai in Japanese).

As the number of his followers grew, he founded a monastic community and codified the principles according to which the monks should live. The Buddha continued to preach and travel for 45 years, until his death in 483 BC. Buddhists believe that he is just one of the many Buddhas who have appeared in the past and who will continue to appear in the future.

Approximately 140 years after Buddha's death, the Buddhist community diverged into two schools: Hinayana and Mahayana, known as the Lesser Vehicle and the Greater Vehicle, respectively. The distinction was made by the Mahayana, and they could just as easily be defined as the southern and northern schools. The essential difference between the two is that Hinayana supports those who strive for the salvation of the individual, whereas Mahayana supports those who strive for the salvation of all beings. Traditionally, Hinayana prospered in south India and later spread to Sri Lanka, Myanmar (Burma), Thailand, Cambodia, Indonesia and Malaysia. Mahayana spread to inner Asia, as well as Mongolia, Siberia, Japan, China and Tibet.

Development of Buddhism in Japan Buddhism was introduced to Japan from China via Korea in the 6th century. Shōtoku Taishi, acknowledged as the 'father of Japanese Buddhism', drew heavily on Chinese culture to form a centralised state based on Buddhism. Hōryū-ji is the most celebrated temple from this period.

Nara Period The establishment of the first permanent capital at Heijō-kyō (present-day Nara) in 710 also marked the consolidation of Buddhism and Chinese culture in Japan. In 741, Emperor Shōmu issued a decree for construction of a network of state temples *(kokubun-ji)*. The centrepiece of this network was Tōdai-ji Temple.

Nara Buddhism revolved around six schools, these being Ritsu, Jōjitsu, Kusha, Sanron, Hossō and Kegon. They covered the whole range of Buddhist thought as received from China. Three of these schools still exist: Kegon, Hossō and Ritsu.

Heian Period When Kyoto became the capital of Japan in 794 it became central to the development and teaching of Buddhism. A number of new schools were established. During this period, political power drifted away from centralised government into the hands of the aristocracy, a major source of Buddhist support. The new schools, which introduced Mikkyō (esoteric Buddhism) from China, were independently founded on sacred mountains away from the orthodoxy of the Nara schools.

The Tendai school, derived from Mt Tian-tai in China, was founded by Saichō (762-822), also known as Dengyō Daishi, who established a base at Enryaku-ji Temple on Mt Hiei-zan. The school was only officially recognised a few days after his death, but Enryaku-ji developed into one of Japan's key Buddhist centres and was the source of all the later important schools (Jōdo, Zen and Nichiren).

The Shingon school (derived from the Chinese term for mantra) was established by the priest Kūkai (714-835 – known posthumously as Kōbō Daishi) at Kongōbu-ji Temple on Mt Koya-san and Tō-ji Temple in Kyoto. Kūkai trained for government service but at the age of 18 decided to switch his studies from Confucianism and Taoism to Buddhism. He travelled as part of a mission to Chang-an in China, where he immersed himself in esoteric Buddhism. On his return, his influence included not only spreading and sponsoring the study of Mikkyō, but also compiling the first Chinese-Japanese dictionary and the *hiragana* syllabary.

During this period there was an eventual collapse of law and order and a general feeling of pessimism in society, encouraging the belief in the Mappō or End of the Law theory, which predicted an age of darkness. This set the stage for subsequent schools to introduce the notion of saviour figures such as Amida.

Kamakura Period In this period (1185-1333), marked by savage clan warfare and the transfer of the capital to Kamakura, three schools emerged from the Tendai tradition. The Jōdo (Pure Land) school was founded by Hōnen (1133-1212) and shunned scholasticism in favour of the Nembutsu, a simple prayer that required the believer to recite 'Namu Amida Butsu' ('Hail Amida Buddha') as a path to salvation. This 'no-frills' approach was popular with the common folk.

Shinran (1173-1262), a disciple of Hōnen, broke away to form the Jōdo Shin-shū (True Pure Land) school. The core belief of this school considered that Amida had *already* saved everyone and hence to recite the Nembutsu was an expression of gratitude, not a petition for salvation.

The Nichiren school bears the name of its founder, Nichiren (1222-82), a fiery character who spurned traditional teachings to embrace the Lotus Sutra. His followers learned to recite 'Namu Myōhō Rengekyō', or 'Hail the Miraculous Law of the Lotus Sutra'. Nichiren's strident demands for the religious reform of government caused antagonism all round and he was frequently booted into exile. Yet the Nichiren school increased its influence in later centuries, and many new religious movements in present-day Japan, such as Sōka Gakkai can be linked to it.

Zen The word Zen is the Japanese reading of the Chinese *chan*. Legend has it that Bodshidharma, a 6th century Indian monk, introduced Zen to China. Most historians, however, credit this to Huineng (618-907), a Chinese monk. It took another 200 years for Zen to take root in Japan.

It did so in two major schools: Rinzai and Sōtō. The differences between the schools are not easily explained, but at a simple level Sōtō places more emphasis on seated meditation *(zazen)* and Rinzai on riddles *(kōan)*. The object of meditation for both schools is enlightenment *(satori)*, and Zen emphasises a more direct, intuitive approach rather than rational analysis.

The practice of zazen has its roots in Indian yoga. Its posture is the lotus position: the legs are crossed and tucked beneath the sitter, the back ramrod straight, the breathing rhythmical. The idea is to block out all sensation and empty the mind of thought. A kōan is a riddle that lacks a rational answer. Most are set pieces that owe their existence to the early evolution of Zen in China. In the course of meditating on these insoluble problems, the mind eventually returns to a form of primal consciousness. The most famous kōan was created by the Japanese monk Hakuin: 'What is the sound of one hand clapping?'

Confucianism

Although Confucianism is essentially a code of ethics pervasive throughout north Asia, it has exerted a strong enough influence to become part of Japanese social norms. Confucianism entered Japan via Korea in the 5th century. To regulate social behaviour, Confucius took the family unit as his starting point and stressed the importance of five relationships: master and subject, father and son, elder brother and younger brother, husband and wife, friend and friend. The strict observance of this social 'pecking order' has over the centuries become central to Japanese society.

continued on page 56

BUDDHIST TEMPLES

MARTIN MOOS

Temples *(tera* or *ji)* vary widely in their construction, depending on the type of school and historical era of construction. From the introduction of Buddhism in the 6th century until the Middle Ages, temples were the most important architectural works in Japan, and hence exerted a strong stylistic influence on all other types of building.

There were three main styles of early temple architecture, *tenjiku yō* (Indian), *karayō* (Chinese) and *wayō* (Japanese). All three styles were in fact introduced to Japan via China. Wayō arrived in the 7th century and gradually acquired local character, becoming the basis of much Japanese wooden architecture. It was named so as to distinguish it from karayō (also known as Zen style), which arrived in the 12th century. A mixture of wayō and karayō known as *setchuyō* eventually came to dominate, and tenjikuyō disappeared altogether.

With their origins in Chinese architecture and emphasis on other-worldly perfection, early temples were monumental and symmetrical in layout. A good example of the Chinese influence can be seen in the famous Phoenix Hall at Byōdō-in Temple in Uji (southern Kyoto), a Tang-style pavilion.

The Japanese affinity for asymmetry eventually affected temple design, leading to the more organic – although equally controlled – planning of later temple complexes. An excellent example in Kyoto is Daitoku-ji Temple, a Rinzai Zen monastery, which is a large complex containing a myriad of subtemples and gardens.

Gates

Temples generally have four gates, oriented to the north, south, east and west. The *nandai-mon* is the south gate, usually the largest one. There is also a central gate, *chū-mon*, which is sometimes incorporated into the cloister. The *niō-mon* houses frightful-looking statues of gods such as Raijin (the god of lightning) and Fū-jin (the god of wind).

The following are some common temple features:

kondō or *hondō*	–	main hall, containing the statue of Buddha
kōdō	–	meeting hall
kyōzō	–	sutra repository
sobō	–	dormitory
jikidō	–	dining hall

The layout of a temple tends to be a variation on a basic theme of pavilions, pagodas and cloisters, all constructed of wood.

Right: The wayō-style Phoenix Hall, at Byōdō-in Temple in Uji, dates from the Heian period. It's a fine example of the Chinese influence on this period of Japanese architecture.

MARTIN MOOS

Asuka Era

Asuka-dera style: the pagoda is centred within the cloister.
Shitennō-ji style: all buildings are placed in a line.

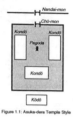

Figure 1.1: Asuka-dera Temple Style

Figure 1.2: Shitennō-ji Temple Style

Nara Era

Hōryū-ji style: the pagoda and kondō are next to one another within the cloister.
Yakushi style: the kondō is central with a pagoda either side, all within the cloister.

Figure 2.1: Hōryū-ji Temple Style

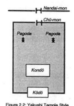

Figure 2.2: Yakushi Temple Style

Pagodas

The Gojū-no-tō, or five storey pagoda, is a major component of temple design. These are elegant wooden towers, symbolising Shaka, the Buddha. Their design is a variation of the Indian stupa, a structure originally intended to hold the remains of Shaka (sometimes with an actual tooth or chip of bone, more often represented by crystal or amber). The spire on top usually has nine tiers, representing the nine spheres of heaven.

Kyoto contains a number of excellent examples of five storey pagodas. Tō-ji Temple (a Shingon seminary) is the best known and the tallest in Japan. Other impressive pagodas include Yasaka-no-tō, and those at Daigo-ji and Kiyomizu-dera temples.

Main Hall

The main hall, known as the kondō, *hondō*, *butsu-den*, *miei-dō*, *amida-dō* or *komponchū-dō*, contains the statue of Buddha, the most holy item in a temple. As the symbol of Shaka, the pagoda was originally given prime position within the temple layout, but as a number of other Buddhas began to gain importance, the kondō became the central structure, as it could contain the images of a variety of Buddhas.

Buddhist Images

There are dozens of images in the Japanese Buddhist pantheon, varying from temple to temple, depending on the religious school or period of construction. Three of the most common images are those of Shaka

Above: Dainichi (the Cosmic Buddha) usually sits with one hand clasped around a raised finger of the other hand – a sexual gesture indicating the unity of being.

(Sanskrit: Sakyamuni), the Historical Buddha; Amida (Sanskrit: Amitabha), the Buddha of the Western Paradise or of light; and Miroku (Sanskrit: Maitreya), the Buddha of the Future.

Kannon (Sanskrit: Avalokitesvara) is the 'one who hears their cries' and is available in no less than 33 different versions, including as the goddess of mercy, a female form popular with expectant mothers. When Christianity was banned, Japanese believers kept faith with the Holy Virgin by creating a clone 'Maria Kannon'.

Jizō, known formally as O-Jizō-san, is often depicted as a monk with a staff in one hand and a jewel in the other. According to legend, this patron of travellers, children and expectant mothers, helps the souls of dead children perform their task of building walls of pebbles on the banks of Sai-no-kawara, the river of the underworld. Believers place stones on or around Jizō statues as additional help.

SHINTŌ SHRINES

Shrines can be called *jinja, jingū, gū* or *taisha*. The original Shintō shrine is Izumo Taisha in Shimane Prefecture, which has the largest shrine hall in Japan. It is said to have been modelled on the Emperor's residence, and its style, known as *taisha-zukuri*, was extremely influential on later shrine design. Shrines tend to use simple, unadorned wood construction, and are built raised above the ground on posts. The roof is gabled, not hipped as with temple architecture. The entrance is generally from the end, not the side, again distinguishing it from temple design. The distinctive roof line of shrine architecture is due to an elaboration of the structural elements of the roof. The crisscross elements are called *chigi* and the horizontal elements are called *katsuogi*.

As Buddhism increased its influence over Shintō, it also affected the architecture. The clean lines of the early shrines were replaced with curving eaves and other ornamental details. Worshippers were provided with shelter by extending the roof or even building a separate worship hall. This led to the *nagare* style, the most common type of shrine architecture. Excellent examples in Kyoto can be found at Shimogamo-jinja and Kamigamo-jinja.

The *gongen* style uses a H-shaped plan, connecting two halls with an intersecting gabled roof and hallway called an *ishi no ma*. This element symbolises the connection between the divine and the ordinary worlds. The best example of this style in Kyoto is at Kitano-Tenman-gū.

Shrine Surroundings

At the entrance to the shrine is the *torii* (gateway) marking the boundary of the sacred precinct. The most dominant torii in Kyoto is in front of Heian-jingū

MASON FLORENCE

Top: The most popular Buddhist images are: Shaka (the Historical Buddha), Amida (the Buddha of Western Paradise or of Light), Yakushi (the Healing Buddha), and Dainichi (see diagram on previous page).
Above: The nagare style is the most common form of shrine architecture.

Left: This depiction of Izumo Taisha, the original Shintō shrine, shows the highly influential taisha-zukuri style of shrine architecture. The roof line displays the crisscross elements or the upward extension of the gables known as chigi, and the horizontal elements, called katsuogi.
Below: The four roof styles which comprise Shintō roof patterns – gabled; square pyramidal; hipped; and hipped with gables.

Shrine, a massive concrete structure a considerable distance south of the shrine.

Fushimi-Inari Taisha Shrine south of Kyoto has thousands of bright vermilion gates lining paths up the mountain to the shrine itself.

Shimenawa, plaited ropes decorated with strips of white paper *(gohei)*, are strung across the top of the torii. They are also wrapped around sacred rocks or trees or above the actual shrine entrance. A pair of stone lion-like creatures called *koma-inu* can often be found flanking the main path. One usually has its mouth open in a roar and the other has its mouth closed.

The *kannushi* (chief priest) of the shrine is responsible for religious rites and the administration of the shrine. The priests dress in blue and white; on special occasions they don more ornate clothes and wear an *eboshi* (a black cap with a protruding, folded tip). *Miko* (shrine maidens) dress in vermilion and white. The ceremonial *kagura* dances performed by miko can be traced back to shamanistic trances.

Mythical Creatures

A variety of fabulous creatures inhabit Japanese folklore and crop up regularly in shops, festivals and shrines:

Tanuki is often translated as badger, but bears a closer resemblance to a North American raccoon. Like the fox, the tanuki is thought of as a mischievous creature and is credited with supernatural powers, but is more a figure of fun than the fox. Statues usually depict the tanuki in an upright position with sombrero-like straw headgear and clasping a bottle of sake. Note the enormous testicles.

Kitsune is a fox, but for the Japanese it also has strong connections with the supernatural and is worshipped in Japan at over 30,000 Inari shrines as the messenger of the harvest god. Fushimi-Inari Taisha is the largest of its kind and is crammed with fox statues.

Maneki-neko, the beckoning cat, is a very common sight outside shops or restaurants. The raised left paw attracts customers and their money.

Tengu are mountain goblins with a capricious nature, sometimes abduct-

Top: The mythical tanuki are mischievous creatures credited with supernatural powers. They usually wear sombrero-like straw headgear and clasp a bottle of sake.
Above: Maneki-neko, the beckoning cat, raises its left paw to attract customers and their money.

ing children, sometimes returning those who were missing. Their unmistakable feature is a long nose.

Kappa are amphibious creatures about the size of a 12 or 13-year-old boy and have webbed hands and feet. They have a reputation for mischief, such as dragging horses into rivers or stealing cucumbers (their favourite food). The source of their power is a depression on top of their heads which must always contain water. A crafty method to outwit a kappa is to bow to it. When the kappa – Japanese to the core – bows back, it empties the water from its head and loses its power. The alternatives are not pleasant. Kappa are said to enjoy ripping out their victim's liver through the anus!

RELIGIOUS SCULPTURE

Fine art in Japan begins with the introduction of Mahayana Buddhism in the 6th century AD. Existing pottery and metalwork skills were turned to the production of Buddhist images. During the late Heian era, native sculpture techniques flourished and a recognisable Japanese style appeared. A knowledge of the different types of Buddhist sculptures found in Japanese temples is a good step to understanding Buddhism itself. The images fall into four main groups, each of which represents a different level of being in the Buddhist cosmology.

At the head of Japanese Buddhism's hierarchy are *nyorai*, or Buddhas. These are beings who have attained enlightenment (nirvana) and freed themselves from the cycle of rebirth. Nyorai images are conspicuous by their simple robes, a lump on the head symbolising wisdom and a head of tight 'snail shell' curls. The major nyorai are: Shaka (the Historical Buddha), one hand raised in a preaching gesture; Yakushi (the Healing Buddha), making the same gesture with one hand while the other clutches a vial of medicine; Amida (the Buddha of Western Paradise or of Light), usually seen sitting with knuckles together in a meditative posture; and Dainichi (the Cosmic Buddha), usually portrayed in princely attire, sitting with one hand clasped around a raised finger of the other hand (a sexual gesture indicating the unity of being). Nyorai are usually portrayed with two bodhisattvas in a triad configuration.

After Buddhas, the next most important beings are *bosatsu* (bodhisattvas). These are beings who have put off their own entry into nirvana in order to help others attain enlightenment. Images of bosatsu are more human in appearance than nyorai and most easily distinguished from the latter by a topknot of hair or a crowned headpiece, sometimes with smaller figures built into the crown. The most common bosatsu in Japanese temples is Kannon, the goddess of mercy. Also common, both in temples and around the countryside, are images of Jizō, often depicted carrying children in their arms. The next group of beings are not native to Buddhism, but were borrowed from Hinduism to serve particular purposes in the Buddhist cosmology. These are *ten* (heavenly beings or devas). While some appear as beastly ogres, others are human in appearance. The most common of these are *niō* (guardians), often found in the gates leading up to temples.

Finally, there are the *myō-ō* (kings of wisdom or light). These beings serve as protectors of Buddhism and were introduced to Japan along with esoteric Buddhism in the 9th century. The most common myō-ō image is Fudō Myō-ō, usually depicted clutching an upright sword.

WHAT TO DO AT TEMPLES & SHRINES

There are no steadfast rituals you must follow when visiting temples and shrines, though most Japanese do pray briefly and have a strong penchant for having their fortunes told.

Buddhist temples generally charge an admission fee of between ¥300 and ¥600. An additional fee is sometimes necessary to visit a museum of temple treasures, the temple gardens or for a cup of tea. Talismans and fortunes are often on sale near the entrance or in one of the halls. An attractive souvenir available for about ¥1000 at many temples is *shūin-chō*, a cloth-covered, pocket-sized booklet with a concertina of folding pages. For a small fee, you can ask a temple monk to give an artistic touch to your booklet by adding calligraphy. As with railway stations and many tourist attractions, temples often provide ink pads and stamps for visitors to print souvenir logos in their booklet.

The central Buddha image, in the main hall, has offerings of incense sticks, food or flowers placed before it. In front of the hall is an offering box *(saisen-bako)*. Visitors stand in front of the hall, toss a coin (or coins) into the box, press their palms together and pray.

Unlike many Buddhist temples, no entrance fee is charged for entering most Shintō shrines. Before prayer, visitors are expected to rinse their hands and mouth with pure water. In a small pavilion *(temizuya)*, a stone ablution basin *(chōzuya)* and bamboo ladle *(hishaku)* are provided for this purpose. Rinse both hands before pouring water into a cupped hand to rinse the mouth.

MASON FLORENCE

Above: A worshipper rings the shrine bell to awaken the gods.

Above the offering box hangs a long rope with a bell attached. Visitors toss a coin into the box, then grab and shake the rope to 'wake the gods', bow twice, clap loudly twice, bow again twice (once deeply, once lightly), and then step back and to the side. It is considered improper to turn one's back on the shrine.

Amulets are popular purchases at shrines. *O-mamori*, special talismans, are purchased at shrines to ensure good luck or ward off evil – taxi drivers often have a 'traffic safety' one dangling from the rear-view mirror. Votive plaques *(ema)* made of wood with a picture on one side and a blank space on the other are also common. On the blank side visitors write a wish, for example success in exams, luck in finding a sweetheart or safe delivery of a healthy child. Dozens of these plaques can be seen attached to boards in shrine precincts.

Fortunes *(o-mikuji)* are selected by drawing a numbered bamboo or steel rod from a box and picking out the associated fortune slip. Luck is classified as *dai-kichi* (great good fortune), *kichi* (good fortune), *shō-kichi* (middling good fortune) and *kyō* (bad luck). If you like the fortune slip you've been given, you can take it home. If you've drawn bad luck, you can tie it to the branch of a tree in the shrine grounds – presumably some other force can then worry about it.

Neighbourhood Shrines

Every neighbourhood in every Japanese town or city has its own tiny shrine to Jizō. Pieces of clothing or red bibs draped around Jizō figures are an attempt to cover the souls of dead children. An annual August children's festival *(Jizō-bon)* features two days of praying and playing around the Jizō shrine by the local children dressed in *yukata* (a light kimono for summer or bathing in a ryokan).

The shrines are located by *fū-sui* (known in Chinese as feng shui), a specifically Asian form of geomancy. It is impossible (or bad luck) to move them, so they are found almost everywhere, often notched into concrete walls or telephone poles.

These shrines are maintained by the local community, each person contributing a regular small sum of money. The person responsible for the shrine changes on a yearly basis, but everyone in the area will leave offerings for Jizō, usually something they themselves have excess of – fruit, chocolate or sake.

continued from page 49

Christianity

Portuguese missionaries introduced Christianity to Japan in the 16th century. In 1549, Francis Xavier landed at Kagoshima on Kyūshū. At first, the daimyō seemed eager to convert, although gaining trade advantages for Portugal, then building its empire in Asia, was just as important, if not more so.

The initial tolerance that had been shown by Oda Nobunaga was reversed by his successor, Toyotomi Hideyoshi, who saw the religious missionaries as an insidious colonial threat. Sectorial differences revealed themselves in the fight between the Jesuits and Franciscans over Japanese souls to 'balance the account'. Christianity was banned in 1587, and 26 Christians (both Japanese and foreign) were crucified in Nagasaki 10 years later. After expelling the remaining missionaries in 1614, Japan closed itself to the outside world for several centuries. The Christian faith survived in hiding during this period, mainly on Kyūshū. Christian missionaries were allowed back at the beginning of the Meiji era and built churches, hospitals and schools, many of which still exist.

It is difficult to judge the true extent of Christian influence in contemporary Japan. While many parents send their children, particularly girls, to Christian schools because of the increased exposure to English and international connections they receive there, the students largely consider themselves Buddhist or nonreligious. Mormons are active in Japan and have had relative success. However, many of their converts are simply younger Japanese trying to rebel against their parents, and often their enthusiasm wanes.

New Religions

A number of new religions have appeared since the Meiji period. They cover a wide range of beliefs, from personality cults to faith healing and UFOs. By far the largest of these new religions is Sōka Gakkai (Creative Education Society). Founded in the 1930s, it follows Nichiren's teachings and numbers over 20 million followers.

The millennial Aum Shinrikyō sect became instantly famous worldwide in 1995 with its poison gas attack on the Tokyo subway system. Under the influence of guru Shōkō Asahara, the sect had decided to speed up the apocalypse they are imminently expecting. For some time afterwards, rubbish bins disappeared from subway stations all over Japan. A number of the key Aum Shinrikyō members are still at large and their mug shots can be seen on police posters all over Japan.

Religious Services in English

Kyoto City Church (Interdenominational; Map 8)
(☎ 222-1854) near Dōshisha University north of Imadegawa-dōri; services 6 pm Sunday, bible study Wednesday evening and a coffee house on Friday night

Kyoto International Chapel (Protestant non-Pentecostal)
(☎ 0774-64-0754) at Kyō-Tanabe (south Kyoto); services 10 am Sunday

Kyoto Lutheran Church (Protestant; Map 8)
(☎ 781-3903) a few minutes walk east of the Keihan line Demachiyanagi station; services 10.30 am Sunday

Kyoto St Agnes Episcopal Church (Interdenominational; Map 7)
(☎ 0775-78-8015) a few minutes walk north of the Karasuma line Marutamachi subway station; services 8.30 am Sunday

Shin-Ai Catholic Kindergarten (Roman Catholic)
(☎ 822-8952) next to the Kyoto Royal Hotel near the Sanjō-dōri and Kawaramachi-dōri intersection; services 3 pm Sunday

St Mary's Church (Anglican/Episcopal; Map 10)
(☎ 771-2581) near the north-east corner of Heian-jingū; services 8 am Sunday followed by breakfast

Members of the Bahai'i faith can call ☎ 712-0447 for information on local gatherings.

LANGUAGE

See the Language chapter at the back of this book for information about Japanese language and Kyoto dialect.

A	B
C	D	E
F	G

Architecture of 'old' Kyoto:
A: A traditional sweet shop. B: The Gion-Shinbashi area preserves lovely wooden house fronts. C: Restaurant facade, eastern Kyoto. D: Stepping out in the old fashioned way. E: A neighbourhood shrine. F: Gion scenes. G: Making an understated entrance is an old Japanese virtue.

A	B
C	
D	E

A: One of the many gates to Kitano-Tenman-gū Shrine, western Kyoto.
B: Moss garden at Sanzen-in Temple, Ōhara.
C: The Nandai-mon (main gate) at Tō-ji Temple, close to the Kyoto city centre.
D: A walking path constructed of tiles at Nison-in Temple, Arashiyama.
E: Shōrin-in Temple, Ōhara, flanked by huge camphor trees.

Facts for the Visitor

WHEN TO GO

Kyoto is a city with countless attractions at any time of the year, even during the muggy height of summer. While spring and autumn are probably the best times to visit in terms of weather, they are also the most popular with Japanese tour groups and school excursions so the crowds can be quite severe. Other jam-packed periods are New Year, Golden Week (late April to early May), Obon in August and any national holiday (see the Public Holidays & Special Events section in this chapter).

Winter in Kyoto is quiet and, despite the often unbearable cold, it's a viable option if you have an aversion to crowds. Likewise, Kyoto's sticky summer heat can keep enough people indoors to offer occasional solitude. During these slow months, Kyoto city sponsors a series of intriguing 'off-season' tours worth looking into (see the Organised Tours section in the Getting Around chapter).

The ephemeral cherry blossom season *(hanami)* usually starts in April and lasts about a week. Japanese become pervaded with 'cherry blossom mania' and descend on favourite spots in hordes. Top spots include the Path of Philosophy, Maruyama-kōen Park and Heian-jingū Shrine, Arashiyama and the Imperial Palace Park. A good place to see the cherry blossoms without the crowds is the Kamo-gawa River north of Demachiyanagi station.

Autumn colours are similarly spectacular and attract huge numbers of leaf-gazers. Popular viewing spots include Ōhara, Kurama and Shūgaku-in Rikyū Imperial Villa, Sagano and Takao and Tōfuku-ji Temple. Perhaps the best place to enjoy the foliage away from the crowds is in the Takao region.

See the Things to See & Do chapter for the locations of the above-named sights.

Planning Your Itinerary

There is no limit to amount of time you could spend exploring Kyoto. In addition to droves of cultural landmarks, Kyoto's greatest asset is the nearby mountains with hiking trails and peaceful, pristine nature. For pleasant day trips out of the city, try the northern Kitayama mountains or the areas west of the city around Takao, both of which are well serviced by bus and train.

The city's one major drawback is that its fame attracts huge numbers of visitors, particularly during holidays and festivals. An early start to the day is the best way to catch a glimpse of 'old Kyoto', but sooner or later you are bound to collide with the tour-group crowds. The best advice is to avoid spending all your time on the major attractions but just spend some time wandering the backstreets.

The absolute minimum stay would be two days, in which you could just scratch the surface of sights around Kyoto station and the Higashiyama area in eastern Kyoto. Five days will give you time to add Arashiyama, western and central Kyoto. Ten days would allow you to cover these areas plus northern, southern and south-eastern Kyoto and leave a day or so for places further afield.

Kyoto is an excellent place to indulge specific cultural interests, whether they be the arts, Buddhism or folkcrafts. The best place to find information on such activities is the Tourist Information Center (TIC), eg details are available on Zen temples which accept foreigners as students of meditation, specialist museums, Japanese gardens and villas, Japanese culinary arts and natural-food outlets, traditional crafts, Japanese drama, *chanoyu* (tea ceremony) and *ikebana* (flower arranging).

Whatever your time limit, try not to over-do the number of sights you visit. Quite apart from the sensory overload, intensive sight-seeing entails a heavy outlay on admission fees. If you don't find temples to your liking, don't visit them. Many of the city's greatest aspects can be enjoyed for free and Kyoto is particularly suited to rambling through the backstreets.

Kyoto also makes an excellent base for

travel in western Japan and is a logical place to begin (or end) a Japan Rail Pass trip (see the Train section in the Getting There & Away chapter). For exploring the Kansai District, Kyoto is by far the best choice considering its wealth of accommodation and its proximity to renowned sights such as Lake Biwa-ko and Himeji. Osaka and Kōbe are under an hour away by train and not much further is Nara, one of Japan's major religious sites (see the Excursions chapter).

ORIENTATION

Kyoto sits in the southern part of Kyoto Prefecture (Kyoto-fu), one of Japan's 47 prefectural regions. The city is commonly divided into five sections designating the central *(raku-chū)*, eastern *(raku-tō)*, northern *(raku-hoku)*, western *(raku-sai)* and southern *(raku-nan)* areas of town, plus *raku-gai*, which refers to the outskirts of the city.

Kyoto has retained a rectangular grid system based on the classical Chinese concept. This

Kyoto Highlights

Sites	Locations	Description
Temples		
Kiyomizu-dera	eastern Kyoto	hillside views from huge wooden veranda
Sanjūsangen-dō	eastern Kyoto	1001 Buddhist Kannon statues
Ginkaku-ji	eastern Kyoto	15th century *shōgun's* 'Silver Pavilion'
Higashi & Nishi Hongan-ji	Kyoto station area	enormous wooden structures
Tō-ji	Kyoto station area	tallest pagoda in Japan; two monthly markets
Sanzen-in	Ōhara (northern Kyoto)	picturesque Yusei-en Garden
Byōdō-in	Uji (southern Kyoto)	11th century Phoenix Hall
Mampuku-ji	southern Kyoto	Ming dynasty Chinese-style buildings
Kurama-dera	Kurama (northern Kyoto)	mountain path leading to Kibune village
Nanzen-ji	eastern Kyoto	quiet temple complex with imposing gate
Shrines		
Yasaka-jinja	eastern Kyoto	colourful gate overlooking Shijō-dōri
Heian-jingū	eastern Kyoto	colourful replica of 8th century imperial palace
Fushimi-Inari Taisha	southern Kyoto	paths with thousands of vermilion *torii* (gates)
Kitano-Tenman-gū	northern Kyoto	lively flea market on 25th of each month
Shimogamo-jinja	northern Kyoto	pleasant wooded Tadasu-no-mori entry path
Kamigamo-jinja	northern Kyoto	striking conical sand mounds in peaceful setting
Villas		
Shūgaku-in Rikyū	northern Kyoto	sprawling imperial estate at foot of Mt Hiei-zan
Katsura Rikyū	south-western Kyoto	delightful stroll garden and buildings
Gardens		
Ryōan-ji Temple	northern Kyoto	classic Zen rock garden
Daitoku-ji Temple	northern Kyoto	numerous subtemples with Zen gardens
Nijō-jō Castle	central Kyoto	lovely Ninomaru Palace garden
Kōdai-ji Temple	eastern Kyoto	delicate landscape with mountain backdrop
Tenryū-ji Temple	western Kyoto	14th century Zen garden
Saihō-ji Temple	south-western Kyoto	plush moss gardens
Museums		
Kyoto National Museum	eastern Kyoto	superb collection of temple treasures
Kawai Kanjirō Memorial Hall	eastern Kyoto	pottery studio in rustic old home
Museum of Kyoto	central Kyoto	impressive exhibits on historical Kyoto

system of numbered streets running east-west and avenues running north-south makes it relatively easy to find your way around. Addresses are indicated with the name of the closest intersection and their location north *(agaru)* or south *(sagaru)* of that intersection. Likewise, east *(higashi-iru)* or west *(nishi-iru)* indicate a cross-town direction.

Kyoto station is in the south of the city, and from there Karasuma-dōri runs north past Higashi Hongan-ji Temple, the commercial centre of town and the Imperial Palace. The commercial and nightlife centres are between Shijō-dōri and Sanjō-dōri (to the south and north of the centre respectively) and between the Gion District and Karasuma-dōri (to the east and west respectively). The less populated northern parts of the city have a far greener feel, and you can still find people tending rice fields sandwiched between apartment buildings. Most of the south has been overrun with industry.

Although many of the major sights are in the city centre, the best of Kyoto's sightseeing is on the fringes of the city in the north, east and west. Due north through the Kitayama mountains, quaint rural villages dot the landscape up to the Sea of Japan and Wakasa-wan Bay, while south-west flatlands follow the path of the Yodo-gawa River toward Osaka and Seto Inland Sea. West of town are the Tanba mountains and Hyōgo Prefecture and east, just over Mt Hiei-zan and the Higashiyama mountains, is Shiga Prefecture and the city's main source of water, Lake Biwa-ko.

Efficient bus services crisscross the city. The quickest way to travel between the far north and south of the city is to take the Karasuma line subway, while the Tōzai line subway is convenient for moving between east and west in central Kyoto and also for reaching Yamashina and Daigo in the southeast of the city.

MAPS

Available free at the TIC, *Tourist Map of Kyoto-Nara* fulfills most mapping needs and includes a simplified map of the subway and bus systems. *Walking Tour Courses in Kyoto*

roughly details ways to see the sights on foot. Also available is the *Kyoto Transportation Guide* map which has detailed information on bus routes in the city and some of the major stops written in both English and Japanese. Some find that the Japanese-only version, available at major bus stops, is more useful, as all names are written in Japanese and it is more detailed. Also at the TIC, the *Useful Information* sheet has lists of admission prices and opening hours of the main sights, as well as a list of inexpensive restaurants with an accompanying map.

Another map intended for long-term foreign residents is the *Guide to Kyoto*, available free at the Kyoto International Community House (KICH; see the Useful Organisations section later in this chapter). There are many other useful maps for sale at local English-language bookshops, some practical for excursions outside Kyoto. Kōdansha's *Kyoto-Osaka: A Bilingual Atlas* is a mini-atlas of the region and Shōbunsha's *Tourist Map of Kyoto* includes some brief historical information and small maps of Nara, Osaka and Kōbe.

San-Art's *Kyoto Information Map*, decent value at ¥300, is a guide magazine with comic book-style maps, basic bilingual explanations and interesting tidbits on many of the city's major sights.

Serious hikers should pick up Shōbunsha's *Kyoto Kitayama* maps (dividing the northern mountain region into two detailed volumes), though they are only available in Japanese. These can be found at most local bookshops. If you're seeking hard-to-find references such as topographical or survey maps check out Kansai Map Center (☎ 761-5141), a small store run out of a private home near Kyoto University (Map 8), a few hundred metres east of the Imadegawa-dōri and Higashiyama-dōri intersection.

Taking top prize in creative mapping is the recent *Kyoto Green Map* (¥500), the first in Asia of a worldwide network of eco-specific city maps outlining everything from organic food markets and recycling centres to illegal waste dumps. You can track one down by phoning ☎ 702-6548.

TOURIST OFFICES
Local Tourist Offices
The best source of information on Kyoto and the Kansai region is the Japan National Tourism Association's (JNTO) TIC (Map 11; ☎ 371-5649); it's just a couple of minutes walk north of Kyoto station, on the ground level of Kyoto Tower on Karasuma-dōri. It's open from 9 am to 5 pm on weekdays, to noon on Saturday, closed Sunday and holidays.

The helpful staff have maps, literature and an amazing amount of information on Kyoto at their capable fingertips. The TIC also functions as a tourist information office for the whole of Japan, so to cope with the daily flood of visitors, it deals with inquiries by numbers and imposes a lightly enforced time limit. Full details of accommodation are available and staff here at the Welcome Inn counter can make reservations for you. Volunteer guides can also be arranged through the TIC if you allow the staff a day's notice.

Reservations are necessary to visit the Kyoto Imperial Palace, the imperial villas and Saihō-ji Temple (Koke-dera). Details are provided in the relevant sections of the Things to See & Do chapter, and the TIC can also explain the procedure. Reservations for Katsura Rikyū Imperial Villa and Shūgaku-in Rikyū Imperial Villa must be organised at the relevant offices, and cannot be arranged by the TIC.

There is a Kyoto city tourist information centre (☎ 343-6656), open daily from 8.30 am to 7 pm, inside the new Kyoto station building (Map 11), just across from Cafe du Monde, though it's more geared toward assisting Japanese visitors. However, this office can be of great assistance when the TIC is closed.

On the 9th floor of the station building, the Kyoto Tourism Federation (Map 11; ☎ 371-2226) distributes information on outlying destinations in Kyoto Prefecture (it has very little on the city itself). Though most literature is only in Japanese, there is a useful English map of Kyoto Prefecture worth picking up for excursions. It's open daily from 9.30 am to 6 pm. Also, on the south-side concourse inside Kyoto station, there is a tourist information counter staffed by local volunteers of the Systemized Goodwill Guide group – again, sufficient for a few quick questions, but anything further would best be taken over to the TIC.

If you're looking to read about Kyoto on the way from Kansai international airport (KIX; Map 1), drop in at the Kansai TIC (☎ 0724-56-6025) on the 1st floor of the international arrivals lobby. They can provide information on the Kansai region and is open from 9 am to 9 pm daily.

The Japan Travel-Phone (☎ 371-5649) provides travel-related information and language assistance in English, seven days a week from 9 am to 5 pm. It can be particularly useful if you arrive when the TIC is closed.

JNTO Offices Abroad
JNTO offices overseas include:

Australia
   (☎ 02-232-4522) Level 33, Chifley Tower, 2 Chifley Square, Sydney, NSW 2000
Canada
   (☎ 416-366-7140) 165 University Ave, Toronto, Ontario M5H 3B8
China
   (☎ 2525-5295) Suite 3606, Two Exchange Square, 8 Connaught Place, Central, Hong Kong
France
   (☎ 01 42 96 20 29) 4-8 rue Sainte-Anne, 75001 Paris
Germany
   (☎ 069-20353) Kaiserstrasse 11, 60311 Frankfurt am Main 1
South Korea
   (☎ 02-752-7968) 10 Da-Dong, Chung-Ku, Seoul
Switzerland
   (☎ 022-731-81-40) 13 Rue de Berne, 1201 Geneva
Thailand
   (☎ 02-233-5108) Wall Street Tower Building, 33/61, Suriwong Rd, Bangkok 10500
UK
   (☎ 0171-734-9638) 20 Saville Row, London WIX 1AE
USA
   Chicago: (☎ 312-222-0874) Suite 770, 401 North Michigan Ave, IL 60611
   Dallas: (☎ 214-754-1820) Suite 980, 2121 San Jacinto St, TX 75201
   Los Angeles: (☎ 213-623-1952) Suite 1611, 624 South Grand Ave, CA 90017
   New York: (☎ 212-757-5640) Suite 1250, One Rockefeller Plaza, NY 10020
   San Francisco: (☎ 415-989-7140) Suite 601, 360 Post St, CA 94108

DOCUMENTS
Visas

Most visitors who are not planning to engage in any remunerative activities while in Japan are exempt from obtaining visas and will be given a landing stamp in their passport upon arrival. Stays of up to six months are permitted for citizens of Austria, Germany, Ireland, Mexico, Switzerland and the UK. Stays of up to three months are permitted for citizens of Argentina, Belgium, Canada, Denmark, Finland, France, Iceland, Israel, Italy, Malaysia, Netherlands, New Zealand, Norway, Singapore, Spain, Sweden, the USA and a number of other countries.

Visitors from Australia and South Africa are among those nationals still requiring a visa. This is usually issued free, but passport photographs are required and a return or onward ticket must be shown.

As well as the information below on visas and regulations, check with your nearest Japanese embassy or go to the Japanese Ministry of Foreign Affairs Web site (www.mofa.go.jp/), where you can check out the 'Guide to Japanese Visas', read about working-holiday visas and find details on the Japan Exchange & Teaching (JET) program, which sponsors native English-speakers to come to Japan to teach in the public school system.

Working-Holiday Visas Australians, Canadians and New Zealanders between the ages of 18 and 25 (the age limit can be pushed up to 30) can apply for a working-holiday visa. This visa allows a six month stay and two six month extensions. It aims to enable young people to travel extensively during their stay, and for this reason employment is supposed to be part-time or temporary, although in practice many people work full time. If you are arriving on a working-holiday visa you may like to contact the Tokyo-based Japan Association for Working Holiday Makers (☎ 03-3389-0181).

A working-holiday visa is much easier to obtain than a working visa and is popular with Japanese employers. Applicants must apply for the visa within their own countries and have the equivalent of A$4000 of funds and an onward ticket from Japan.

Working Visas Requirements for working visas are becoming increasingly strict. Immigration laws introduced in 1990 designate legal employment categories for foreigners and specify standards of experience and qualifications. Arriving in Japan and looking for a job has become a tougher proposition, though many people still do it. In cases where an employer is willing to sponsor you, it is necessary for the employer to obtain a Certificate of Eligibility. Following this, you must apply for a working visa at a foreign visa office, not within Japan.

Visa Extensions

With the exception of those nationals whose countries have reciprocal visa exemptions and who can stay for six months, 90 days is the limit for most people. Though it has become difficult to do so, to extend a tourist visa beyond the standard three months, apply at the Kyoto branch of the Osaka Immigration Bureau (Map 10), on the 4th floor of the Dai Ni Chihō Godochosha building, 34-12 Higashi Marutamachi, Kawabata Higashi-iru, Sakyō-ku. You must provide two copies of an Application for Extension of Stay (available at the bureau), a letter stating the reasons for the extension and supporting documentation, as well as your passport. There is a processing fee of ¥4000; be prepared to spend well over an hour to complete the process.

The Kyoto branch is best reached from Marutamachi station on the Keihan line. To get there take the No 4 exit, turn left and continue east past a church until the second traffic light. The bureau is in the five storey building on your left.

The Osaka Immigration Bureau has an English-language visa information line at its Osaka headquarters (☎ 06-774-3409), though you can usually have most questions about visas answered in English by calling the Kyoto branch (☎ 752-5997). Both offices are open Monday to Friday from 9 am to noon and 1 to 4 pm.

Many long-term visitors to Japan get around the extension problem by briefly leaving the country, usually going to South Korea, though these days immigration officials can be very unwelcoming on return and in many cases such 'tourist visa returnees' are turned back at the entry point.

Alien Registration Card

Anyone, and this includes tourists, who stays more than 90 days is required to obtain an Alien Registration Card (Gaikokujin Toroku Shomeisho). The card can be obtained at the municipal office of the city, town or ward in which you're living, but moving to another area requires that you re-register within 14 days. To register, you will need your passport, an application form and two passport-size photographs.

You must carry your Alien Registration Card at all times as the police can stop you and ask to see the card. If you don't have it, you will be taken to the police station and will usually have to wait there until someone fetches it for you.

Photocopies

As with travel anywhere, it is a good idea to keep photocopies of any vital documents (passport data pages, birth certificate, credit cards, airline tickets etc), as well as a record of travellers cheque serial numbers and an emergency stash of about US$50, in a place separate from your daily valuables. Also leave a copy of all these things (except perhaps the cash) with someone at home. Copies can be made at nearly any of Japan's convenience stores for ¥10.

Travel Insurance

Despite Japan still being one of the safest places in the world to travel (where a paper bag full of cash left on the train stands a strong chance of being turned in for you to claim), travel insurance to cover theft, property loss and medical problems is a wise idea. With such a wide variety of policies available, it may be best to consult your travel agent for recommendations. Some policies offer a choice between lower and higher medical expense options; choose the high-cost option for Japan. The international student travel policies handled by STA Travel or other student travel organisations are usually good value.

Driving Licence & Permits

Those planning on driving in Kyoto (though it's really not recommended) need their home country's driver's licence and an International Driving Permit. Providing you have these, renting a car is no problem at all – finding somewhere to park is another matter. For motorbikes up to 250cc (including scooters), the same combination will suffice. However, anything over 250cc will require a special motorcycle licence rating and corresponding stamp in the international permit. While in past years the police were fairly ignorant when handed foreign driving documents, recently they've produced a handy book of worldwide licence types (and their restrictions), so think twice before trying to pull one over on the cop who pulls you over.

Hostelling International Card

Youth hostel accommodation is popular in Japan and there are over 350 hostels nationwide. If you are planning on hostelling around Japan, it is best to set up an international youth hostel membership before you leave home.

Foreign nonmembers can stay at any hostel in Japan, but must pay a ¥600 premium (sometimes ¥1000 – the same as Japanese nonmembers pay) on top of the regular cost. If you collect six stamps from any one or a combination of Japan's hostels (a total cost of ¥3600), this entitles you to a year's Japan Youth Hostels (JYH) membership (Japan only). If you know, however, you will be staying at hostels for more than six nights, you can save ¥800 by purchasing a 'guest card' for ¥2800, actually a set of six member stickers, good for one night each. International YH cards can *only* be arranged in Japan if you can prove you have lived in the country for over a year.

The combination of national, prefectural and privately run hostels makes the entire system rather complex and it's further complicated by considerable variations in prices and rules between hostels. For details, contact the JYH Kyoto branch (☎ 462-9185, or ☎ 03-3288-1417 in Tokyo). JYH publishes annually a comprehensive map of hostels in Japan which can be picked up at the TIC, JYH office or any hostels.

Student & Youth Cards

In some cases, a valid international student card will get you discounts on entry fees to sights (at most museums and temples the cut-off age for discounts is high school students) and on long-distance train travel, but generally it will not be particularly useful. The card might also save you some money at movie theatres.

EMBASSIES
Japanese Embassies Abroad

Australia
  (☎ 06-273-3244) 112 Empire Circuit, Yarralumla, Canberra, ACT 2600. There are also consulates in: Brisbane (☎ 07-3221-5188); Melbourne (☎ 03-9639-3244); Perth (☎ 08-9321-7816); and Sydney (☎ 02-9231-3455).
Canada
  (☎ 613-241-8541) 255 Sussex Drive, Ottawa, Ontario K1N 9E6. There are also consulates in: Edmonton (☎ 403-422-3752); Montreal (☎ 514-866-3429); Toronto (☎ 416-363-7038); and Vancouver (☎ 604-684-5868).
China
  (☎ 10-6532-2361) 7 Ritan Lu, Jianguomenwai, Beijing. There is also a consulate in Hong Kong (☎ 2522-1184), 47th Floor, One Exchange Square, 8 Connaught Place, Central.
France
  (☎ 01 48 88 62 00) 7 Ave Hoche, 75008 Paris
Germany
  (☎ 0228-81910) Godesberger Allee 102-104, 53175 Bonn
Ireland
  (☎ 1-269-4033) Nutley Bldg, Merrion Centre, Nutley Lane, Dublin 4
New Zealand
  (☎ 04-473-1540) 7th Floor, Norwich Insurance House, 3-11 Hunter St, Wellington 1. There is also a consulate in Auckland (☎ 09-303-4106).
Singapore
  (☎ 235-8855) 16 Nassim Rd, Singapore 258390
Thailand
  (☎ 02-252-6151) 1674 New Petchburi Rd, Bangkok 10320

UK
  (☎ 0171-465-6500) 43-46 Grosvenor St, London W1X 0BA
USA
  (☎ 202-238-6700) 2520 Massachusetts Ave NW, Washington, DC 20008-2869. There are also consulates in: Anchorage (☎ 907-279-8428); Atlanta (☎ 404-892-2700); Boston (☎ 617-973-9772); Chicago (☎ 312-280-0400); Honolulu (☎ 808-536-2226); Houston (☎ 713-652-2977); Kansas City (☎ 816-471-0111); Los Angeles (☎ 213-617-6700); New Orleans (☎ 504-529-2101); New York (☎ 212-371-8222); Portland (☎ 503-221-1811); and San Francisco (☎ 415-777-3533).

Foreign Embassies in Tokyo

Most countries have embassies in Tokyo (telephone area code ☎ 03), some of which are listed below. Visas are generally substantially more expensive in Japan than in neighbouring countries. It's best to call the visa office first to confirm opening times.

Australia
  (☎ 5232-4111) 2-1-14 Mita, Minato-ku
Canada
  (☎ 3408-2101) 7-3-38 Akasaka, Minato-ku
China
  (☎ 3403-3380) 3-4-33 Moto-Azabu, Minato-ku
France
  (☎ 5420-8800) 4-11-44 Minami-Azabu, Minato-ku
Germany
  (☎ 3473-0151) 4-5-10 Minami-Azabu, Minato-ku
India
  (☎ 3262-2391) 2-2-11 Kudan-Minami, Chiyoda-ku
Indonesia
  (☎ 3441-4201) 5-2-9 Higashi-Gotanda, Shinagawa-ku
Ireland
  (☎ 3263-0695) 8-7 Sanbanchō, Chiyoda-ku
Malaysia
  (☎ 3476-3840) 20-16 Nampeidaichō, Shibuya-ku
Netherlands
  (☎ 5401-0411) 3-6-3 Shiba-kōen, Minato-ku
New Zealand
  (☎ 3467-2271) 20-40 Kamiyamachō, Shibuya-ku
Philippines
  (☎ 3496-2731) 11-24 Nampeidaichō, Shibuya-ku
Russia
  (☎ 3583-4224) 2-1-1 Azabudai, Minato-ku
Singapore
  (☎ 3586-9111) 5-12-3 Roppongi, Minato-ku
South Korea
  (☎ 3452-7611) 1-2-5 Minami-Azabu, Minato-ku
Sweden
  (☎ 5562-5050) 1-10-3 Roppongi, Minato-ku
Taiwan (Association of East Asian Relations)
  (☎ 3280-7811) 5-20-2 Shirogane-dai, Minato-ku

FACTS FOR THE VISITOR

Thailand
  (☎ 3441-1386) 3-14-6 Kami-Osaki, Shinagawa-ku
UK
  (☎ 3265-5511) 1 Ichibanchō, Chiyoda-ku
USA
  (☎ 3224-5000) 1-10-5 Akasaka, Minato-ku

Foreign Consulates in Osaka

Several countries also have consular representation in Osaka (telephone area code ☎ 06). These include:

Australia
  (☎ 941-8601) 29F, Twin 21 Mid-Tower,
  2-1-61 Shiromi, Chūō-ku
Canada
  (☎ 212-4910) 12F, Dai-san Shoho Building,
  2-2-3 Nishi-shinsaibashi, Chūō-ku
China
  (☎ 445-9481) 3-922 Utsubo-hon-machi, Nishi-ku
France
  (☎ 946-6181) 24F, Ōbayashi Building,
  4-33 Kitahama-higashi, Chūō-ku
Germany
  (☎ 440-5070) 35F, Umeda Sky Building, Tower
  East, 1-1-88 Ōyodo-naka, Kita-ku
Netherlands
  (☎ 944-7272) 33F, Twin 21 Mid-Tower,
  2-1-61 Shiromi, Chūō-ku
New Zealand
  (☎ 942-9016) 28F, Twin 21 Mid-Tower,
  2-1-61 Shiromi, Chūō-ku
Philippines
  (☎ 910-7881) 101-301 Advan City Building,
  2-3-7 Uchiawajichō, Chūō-ku
Russian Federation
  (☎ 848-3452) 2-2, Nishi Midorigaoka 1-Chome,
  Toyonaka-shi
Singapore
  (☎ 261-5131) 14F, Kokusai Building,
  2-3-13 Azuchi-machi, Chūō-ku
South Korea
  (☎ 213-1401) 2-3-4 Nishi-shinsaibashi,
  Chūō-ku
Thailand
  (☎ 243-5563) 4F, Kono-ike East Building,
  3-6-9 Kitakyohoji-machi, Chūō-ku
UK
  (☎ 281-1616) 19F, Seiko Osaka Building,
  3-5-1 Bakuro-machi, Chūō-ku
USA
  (☎ 315-5900) 2-11-5 Nishi-Tenma, Kita-ku

CUSTOMS

Customs allowances include the usual tobacco products, three 760ml bottles of alcoholic beverage, 57g of perfume, and gifts and souvenirs up to the value of ¥200,000. Liquor is not cheap, so it might be worth bringing some for personal consumption or as a gift. The penalties for importing drugs are very severe.

Although observance of Japanese laws regarding the publication of photographs showing pubic hair is much diminished nowadays, it is likely that anything slightly pornographic will be confiscated at customs. Don't be surprised if customs agents produce comic-like sketches of guns, drugs, porno magazines and the like to illustrate a well rehearsed list of 'Do you have any ...' questions.

There are no limits on the import of foreign or Japanese currency. The export of foreign currency is also unlimited, but a ¥5 million limit exists for Japanese currency.

MONEY
Costs

Japan, as notorious as it is for being prohibitively costly, is often more affordable than many assume – it's just a matter of seeking out the cheaper options. In recent years there has been a noticeable rise in big supermarkets, discount shops and other forms of price-cutting, finally giving consumers more choice in what they pay for goods and services. One area where this rule does not apply is drinking, a pastime which will quickly see all that yen quickly evaporate.

For the traveller, compared to other parts of Japan, Kyoto cannot be strictly called expensive or cheap. The city has droves of starving college students right up to a regular stream of ultrawealthy tourists, and can accommodate for every budget in between. A skeleton daily budget would be ¥6300. This means taking the cheapest accommodation (¥2800 for a youth hostel or *gaijin house* dorm bed), eating modestly for another ¥2500 and spending just ¥1000 on local transport. Add at least ¥2500 for extras like snacks, drinks, admission fees and entertainment and you're looking at roughly ¥9000. More expensive accommodation will cost around ¥5500 to ¥8000 for a budget-range business hotel, and anywhere from ¥14,000 to ¥34,000 for something more luxurious.

For stays in traditional surroundings, per person prices range from about ¥4500 per night in one of the cheaper *minshuku* (guesthouses), or Japanese inns, to over ¥50,000 in a top-flight *ryokan* (traditional inn).

Food costs can be kept within reasonable limits by taking set meals. A fixed 'morning service' breakfast *(mōningu sābisu* or *setto)* is available in most coffee shops for around ¥500. Lunchtime set meals *(teishoku)* cost about ¥750. Cheap noodle places, often found at stations, charge around ¥350 for a filling bowl of noodles. Alternatively, you can buy a takeaway *bentō*, or Japanese-style boxed lunch, for around ¥500 from local kiosks, convenience shops or department stores. For an evening meal, there's the option of a set course again or a single order – ¥800 should cover this. An evening meal and a couple of glasses of beer at one of Kyoto's *nomiya* or *izakaya* (traditional pubs) will cost around ¥2500. Expect to pay more for a meal at any of the larger western-style hotels. Average prices at youth hostels are ¥450 for a Japanese breakfast and ¥700 for dinner.

Some other costs to consider include: museum admission (¥400 to ¥800), movie tickets (¥1600 to ¥2000), foreign magazines (¥700), local English newspapers (¥120 to ¥140), 36 exposure colour film, without processing (¥420), a glass of orange juice at a coffee shop (¥450), a cocktail in an average-priced bar (up to ¥1000), shirt dry-cleaning (¥200) and cigarettes (¥220 to ¥250).

Transport costs for trips to the sights around Kyoto can be expensive, but unless you are going to be travelling to other parts of Japan, it's dubious whether it's worth getting a Japan Rail Pass for local excursions. If you want to avoid emptying your wallet at an alarming rate, you should only use taxis as a very last resort. Kyoto has fast, efficient public transport, so it's only on those late-night binges that you need a taxi anyway. For *shinkansen* (bullet train) trips and domestic flights, discounted tickets are available at some discount shops (see the Discounts entry later in this section for more information on cheap tickets).

Cash

Cold hard yen is the way to pay in Japan. While credit cards are becoming more common in Kyoto, cash is still much more widely used, and travellers cheques are rarely accepted as payment.

Carrying Money

The Japanese are generally used to a very low crime rate, and often carry huge wads of cash for the almost sacred ritual of cash payment. Most foreign travellers in Kyoto can safely copy this habit but, as always, take the usual precautions.

Travellers Cheques

Travellers cheques are fairly commonplace nowadays, though they can only be cashed at authorised money changers (most banks and some hotels). It is not possible to use foreign currency travellers cheques in stores and restaurants. In most cases the exchange rate for travellers cheques is slightly better than cash. In order to cash travellers cheques or make cash advances at banks, you will need to show your passport or a valid alien registration card.

ATMs

Automatic teller machines are becoming as common as vending machines in Kyoto, and there are several locations in the city which can provide services for most major international banks and credit card companies. Bear in mind that ATMs generally close at 7 pm. There are exceptions, like in Kyoto station where the ATMs are open from 5.30 am to 11 pm, but they are few and far between. The majority of ATMs are equipped with English instructions.

In the Kyoto station area, try the 2nd level of the complex, just to the right (where the coin lockers are) outside the turnstiles from the JR tracks. Alternatively, there are several machines in the basement of the Kyoto Tower building across the street from the station.

In the city centre, try the All Card Plaza (Map 10) in the Teramachi shopping arcade just north of Shijō-dōri, the 7th floor 'card corner' in the Takashimaya department store

FACTS FOR THE VISITOR

(Map 10) or in the Zest shopping arcade (Map 10) under Oike-dōri.

Credit Cards

The use of plastic money is becoming more widespread in Japan. The most commonly accepted foreign credit card is Visa, though MasterCard, Diners Club and American Express are also becoming better represented. Do not assume, however, that restaurants and bars accept credit cards; always check first. While most large hotels and *some* traditional inns accept credit cards, most cheaper accommodation like youth hostels and guesthouses do not. In general, it is better to carry plenty of cash than to rely on credit cards.

For cash advances of amounts up to ¥40,000, any of the above-mentioned ATMs should suffice. For larger amounts, Visa card-holders can also get cash advances at Sumitomo bank (Map 9), on the corner of Shijō-dōri and Karasuma-dōri or at the Sumitomo branch a few minutes walk east on the 1st floor of the Hankyū department store (Map 10). Currently there is no representation for international card-holders in Kyoto, and for inquiries it is often best to call the number in your home country on the back of your card, or try their offices in Tokyo; the telephone numbers (area code ☎ 03) of the Tokyo offices are:

American Express
  (☎ 3220-6100; 0120-020-120, toll-free)
Diners Club
  (☎ 3499-1311)
MasterCard
  (☎ 5350-8051)
Visa
  (☎ 5251-0633)

International Transfers

International transfers can be handled at most major banks, though many require that you hold an account with them in order to process the paperwork. If you are having money sent to a bank in Japan, make sure you know *exactly* where the funds are going: the bank, branch and location.

Telex or telegraphic transfers are much faster, though more expensive, than mail transfers. A credit-card cash advance is a quick and worthwhile alternative.

For sending money home, perhaps the easiest and cheapest option is a postal money order, which can be bought at the central post office near Kyoto station and safely sent by registered mail.

Currency

The currency in Japan is the *yen* (¥), and banknotes and coins are easily identifiable. There are ¥1, ¥5, ¥10, ¥50, ¥100 and ¥500 coins, and ¥1000, ¥5000 and ¥10,000 banknotes. The ¥1 coin is of lightweight aluminium, and the ¥5 (known to bring good luck) and ¥50 coins have a hole in the middle.

Exchange Rates

Currency exchange rates are:

Australia	A$1	=	¥87.59
Canada	C$1	=	¥94.66
France	FR1	=	¥23.57
Germany	DM1	=	¥79.10
Hong Kong	HK$1	=	¥18.27
New Zealand	NZ$1	=	¥73.48
Singapore	S$1	=	¥82.66
UK	UK£1	=	¥232.72
USA	US$1	=	¥141.64

Changing Money

You can change cash or travellers cheques at an 'Authorised Foreign Exchange Bank' (signs will always be displayed in English) or at some of the large hotels and stores. Some post offices also exchange money – look for the 'Authorised Foreign Exchange' sign. The safest and most practical way to carry your money is in travellers cheques, preferably in US dollars, although other major currencies are acceptable. Although Korean and Taiwanese currency has become easier to change in recent years, it is still a good idea to change it into US dollars or yen first if you are coming from those countries. No black market exists in Japan, and rates vary little, if at all, between banks.

Most major banks are located near the

Shijō-dōri and Karasuma-dōri intersection, two stops north of Kyoto station on the Karasuma line subway. The Tokyo-Mitsubishi bank (Map 9), on the south-east corner of the intersection, is quite convenient for changing money and buying travellers cheques. For more complex services like wire transfers, there is another branch (Map 9) of the same bank a few hundred metres north of the intersection on the east side of Karasuma-dōri. For those arriving yenless at Kyoto station, there is a Tokyo-Mitsubishi branch inside the terminal building.

Tipping & Bargaining

Those who blast Japan for being so expensive often do not figure into their overall travel costs the absence of tipping. There is no situation, be it for taxi drivers, tour guides, waiters and waitresses, hotel porters, room service or maids, in which it is considered compulsory to tip. You may even send the pizza delivery person into a fit if you do try to tip. As nobody expects a tip, it's probably best to keep it that way. One possible exception is that if you feel your maid at a top-flight ryokan has given service surpassing that of a fairy godmother, leave a small present, perhaps a souvenir from your home country. If you give cash, the polite way is to place it in an envelope.

With the exception of antique shops and flea markets (where there is *always* a premium built into the first quoted price), bargaining in Japan is also virtually nonexistent. Possible exceptions are camera and electronic stores (in particular those dealing in used goods). Bear in mind, however, that store clerks are not open to the kind of haggling that is the norm in India or China. A polite request is all that is required. To try and bargain down prices at a regular souvenir shop would appear as tactless as asking a clerk at Harrod's to give you a special price on a necktie or bottle of perfume.

Taxes & Refunds

Japan's 3% consumer tax was made even more unpopular in April 1997 when it was raised to the current 5% level. Visitors on a tourist visa can, however, avoid this 5% consumption tax on purchases made at major department stores and duty-free stores such as the Kyoto Handicraft Center (Map 10). For a refund on general purchases, check first that the department store has a service desk for tax refunds. When you make the purchase the tax will be included; take the purchase, receipt and your passport to the service desk for an immediate refund. The exemption applies only for tourists with a visitors stamp in their passport, not for registered foreigners on other visas.

If you eat at expensive restaurants and stay at 1st class accommodation, you will often encounter a service charge – a disguised form of tipping – which varies from 10% to 15%. A local tax of 5% is added to restaurant bills exceeding ¥5000 or for hotel bills exceeding ¥10,000. This means it is sometimes cheaper to ask for separate bills. At *onsen* (hot-spring) resorts, a separate onsen tax can apply. This is usually 5%, and applies also at cheap accommodation, even youth hostels.

Discounts

There are several discount ticket/coupon shops in Kyoto selling everything from telephone cards and movie tickets to beer and department store gift certificates (usually anywhere from 5% to 10% below cost). Much of the supply comes from company employees (so much for the all-honest image) flogging off tickets from the company coffer or promotional gifts for cold cash.

One of the best selling items, however, is shinkansen tickets, sold for up to 10% off their original price (usually saving you just enough to buy a cheap lunch), though some restricted travel dates apply.

There are two such shops around Kyoto station, both called Tōkai, one (Map 11) on the north side near the TIC and the other on the south side, on the ground level of Avanti shopping centre (Map 11). In the centre of town, you will find a Ticket King outlet near the Shijō-dōri and Ōmiya-dōri intersection (Map 9).

FACTS FOR THE VISITOR

DOING BUSINESS

Although the reigning business centre of Kansai is Osaka, Kyoto is not surviving off tourism revenue alone. The city has an entrepreneurial spirit and a surprising range of businesses. In addition to traditional cottage industries such as weaving and handicrafts, several of Japan's leading high-tech firms such as Kyocera, Murata, Nintendo and Omron have their headquarters here. Kyoto also has an array of business-related facilities such as the Kyoto International Conference Hall (Map 4), Kyoto Research Park (Map 6) and Kansai Science City's Keihanna Plaza.

One useful organisation is the Kyoto Convention Bureau (KCB; Map 9), which provides services such as introductions to convention facilities, accommodation and, through selected tour operators worldwide, can arrange incentive package tours. Information can be found through JNTO offices (see the Tourist Offices section earlier in this chapter) worldwide or write to KCB through Kyoto Chamber of Commerce, Ebisugawa, Nakagyō-ku, Kyoto 604, or phone ☎ 212-4110; fax 212-4121. Its email address is hellokcb@mbox.kyoto-inet.or.jp; its Web site is at web.kyoto-inet.or.jp/org/hellokcb.

Another interesting organisation with useful information on the Internet is the Osaka-based Kansai International Public Relations Promotion Office (KIPPO). Its Web site (www.ksi.cae.ntt.jp/kippo/) has links to other groups such as the Japan External Trade Organization (JETRO).

A useful reference for turning up business contacts is Nippon Telephone & Telegraph Corporation's (NTT) Townpage, an English telephone directory complete with an extensive index of Internet listings. This can be picked up at KICH (Map 10; ☎ 752-3010) or by contacting NTT (☎ 06-944-7504).

POST & COMMUNICATIONS
Post

Most local post offices are open Monday to Friday from 9 am to 5 pm. Kyoto's central post office (Map 11; ☎ 365-2467), on the north side of Kyoto station, is open from 9 am to 7 pm on weekdays, to 5 pm on Saturday and to 12.30 pm on Sunday and holidays. Poste restante mail can be collected here. There is a philactic counter on the 1st floor where you can purchase unique stamps to post or collect. There's also an after-hours service counter on the south side of the building open 24 hours a day for air mail, small packages, and special express mail service.

The large Nakagyō post office (Map 9; ☎ 255-1112) on the Higashinotōin-dōri and Sanjō-dōri intersection is also open until 7 pm on weekdays, but is closed on weekends. There is a 24 hour service window on the west side of the building. If you've just got to mail something on a Sunday, try the post office on the 7th floor of the Takashimaya department store (next to the NTT office; Map 10).

Postage costs are: postcards ¥50 domestic, ¥70 international; aerograms ¥90 worldwide; while letters up to 10g cost ¥90 within Asia, ¥110 to North America, Europe, Oceania and the Middle East, and ¥130 to Africa and South America.

All post offices offer a reliable international Express Mail Service (EMS); there is also a Kyoto branch of Federal Express (☎ 672-8006, or Tokyo number toll-free ☎ 0120-003-200) in the far south of town. The daily cut-off time to post packages is 5 pm; Fed-ex can also provide pick-up service, but requires a full day's notice. For domestic express delivery services 24 hours a day, the services known as *takyūbin* that are handled by most convenience stores are cheap and efficient.

Telephone

The area code for greater Kyoto is ☎ 075; unless otherwise indicated, all numbers in this book fall into this area. Japanese telephone codes consist of an area code plus a local code and number. You do not dial the area code when making a call in that area. When dialling Japan from abroad, the country code is ☎ 81, followed by the area code (drop the 0) and the number. Area codes for some of the main cities are:

Fukuoka/Hakata	092
Hiroshima	082

Kōbe	078
Matsuyama	0899
Nagasaki	0958
Nagoya	052
Nara	0742
Narita	0476
Osaka	06
Sapporo	011
Sendai	022
Tokyo	03
Yokohama	045

Local Calls The Japanese public telephone system is very well developed. There are a great many public phones and they work almost 100% of the time – it is very unusual to see a vandalised phone in Japan. Telephone services within Japan are principally handled by NTT (Nippon Telegraph & Telephone Corporation).

Local calls from pay phones cost ¥10 per minute (¥10 will buy you three minutes if calling from a private phone); long-distance or overseas calls require a handful of coins; unused coins are returned at the end of the call. Though prepaid phonecards *(terefon kādo)* have been in use nationwide since the mid-1980s, the recent wave of cellular phone use has caused a sharp decline in their use. In general it's much easier to buy a phone card when you arrive rather than worry about always having coins on hand. Phone cards are sold in ¥500 and ¥1000 denominations (the latter earns you an extra ¥50 in calls) and can be used in most green or grey pay phones. They are available from vending machines and convenience stores, come in a myriad of designs and are also a collectable item.

Directory information is reached by dialling ☎ 104 (the charge is ¥30, in ¥10 coins or deducted from a phone card) and has English-speaking operators on call from 9 am to 8 pm. For domestic collect calls, dial ☎ 106.

International Calls Overseas call telephones have become increasingly common. The rates have also become more competitive as a result of market liberalisation. Kokusai Denshin Denwa (KDD) operates alongside its newer competitors, International Telecom Japan (ITJ) and International Digital Communication (IDC).

Both paid and reverse-charge (collect) overseas calls can only be made from grey ISDN phones. Thanks to NTT's efforts to curb the use of illegal, remagnetised telephone cards, many of the pay phones designed for international calls can no longer accept phone cards (only ¥100 coins). Once you're connected, calls are charged by the unit (no three minute minimum), each of which is six seconds, so if you haven't got much to say you could phone home for just ¥100.

As in other parts of the world, you save money by dialling late at night. Economy rates with a discount of 20% apply from 7 to 11 pm Monday to Friday, and all day to 11 pm on weekends and holidays. From 11 pm to 8 am a discount rate brings the price of international phone calls down by 40% seven days a week. Note that you can also make cheaper domestic calls by dialling outside the standard hours.

To place an international call through the operator, dial ☎ 0057 – international operators all seem to speak English. To make the call yourself, simply dial ☎ 001 (KDD), ☎ 0041 (ITJ) or ☎ 0061 (IDC) – there's little difference in their rates – then the international country code, the local code and the number.

Another option is to dial ☎ 0039-111 for home country direct, which takes you straight through to a local operator in the country dialled. You can then make a reverse-charge call or a credit-card call with a telephone credit card valid in that country. In some hotels or other tourist locations, you may find a home country direct phone where you simply press the button labelled USA, UK, Canada, Australia, NZ or wherever, to be put through to your operator.

Connecting a Phone Having a home telephone connected is quite simple. You can apply at any NTT office (about 15 minutes to complete the paperwork) and must also buy a phone line, which costs about ¥70,000 if you buy from NTT, but only ¥55,000 to ¥60,000 from someone who no longer wants their line. 'Used' phone lines are advertised at the Kyoto International Community House and in *Kansai Time Out*.

Fax, Telegraph & Email

Most larger hotels offer domestic and international fax services. As well, you can send and receive faxes at KICH (see the Useful Organisations section later in this chapter).

Telegraph services can be handled at any NTT branch in town. Rates begin at 25 letters for ¥700. For information on domestic telegrams, call ☎ 115 or to transmit overseas, ☎ 03-3344-5151 (toll-free).

For email, phone jacks in Japan are compatible with most modems and many of the newer grey-coloured pay phones are equipped with jacks to hook up on the road. For details on places to check and receive email in Kyoto, see the Internet Cafes boxed text on this page.

INTERNET RESOURCES

For travel information and general tidbits on Kyoto, there are a myriad of Web sites worth checking. The following are a good place to begin and will lead to plenty of other links:

Japan National Tourism Association
www.jnto.go.jp
Kansai Time Out magazine (Kansai area)
www.kto.co.jp
Kyoto Prefecture (the greater Kyoto area)
pref.kyoto.jp/index_e.html
Kyoto Visitor's Guide (Kyoto-specific information)
www.kyoto-inet.or.jp/city-office/kankou/visitor/index.html

Of the seemingly infinite number of Kyoto photo galleries on the Web, two in particular stand out for originality.

'The Play of Light – Kyoto at Night'
by American photographer David Culton; a wonderful collection of black and white images shot in Kyoto after dark (www.butaman.ne.jp:8000/divad/).
'Soft Focused Kyoto'
by Tsutomu Otsuka; an impressive selection of colour photos shot through a special soft-focus lens (web.kyoto-inet.or.jp/people/gordon/soft/Kyoto/index.html).

Internet Cafes

Along with the intensifying popularity of the Internet boom in Japan, cybercafes have been springing up in Kyoto, with more and more places offering public Internet access.

The cheapest cafe in town is Meix Internet Cafe (☎ 213-1201), on Karasuma-dōri (Map 7), a one minute walk south of the Imperial Palace. Here Internet access (including email service) costs only ¥350 per two hours. Meix is open from noon to 7 pm (closed Sunday).

Buttercups cafe (Map 8; ☎ 751-9537) has one terminal available for surfing for ¥250 per 30 minutes. You can send email for ¥50 per batch (typing time free) and also use the cafe's email (bttrcps@dd.iij4u.or.jp) to receive – your own mail box is created free of charge. Printouts cost ¥30 per page.

Another similar yet more expensive (even with free coffee and tea) option is Net Surf (☎ 221-2707) across the street and just east from Daimaru department store (Map 10) on Shijō-dōri. There is a one-off fee (¥500) to become a member, whereafter surfing will cost ¥800 per hour; nonmembers pay ¥1000. The cafe also offers a one month, all-you-can-surf special for ¥8000.

There are several places in Kyoto offering reasonable (or free) access to the Internet, without the benefit of email. NTT has a few demonstration showrooms about town where it's possible to surf for free; the most accessible of these is on the 7th floor of Takashimaya department store (Map 10) at the intersection of Shijō-dōri and Kawaramachi-dōri.

Another reasonable option (and easier for getting English support) is the Kyoto Prefectural International Center on the 9th floor of the Kyoto station building (Map 11), where you can surf for ¥250 per 30 minutes, though there is no email service yet. ■

BOOKS

With books on culture, arts, economics, travel and literature both from foreign writers and in translation, there are hundreds of titles to choose from in Japan. There's no real need, however, to stock up on books, particularly about Kyoto and Japan in general, before you leave home. Kyoto has several excellent bookshops (see the Kyoto Bookshops boxed text in this section).

Lonely Planet

For further exploration of the Kansai area

and beyond, Lonely Planet's *Japan* (6th edition), is the most complete Japan guide available. LP publishes a superb city guide *Tokyo* (3rd edition), a pocket-size *Japanese phrasebook*, *Japanese audio pack* (including phrasebook and CD or cassette), and also *Japan*, a selection from its video series.

An excellent contemporary nonfiction book on the country is Alex Kerr's *Lost Japan* (1996), from the popular Lonely Planet 'Journeys' series. Kerr spent 20 years living on the outskirts of Kyoto and shares his candid views of the city and its people in the provocative chapter 'Kyoto Hates Kyoto'.

Guidebooks

The guide you're holding in your hand is to date the most comprehensive guide available to Kyoto, though there are several other worthwhile books.

Perhaps the most detailed guide to Kyoto's cultural attractions is *Kyoto – A Cultural Guide to Japan's Ancient Imperial City* by John & Phyllis Martin. *Exploring Kyoto* by long-term Kyoto resident Judith Clancy is an excellent 'on foot' guide with more than 25 well documented walks and hikes throughout the city.

Former Kyoto resident Diane Durston is one of the world's leading experts on Kyoto and its vanishing traditions. Her *Old Kyoto – A Guide to Traditional Shops, Restaurants & Inns* is a must for those in search of specific Kyoto handicrafts. It also provides detailed information on atmospheric old ryokan and restaurants. The material for this book later appeared as *The Living Traditions of Old Kyoto*, in a lavish coffee-table format. Durston's *Kyoto, Seven Paths to the Heart of the City* is an informative, well illustrated tool for those interested in exploring some of Kyoto's traditional neighbourhoods.

Gouverneur Mosher's classic title *Kyoto – A Contemplative Guide* was originally published in 1964, yet still gives a taste of the amazing scope for exploration possible in Kyoto. Though the transport information is decades out of date (in fact some of the last streetcars described were retired in 1997), it's well worth a read. A wonderful collection of poems and prose describing the yearly changes in the Kyoto landscape is Harold Stewart's hard-to-find *By The Old Walls of Kyoto* (1981).

Anyone planning to tour Osaka and Kōbe should look out for John Ashburne's *The Best of Kansai*. It's full of refreshingly opinionated advice on what to see, do and eat in the region.

Those anticipating a long stay may want

Kyoto Bookshops

Kyoto has several mega-bookshops, the biggest of which is Maruzen (Map 10; ☎ 241-2161), on Kawaramachi-dōri between Sanjō-dōri and Shijō-dōri. On the 6th floor is an extensive selection of English-language books, magazines and maps, a limited number of French, German and Spanish-language books, and plenty of books about Kyoto and Japan. Opening hours are daily from 10 am to 8 pm (closed the third Wednesday of each month).

Kinokuniya (☎ 253-3151), in the Zest underground shopping arcade (Map 10), also has a large selection of English-language books and magazines, and is open daily from 10.30 am to 8.30 pm (also closed on the third Wednesday of each month).

Muse (☎ 705-3090), an imported book seller on Shirakawa-dōri in Saikyō-ku, has been attracting attention since opening in late 1997. Challenging Japan's complex distribution network by direct import, Muse undercuts the biggies by selling all books for the equivalent of the US list price, instead of upping its value in yen. It stocks over 8000 titles, and has a 400,000 title database via the Internet where customers can order everything from Bashō to Hemingway. You can contact Muse by email (kiyota@musegate.com or mews@bookshop.co.jp) or visit its Web site (www.musegate.com).

For art and architecture, try Media Shop (☎ 255-0783), near the Sanjō-Kawaramachi intersection (Map 10). It's open daily from 11 am to 10 pm. Another excellent shop with an extensive variety of architectural titles (many in English) is Tairyū-dō (☎ 231-3036) just south of the Imperial Palace (Gosho) on Shin Sawaragichō-dōri. It's open from 9 am to 7 pm daily, except Sunday morning.

If you want to trade a book you've read, there is a small self-service bookswap at Buttercups cafe (Map 8). Books can also be borrowed (and returned) on an honour system from the YWCA (Map 7). ■

to pick up a copy of *Easy Living in Kyoto*, full of practical advice for foreign residents. It's free and is available from KICH (see the Useful Organisations section later in this chapter).

History

Virtually any Japanese history book is full of data on Kyoto, but there are several books in particular worth looking for.

For general Japanese history, *Japan – Its History & Culture* by W Scott Morton is a worthy read. Anyone studying Japanese language and history might check out *Japanese History – 11 Experts Reflect on the Past*, part of Kodansha's multipurpose Bilingual Books series.

Historical Kyoto by Herbert Plutschow offers perhaps the most detailed history of the city, while *The Temples of Kyoto* by Donald Richie & Alexandre Georges, a handsome little coffee-table book, is an enamoured look at 21 of the city's most celebrated temples.

For a visual perspective on Japan's intriguing past, there are two excellent photo books each featuring numerous images from Kyoto. *Early Japanese Images* by Terry Bennett and *Japan – Caught in Time* by Hugh Cortazzi & Terry Bennett both offer a rare glimpse into old Japan.

Religion

Good primers include *Japanese Religion – A Cultural Perspective* by Robert S Elwood & Richard Pilgrim and *Religions of Japan – Many Traditions within One Sacred Way* by H Byron Earhart.

Probably the best introduction to Zen is *Zen and Japanese Culture* by Daisetzu T Suzuki. Peter Matthiessen gives a personal account of his Zen experiences in *Nine Headed Dragon River*.

Business

There is a mountain of tomes purporting to unlock the secrets of Japanese business. *The Art of Japanese Management – Applications for American Executives* has been around for a while, but is still a good introduction.

For nuts and bolts information, there's the *Japan Company Handbook* (Toyo Keizai) detailing listed companies. *Nippon 1997* (JETRO) is an annual statistical publication. Other annual publications include *Survey of Japanese Corporations Overseas* (Toyo Keizai), *Japan Trade Directory* (JETRO), *Japan Economic Alamanac* (the *Nikkei Weekly*), and *Japan – An International Comparison* (Keizai Kōhō Center, or Japan Institute for Social and Economic Affairs).

More-practical guides include *Setting Up an Office in Japan* (American Chamber of Commerce in Japan, 1993), *Setting Up and Operating a Business in Japan* by Helene Thian (Tuttle, 1990), and *Setting Up Enterprises in Japan – Guidelines on Investment, Taxation and Legal Regulations* (JETRO, 1993). JETRO's *Investment Japan – A Directory of Institutions and Firms Offering Assistance to People Seeking to Set Up a Business in Japan* is a comprehensive listing of useful contacts across all industries. The *Japan Yellow Pages* is published by Japan Yellow Pages Ltd (☎ 03-3239-3501).

Arts

If you want to delve deeper into the performing arts you may find useful: *Kabuki* and *The Kabuki Guide* by Gunji Masakatsu; *Kabuki – Backstage, Onstage: an Actor's Life* by Nakamura Matazo; *The Kabuki Handbook* by Aubrey & Giovanna Halford; *Five Modern Nō Plays* by Mishima Yukio; *A Guide to Nō* by PG O'Neill; *A Guide to Kyōgen* by Don Kenny; and *The Bunraku Handbook* by Hironaga Shuzaburō.

Donald Richie's *Japanese Cinema – An Introduction* is a brief but useful guide for the beginner interested in Japanese film and its history.

In the wide-ranging area of crafts, the *Japan Crafts Sourcebook* compiled by the Japan Craft Forum is comprehensive and beautifully illustrated, covering an extensive array of traditional Japanese crafts including ceramics, textiles, lacquerware, wood and bamboo craft, Japanese papermaking and metalwork.

Countless books have been published on ikebana. One of the more handsome is *Rikka*

– *The Soul of Japanese Flower Arrangement* by Fujiwara Yuchiku, providing a detailed treatment of the upright form.

Just as countless are the number of books on Japanese gardens. The most integrated coffee-table book, encompassing history, philosophy and form, is Mark Peter Keane's superb *Japanese Garden Design*. Also look for *A Celebration of Japanese Gardens* by Hibi Sadao; *Japanese Residences and Gardens* by Fujioka Michio; *Elements of Japanese Gardens* by Yoshikawa Isao; *Hedges and Ground Cover for Your Garden* by Suzuki & Aizeki; *A Thousand Mountains – A Million Hills* by David E Engel; and the photo-driven *Japan – The Living Gardens* by Johnny Hymas. The best English guidebook available for touring Kyoto's gardens is *A Guide to the Gardens of Kyoto* by Marc Treib & Ron Herman.

Also worth a mention are three reasonably priced, compact books from Mitsumura Suiko Shoin: *Invitation to Tea Gardens* by Preston Houser and *Zen Gardens* by Tom Wright (both containing photos by Mizuno Katsuhiko), and *Invitation to Kyoto Gardens* by Yamamoto Kenzo.

The praiseworthy *Kyoto Gardens – A Virtual Stroll Through Zen Landscapes* (Lunaflora, Yorba Linda, California, 1996) is a masterpiece CD Rom taking the viewer on an up-close, interactive journey through 24 of Kyoto's most exquisite gardens.

Two books on local architecture worth looking out for are *The Architectural Map of Kyoto*, a painstakingly detailed guide to Kyoto's ancient and modern buildings (written in Japanese, with English footnotes) and *Light in Japanese Architecture* by Henry Plummer, a thoughtfully written and brilliantly illustrated bilingual treatment of both traditional and contemporary Japanese architecture.

General

Kyoto Encounters is J Thomas Rimer's provocative collection of reflections on Kyoto in literature, prose and photos, including notables spanning the globe from Bashō to Rudyard Kipling.

In *Introducing Kyoto* Herbert Plutschow provides a basic overview of Kyoto's history, culture and sights illustrated with colour photos. The similar *Kyoto & Nara – The Soul of Japan* by Philip Sandoz, with photos by Morita Toshitaka, takes in the ancient capital of Nara as well.

The Spirit of Kyoto is another colourful collection of classical Kyoto images shot by noted local photographer Mizuno Katsuhiko.

NEWSPAPERS & MAGAZINES

All four of Japan's English-language daily newspapers – the *Japan Times*, *Daily Yomiuri*, *Mainichi Daily News* and *Asahi Evening News* can be found at selected bookshops, most major hotels and often at newspaper stands *(kiosk)* in train and subway stations.

Those with more eclectic interests should keep an eye out for the praiseworthy (and nonprofit) *Kyoto Journal*, which publishes in-depth articles on Asian culture and issues, as well as artwork by Kyoto residents and others. It's also available at local bookshops, or by calling ☎ 761-1433.

Useful Publications

The monthly *Kyoto Visitor's Guide* is the best source of information on cultural and tourist events. It's available free at the TIC, Maruzen bookshop, Kyoto International Community House and most major hotels.

Another excellent source of information on Kyoto and the rest of the Kansai area is *Kansai Time Out*, a monthly English-language listings magazine (¥300). For short-term visitors, new arrivals or veteran expats in need of more than tourist happenings, *Kansai Time Out* is by far the best spent ¥300 going. Apart from lively articles, it has a large section of announcements and ads for employment, travel agencies, clubs, lonely hearts etc. It's available at Maruzen and Kinokunia bookshops, or by calling ☎ 078-232-4516 (Kōbe).

Kansai Flea Market is a free monthly aimed at foreign residents with work and housing listings, as well as entertaining personals. It can be picked up at several places in town including bookshops, bars and the TIC.

RADIO & TV
Radio
Within the past decade or so there has been a major growth in FM radio stations and community FMs throughout Japan. Kyoto's best station with bilingual broadcasts and decent music is Alfa Station (89.4 FM; Map 4), but there are several others in Kansai that will transmit in Kyoto.

76.5 FM COCOLO	(multilingual)
80.2 FM 802	(Japanese/English)
85.1 FM Osaka	(Japanese/English)
89.9 Kiss FM Kōbe	(Japanese/English)

TV
Unless you are fortunate enough to have a TV in your hotel room which is hooked up to a satellite system to bring in English programming, there is not much in the way of English on TV. In any case, catching a few minutes of Japanese TV can prove to be a cultural experience, a never-ending presentation of the bizarre (both in programs and commercials).

If you're craving a bit of international news, either CNN or BBC runs on a widescreen set at KICH, and at the Kyoto Prefectural International Center, during their opening hours (see the Useful Organisations section later in this chapter).

PHOTOGRAPHY & VIDEO
Photography is one of Japan's great pastimes. As such, you can be sure that you're never too far from a new roll of film. Colour print film and disposable cameras are found everywhere, from train station kiosks to convenience stores. While most prices are fairly competitive, you're always better off buying a multipack of film at a camera store (these offer substantial savings over purchasing individual rolls).

For amateur and professional supplies including slide film, black and white film and all the latest gadgets, Kyoto's best shop is Medic (Map 10; ☎ 256-6651), on the west side of Kawaramachi-dōri, about 50m north of Sanjō-dōri. It also offers reliable processing services.

Another popular place to have print film developed is at the Yellow Camera chain (with several branches in Kyoto), easy to spot by its all-yellow facade. One hour processing tends to be slightly more expensive than overnight, but it is offered at many local shops. Japanese labs usually print on what's called *sābisu saizu* (service size), which is about two-thirds of the standard size in most countries (four by six inches). Unless you're happy with this size, ask to have your photos printed on *hagaki* (postcard) size paper.

For black and white film or slide processing three of Kyoto's best labs are Create (Map 9; ☎ 252-1728), south of the Imperial Palace Park on Ebisugawa-dōri, Horiuchi Color (Map 10; ☎ 223-5321), just south of Oike-dōri on Yanaginobanba-dōri, and Kodak Imagica (Map 10; ☎ 252-0577), about 100m north of Shijō-dōri on Fuyachō-dōri. All often offer discounts on large processing orders (usually more than 20 rolls).

Photographers will do their best picture-taking early in the morning and at dusk. Not only are these the hours when light quality is at its best, you'll also have the best chance of making sure your photos are not encroached upon by swarms of tourists.

Though in Japan it is more often a case of being asked to join in another's snapshot, in general Japanese people are happy to have their photos taken. It never hurts, however, to ask before you shoot. Even the fully dressed *geisha* shuffling through the streets of the entertainment district will often stop to pose if asked politely (just try to make it quick, as they are always hurrying to and from appointments and don't like to wait while you change film or set up your tripod).

If you haven't already experienced the thrill, Kyoto is full of *purika*, self-service miniphoto booths where people cram in to be photographed in front of various backgrounds or with Japanese pop stars. For a few hundred yen you can take home your very own sheet of photo stickers to impress your friends.

TIME

Despite Japan's east-west distance, the country is all in the same time zone, nine hours ahead of Greenwich Mean Time (GMT). Thus, when it is noon in Japan, it is 5 pm the previous day in Honolulu, 7 pm in San Francisco, 10 pm in New York, 3 am in London, 11 am in Hong Kong, 1 pm in Sydney and 3 pm in Auckland. Daylight-saving time is not applied in Japan.

Many clocks, in particular those in train and bus stations, operate on a 24 hour clock and most timetables for public transport are based on this system.

Calendars and Dates

In 1873 the Japanese switched from the lunar calendar to the Gregorian calendar used in the west. As throughout Asia, official public holidays are dated according to the Gregorian calendar, while traditional festivals and events still follow the lunar system.

Years are counted in Japan according to two systems: western and imperial. The western system sets the date from the birth of Christ, while the imperial system calculates the year from the accession of the most recent emperor. The reign of each emperor is assigned a special name; thus the span of the previous emperor, Hirohito (1926-89), is known as the Shōwa (Enlightened Peace) era, meaning 1988 was Shōwa 63. The present emperor, Akihito, who ascended the throne in 1989, reigns in the Heisei (Achievement of Lasting Peace) era, so 1997 was Heisei 8, and 2000 equals Heisei 11. ■

ELECTRICITY

The Japanese electric current is 100V AC, an odd voltage not found elsewhere in the world, though most North American electrical items, designed to run on 117V, will function reasonably well on the Japanese current.

While Tokyo and eastern Japan are on 50 Hz, Kyoto and the rest of western Japan are on a cycle of 60 Hz. Identical to North American plugs, Japanese plugs are of the flat, two pronged variety.

LAUNDRY

While most youth hostels and some inns are equipped with laundry facilities, most hotels are not. Unless you're prepared to pay for (expensive) hotel laundry services, the next-best option is to find a *koin randorii* (coin laundry). Like most Japanese cities, Kyoto has plenty of these. Costs average from ¥200 to ¥400 per load; dryers run for seven to 10 minutes for ¥100.

Kyoto has plenty of capable dry-cleaners. While most are expensive compared to what you may be used to, one of the better deals is on *Y-shatsu* (white shirts) or *cat shatsu* (cutter shirts), regular cotton button-down business shirts which cost around ¥150 to ¥200 to clean and press.

WEIGHTS & MEASURES

Japan uses the international metric system. One odd exception is the size of rooms, which is often given in *tatami* (woven straw floor matting) measurements known as *jō*. Most bedrooms range from about four to eight jō, while large rooms in some temples can have over 100 tatami covering the floor. Tatami sizes vary regionally in Japan, which can tend to complicate things. In Tokyo a tatami measures 1.76 by 0.88m, while Kyoto tatami are slightly larger at 1.91 by 0.96m.

HEALTH

Travel health depends on your predeparture preparations, your day-to-day health care while travelling and how you handle any medical problem or emergency that does develop. However, looking after your health in Japan should pose few problems, since hygiene standards are high and medical facilities are widely available, though expensive. There are very few health risks in Japan to speak of, aside perhaps from an over abundance of secondary smoke, and the average life expectancy among the Japanese is now 80 years for women and 74 for men, a sure sign that they are doing something right.

Travel Health Guides

There are a number of useful guides on travel health:

Staying Healthy in Asia, Africa & Latin America
by Dirk Schroeder, Moon Publications, 1994. Probably the best all-round guide to carry; it's compact, detailed and well organised.

Travellers' Health
by Dr Richard Dawood, Oxford University Press, 1995. Comprehensive, easy to read, authoritative and highly recommended, although it's rather large to lug around.

Travel with Children
by Maureen Wheeler, Lonely Planet Publications, 1995. Includes advice on travel health for younger children.

There are also a number of excellent travel health sites on the Internet. From the Lonely Planet Web site (www.lonelyplanet.com) there are links to the World Health Organization and the US Centers for Disease Control & Prevention.

Predeparture Planning

No immunisations are required for Japan though, despite the very low risk factor, you may want to consider vaccinations against Hepatitis A and B. The former is transmitted by contaminated food and drinking water and the latter is spread through contact with infected blood, blood products or body fluids. It is also wise to keep up to date with your tetanus and diphtheria and polio shots (boosters are recommended every 10 years). Tap water is safe to drink and the food is almost uniformly prepared with high standards of hygiene. It is advisable to take out some form of health insurance (see the Documents section earlier in this chapter).

Medical Assistance

Medical care in Japan is relatively expensive. Although the cost of a basic consultation is cheap (about ¥3000) the costs really start to add up with any further examinations, especially with the tendency of Japan's doctors to over-prescribe medicines. If you do need to visit a hospital in Kyoto, it is not usually necessary to have cash in hand; most hospitals will admit people on a pay-later basis. Credit cards are very rarely accepted.

The TIC has lists of English-speaking doctors and hospitals in Kyoto. Japan has a 24 hour multilingual HIV/AIDS hotline (☎ 0120-46-1995, toll-free) which can provide advice on prevention and dealing with the disease.

Hospitals and clinics have limited walk-in hours and can be contacted for appointments.

For nonemergency medical care in Kyoto, the Japan Baptist Hospital (Map 8; ☎ 781-5191) is popular with foreign residents and has English-speaking doctors. It's in northeast Kyoto; to get there, take bus No 3 from Shijō Kawaramachi station on the Hankyū line and get off at the Baptist Byōin-Mae stop. It's a short walk up the hill. Walk-in hours are from 8.30 to 11 am and 1 to 3.45 pm; closed Saturday afternoon, Sunday and holidays.

For an emergency clinic open on Sunday

Medical Kit Check List

A small medical kit is worth carrying, even though most items will usually be readily available in Japan. Your kit could include:

☐ **Aspirin** or **paracetamol** – for pain or fever.
☐ **Antihistamine** (such as Benadryl) – useful as a decongestant for colds, allergies, to ease the itch from insect bites or stings or to help prevent motion sickness.
☐ **Kaolin preparation** (Pepto-Bismol), Imodium or Lomotil – for stomach upsets.
☐ **Antiseptic** and **antibiotic powder** or similar 'dry' spray – for cuts and grazes.
☐ **Calamine lotion** – to ease irritation from bites or stings.
☐ **Bandages** and **band-aids** – for minor injuries.
☐ **Scissors, tweezers** and a **thermometer** – mercury thermometers are prohibited by airlines.
☐ **Insect repellent, sunscreen (**can be difficult to find in Japan) and **chapstick**.

If you're shortsighted, bring a spare pair of glasses and your prescription. If you require a particular medication, take an adequate supply as it may not be available locally. Take the prescription with the generic rather than the brand name, which may be unavailable, as it will make getting replacements easier. It's a wise idea to have the prescription with you to show you legally use the medication.

Although oral contraceptives are available from clinics specialising in medical care for foreigners, it is preferable to bring adequate supplies with you. It was only in 1990 that the marketing of oral contraceptives was officially authorised in Japan. Condoms are widely available, but visitors are advised to bring their own or buy a foreign brand. ∎

and public holidays, try the Kyoto Holiday Emergency Clinic (Map 6; ☎ 811-5072). For emergency dental problems call the Kyoto Holiday Emergency Dental Clinic (Map 7; ☎ 441-7173) or Igarashi Dental Clinic (Map 3; ☎ 392-0993).

Some other hospitals and clinics around town include:

Hashimoto Pediatric Clinic
 (Map 2; ☎ 581-0015) Hirata-chō 24-6,
 Nagitsuji, Yamashina-ku
Kyoto City Hospital
 (Map 6; ☎ 311-5311) Higashi-takada-chō 1-2,
 Mibu, Nakagyō-ku
Kyoto Prefectural University Hospital
 (Map 8; ☎ 251-5111) Hirokoji-agaru,
 Kawaramachi-dōri, Kamigyō-ku
Tomita Maternity Clinic
 (Map 9; ☎ 221-1202) Sanjō-agaru,
 Shinmachi-dōri, Nakagyō-ku

Pharmacies
Pharmacies are found in any neighbourhood in the city and are easily spotted by their colourful outdoor displays of shampoo and other pharmaceutical products.

Emergencies
The nationwide number for police *(keisatsu)* is ☎ 110; phone ☎ 119 for an ambulance *(kyukyu-sha)*. The person answering the phone may not always speak English.

Police boxes, or *kōban*, are small police stations typically found at city intersections. Most can be recognised by the small, round red lamp outside. They are a logical place to head in an emergency, but remember that the police may not always speak English.

If you need to use English and want help finding the closest suitable service, try Japan Travel-Phone (☎ 371-5649) or Japan Helpline (☎ 0120-461-997, toll-free), which is an emergency number operating 24 hours a day, seven days a week. Don't clog the line unless you really do have an emergency.

There is a local police consultation telephone helpline (☎ 441-8580) with limited English, open Monday to Friday from 9 am to 5 pm. Another option for women is consulting

the YWCA (Map 7; ☎ 431-0351), which can be very helpful with things like locating doctors and assistance for getting to hospitals.

Counselling & Advice
Adjusting to life in Japan can be tough but there are several places to turn to for help. KICH (Map 10) offers multilingual counselling services, as does the Kyoto Prefectural International Center in Kyoto station (Map 11; see the Useful Organisations section later in this chapter). If you need to urgently speak with someone, try the 24 hour Japan Helpline (☎ 0120-461-997, toll-free).

For professional psychiatric assistance, the private Aoibashi Family Clinic (Map 7; ☎ 431-9150) has foreign staff and offers counselling in English from 10 am to 5 pm, except Sunday; by appointment only.

TOILETS & PUBLIC BATHS
Toilets
To sit or squat ... that is the question. In Kyoto you will come across both western-style and Asian squat toilets (though generally the latter are on the way out). When you are compelled to squat, the correct position is facing the pipes, away from the door. Some squatters are equipped with a handlebar fixed to wall. Also, be sure not to lose the contents of your pockets on the floor, or worse, in the basin.

In some public western-style toilets you are discouraged from flushing tissue or 'other foreign objects', and there is often a small trash bin found by the toilet. In homes and inns, separate toilet slippers are usually provided just inside the door. These are for use in the toilet only, so remember to change out of them before you exit, or you can expect some horrified looks as you reappear onto the tatami with them still on.

Public toilets do not always provide toilet paper, so it is a very good idea to keep some on hand (you can usually find packets of tissues used for advertising handed out on street corners). You will find that most train and subway station toilets are equipped with tissue vending machines (about ¥50 per pack). You can also usually find a toilet in a big hotel or fast-food restaurant if you are in a jam, and in some convenience stores.

Bear in mind that many public toilets are unsegregated, and it is common for women on their way to the toilet to be shocked when they pass men busy at the urinal. Likewise, for many visiting men this co-ed feature adds a new dimension to the term 'stage fright'. It is also unexceptional to see men urinating in public, but as one might suspect, women do not enjoy the same freedom (see the Etiquette section in the Facts about Kyoto chapter). Public toilets are free in Japan. The kanji script for 'toilet' is 手洗い, for 'men' is 男, and for 'women' is 女.

Public Baths

Due to the large number of old houses lacking bathing facilities, Kyoto has a large number of *sentō* (public bath houses) and a visit to one of these can be a worthwhile experience. Sentō are frequently mistaken with *onsen* (hot-spring baths), but while both are essentially places to get clean and relax, they are in fact different. Sentō are simply neighbourhood bath houses, while onsen are baths using deep natural spring water with mineral qualities that do not flow from the tap. For more on Japanese bathing etiquette and a listing of sentō in Kyoto, see The Japanese Bath boxed text in the Things to See & Do chapter.

WOMEN TRAVELLERS

Overall, Japan is a safe country to travel in and serious crimes against women are rare. However, women should be aware of the wandering hands that appear on jam-packed public transport. Frequently Japanese women will put up with this interference as many feel drawing attention to it is somehow worse than tolerating the discomfort. In most cases, should you face such a situation, nudge your way away to a different corner of the sardine can; otherwise, a loud complaint will shame the perpetrator into withdrawing his hand.

Women's roles in the Japanese mass media are something that many western women find difficult to accept. This ranges from forms of advertising that many see as overly 'sexist' to *manga* (comics) and other newspapers and magazines where women are portrayed in exploitative situations. Such publications are widely read by men (and women) in trains and other public places, and it can be disconcerting to find yourself seated next to someone reading one.

There are a variety of helpful contacts and women's services in Kyoto, and the YWCA (see the Useful Organisations section) is a good place to begin. The YWCA offers a free telephone consultation service for foreign women in English, as well as Spanish, Thai, Tagalog (Filipino) and Chinese, on Monday from 3 to 6 pm and Thursday from 3 to 8 pm. You can also arrange long-term accommodation here. There is a useful book of Kansai area contacts for women on display in the lobby.

Recently the Kyoto police launched a women's telephone consultation service staffed by local policewomen. It provides advice and information on sex offenders (like *chikan*, men who lurk in the shadows of narrow streets after dark looking to assault young woman), rape and sexual harassment, a relatively new concept in Japan. The helpline can contacted on ☎ 411-0110, Monday to Friday from 9 am to 5 pm. There are English-speaking staff, and though they're not always on duty, you can arrange a time to call back to speak with one of them.

Kansai Time Out is a good source to locate women's groups, meetings and activities. See also the Dangers & Annoyances section later in this chapter for general information on safety.

GAY & LESBIAN TRAVELLERS

Homosexuality has been enjoying a minor boom of late in Japan's mass media and scandalous gay love affairs have the subject of more than one Japanese soap opera. Yet while the country has on the whole become slightly more open-minded toward gay lifestyles, most people remain fairly restrained. Notoriously, many Japanese gay men are known to enter corporate Japan, marry and have kids to fulfil societal expectations, then pursue their true needs behind this veil.

Many Japanese, especially young women, in their drive to embrace new cultures, go to 'gay bars', which are not quite as you might imagine them in the west. Many of these *gei-bā* are not places where gay people hang out, but are popular because they are staffed by transvestites or transexuals with whom a largely straight clientele satisfies their curiosity by chatting.

While there is a sizable gay community in Kyoto and a number of establishments where gays do congregate, they will take a fair amount of digging to find. There is a far more active scene in Osaka, and many of Kyoto's gay residents choose to make the one hour train trip. If you are in Kyoto on the right day of the month, however, *the* gay event in town is the monthly *sutoraito jai nai* night (not straight night) at the Metro (see the Entertainment chapter for details).

If you are on your way to the Kansai area, it is worth writing to a group called Out and About, which organises local gay events and outings. Its address is: PM Box 104, Room 20, Nishigami Building, Doyama-chō 7-10, Kita-ku, Osaka 530.

On the Internet the following organisations also may be of help:

Hyper Stag
    www.gavie.or.jp/jp/hpstag/index.html
Gay Net Japan
    www.gnj.or.jp/gaynet/
Planet Rainbow
    www.kt.rim.or.jp/rainbow/

DISABLED TRAVELLERS

Though Kyoto has made a tolerable attempt at equipping city streets and public facilities for easy access, its narrow streets and the terrain of sights such as temples and shrines make it a challenging city for disabled people, especially for those confined to wheelchairs. Both the Kyoto TIC and the city tourist information centre in the new Kyoto station building have wheelchairs that can be borrowed free of charge.

AD-Brain (the same outfit which pub-

lishes the monthly *Kyoto Visitor's Guide)* has produced a basic city map for disabled people and senior citizens showing wheelchair access points in town and giving information on public transport access etc. The map is available at the TIC. You might also try contacting the disabled welfare section at Kyoto City Hall (Map 10; ☎ 251-2385), or the Kyoto City Association for Disabled Persons (Map 9; ☎ 822-0770), which publishes the very detailed *Handy Map* guidebook on local facility accessibility, presently in Japanese only.

One place which may be worth contacting is the Yoriai-no-kai (☎ 314-7726), an activity centre for events, meetings, information and selling of goods. It's west of Nishiōji-dōri on Takoyakushi-dōri.

MK Taxi (☎ 721-2237) can accommodate wheelchairs in many of its cars and is an attractive possibility for anyone interested in touring the city by cab. Facilities for the visually impaired include musical pedestrian lights at many city intersections and raised bumps on railway platforms for guidance.

SENIOR TRAVELLERS

Generally speaking, from a travel perspective, seniors get far less of a break in Japan than they might in say Europe or North America. Though in some areas of society benefits are built in and discounts are offered to seniors, these are mostly designed for local people (who, by the way they elbow their way onto buses and to the front of the queue, can fend for themselves).

KYOTO FOR CHILDREN

Travelling with kids in Kyoto is relatively easy, as there is plenty to keep them occupied. Luckily, most of these kid-friendly attractions seem to fascinate adults equally.

In general, the cost of public transport is half-price for children under 12. Likewise, many of the city's attractions and hotels also offer discounted rates for children. The western part of town gets high marks with kids: in the Uzumasa area there is Tōei Uzumasa Eiga Mura (Movie Village), Kyoto's answer to a Universal Studios theme park;

MASON FLORENCE

The Iwatayama Monkey Park in Kyoto's hills is certain to entertain the children.

of seeing their Japanese counterparts parading down the street dressed in traditional costume. In addition, even at the most 'traditional' of Kyoto's many festivals, there are usually several carnival-like attractions and games to win prizes (see the Festivals boxed text later in this chapter).

A useful guide on taking the kids along is Lonely Planet's *Travelling with Children* by Maureen Wheeler.

USEFUL ORGANISATIONS
Kyoto International Community House (KICH)

KICH (Map 10; ☎ 752-3010), near Nanzen-ji Temple in eastern Kyoto, is an essential stop for those planning a long-term stay and can be quite useful for short-term visitors as well. With a day's notice it is possible to arrange a local home visit through KICH. In-house services include typewriter rental, fax and library. There's a lobby area with wide-screen English-language TV news and a notice board with messages regarding work, accommodation, sayonara sales (where foreigners leaving Japan sell household goods, bicycles etc) and so on.

KICH is an excellent place to meet both expats and Japanese. It offers free Japanese-language classes as well as tea ceremony, *nō* and *koto* classes for a minimal fee. To get a taste of these subjects, you can sit in on a lesson for free or ¥1000 (depending on the class). If you would like to meet a Japanese family at home, you can also make arrangements here (let them know a day or two advance).

KICH is open from 9 am to 9 pm, closed Monday (plus Tuesday following a national holiday).

Other Organisations

Another useful resource in the heart of town, a few minutes walk north of the intersection of Shijō-dōri and Karasuma-dōri, is the Japan Foundation (Map 9; ☎ 211-1312) on the 8th floor of the Yasuda Kasai Kaijō building. It has a well stocked library, message board, monthly lectures and seminars, and screens free Japanese movie classics for

the entertaining Iwatayama Monkey Park with paddle boats in nearby Arashiyama; and the excitement of shooting the rapids from Kameoka down to Arashiyama on the Hozugawa River ride.

Other sights to consider are the Kyoto Municipal Zoo, where you can recharge the tots when visiting the Heian-jingū area in Okazaki. For a ride on an authentic steam train, there is the Umekoji Steam Locomotive Museum west of Kyoto station; another possibility if you plan to visit southern Kyoto is Castle Land in the grounds of Fushimi Momoyama-jō Castle.

Of course, there is always the option of a nature walk around the foothills of the city. If this doesn't do the trick, there are plenty of trademark game centres scattered around town with all the latest in high-tech video games.

You should also consider the surprising number of festivals in Kyoto, as they are not only culturally rich, but often involve kids as participants. Many foreign kids get a kick out

foreign visitors on Wednesday at 2 pm. The office is open from 10 am to 5 pm, closed weekends.

The Kyoto Prefectural International Center (☎ 342-5000; Map 11) is a multifunction resource centre with information on the Kyoto Prefecture region. It has a small library of travel literature, English TV news and offers Internet access (see the Internet Cafes boxed text in this chapter). The centre is open daily from 10 am to 6 pm, closed on the second and fourth Tuesday of the month.

The YWCA (Map 7; ☎ 431-0351), west of the Imperial Palace Park at Muromachi-dōri, Demizu-agaru, offers counselling and long-term accommodation for women. It's open Monday to Friday from 10 am to 8 pm, Saturday from 11 am to 5 pm, closed Sunday and public holidays.

LIBRARIES

Though there are several public and university libraries in Kyoto, some with reasonable English collections, the best and most accessible books are at the libraries of the Kyoto International Community House and Japan Foundation (see the previous Useful Organisations section), each with several thousand titles in English.

While the Japan Foundation has a particularly strong collection on Japanese history, culture and arts, KICH also has newspapers and magazines in various languages, and a large collection of travel guides and maps. If there are specific areas of research, the staff at either of these facilities should be able to provide leads on other public or private collections in town.

For travel guides and books on Japan, the Kyoto Prefectural International Center is also worth a look.

CAMPUSES

Kyoto has always been at the forefront of Japan's education system and today, second only to Tokyo, Kyoto is Japan's major university centre. There are 37 universities and junior colleges representing about 10% of the city population. The campuses are good areas to meet young Japanese and most have

school festivals in autumn worth checking out.

Among the largest schools are:

Bukkyō University (Map 4; Buddhist)
Dōshisha University (Map 8; Liberal Arts)
Kyoto Sangyō University (Map 4; Liberal Arts)
Kyoto University (Map 8; Liberal Arts)
Kyoto University of Foreign Studies (Map 5; Foreign Languages)
Ritsumeikan University (Map 3; Liberal Arts)

CULTURAL CENTRES

International culture centres are represented in Kyoto by Britain, Germany, France and Italy (in 1995 the American centre was absorbed into the Osaka branch). Each features libraries and sponsors art exhibitions, lectures and seminars relating to their respective country, and cross-cultural exchange.

British
  The British Council (Map 8; ☎ 791-7151) is on Nishimachi-dōri, north-west of the Imadegawa-Shirakawa intersection; open from 10 am to 6 pm, closed weekends and public holidays.
French
  Institut Franco-Japonais du Kansai (Map 8; ☎ 761-2105) is on Higashiōji-dōri, south of Imadegawa-dōri; open from 9.45 am to 6.15 pm (to 5.45 pm Saturday), closed Sunday.
German
  Goethe Institute Kyoto (Map 8; ☎ 761-2188) is on Kawabata-dōri, south of Imadegawa-dōri; open from 9 am to 5 pm, closed weekends and public holidays.
Italian
  Instituto Italiano di Cultura di Kyoto (Map 8; ☎ 751-1868) is on Higashiōji-dōri, south of Imadegawa-dōri; open from 10 am to 6 pm, closed weekends and public holidays.

DANGERS & ANNOYANCES

Despite still being one the safest places in the world to travel, it is highly advisable not to get too comfortable in Japan. The country has its fair share of wierdos and Kyoto is by no means an exception.

There have been numerous cases of foreign women being groped, assaulted in public places and even raped. Japanese women are notoriously hesitant in reporting sexual crimes, so the statistics may not reflect reality. In general, it is best to stay on well travelled,

Mushroom Danger

While boars and bears pose a threat to hikers, a less suspecting mountain hazard is a confrontation with *homo sapiens* gatherers of Japan's prized *matsutake* mushrooms. During harvest season in early autumn, culinary demand for these furry spores commands inconceivable prices. As such, forested areas where they thrive in very limited quantities are highly protected by whoever has the legal area rights to collect the fungi.

Signs posted in Japanese warn hikers (and potential poachers) to keep out, and foreigners who have wandered innocently into off-limits areas have at times created problems with the locals. There allegedly exists an unwritten code that anyone found even walking in such areas will be held responsible for three times the amount of money the person renting the rights to the land has shelled out.

It is helpful to be aware of matsutake season (usually September and October) and also to think twice about pressing on if you see a signpost you cannot read. Often the sign won't even have the word 'matsutake' on it, so be especially careful at this time. ■

well lit streets at night and remember you will be safer going out in a group of people.

Generally speaking, Kyoto is quite safe, and the only specific danger spot to be aware of is the west bank of the Kamo-gawa between Sanjō-dōri and Shijō-dōri, a popular summer hangout for couples and Kyoto youth, including some wanna-be gangs. There have been several recent incidents of foreign men being attacked by these gangs, although the problem appears to have declined of late.

Theft of bicycles can also be a problem, and bicycles should always be locked up (see also the Bicycle section in the Getting Around chapter).

LEGAL MATTERS

With the ever-increasing number of foreigners living in Japan, there has been a natural rise in the need for legal services catering to non-Japanese.

Theoretically, foreigners in Japan are extended the same rights as Japanese nationals, though suspicious police and language barriers have at times been reported to have placed foreigners at a legal disadvantage. If there are language problems when dealing with the police, you have the right to request an interpreter, provided at their expense. Though Japanese enjoy watching the practice in movies and on American TV shows, there is no custom in Japan of demanding to see a lawyer on the spot.

For legal advice and contacts for English-speaking lawyers, the best place to turn is KICH (☎ 752-1187), which also offers free legal counselling to foreigners.

BUSINESS HOURS

Shops in town are typically open from 10 am to 7 or 8 pm. Shopping (or sightseeing for that matter) on Sunday, the only free day for most working Japanese, should be avoided at all costs – unless you've always dreamed of being a sardine.

Kyoto's six major department stores are open from 10 am to 7.30 pm and each closes one day a week (though this day varies through the year). If one is closed you stand a good chance of finding another one open close by. If in doubt, phone first. On Shijō-dōri are Daimaru (Map 10; ☎ 211-8111), Fujii Daimaru (Map 10; ☎ 221-8181), Takashimaya (Map 10; ☎ 221-8811) and Hankyū (Map 10; ☎ 223-2288), and at Kyoto station (inside of and north of respectively) are Isetan (Map 11; ☎ 352-1111) and Kintetsu (Map 11; ☎ 361-1111).

Though most companies technically operate on a 9 am to 5 pm, five day work week, many stay in business on Saturday morning as well. See the earlier Post & Communications section for post office hours.

Banks are open Monday to Friday from 9 am to 3 pm, and closed on Saturday, Sunday and national holidays. Procedures can be time-consuming at some banks. If you're caught cashless outside regular banking hours, try a large department store or major hotel. (By the way, interest rates are next to nothing in Japan – usually less than 1% – but opening a savings account at a bank is a fairly simple process; you just need to provide a passport and spend about 20 minutes filling out the paperwork.)

For those late-night cravings, beer and cigarette vending machines shut down after 11 pm, though there seems to be a 24 hour convenience store on nearly every corner of town, some of which stock booze and tobacco.

PUBLIC HOLIDAYS & SPECIAL EVENTS

Japan has 13 national holidays. When a public holiday falls on a Sunday, the following Monday is generally taken as a holiday. As with visiting Kyoto on any of these days, you can also expect a near sell-out for travel and lodging during the New Year (29 December to 6 January), Golden Week (last week in April to first week in May) and during Obon (Festival of the Dead) from 13 to 16 August when most Japanese travel back to their home town.

Public Holidays

Ganjitsu
   (New Year's Day) 1 January
Seijin-no-hi
   (Adult's Day) 15 January
Kenkoku Kinen-bi
   (National Foundation Day) 11 February
Shumbun-no-hi
   (Spring Equinox Day) 21 March (approximately)
Midori-no-hi
   (Green Day) 29 April
Kenpō Kinen-bi
   (Constitution Memorial Day) 3 May
Kodomo-no-hi
   (Children's Day) 5 May
Keirō-no-hi
   (Respect for the Aged Day) 15 September
Shūbun-no-hi
   (Autumn Equinox Day) 23 September (approximately)
Taiiku-no-hi
   (Sports Day) 10 October
Bunka-no-hi
   (Culture Day) 3 November
Kinrō Kansha-no-hi
   (Labor Thanksgiving Day) 23 November
Tennō Tanjōbi
   (Emperor's Birthday) 23 December

Festivals

Kyoto's greatest Living Treasures are its vivacious festivals *(matsuri)*. The city hosts

some 500 of these colourful events throughout the year, and almost any visit should provide the chance to catch at least one.

Most of these celebrations have their roots in ancient Buddhist and Shintō rituals, from ceremonies for a bountiful harvest to fertility rites or prayers for success in business. Today, however, many people attend for the sheer fun and fanfare. Photo opportunities abound with elaborate floats, people dressed in period costume, geisha, tea ceremonies, and traditional drama and dances. At many of the festivals, both participants and spectators dress up in kimono or *yukata* (summer kimono).

These spectacular festivals are testimony to the ancient culture of the city, and some have been celebrated for over 1000 years. Interestingly, even some of the most traditional events incorporate modern features, right down to amusement park games for kids, cotton candy and the ever-popular fried squid-on-a-stick.

Festival time has its advantages and disadvantages. While there are often special openings of temple buildings and treasures, you will often be struggling through the crowd to get a view. While some temples and shrines waive entry fees on festival days, there are sometimes other fees involved (usually for tea ceremony, good luck charms or food). Some matsuri, especially the 'big three' (the Aoi, Gion and Jidai festivals) attract hordes of spectators from out of town, so it is important to book accommodation well in advance.

It's best to arrive early (around an hour or so before the main event) and try to stake out a suitable place to view the spectacle. If you're not sure where to set up camp, look for the always-present pack of Japanese photographers with step ladders and other fancy gadgets – they will probably be positioning themselves in prime photo-taking territory.

There have been several books published on Japanese festivals; perhaps the best and most colourful is the coffee-table *Matsuri* by Gorazd Vilhar & Charlotte Anderson. Helen Kay's exhaustive *Japan Festival Guide* lists some 800 festivals throughout the country.

Festivals

Hatsumōde
1 to 3 January; involves paying the first visit of the New Year to a Shintō shrine, where prayers are said to bring health and good fortune during the ensuing year. Kyoto's two most-visited shrines on this occasion are Yasaka-jinja (Map 10) and Heian-jingū (Map 10).

Karuta Hajime
3 January; at Yasaka-jinja Shrine from 1 pm, pairs of women dressed in Heian-era court costumes play *hyaku-nin-isshu*, an ancient Japanese card game.

Kemari Hajime (Kick Ball Game)
4 January; at Heian-jingū Shrine from 2 pm, men in elaborate Heian-era court costumes play *kemari*, a traditional court ball game. It's the first of several such events during the year.

Hatsu Ebisu or Tōka Ebisu
8 to 12 January; at Ebisu-jinja Shrine (Map 10) a party is held for Ebisu, the patron deity of merchants and one of the beloved Shichi Fuku Jin (Seven Luck Gods); local merchants and people go to pray for a prosperous year.

Tōshiya (Archery Contest)
15 January; at Sanjūsangendō Temple (Map 6) from 8 am to 4 pm. This is the largest of Kyoto's three archery events in January and dates to a 1606 feat by a samurai who is said to have shot 51 arrows in rapid succession along the veranda of the temple. Hundreds of kimono-clad archers gather for a competition of accuracy and strength, trying to shoot as many arrows as possible into a 1.5m-diameter target 118m away.

Setsubun
2 to 4 February; this signals the last day of winter according to the lunar calendar. People go to various temples and bless their homes, driving off demons, sickness and misfortune by scattering roasted soybeans *(mamemaki)* in and around the house while shouting *'Oni-wa-soto, Fuku-wa-uchi'* (Out with devils, In with luck). You can enjoy the revelry at Imamiya-jinja Shrine (Map 4) and Yasaka-jinja (Map 10) from 1 to 3 pm.

Godai Rikison Ninno-e
23 February; at Daigo-ji Temple (Map 2), participants lift two gigantic rice cakes (150kg for men, 90kg for women!). The winner is the one who keeps it in the air longest.

Baika-sai
25 February; at Kitano-Tenman-gū Shrine (Map 4) this festival features colourful plums and geisha. It's a rare open-air tea ceremony, and provides great photo opportunities (it's timed with the market).

Sagano O-taimatsu
15 March; at Seiryō-ji Temple (Map 12) this commemorates Shaka's (the Historical Buddha's) death with Nembutsu Kyōgen (Buddhist Miracle Plays) at 2 pm. At 7.30 pm three enormous torches are set ablaze to divine the coming harvest.

Kanno-chakai (Flower Viewing Festival)
1 to 21 April; at Heian-jingū (Map 10), there is tea ceremony (¥600) and cherry blossom viewing.

Yasurai Matsuri
Second Sunday in April; at Imamiya-jinja (Map 4) from noon to 4 pm; a rite against plague, with dancers in demon costumes and with flaming red hair. Large parasols are paraded through the streets to collect 'disease-causing spirits', which are taken to the shrine to be exorcised.

Taiko Hanami Gyōretsu
Second Sunday in April; at Daigo-ji (Map 2), a parade re-enacts in full period costume a cherry blossom party which Toyotomi Hideyoshi held in 1598. As a result of this party, the temple's abbot was able to secure Hideyoshi's support for the restoration of the dilapidated temple complex.

Mibu Kyōgen
21 to 29 April; at Mibu-dera Temple (Map 9) from 5.30 pm; Buddhist miracle plays are held to teach Buddhist doctrine through pantomime. This has been held every spring for the last 700 years.

Aoi Matsuri (Hollyhock Festival)
15 May; dates to the 6th century and commemorates the successful prayers of the people for the gods to stop calamitous weather. Today, the procession involves imperial messengers in oxcarts and a retinue

of 600 people dressed in traditional costume; hollyhock leaves are carried or used as decoration. The procession leaves around 10 am from the Imperial Palace (Map 8) and heads for Shimogamo-jinja Shrine (Map 8) where ceremonies take place. It sets out again at 2 pm and arrives at Kamigamo-jinja Shrine (Map 4) at 3.30 pm.

Mifune Matsuri
Third Sunday in May; takes place on boats in the Arashiyama area (Map 12), west of Kyoto; one of Kyoto's most colourful festivals, it starts at 1 pm.

Kibune Matsuri
1 June; at Kibune-jinja Shrine (Map 2) in the mountains north of Kyoto; yet another festival held in the interests of good harvest, carrying *mikoshi* (portable shrines) along the Kibune-gawa River.

Takigi Nō
1 and 2 June; at Heian-jingū (Map 10); a festival of nō drama held by flaming torchlight in the outdoor courtyard of the shrine. Tickets for this special event cost ¥2500 in advance, ¥3300 on the day of performance (phone ☎ 761-0221 for details).

Takekiri E-shiki
20 June; at Kurama-dera Temple (Map 2); a bamboo-cutting festival dating back to an event 1000 years ago, when a priest of Kurama-dera defeated two evil serpents with the aid of Bishamon-tei, the Buddhist guardian enshrined at the temple. Today, eight priests dressed in robes and hoods of *yamabushi* (mountain priests) form two teams and race to hack to pieces four lengths of green bamboo symbolising the serpents. The festival begins at 2 pm.

Mitoshiro Nō
1 July; at Kamigamo-jinja (Map 4); nō, kyōgen and dances are offered from 1 pm for the protection of rice crops from insects.

Gion Matsuri
17 July; perhaps the most renowned of all Japanese festivals, this month long fanfare involves a myriad of events. Yoi-yama is held on the 16th, when over 200,000 people throng the Shijō-Karasuma area, and reaches a climax on the 17th, when a Yamaboko-junkō parade of over 30 floats is held to the accompaniment of flutes, drums and gongs. On the three evenings preceding the 17th, people gather on Shijō-dōri, many dressed in beautiful light summer kimono, to look at the floats and carouse from one street stall to the next. Events last through July.

Gion Matsuri was initiated in 869 AD, when plague had ravished the city. The festival was offered as a prayer of relief to the god Susanō-no-Mikoto (the son of the gods, which according to Japanese mythology gave birth to Japan).

Osuzumi
20 July; at Jōnan-gū Shrine (Map 3); people gather here from 5pm to enjoy the cooling down of the summer heat.

Hiwatari Matsuri
28 July; at Tanuki-dani Fudō-in Temple (Map 4), on the mountain behind Shisen-dō Temple; this festival incorporates a fire walk.

Hassaku
1 August; Geisha and *maiko* (apprentice geisha) make obligatory appreciation rounds to teachers and Gion (Map 10) teahouses. Also on 1 August the Nagoshi-no-shinji is held at Shimogamo-jinja (Map 8) to bring closure to the heat of summer.

Mantō-e
14 to 16 August; at Higashi Ōtani Cemetery, the graveyard of Higashi Hongan-ji Temple (Map 11), where 10,000 candle-lit lanterns welcome home the dead.

Daimon-ji Gozan Okuribi
16 August; mistakenly referred to by many as Daimon-ji-yaki (literally, burning of Daimon-ji), this is performed to bid farewell to the souls of ancestors. Enormous fires are lit on five mountains in the form of Chinese characters or other shapes. The main fire is the character for *dai*, or great, on Daimonji-yama (Map 6), panning left to right and lit at 10 minute intervals. The first fires are lit at 8 pm. It is best to watch from the banks of the Kamo-gawa River or pay for a rooftop view from a hotel.

Sentō Kuyō
23 to 24 August; at Adashino-Nembutsu-ji Temple (Map 12) in Sagano. This is a dedicatory mass to the souls of the countless *jizō* statues at this temple representing the dead of the relatives attending the colourful ceremony. Reserve in advance by post by 15 June. There is a ¥1000 fee (children under 12 free).

Karasu Zumō
9 September; at Kamigamo-jinja (Map 4); also called crow wrestling, from 10 am young boys compete in bouts of sumō wrestling. The festival is named for a legendary blackbird who came to rest on the arrow of Japan's first emperor, Jimmu.

Tsukimi
Mid-September; moon viewing festivals take place at several places, including Daikaku-ji Temple (Map 12) and Shimogamo-jinja (Map 8). At this time of year *(Jūgoya)*, literally the night of the 15th (full) moon, the Japanese traditionally decorate their verandas, temples and shrines with *susuki* (pampas grass) reeds in a vase, *tsukimi-dango* (rice dumplings), steamed *sato-imo* (taro potatoes) and autumn fruits, all facing the moon as an offering. Tsukimi has its roots in a harvest celebration.

Nijū-go Bosatsu Oneri Kuyō
Third Sunday in October; at Sokujō-in Temple (Map 6); from 1 pm, a colourful procession of 25 children, wearing elaborate costumes of gold brocade, assume roles of the different Bodhisattvas and parade around the temple.

Jidai Matsuri (Festival of the Ages)
22 October; though one of Kyoto's big three, this festival is of recent origin, dating to 1895. More than 2000 people dressed in costumes ranging from the 8th to the 19th centuries parade from the Imperial Palace (Map 8) to Heian-jingū (Map 10).

Kurama-no-Hi Matsuri (Fire Festival)
22 October; this festival is traced to a rite using fires to guide the gods of the nether world on their tours around this world. Mikoshi are carried through the streets and accompanied by young men in loincloths and with giant flaming torches. The festival climaxes at 10 pm at Yuki-jinja Shrine in Kurama (Map 2).

Yōkō-sai
29 October; at Kitano-Tenman-gū (Map 4); features a ceremony from 2 pm in memory of exiled scholar Lord Sugawara Michizane (845-903); people dress in elaborate Heian-era costumes and recite ancient poems.

Arashiyama Momiji Matsuri
Second Sunday in November; in the Arashiyama area (Map 12); a procession of boats moves along the Oi-gawa River (a fantastic photo opportunity).

Shichi-go-san
15 November; a nationwide event in which proud parents dress kids aged seven, five and three in colourful kimono, and visit local shrines to pray for their health and happiness. Heian-jingū (Map 10) and Yasaka-jinja (Map 10) are popular places for this event.

Fude Kuyō
23 November; in the grounds of Tōfuku-ji Temple (Map 3), this service is for used calligraphy brushes.

O-susu-harai
20 December; at Higashi Hongan-ji Temple (Map 11); from 9 to 10.30 am, as a line of people kneel and beat the tatami with wooden mallets, soot-sweeping monks and devotees of the temple don masks and whisk away the dust with gigantic paper fans, ceremonially cleansing the spirit to mark the end of the year.

Ominugui-shiki
25 December; at Chion-in Temple (Map 10); another temple-cleaning ceremony, this time of a Buddhist statue, to the sensational accompaniment of several hundred monks chanting sutras.

Ōmisoka (New Year's Eve)
31 December; sacred fire-kindling festival *(Okera Mairi)* named for the herb burned in the lanterns at Yasaka-jinja (Map 10). It's customary to consume *toshikoshi soba* (buckwheat noodles) before setting out to the shrine to see off the old year and welcome in the new. It is believed that returning home with a bit of sacred flame on *kitchō-nawa* rope from the shrine will fend off illness in the new year. The activities continue from about 7 pm to 1 am, with huge crowds from about 11 pm. ■

There is also an excellent video produced by the *Kyoto Shimbun* newspaper, called *Grand Festivals of Kyoto – A Journey Through The Seasons*. It's 60 minutes long and is available in both PAL and NTSC formats at major bookshops, or call the *Kyoto Shimbun* (☎ 222-2111).

See the Festivals boxed text in this section for a partial listing including Kyoto's major festivals (though there are many more worthwhile events). Dates and times can vary from year to year, so check with the TIC, the *Kyoto Visitor's Guide* or *Kansai Time Out* (the latter has festival listings for the Kansai region). Also see the Entertainment chapter for details on geisha dances.

Antique & Craft Fairs The Antique Grand Fair is a major event, with over 100 dealers selling a wide range of Japanese and foreign curios. It is held thrice-yearly (March, June and November) at Pulse Plaza (Map 3) in Fushimi (southern Kyoto). From Takeda station on the Karasuma subway line, there are free shuttle buses – a five minute ride – departing for the fair. Entry to the fair is free. Ring ☎ 541-7025 for more information.

Kyoto holds several large annual pottery events, which are great opportunities for finding deals on both local wares and ceramics from around Japan.

Toki-ichi
  9 to 12 July; a large pottery fair at Senbon Shaka-dō Temple (Map 4; ☎ 461-5973) with around 30 vendors selling various wares.
Toki Matsuri
  18 to 20 July; a famed ceramics bazaar held at Kiyomizu-danchi (Map 6; ☎ 581-6188), with some 60 vendors selling primarily Kiyomizu-yaki style pottery.
Toki Matsuri
  7 to 10 August; on Gojō-zaka (Map 6), the sloping stretch of Gojō-dōri near Kiyomizu-dera Temple, this is one of Japan's greatest pottery fairs, with around 450 vendors.

Kyoto Film Festival This annual event was inaugurated in December 1997. It features a myriad of Japanese and foreign films shown at several venues and is currently scheduled to be held every other year. To find out more

call ☎ 752-4840, or check the festival Web site (web.kyoto-inet.or.jp/org/film-fes/).

Fireworks The Japanese are among the world's biggest fireworks enthusiasts, and during summer in Kyoto a cherished local pastime (especially among young people) is gathering on the banks of the Kamo-gawa to set off low-calibre explosives and twirl sparklers. For those more into the heavy artillery, there are several chances to view major displays in early August – including those on the Kamo-gawa, down south in Uji (Map 2) and from the shores of Lake Biwa-ko (Map 2; see also the Excursions chapter). Check *Kansai Time Out*, *Kyoto Visitor's Guide* or with the TIC for up-to-date details. Before you go, however, you may want to practise two Japanese exclamations – *sugoi* (wow!) and *kirei* (beautiful!) – holler either of these at the right time and you'll fit right in!

Night Illumination at Temples & Shrines In the evening during the peak foliage times of spring and autumn, several temples and shrines light up their grounds to create an incredible scene of pink cherry blossoms or blazing maples. Dates and places change slightly from year to year, though in spring (from the beginning of April through mid-May) they're typically held at Kiyomizu-dera (Map 6), Kōdai-ji Temple (Map 10) and Hirano-jinja Shrine (Map 4); in autumn (from mid-November to late November) at Kiyomizu-dera, Kōdai-ji, Shōren-in (Map 10), Eikan-dō (Map 10), Enkō-ji (Map 4) and Tenryū-ji (Map 12) temples. The illumination is usually from dusk till about 9.30 pm; bring a sweater or jacket with you, as the nights can become suddenly cool. Also bring a tripod if you have any plans of taking decent photos. The TIC can provide up-to-date details on places and times.

WORK
Kyoto's popularity makes it one of Japan's most difficult cities in which to find work. Despite this fact and increasingly strict immigration policies, there is a relatively quick turnaround of many resident foreigners, so it

is often just a case of patience until something comes up. Still, anyone looking to work in Kyoto should make sure they have enough money to survive on for a while and *definitely* be prepared to wait.

Many who would prefer to live in Kyoto end up commuting to jobs in Osaka or other neighbouring cities, at least until they find something closer to home. Aside from the English-teaching racket, other popular jobs include bar hostessing (mainly women), work in restaurants and bars, and carpentry. While most of Japan's modelling and acting work comes out of Tokyo, Kyoto's own Tōei Uzumasa Eiga Mura movie studios occasionally hire foreigners as extras to appear in Meiji period films. For this or any other type of local work, the best place to look is in *Kansai Time Out*, the Kansai flea market newsletter or on the message board at KICH.

It is illegal to work in Japan without a proper visa, though many enter on a tourist visa to search for work and try to first sign a contract and arrange visa sponsorship. Once this is handled, you'll just need to make a short trip out of the country – most go to Korea – before returning to begin work (see the Visas section earlier in this chapter).

Getting There & Away

While there is no major international or domestic airport in Kyoto, the city is within easy reach of both Osaka's Itami airport (domestic traffic) and Kansai international airport (KIX), neither of which suffers the acute overcrowding experienced at Tokyo's Narita international airport.

AIR
Airports
With the opening of KIX (Map 1) in 1994, Kansai is now the first port of call for many visitors to Japan. Built on an artificial island in Osaka-wan Bay, it is Japan's first ultra-modern, 24 hour airport with a weekly traffic of more than 500 flights from 75 cities worldwide. The massive terminal is a stimulating building to explore and there are plenty of opportunities to make use of your leftover yen.

Itami airport (Map 1) has frequent flights between Tokyo and Osaka (about 70 minutes) but unless you are very lucky with connections you'll probably find it more convenient and cheaper to take the *shinkansen* (bullet train). The trip to Kansai international airport from Kyoto can be quite expensive and time-consuming; so if you are arriving in Osaka by air from another Japanese city, Itami is the more convenient of the two airports for reaching Kyoto. See the Getting Around chapter for details on transport to and from the airports.

Airlines
Major airline offices in Kyoto include:

All Nippon Airways (ANA)
(Map 10; ☎ 211-5471) near the intersection of Oike-dōri and Teramachi-dōri
Japan Airlines (JAL)
(Map 11; ☎ 0120-255-931 toll-free) Kyoto station building
Japan Air System (JAS)
(Map 9; ☎ 371-0933) near the intersection of Bukkōji-dōri and Karasuma-dōri

Most foreign airlines have offices (☎ 0120 numbers are toll-free) in Osaka, including:

Air France	☎ 06-641-2425
Air New Zealand	☎ 0120-300-747
Alitalia	☎ 06-341-3951
American Airlines	☎ 0120-000-860
Ansett Australia	☎ 0120-800-747
Canadian Airlines International	☎ 06-252-4227
Cathay Pacific Airways	☎ 06-245-6731
Delta Air Lines	☎ 0120-333-742
Garuda Indonesia	☎ 06-445-6985
KLM-Royal Dutch Airlines	☎ 0120-868-862
Korean Air	☎ 06-264-3311
Lufthansa Airlines	☎ 06-341-4966
Northwest Airlines	☎ 0120-120-747
Qantas Airways	☎ 0120-207-020
Scandinavian Airlines	☎ 0120-678-101
Swissair	☎ 0120-667-788
Thai Airways International	☎ 06-202-5161
United Airlines	☎ 0120-114-466

Buying Tickets
With practically every major international carrier flying into KIX there is brisk competition for customers. The best place to look for bargains is through discount travel agents (see the Travel Agents section later in this chapter). Most offer cheap tickets through the airlines or consolidators, who snap up large quantities of seats in bulk from the airlines. Fares to Japan vary greatly from season to season, and during major Japanese holidays planes fill up and fares skyrocket (see the Public Holidays & Special Events section in the Facts for the Visitor chapter). Many deals also depend on whatever 'price wars' the airlines are waging at the time you purchase your ticket. Most discount tickets are nonrefundable and will carry severe restrictions such as a 60 day maximum stay, unchangeable dates, or weekday travel only.

There are occasionally good deals to be found on one way tickets to/from KIX (costing around 60% to 70% of the normal return fare), but in many cases the fares end up just marginally cheaper than if you were to purchase a return ticket. Japan can often be included on special tickets such as round-the-world or multistop excursion itineraries; routes offered depend on which airline (or combination of airlines) you book with. It is best to check with a discount agency for what's available closer to when you are planning your itinerary. Once in Kyoto, check in the back of *Kansai Time Out* for the latest discounted fares available from KIX, and see the Travel Agents section at the end of this chapter for recommended agents.

Travellers with Special Needs

Most international airports and carriers offer an array of special services for travellers with special needs. Services can include wheelchair porters, child escorts and special meals, from vegetarian to religious-specific.

It is best to call the airline you are flying with to confirm how they can provide for your particular needs. When you reconfirm your flight (at least 72 hours prior to departure), check that whatever you have requested

---

Air Travel Glossary

Apex Apex, or 'advance purchase excursion', is a discounted ticket which must be paid for in advance. There are penalties if you wish to change it.

Baggage Allowance This will be written on your ticket and usually includes one 20kg item to go in the hold, plus one item of hand luggage.

Bucket Shops These are unbonded travel agencies specialising in discounted airline tickets.

Budget Fares These can be booked at least three weeks in advance, but the travel date is not confirmed until seven days prior to travel.

Bumped Just because you have a confirmed seat doesn't mean you're going to get on the plane (see Overbooking).

Cancellation Penalties If you have to cancel or change an Apex or other discounted ticket, there are often heavy penalties involved; insurance can sometimes be taken out against these penalties. Some airlines impose penalties on regular tickets as well, particularly against 'no-show' passengers.

Check-in Airlines ask you to check in a certain time ahead of the flight departure (usually one to two hours on international flights). If you fail to check in on time and the flight is overbooked, the airline can cancel your booking and give your seat to somebody else.

Confirmation Having a ticket written out with the flight and date you want doesn't mean you have a seat until the agent has checked with the airline that your status is 'OK' or confirmed. Meanwhile you could just be 'on request'.

Courier Fares Businesses often need to send urgent documents or freight securely and quickly. Courier companies hire people to accompany the package through customs and, in return, offer a discount ticket which is sometimes a phenomenal bargain. In effect, what the companies do is ship their freight as your luggage on the regular commercial flights. This is a legitimate operation, but there are two shortcomings – the short turnaround time of the ticket (usually not longer than a month) and the limitation on your luggage allowance. You may have to surrender all your allowance and take only carry-on luggage.

Discounted Tickets There are two types of discounted fares – officially discounted (such as promotional fares) and unofficially discounted. The lowest prices often impose drawbacks like flying with unpopular airlines, inconvenient schedules or unpleasant routes and connections. Discounted tickets only exist where there is fierce competition.

Economy Class Tickets Economy class tickets are usually not the cheapest way to go, though they do give you maximum flexibility and they are valid for 12 months. If you don't use them, most are fully refundable, as are unused sectors of a multiple ticket.

Full Fares Airlines traditionally offer 1st class (coded F), business class (coded J) and economy class (coded Y) tickets. These days there are so many promotional and discounted fares available that few passengers pay full economy fare.

ITX An ITX, or 'independent inclusive tour excursion', is often available on tickets to popular holiday destinations. Officially it's a package deal combined with hotel accommodation, but many agents will sell you one of these for the flight only and give you phoney hotel vouchers in the unlikely event that you're challenged at the airport.

Lost Tickets If you lose your airline ticket an airline will usually treat it like a travellers cheque and, after inquiries, issue you with another one. Legally, however, an airline is entitled to treat it like cash and if you lose it then it's gone forever. Take good care of your tickets.

MCO An MCO, or 'miscellaneous charge order', is a voucher that looks like an airline ticket but carries

is in fact on record. You should also remind the agent at the check-in counter.

Arrival in Osaka

Most people travelling to Kyoto from abroad arrive at KIX. It is dramatically better equipped than its predecessor, Itami airport (now handling domestic traffic only). There are information counters throughout the complex with English-speaking staff, as well as a small Tourist Information Center (TIC) in the international arrivals lobby. Nearly all signs are posted in English as well as Japanese, so finding your way around should not be a problem. After clearing customs, it is a short walk to public transport (straight out the doors for buses and up the escalators or elevators for train connections). KIX offers short-term and long-term baggage storage for ¥350 to ¥1000 per day, depending on the size of the bag. You pay the bill when you pick up your bag.

---

no destination or date. It can be exchanged through any International Association of Travel Agents (IATA) airline for a ticket on a specific flight. It's a useful alternative to an onward ticket in those countries that demand one, and is more flexible than an ordinary ticket if you're unsure of your route.

No-Shows No-shows are passengers who fail to show up for their flight. Full-fare passengers who fail to turn up are sometimes entitled to travel on a later flight. The rest are penalised (see Cancellation Penalties).

On Request This is an unconfirmed booking for a flight.

Open Jaw Tickets These are return tickets where you fly out to one place but return from another. If available, this can save you backtracking to your arrival point.

Overbooking Airlines hate to fly empty seats and since every flight has some passengers who fail to show up, airlines often book more passengers than they have seats. Usually excess passengers make up for the no-shows, but occasionally somebody gets bumped. Guess who it is most likely to be? The passengers who check in late.

Point-to-Point Tickets These are discount tickets that can be bought on some routes in return for passengers waiving their rights to a stopover.

Promotional Fares These are officially discounted fares like Apex fares, available from travel agents or direct from the airline.

Reconfirmation At least 72 hours prior to departure time of an onward or return flight, you must contact the airline and 'reconfirm' that you intend to be on the flight. If you don't do this the airline can delete your name from the passenger list and you could lose your seat.

Restrictions Discounted tickets often have various restrictions on them – Apex is the most usual one. Others are restrictions on the minimum and maximum period you must be away, such as a minimum of 14 days or a maximum of one year.

Round-the-World Tickets RTW tickets are just that. You have a limited period in which to circumnavigate the globe and you can go anywhere the carrying airlines go, as long as you don't backtrack. These tickets are usually valid for one year, the number of stopovers or total number of separate flights is worked out before you set off and they often don't cost much more than a basic return flight.

Stand-by This is a discounted ticket where you only fly if there is a seat free at the last moment. Stand-by fares are usually only available on domestic routes.

Tickets Out An entry requirement for many countries is that you have a ticket out of the country. If you're unsure of your next move, the easiest solution is to buy the cheapest onward ticket to a neighbouring country or a ticket from a reliable airline which can later be refunded if you do not use it.

Transferred Tickets Airline tickets cannot be transferred from one person to another. Travellers sometimes try to sell the return half of their ticket, but officials can ask you to prove that you are the person named on the ticket. This is unlikely to happen on domestic flights, but on an international flight tickets may be compared with passports.

Travel Agencies Travel agencies vary widely and you should choose one that suits your needs. Some simply handle tours, while full-service agencies handle everything from tours and tickets to car rental and hotel bookings. If all you want is a ticket at the lowest possible price, then go to an agency specialising in discounted tickets.

Travel Periods Some officially discounted fares, Apex fares in particular, vary with the time of year. There is often a low (off-peak) season and a high (peak) season. Sometimes there's an intermediate or shoulder season as well. Usually the fare depends on your outward flight – if you depart in the high season and return in the low season, you pay the high-season fare. ■

For further inquiries about the airport and services call KIX's 24 hour information line (☎ 0724-552-500).

Leaving Osaka
As most flights out of Japan depart on time, it is a good idea to allow yourself plenty of time to arrive at the airport. International flights require you be at the airport two hours prior to departure time; for domestic flights ·you should allow at least an hour. The KIX terminal has a stunning assortment of shops and restaurants to make sure you won't be bored should you arrive early. There are also shower facilities, costing ¥1200, beyond the passport counters; only those who have cleared immigration *leaving* Japan can use them.

If you are flying to another city in Japan, be sure to check which airport you are leaving from as there are domestic departures from both KIX and Itami. There is an international departure tax at KIX of ¥2650, which must be paid in yen.

USA & Canada
West-coast flights to Osaka cross the Pacific and cost US$830 return in the low season (US$1250 in the high season). From the east coast, flights generally take the northern route over Alaska and cost US$1180 in the low season (US$1600 in the high season). There a major time change and a date change as you cross the International Date Line.

The major carriers between KIX and North America are Northwest, United, Canadian, JAL, ANA and Korean Airlines. The cheapest fares are often on Korean, but you fly a couple of hours in the opposite direction to Seoul to make connections. Often fares to South-East Asia differ little from Japan and for those continuing onto places like Thailand or the Philippines, it can be cost-effective to include Japan as a stopover.

Europe
Most direct flights between Europe and Japan fly into Tokyo and from there you make a connection to Kansai. There are, however, an increasing number of direct flights to/from KIX. London-Osaka return in the low season costs £500. The most direct route is across Scandinavia and Russia; flights which a stopover in Tokyo or Moscow can take from two to four hours longer than a direct flight. A few flights still stop in Anchorage, Alaska, and there are a number flying the trans-Asian routes across the Middle East and south Asia.

Australia & New Zealand
Flights between Australia and Japan are shared between JAL, ANA, Qantas and Ansett, all with direct flights to/from KIX. You can fly from most Australian state capitals direct to KIX and there is only a one or two hour time change. Sydney-Osaka flights cost A$1309 in the low season.

From New Zealand, either with Air New Zealand or JAL, there are about five flights a week connecting Auckland with KIX and another two flights weekly to Christchurch.

Asia
Most Asian nations have regular air links with Japan, the most frequent being with China (Hong Kong), Thailand (Bangkok), Singapore and South Korea (close and inexpensive for a short holiday or to renew an expiring visa). Compared to the early 1990s, fares have dropped dramatically, making the possibility of excursions around the region more viable. There are regularly cheap excursion fares from Japan which allow stops in several Asian cities.

China Of the Asian air links, Hong Kong has the highest frequency of daily flights to KIX. There are several daily flights on Cathay Pacific, as well as on JAL, ANA and JAS. Hong Kong-Osaka return costs US$900.

There are also flights to KIX from Beijing, Shanghai, Guangzhou and Dalian on all the Japanese carriers as well as on Air China, China Eastern Airways and China Southern Air. Beijing-Osaka costs US$892 return.

South Korea There are daily flights between Seoul and KIX on several airlines including JAL, ANA and Asiana, though Korean Airlines has the most flights (three a day) and usually offers the best fares. There are also several weekly flights from Chejudo Island, Taegu and Pusan. From Pusan you could instead take a ferry to Shimonoseki at the westernmost tip of Honshū. A flight to Seoul will cost US$272 return.

Taiwan There are daily departures from Taipei on both Japan Asia Airlines· and Cathay Pacific, and around four flights weekly on Singapore Airlines. Taipei-Osaka return costs US$441.

Other Asian Countries There are daily flights from Bangkok to Osaka on both Thai and ANA with fares costing US$787 return in the low season (US$874 in the high season). From Singapore on Singapore Airlines, JAL or ANA costs US$899 return; from Indonesia (Jakarta/Denpasar) on Garuda, Continental or Japan Asia Airlines a return flight will cost US$1355.

From the Philippines (Manila) a return flight to Osaka is US$646 and from Malaysia (Kuala Lumpur) it's US$899 return. From Vietnam (Ho Chi Minh City) a return flight costs US$660.

Other Asian countries with limited weekly flights to KIX include India, Nepal and Myanmar (Burma). Check in *Kansai Time Out* for current flight schedules and fares.

Domestic Air Services

All larger airports in Japan have regular flights to/from Osaka. Bear in mind that Tokyo is serviced by two different airports; Haneda is closer and more convenient to the city centre, while Narita is best for connecting to international flights. For cities closer to Osaka such as Nagoya and Hiroshima, it is usually faster, cheaper and more convenient to travel by shinkansen.

Domestic airfares can be rather expensive and tend to vary little between carriers; they also fluctuate slightly between seasons (see Airlines earlier for ANA, JAL and JAS offices in Kyoto). Many local travel agents offer packages for short excursions to places such as Nagasaki – prices typically include

airfare and a few nights accommodation for around the same as the airlines charge for a return fare.

The following are typical one way prices for flights from Osaka (Itami or KIX) to several major areas in Japan:

Fukuoka	¥15,600
Kagoshima	¥19,500
Kōchi	¥12,000
Kumamoto	¥16,650
Matsuyama	¥11,900
Nagasaki	¥18,800
Niigata	¥16,400
Ōita	¥13,450
Sapporo	¥29,050
Sendai	¥22,700
Takamatsu	¥10,000
Tokyo	¥15,850

BUS

Japan Railway (JR) buses run four times a day between Osaka and Tokyo via Kyoto and Nagoya (passengers change at Nagoya). The express bus between Kyoto and Nagoya takes about 2½ hours (¥2500). The journey between Nagoya and Tokyo takes about 6¼ hours (¥5100). Other companies competing with JR on the route include Meihan and Nikkyū. All buses leave from Kyoto station (Map 11).

Popular overnight buses (JR Dream Bus and Keihan Bus) run nightly between Kyoto station and Tokyo (either Yaesu bus terminal which is next to Tokyo station, or to Shinjuku station – departures in both directions), taking about eight hours. There are JR departures for Tokyo station at 10 and 11 pm, arriving at 6 and 7 am respectively, and a Shinjuku-bound bus at 10.50 pm arriving at 6 am; these depart from the northern side of Kyoto station, near the central post office.

The Keihan Bus leaves for Shinjuku at 10.50 pm on the Hachijō-guchi (south) side of Kyoto station from in front of the Hotel Keihan, also picking up at Sanjō station (Map 10) on the Keihan line at 11.10 pm and arriving at Shinjuku at 6 am. Tickets are ¥8180 one way, but if you're returning within one week a return ticket works out cheaper

(¥14,480). You just might be able to grab some sleep in the reclining seats; if you find dozing off a bit of a struggle, console yourself with the thought that you are saving on accommodation and will be arriving at the crack of dawn to make good use of the day. Though it is often possible to just show up and get a seat, reservations and advance purchase are recommended. Call JR buses on ☎ 341-0489 or go to the ticket counters in most JR stations. For Keihan buses, call ☎ 661-8200. Most local travel agents can also issue these tickets in a few minutes for a nominal fee.

Other JR bus possibilities include Kanazawa (¥4060), Tottori (¥3780), Hiroshima (¥8070), Nagasaki (¥11,310), Kumamoto (¥10,800) and Fukuoka (¥10,500).

For buses to/from the airports, see the Getting Around chapter.

TRAIN
Japan's expansive and highly efficient railway services make train travel an ideal way of getting around the country. Kyoto is reached from many places by JR, and there are also several private lines connecting Kyoto with Nagoya, Nara, Osaka and Kōbe.

Shinkansen
The fastest and best known train services in Japan are JR's shinkansen (literally, new trunk line). Kyoto station is reached on the JR Tōkaidō line (one of four major shinkansen routes), which runs between Tokyo and Osaka and continues west to Kyūshū as the Sanyō line. Three types of trains run on this route: the *kodama* (echo), which makes stops at all local shinkansen stations, *hikari* (light), which makes limited stops, and the ultrafast *nozomi* (hope), which reaches speeds of over 300km per hour. All trains are well equipped with facilities including coffee shops, pay phones and mobile food cart services (notice the subtle bow as vendors exit each car). If you don't share the Japanese passion for cigarettes, there are a limited number of nonsmoking cars *(kin-en-sha)* which can be requested when booking. Unreserved carriages are frequently packed

and without a reserved seat during peak travel times you may find yourself standing for the entire trip. Green Car (1st class) carriages offer slightly more spacious seating and you may even find a *Time* or *Newsweek* magazine in the rack.

Japan Rail Pass
One of Japan's few travel bargains is the unlimited-use Japan Rail Pass. As the cost of a seven day pass is about the same as buying a return shinkansen ticket between Kyoto and Tokyo, you stand a good chance of getting your money's worth if you're planning to cover some distance. The pass lets you use any JR train and bus service: for seven days a pass costs ¥28,300, 14 days for ¥45,100 or 21 days for ¥57,700. Green Car passes cost about 30% more. Children aged six to 11 get a 50% discount. Although the pass cannot be used for the super-express nozomi shinkansen, it is OK for everything else. The only additional surcharge levied on the pass is for overnight sleepers.

The pass can *only* be purchased overseas and cannot be used by foreign residents in Japan. The clock starts to tick on the pass as soon as you validate it, which can be done at most major JR stations, including the one in Kansai international airport if you're intending to jump on a JR train immediately. Don't validate it if you're just going into Kyoto and plan to hang around in the city for a few days. It is not worth using the pass up for short trips around the Kansai area; try to plan for long-distance travel, either finishing with the pass the day you arrive or validating it when you leave.

Rail pass-holders are entitled to reserved seating; just take your pass to the Green Window ticket counter *(midori-no-madoguchi)* and you will be given a ticket indicating carriage and seat number.

For ticket costs or schedule inquiries, check with the TIC or call JR West's Infoline on ☎ 371-0036.

Getting to Kyoto
Kyoto is easily reached from Tokyo and from cities throughout the Kansai region.

Tokyo-Nagoya The JR shinkansen line is the fastest and most frequent rail link. The hikari super-express takes two hours and 40 minutes from Tokyo station and a one-way ticket including surcharges costs ¥13,220.

Unless you're travelling on a Japan Rail Pass or are in an extreme hurry, there are cheaper ways to make the trip. Travelling by local train takes around eight hours and involves at least two (often three or four) changes along the way. The fare is ¥7980; check JR schedules for frequency and changes.

Another interesting option during university vacation periods (2 February to 20 April, 20 July to 10 September, 10 December to 20 January) is the *seishun jū-hachi kippu*, literally a 'youth 18 ticket'. Theoretically aimed at Japanese university students, these tickets can be used by people of any age. Basically, they allow you to buy a book of five train tickets to anywhere in Japan for ¥11,300 (¥2260 each); the only catches being that you can only travel on local trains and each ticket must be used within 24 hours. However, even if you only use two of the five tickets to travel between, say, Kyoto and Tokyo, you'll still be saving money. These tickets can be purchased at most JR ticket counters during the valid periods.

From Nagoya, the shinkansen takes less than an hour to Kyoto and costs ¥5980. You can save around half the cost by taking regular express trains, but you will need to change trains at least once and can expect the trip to take about three hours.

Osaka Regular JR Tōkaidō Main (Kyoto) line express trains make the 30 minute trip between Osaka and Kyoto for ¥540. If you have money to burn, or a Japan Rail Pass, you can take the JR shinkansen line between Shin-Osaka and Kyoto – the trip takes only 16 minutes (¥1380). To connect between central Osaka and Shin-Osaka, you can take either the JR Tōkaidō Main (Kyoto) line or the Midō-suji subway line from JR Osaka station.

There are also two private lines which connect Osaka and Kyoto. The Hankyū Kyoto line runs between Osaka (Hankyū Umeda station, next to JR Osaka station) and Kyoto (Kawaramachi station). The fastest trip takes 47 minutes and costs ¥390. The Keihan Main line runs between Yodoyabashi station (on the Midō-suji subway line, convenient for connections from Shin-Osaka, Osaka and Namba) in Osaka and Demachi-yanagi station in northern Kyoto. In Kyoto, it also stops at Shichijō, Shijō and Sanjō (its main station). The fastest trip from Yodoyabashi to Sanjō takes 40 minutes and costs ¥400.

If you arrive in Osaka at the Osaka-kō or Nan-kō ferry ports, you will find convenient subway connections to JR Osaka station, Keihan Yodoyabashi station or the Hankyū Umeda station en route to Kyoto. From Osaka's Itami airport, take the Osaka mono-rail to Minami Ibaraki (30 minutes, ¥380) and connect to the Hankyū Kyoto line for Kawaramachi (about 30 minutes, ¥310). For details on reaching Kyoto from KIX, see To/From the Airports in the Getting Around chapter.

Nara Without a valid Japan Rail Pass, the best option is the Kintetsu Kyoto line linking Kyoto station and Kintetsu Nara station in 35 minutes by limited express *(tokkyū*; ¥1110 one way). If you take a local or regular express train on this line, the ticket price drops to ¥610 for the 45 minute ride, but you may need to change at Yamato-Saidai-ji, itself a five minute train ride from Kintetsu Nara station.

The JR Nara line connects Kyoto with JR Nara station once an hour by express *(kaisoku)* in 47 minutes (¥690 one way). By local train *(kaku-eki)* this trip takes about one hour.

Kōbe Regular JR Tōkaidō (Sanyō) line *shin kaisoku* express trains make the 55 minute trip between Kōbe (Sannomiya station) and Kyoto for ¥1050. There is also a shinkansen stop at Shin-Kōbe station, about 1.5km north of Sannomiya station.

To reach central Kyoto, the easiest (and cheapest) way from Kōbe is by Hankyū express. Ride from Hankyū Sannomiya station, beside the JR station, and change

GETTING THERE & AWAY

trains at Osaka's Jūsō station to connect for a Kawaramachi-bound tokkyū (stopping at Ōmiya, Karasuma and Kawaramachi stations in Kyoto). The trip takes about 70 minutes and costs ¥600.

From the Merikan Park ferry terminal at Kōbe-kō Port, JR Motomachi station is about a 10 minute walk; the station is one stop west of Sannomiya station.

Kyūshū Kyoto is serviced by shinkansen on the JR Sanyō line from Hakata station (in Fukuoka, northern Kyūshū). The trip takes just under four hours and costs ¥15,010. Other places to pick up the train along this route include Shimonoseki (three hours, ¥13,760), Hiroshima (1¾ hours, ¥10,590) and Okayama (one hour, ¥7130).

The North Kyoto is reached from the northern cities of Kanazawa and Fukui by the JR Hokuriku and Kosei lines (running along the west coast of Lake Biwa-ko). From Sea of Japan cities such as Obama and Maizuru, take the JR Obama line to Ayabe and change to the San-in line coming from Kinosaki. To reach central Kyoto, it is best to get off at JR Nijō station (the last express stop before Kyoto station) and connect to the Tōzai line subway (see the Subways section in the Getting Around chapter).

Trans-Siberian Though it is a seldom-used option for getting in and out of Japan, those with plenty of time to travel, and to arrange bookings and visas, might consider the Trans-Siberian railway. The most popular routes are the Chinese Trans-Mongolia and Russian Trans-Manchuria, which begin or end in China, from where there are frequent flights and ferries to Japan. Also, the Trans-Siberian has become popular among young Japanese backpackers and it's now much easier to find information about and make travel plans for. The best way to plan your itinerary is through a local discount travel agent – most can assist with the full range of arrangements.

There are several guides to travelling on the Trans-Siberian – look for Robert Strauss'

Trans-Siberian Handbook. Anyone making their way to/from Japan via China should pick up a copy of Lonely Planet's *China* guidebook which includes details on Trans-Siberian journeys.

CAR & MOTORCYCLE

The Meishin Expressway runs between major interchanges at Nagoya and Kōbe and accesses Kyoto best from the Kyoto-Minami off-ramp (it will leave you on Route 1, a few kilometres south of the city centre). Kyoto is also accessible from Osaka on Route 1, Nishinomiya (Kōbe area) on Route 171, from the western hills on Route 9, or from the north (Sea of Japan) on the Shūzan Kaidō (Route 162).

See the Getting Around chapter for information on car and motorcycle rental.

BICYCLE

Kyoto is accessible from all directions and there are some lovely rides into the city, especially from the north (Sea of Japan and Kitayama regions), east (via Mt Hiei-zan and Lake Biwa-ko in Shiga Prefecture) and the mountains north-west of the city. Details on these rides can be found in the excellent guide *Cycling Japan* by Bryan Harrell, who also publishes the English-language cycling newsletter, *Oikaze* (for information on these publications phone ☎ 03-3485-0471).

HITCHING

Hitching can be an amusing and money-saving way to travel around Japan, in particular to areas where trains and buses don't run to. Whether on the highway or by local road, there are a number of feasible routes for thumbing in and out of Kyoto.

For long-distance hitching, the best bet is to head for the Kyoto-Minami interchange of the Meishin Expressway which is about 4km south of Kyoto station. Take the Toku No 19 bus – make sure the *kanji* (Chinese character) for 'special' *(toku)* precedes the number – from Kyoto station and get off when you reach the Meishin Expressway signs.

From here you can hitch east toward Tokyo or west to southern Japan. It is a good

MARTIN MOOS

MASON FLORENCE

MASON FLORENCE

MASON FLORENCE

MASON FLORENCE

	A	
B	C	D
	E	

A: Early morning view of Seto-Ōhashi Bridge.
B: Waterfall on the Katsura-gawa River.
C: White swan on the Katsura-gawa River.
D: Rarely is a shadow your only company at busy Kyoto station.
E: The view from Kyoto Tower mercifully excludes the tower itself.

MASON FLORENCE

MASON FLORENCE

MARTIN MOOS

MASON FLORENCE

MARTIN MOOS

MASON FLORENCE

A	B
C	D
E	F

A: The moat surrounding Nijō-jō Castle. B: The gardens of Sentō Gosho Palace in *kōyō* (autumn foliage) season. C: Close-up view of Himeji-jō Castle, Himeji. D: A stolen moment of 'borrowed scenery' at Shūgaku-in, Rikyū Imperial Villa. E: Fushimi Momoyama-jō Castle, southern Kyoto. F: A *haiku*-in-waiting: autumn maple at Sentō Gosho Palace.

idea before heading out to make signs in kanji of intended destinations; these can prove very helpful in a country where many still stare in bewilderment at hitchhikers, wondering what in the world could be wrong with the person's thumb!

For serious hitching, try to pick up a copy of William Ferguson's comprehensive *The Hitchhikers' Guide to Japan*. Despite Japan's remarkable safety record, taking a ride with a total stranger any place in the world demands a certain level of caution. If the situation looks risky, pass up the ride.

BOAT

Though in ancient days river transport into the city from Kyoto's western hills was commonplace, these days such travel is solely for the benefit of tourists – it can make an interesting way to arrive in the Arashiyama area (see the Kiyotaki River Hike boxed text in the Things to See & Do chapter).

Domestic Ferries

Domestic overnight ferries are an excellent way to save time and one night's accommodation costs, if you're willing to forgo the scenery after dark.

From Kyoto, many travellers head for Osaka or Kōbe to catch ferries to Shikoku (Takamatsu, Kōchi and Matsuyama), Kyūshū (Beppu, Miyazaki and Kagoshima) and as far south as Naha on Okinawa Island (34 hours, ¥15,750). From Naha there are ferries to Taiwan (22 hours, ¥15,600).

From the cities north of Kyoto on the Sea of Japan you can also catch ferries as far north as Hokkaidō. Two popular routes, with daily departures, are Maizuru to Otaru (29 hours, ¥6710) and Tsuruga to Otaru (36 hours, ¥7420).

The TIC can provide detailed information on various routes and up-to-date schedules.

Ferries to Korea & China

There are twice weekly ferries to/from Osaka-Kōbe and Shanghai, China, as well as from Kōbe to Tenshin. The cost is about ¥20,000 and ferries take about 24 hours. Check with the TIC for current departure schedules.

Many travellers also arrive or depart from Pusan (South Korea) via Shimonoseki, or Hakata (northern Kyūshū). One way fares begin at ¥8500 and the trip takes about 14 hours overnight. There are also high-speed jetfoil services costing ¥12,400 which take just under three hours.

TRAVEL AGENTS

Kyoto has several good central travel agents who can arrange discount air tickets, visas, car rental, accommodation and other services. Worth trying are A'cross Travellers' Bureau (Map 9; ☎ 255-3559) or No 1 Travel (Map 10; ☎ 251-6970).

On the ground level of Kyoto Tower (Map 11), about 50m east of the TIC, is the main Kyoto branch of the Japan Travel Bureau (JTB; ☎ 341-6631). It can arrange train and bus tickets, as well as air tickets (through the two discount agents mentioned above). JTB is also the place to discuss package tours of the Kansai region. Another outlet of JTB, staffed by foreigner-friendly English-speakers, is the JTB Kansai Sunrise Center (☎ 341-1413) on the 8th floor of the nearby Nihon Seimei Kyoto Santetsu building.

Warning

The information in this chapter is particularly vulnerable to change: prices for international travel are volatile, routes are introduced and cancelled, schedules change, special deals come and go, and rules and visa requirements are amended. Airlines and governments seem to take a perverse pleasure in making price structures and regulations as complicated as possible. You should check directly with the airline or a travel agent to make sure you understand how a fare (and ticket you may buy) works. In addition, the travel industry is highly competitive and there are many lurks and perks.

The upshot of this is that you should get opinions, quotes and advice from as many airlines and travel agents as possible before you part with your hard-earned cash. The details given in this chapter should be regarded as pointers and are not a substitute for your own careful, up-to-date research. ■

GETTING THERE & AWAY

Getting Around

TO/FROM THE AIRPORTS
Kansai International Airport (KIX)

The fastest, most convenient way between KIX (Map 1) and Kyoto is the special JR 'Haruka' airport express which makes the trip in 75 minutes for ¥3490. All seats are reserved on this train but can usually be purchased at the airport or Kyoto station (Map 11) on the day of travel. If you're leaving from KIX at an especially busy time, you might want to stop at a local travel agent to pick up your train tickets in advance to be sure of getting a seat.

Another convenient, though equally expensive, option is MK Taxi (☎ 721-2237) airport limo service which will pick up anywhere in Kyoto city and deliver you to KIX for ¥3530 – reservations are necessary.

If you have time to spare, you can save some money by taking Japan Railway's (JR) Kanku Kaisoku (express) between the airport and Osaka station and then taking a regular shinkaisoku (limited express) to/from Kyoto. The total journey takes about 90 minutes with good connections and costs ¥1800.

The Keihan Airport Limousine Bus is a direct KIX-Kyoto service taking about 105 minutes with drop-off points at Kyoto station, the ANA Hotel (Map 9) and Sanjō station (Map 10) on the Keihan Main line. Tickets cost ¥2300 (children ¥1150). If you're heading to KIX from Kyoto reservations are recommended; call ☎ 682-4400 between 9 am and 7 pm. Taxi service (charged separately) to bus departure points can also be arranged by calling the Keihan Taxi Reservation Center (☎ 602-8162).

For those travelling on Japanese airlines (JAL and ANA), there is an advance check-in counter inside the JR ticket office in Kyoto station. To use this service, you must already hold a train ticket to the airport.

Osaka Itami Airport

This airport (Map 1) is the main terminal for domestic flights in and out of Kansai, and there are frequent airport limousine buses running between here and Kyoto station (the bus stop is on the south side of the station in front of the Avanti building). Buses also run between the airport and some hotels around town, but on a less regular basis (check with your hotel). The journey takes around an hour and costs ¥1280.

BUS

Kyoto has an intricate network of bus routes providing an efficient way of getting around at moderate cost. Many of the routes used by visitors have announcements in English. The core timetable for buses is between 7 am and 9 pm, though a few run earlier or later.

The main bus terminals are Kyoto station on the JR line, Sanjō station on the Keihan line, and Karasuma-Shijō station on the Hankyū line. The bus terminal at Kyoto station is on the north side and has three main departure bays (departure points are indicated by the letter of the bay and number of the stop within that bay). Kyoto Bus (☎ 871-7521, Japanese language only) can also provide information on their routes into the Kyoto countryside, or check with the Tourist Information Center (TIC) for details.

The TIC's *Kyoto Transportation Guide* is a good map of the city's main bus lines, with a detailed explanation of the routes and a Japanese/English communication guide on the reverse side. Since this map is intended for tourists it is not exhaustive. Those who can read a little Japanese should get a copy of the regular Japanese bus map available at major bus stops throughout the city.

Bus stops usually display a map of stops in the vicinity on the top section. On the bottom section there's a timetable for the buses serving that stop. Unfortunately, most of this information is in Japanese, and non-speakers will simply have to ask locals for help.

Entry to the bus is usually through the back door and exit is via the front door. Inner-city buses charge a flat fare (¥220) which you drop into the clear plastic receptacle on top of the machine next to the driver on your way out. The machine gives change for ¥100 and ¥500 coins or ¥1000 notes, or you can ask the driver.

On buses serving the outer areas, you take a numbered ticket *(seiri-ken)* when entering. When you leave, an electronic board above the driver displays the fare corresponding to your ticket number.

To save time and money, you can buy a *kaisū-ken* (book of five tickets) for ¥1000, or a prepaid *torafika-kādo* (traffica card) in ¥1000 or ¥3000 denominations which can be used on both subways and buses. Both types can be purchased at bus centres, newsstands or from bus drivers.

There's a one day pass *(ichinichi jōsha-ken)* valid for unlimited travel on city buses and available for ¥700 at bus centres and from the ticket booth near the central exit of Kyoto station. A similar ticket which also allows for unlimited use of the subways costs ¥1200. A two day pass *(futsuka jōshā-ken)* costs ¥2000. The passes can be picked up at any subway station.

Bus No 59 is useful for travel between north-western Kyoto and Sanjō station on the Keihan line. Bus No 5 connects Kyoto station with eastern Kyoto.

Three-digit numbers written against a red background denote loop lines: bus No 204 runs around the northern part of the city and Nos 205 and 206 circle the city via Kyoto station. Buses with route numbers on a blue background take other routes.

When heading for locations outside the city centre, be careful which bus you board. Kyoto city buses are green, Kyoto buses are tan and Keihan buses are red and white.

TRAIN

There are several quick and efficient options for getting around Kyoto by train.

For heading out to Yamashina, excursions into Shiga Prefecture, or into south-western Kyoto you can use the JR Tōkaidō line. The JR San-in Main line runs from Kyoto station into western Kyoto via Nijō station, and the JR Nara line makes stops in southern Kyoto en route to Nara. On a similar course from Kyoto station, the Kintetsu Kyoto line also makes its way to Nara and on to Nagoya.

The Hankyū Kyoto line runs across town under Shijō-dōri from Kawaramachi to Saiin station (en route for Osaka) and also from Katsura station to the Arashiyama area on the Hankyū Arashiyama line. Keifuku trains also go to Arashiyama, running west from Shijō-Ōmiya station on the Keifuku Arashiyama line.

In the southern and eastern parts of town, the Keihan Main line makes underground stops along the Kamo-gawa River, terminating in the north at Demachiyanagi station. From here you can connect to the electric Eiden Kurama line for access to Shū-gakuin, Kurama, Kibune and Yase-yūen (near Ōhara).

Train Stations

With the exception of the gigantic Kyoto station complex, most station facilities are limited to toilets and a kiosk (newsstand). Several of the larger stations like Hankyū Shijō-Kawaramachi and Keihan Sanjō have coin lockers and vendors selling *ekiben* (boxed lunches). Stations can have anywhere from one to more than 10 numbered exits to cause you confusion; in most cases, especially from underground stations, it is quicker to just pick an exit and surface to the street before trying to get your bearings.

Buying a Ticket

All stations are equipped with automatic ticket machines which are simple to operate. Destinations and fares are all posted in both Japanese and English and once you've figured out how much it costs to where you're heading, just insert your money and press the yen amount. Most of these machines can accommodate paper currency in addition to coins (usually just ¥1000 notes).

SUBWAY

Kyoto has two efficient subway lines which operate from 5.30 am to 11.30 pm. The minimum fare is ¥200 (children ¥100).

The quickest way to travel between the

north and the south of the city is to take the Karasuma line subway. There are 15 stops stretching from Takeda (Map 3) in the far south, via Kyoto station, to the Kyoto International Conference Hall (Kokusai-kaikan station) in the far north, near Takara-ga-ike Pond (Map 4). The most useful stops are those in the centre of town.

In October 1997, after eight years under construction at a cost of ¥450 billion (only three years late and twice over-budget), the city completed the much awaited Tōzai line. It traverses town from the west at JR Nijō station (Map 6), meeting the Karasuma line at Karasuma-Oike station (Map 9), and continuing east on to Keihan-Sanjō (Map 10; transfer here for the Keihan lines), Yamashina (Map 2) and south-east to Daigo (Map 2). Though for many the new line has brought greater convenience, one sad casualty of the project was the removal of one of Kyoto's last streetcar lines, along Sanjō-dōri.

CAR & MOTORCYCLE

Kyoto's traffic problems create a trying situation for short trips around town and you will almost always do better on a bicycle or public transport. Unless you have specific needs, don't even entertain the idea of renting a car to tour the city – far more cost and headache than any traveller needs (plus parking ticket fines start at ¥15,000!).

One situation where a car would be practical is for touring some of the outlying rural areas, particularly those to which train lines do not venture (consequently keeping many such places charmingly intact and less travelled). There are several central rental agencies, though you will need to produce an International Driving Permit (see the Documents section in the Facts for the Visitor chapter) and if you cannot find a local to assist you with the paperwork, speaking a little Japanese will help greatly.

Eki Rent-a-Car (Map 11; ☎ 371-3020) is behind the central post office next to Kyoto station. Matsuda Rent-a-Car (Map 11; ☎ 361-0201) is close to the intersection of Kawaramachi-dōri and Gojō-dōri. Nippō Rent-a-Car (Map 9; ☎ 251-7072) has an outlet on Karasuma-dōri, about 100m north of Shijō-dōri. South of the same intersection and on the opposite side of Karasuma-dōri is Nippon Rent-a-Car (Map 9; ☎ 343-0919).

Rates vary greatly and it's a good idea to shop around, but expect to spend at least ¥7000 per day for an ultracompact, or around ¥10,000 for a regular sedan.

Motorcycles are a quick (and dangerous) way to get around town or do a bit of countryside touring. Sakaguchi Shōkai (Map 4; ☎ 791-6338) in the Iwakura area (northern Kyoto) rents a variety of bikes ranging from 50cc scooters (¥3200 per day) to 400cc 'ninja' speed machines (¥14,600).

Remember, driving is on the left-hand side in Japan.

TAXI

For just getting from place to place about town, taxis are a convenient, though expensive way to go. A taxi can usually be flagged down within minutes, around the clock in most parts of the city. There are also a large number of taxi stands (takushi noriba) in town, outside most train/subway stations, department stores etc. Remember, there is no need to touch the back doors of the cars at all – the opening/closing mechanism is controlled by the driver.

Fares start at ¥630 for the first 2km. The exception is MK Taxi (☎ 721-2237) with fares starting at ¥580. If you have a choice, always take an MK taxi – in addition to being cheaper, the drivers are scrupulously polite and can often speak a bit of English.

MK Taxi also provides tours of the city with English-speaking drivers. For a group of up to four people, prices start at ¥13,280 for three hours. Two other companies offering a similar service and competitive prices are Kyōren Taxi Service (☎ 672-5111) and Keihan Taxi Service (☎ 602-8162).

BICYCLE

Kyoto is a great city to explore on a bicycle; with the exception of outlying areas it's mostly flat and there is a new bike path running the length of the Kamo-gawa.

Unfortunately, Kyoto must rank near the

top in having the world's worst public facilities for bike parking (hence the number of bikes you see haphazardly locked up around the city) and many bikes end up stolen or impounded during regular sweeps of the city (in particular near entrances to train/subway stations). If your bike does disappear, check for a poster in the vicinity (in both Japanese and English) indicating the time of seizure and the inconvenient place you'll have to go to pay a ¥2000 fine and retrieve your bike.

Bike Shops & Rentals

An excellent deal is offered by the Green Flag Matsumoto rental shop (☎ 381-4991), Namomiya-cho 2, Saga, Ukyo-ku. If you call a day in advance (or get someone from your hotel or the TIC to do so), it will deliver a bicycle to your lodgings (or any other arranged place) for ¥500. After that, daily rental fees are only ¥100. It's open from 9 am to 5 pm daily, closed Wednesday.

Near Sanjō station on the Keihan Ōtō line, Kitazawa Bicycle Shop (Map 10; ☎ 771-2272) rents out bicycles for ¥200 per hour and ¥1000 per day, with discounts for rentals over three days. It's a 200m walk north of the station next to the river on the east side. A passport is necessary for rental, though one will suffice for a group. It's open daily from 8 am to 5 pm. Nearby on Kawabata-dōri, north of Sanjō-dōri, is Rental Cycle Yasumoto (Map 10; ☎ 751-0595), open from 9 am to 5 pm, with the same rates.

Rent Pia Service Center (Map 6; ☎ 672-0662) is about 70m south of Nishiōji station on the JR Tōkaidō Main line, one stop from Kyoto station. Ask for a map to the store at the TIC. If you take the train, the rental shop will reimburse you for your fare. Expect rental rates of around ¥1100 per day, but different rates apply depending on the kind of bicycle.

Arashiyama has several places for bicycle rental (see the Arashiyama-Sagano District section in the Things to See & Do chapter) and the Higashiyama (Map 10) and Utano (Map 3) youth hostels offer bicycle rental. Most rental outfits require you to leave ID such as a passport or driver's licence.

For more hardcore cyclists touring Japan, or looking for equipment or a professional tune-up, drop by Takenaka (Map 10; ☎ 256-4863), a small, but first-rate bike shop near the south-eastern corner of the Imperial Palace Park in the centre of town. The friendly owner, Mr Takenaka, speaks English and is happy to share his wide knowledge of the region's best cycling routes. He also organises regular Sunday road rides, usually day-long outings into the nearby countryside, and welcomes any riders with a helmet.

For information on the useful resources, *Cycling Japan* and *Oikaze*, see the Getting There & Away chapter.

WALKING

Walking is often the best way to explore the city, taking away the cost and concerns like traffic and parking and allowing you the chance to wander through narrow backstreets where you're far more likely to catch a glimpse of old Kyoto. There are several excellent walking tours and easily accessible hikes outlined in the Things to See & Do chapter. Other sources such as Japan National Tourist Organization's (JNTO) *Walking Tours in Kyoto* brochure may come in handy as well. Before heading out for the day, check weather forecasts and pack accordingly; sunny mornings can quickly turn to rain, and vice versa.

When walking, take caution – the streets are very narrow and taxis and oversized 4WD recreational vehicles often don't slow down for pedestrians.

For an excellent guided walking tour around Kyoto station with 'Johnnie Hillwalker', see the following Organised Tours section.

ORGANISED TOURS

Kyoto city offers a large array of guided services, from docile bus tours to provocative walking escapades through the city's less travelled backstreets. Tour possibilities range from Buddhist temples to beer breweries and these, as well as free guided tours through Kyoto's four imperial properties, are described in the Things to See & Do chapter. Occasionally, there are noteworthy tours by private or public organisations; typically these incorporate historical or architectural themes and the TIC is a good place to inquire if any are taking place during your stay.

One of the greatest ways to acclimatise to Kyoto is to spend a few hours with 'Johnnie Hillwalker,' walking-tour guide extraordinaire. Four days each week (Monday to Thursday), from early March to late November, Hirooka Hajime leads an intimate, three hour English-speaking tour, providing an excellent overview of Kyoto and insights you definitely won't get on a standard city bus tour. The course, starting from the northern side of Kyoto station, covers some of the sights in central and eastern Kyoto. Hirooka worked as a tour guide for Japan Travel Bureau (JTB) for 34 years and came out of retirement to help hapless foreigners find their way around. Per-person prices are ¥2000, or ¥3000 per couple (all fees included). Call ☎ 622-6803 for details.

If you were going to opt for a bus tour, perhaps the best time of year is during the sweltering summer or cold winter, when walking the city sights can take its toll. Special off-season summer tours (Natsu-no-tabi) and winter tours (Kyō-no-furu), with a variety of themes such as *uruwashi* (beauty), *ajiwai* (taste) and *miyabi* (elegance), are organised by the Kyoto city (see the TIC for information) and are reasonably priced at ¥9500 (fees included). Although there are no English-language tours, these provide a great opportunity to see places slightly off the beaten track, some of which are often not open for public viewing.

JTB Sunrise Tours (☎ 341-1413) offers morning, afternoon and all-day bus tours with an English-speaking guide. Morning and afternoon tours cost ¥5200, while all-day tours with a buffet lunch included are ¥10,600.

For people with very little time and lots of money, another effortlessly convenient and time-efficient tour option to consider is a chartered taxi (see the Taxi section earlier in this chapter).

Things to See & Do

Exploring Kyoto is a fascinating and seemingly endless pursuit. As well as the wealth of beautiful temples and shrines that dot the city and its outskirts, there are the imperial palace and villas, the fascinating traditional geisha quarters and teahouses of the Gion District, the trendy boutique and gallery area of Kitayama-dōri and plenty of museums to keep the visitor occupied. There are also some lovely parks, such as Maruyama-kōen, to relax in.

Add to this the myriad of walking possibilities that can be made into the hills surrounding the city (see our suggestions for some walking tours, both around town and out of town, in this chapter), and the excellent opportunities to view and learn Kyoto's famous crafts and tea ceremony, and you will find that in Kyoto you can be happily busy not only for days, but weeks, and even months.

Japanese Key Words

There are a number of easy ways to help you find what you're looking for in Kyoto, simply by knowing a few key Japanese words that commonly appear in place names.

Buddhist temples are most commonly read with a suffix of *-dera*, *-ji*, *-in* or *-dō*, meaning temple, eg Kiyomizu-dera Temple, Ginkaku-ji Temple, Sanjūsangen-dō Temple etc.

In the case of Shintō shrines, the suffix is usually *-jinja*, *-jingū* or *-taisha*, eg Yasaka-jinja Shrine, Heian-jingū Shrine, Fushimi Inari Taisha Shrine etc.

There are two key words used for museum: *-hakubutsukan* or *-bijitsukan*; so Kyoto National Museum is Kyoto Kokuritsu Hakubutsukan and the Nomura Museum is known as the Nomura Bijitsukan. The word *-bijitsukan* also means art gallery.

Parks are known as *-kōen*, eg Maruyama-kōen Park. Finally for gardens, most end with *-en*, eg Shōsei-en Garden.

Even when speaking in English, it is fairly standard to refer to temples, shrines and the like by their Japanese name. ∎

This chapter groups Kyoto's sights under geographical areas of the city to facilitate sightseeing and walking in particular districts. Toward the end of the chapter we have included a complete list of courses in crafts and other activities you can indulge, to provide a break from temple hopping.

KYOTO STATION AREA

The area around Kyoto station, south of the city centre, is a fairly drab part of town. The main sights are Higashi Hongan-ji and Nishi Hongan-ji temples and Tō-ji Temple, though there are a number of other spots worth a look (including the station itself). The TIC is just a couple of minutes walk north of the station.

Kyoto Station

Prior to 1997, Kyoto station (Map 11) was simply an unassuming point of transit. Now it's a minicity towering 16 storeys high. Call it an eyesore or a masterpiece, the station is definitely worth checking out. It is massive and modern, a glass Titanic with a main concourse 27m wide, 60m high and 470m long. The size and design were extremely controversial, and groups such as the Buddhist Association expressed outrage over the proposed height and facade.

As so often happens in Japan, construction proceeded and today the station, with its extensive public spaces, has become a major sightseeing and commercial attraction. For its architecture, stores, restaurants and hotel, you can easily spend hours bobbing amid the throngs.

The JR Tōkaidō Main and Kintetsu lines run through the station, which also acts as the main southern bus terminal. There is a pedestrian walkway connecting the Karasuma Central Gate to the north and Hachi-jō West Gate to the south.

Kyoto Tower

Directly north of the station is one of the

Six Great Views of Kyoto

To get a feel for Kyoto's geomantically aligned grid, it's best see the scenery from above. Viewing the city from overhead also reveals a surprising amount of greenery, and often a better perspective on what really remains of Kyoto's traditional architecture (usually far more than can be seen from ground level). The following are a few of the best spots to take in the sights:

Kyoto station (Map 11)
    In the station building, free entry
Kyoto Tower (Map 11)
    Kyoto station area, ¥770
Kiyomizu-dera Temple (Map 6)
    Southern Higashiyama, ¥300
Mt Daimonji-yama (Map 6)
    Northern Higashiyama, free entry
Iwatayama Monkey Park (Map 12)
    Arashiyama, ¥500
Mt Hiei-zan (Map 2)
    North-eastern Kyoto, cable car fee;
    free entry for hikers

city's greatest architectural blunders – the 131m-high Kyoto Tower (Map 11). The tower is said to represent a 'forever burning candle', but it looks more like a misguided space rocket. Many cite the 1964 construction of the tower as the beginning of the end of Kyoto's once-graceful skyline. The antiquated building houses the Kyoto Tower Hotel; the Tourist Information Center (TIC) is at ground level on the Karasuma-dōri side.

The tower's observation deck offers a panoramic 360° view of the city (on a clear day you can see all the way to Osaka-jō Castle). If you don't feel like shelling out the ¥770 entry fee, you might opt for a slightly less dramatic but free vista from the top of the Kyoto station building. The observation deck is open daily from 9 am to 9 pm.

Nishi Hongan-ji Temple

Nishi Hongan-ji (Map 11) was originally built in 1272 in the Higashiyama mountains by Shinran's daughter, the priestess Kakushin. The temple complex was relocated to its present site in 1591, onto land provided by Toyotomi Hideyoshi. It became the head-

quarters of the Jōdo Shin-shū (True Pure Land) school, which had accumulated immense power. Tokugawa Ieyasu sought to weaken the power of the Jōdo Shin-shū by encouraging a breakaway faction to found Higashi Hongan-ji Temple (*higashi* means east) in 1602. The original Hongan-ji then became known as Nishi Hongan-ji (*nishi* means west). It is now the headquarters of the Hongan-ji branch of Jōdo Shin-shū, with over 10,000 temples and 12 million followers worldwide.

The temple contains five buildings featuring some of the finest examples of the architectural and artistic achievement of the Momoyama period. The Daisho-in Hall has sumptuous paintings, carvings and metal ornamentation. A small garden and Japan's oldest *nō* stages are connected with the hall. The dazzling Chinese-style Kara-mon Gate displays intricate, ornamental carvings and metalwork. The gate has also been dubbed 'Higurashi-mon' (or Sunset Gate), purporting that its beauty can distract one from noticing the setting sun. Both Daisho-in and Kara-mon were transported here from Fushimi-jō Castle in the south of the city.

The *goei-dō* (founder's hall) dates from 1636 and contains a seated statue of Shinran, which he is said to have carved at the age of 71. The elaborate *hondō* (main hall), last reconstructed in 1760, houses a priceless collection of painted sliding screens adorned with phoenixes and peacocks.

Reservations for special tours (in Japanese) can be arranged at the temple office (☎ 371-5181). Check here for current schedules. The temple is about a 10 minute walk north-west of Kyoto station. Admission is free.

Higashi Hongan-ji Temple

In 1602, when Tokugawa Ieyasu engineered the rift in the Jōdo Shin-shū school, he founded this temple (Map 11) as a competitor to Nishi Hongan-ji. Rebuilt in 1895 after a series of fires destroyed all the original structures, it is certainly monumental but less impressive artistically than its rival. The temple is now the headquarters of the Ōtani branch of the Jōdo Shin-shū school.

The two storey Taishidō-mon Gate stands 27m high and features giant doors fashioned out of a single slab of wood. Wade through the sea of pigeons to the hondō – place your shoes in one of the plastic bags and carry them with you so you can exit from the neighbouring building. This hall enshrines a 13th century statue of Amida Nyorai.

In the corridor between the two main buildings you'll find a curious item encased in glass: a tremendous coil of rope made from human hair. Following the destruction of the temple in the 1880s, an eager group of female temple devotees donated their locks to make the ropes that hauled the massive timbers used for reconstruction.

The enormous *taishi-dō* (founder's hall) is one of the world's largest wooden structures, standing 38m high, 76m long and 58m wide. The centrepiece is a self-carved likeness of Shinran, the founding priest of the Jōdo Shin-shū school.

The temple is open from 9 am to 4 pm and admission is free. It only takes a few minutes to wander through the buildings and you can ask at the information office just inside the main gate for an English leaflet. It's a short stroll north of Kyoto station.

About five minutes walk east of the temple, **Shōsei-en Garden** (Map 11) is worth a look. The lovely grounds, incorporating Kikoku-tei Villa, were completed in 1657. Bring a picnic (and some bread to feed the carp) or just stroll around the beautiful Ingetsu Pond. Just when you're caught up in the 'old-Kyoto' moment, note the two love hotels looming in the background outside the wall (modern 'borrowed scenery'). The garden is open daily from 9 am to 3.30 pm. Admission is free.

Period Costume Museum

The Fūzoku Hakubutsu-kan (Map 11) is a museum of wax figures donning costumes representative of different periods in Japanese history; these include samurai warriors, merchants and fire fighters – not a must-see but worth a peek on a rainy day. It is open

from 9 am to 5 pm, closed Sunday, public holidays and from 16 December to 6 January and 1 to 19 June. Admission costs ¥400. From the north-east corner of Nishi Hongan-ji, it's just across Horikawa-dōri.

Sumiya Pleasure House

Shimabara (Map 6), a district north-west of Kyoto station, was Kyoto's original pleasure quarters. At its peak during the Edo period, the area flourished, with over 20 enormous *ageya* – magnificent banquet halls where artists, writers and statesmen gathered in a 'floating world' ambience of conversation, art and fornication. Geisha were often sent from their quarters *(okiya)* to entertain patrons at these restaurant-cum-brothels. By the start of the Meiji period however, such activities had gradually slinked north to the Gion District and Shimabara eventually lost its prominence.

Though the traditional air of the district has dissipated, a few old structures remain. The tremendous Shimabara-no-Ō-mon Gate, which marked the passage into the quarter, still stands as does Sumiya (Map 6), the last remaining ageya, now designated a National Cultural Asset. Built in 1641, this stately two storey, 20 room structure allows a rare glimpse into Edo-era nirvana. With a delicate lattice-work exterior, Sumiya has a huge open kitchen and an extensive series of rooms (including one extravagantly decorated with mother-of-pearl inlay).

Sumiya is open from 10 am to 4 pm, closed Monday. Admission is ¥1000. Special tours (requiring advance reservations and an extra ¥800) allow access to the 2nd storey and are conducted daily (in Japanese only) – call ☎ 351-0024. An English pamphlet is provided, but you might consider arranging a volunteer guide through the TIC. Sumiya is closed during August and from 16 December to 31 January. It is about 15 minutes walk west of Nishi Hongan-ji, or 10 minutes north-west of the Nanajō Mibu-dōri bus stop (bus No 205).

Umekōji Steam Locomotive Museum

A hit with steam train buffs and kids, this

museum (Map 6) features 18 vintage steam locomotives (dating from 1914 to 1948) and related displays. It is in the former JR Nijō station building, which was recently relocated here and thoughtfully reconstructed. Entry costs ¥400, and for another ¥300 you can take a 10 minute ride on one of the smoke-spewing choo-choos (departures at 11 am and 1.30 and 3.30 pm). It's open from 9.30 am to 5 pm, closed Monday.

Tō-ji Temple

This temple (Map 6) was established in 794 by imperial decree to protect the city. In 823, the emperor handed it over to Kūkai (known posthumously as Kōbō Daishi), the founder of the Shingon school. Many of the temple buildings were destroyed by fire or fighting during the 15th century and most of those remaining are from the Momoyama period.

The main gate (Nandai-mon) was moved here in 1894 from Sanjūsangen-dō Temple in the southern Higashiyama area. The *kōdō* (lecture hall) dates from the 1600s and contains 21 images representing a Mikkyō (esoteric Buddhist) mandala. The *kondō* (main hall), rebuilt in 1606, combines Chinese, Indian and Japanese architectural styles and contains statues depicting the Yakushi (Healing Buddha) trinity. In the southern part of the garden stands the five storey Gojū-no-tō Pagoda which, despite having burnt down five times, was doggedly rebuilt in 1643. It is now the highest (57m) pagoda in Japan.

The **Kōbō-san Market** fair is held here on the 21st of each month in addition to a regular market on the first Sunday of each month. Admission to the temple costs ¥500 and there is an extra charge for entry to special exhibitions. A thorough explanatory leaflet in English is provided. It's open from 9 am to 4.30 pm. The temple is a 15 minute walk south-west of Kyoto station.

CENTRAL KYOTO

In the 16th century Toyotomi Hideyoshi ordered a defensive wall to be built around the city, and the area within was called *raku-chū*, or central district. Though the exact boundary is hard to define today, it refers to the area in and around the central business district. Once Kyoto's artistic and cultural centre, the area now bristles with office buildings, department stores, banks, restaurants and bars. While most of raku-chū resembles any other Japanese city, there are several major sights in the area, such as the Imperial Palace, Nijō-jō and numerous museums.

Kyoto Imperial Palace Park

The Imperial Palace is surrounded by a spacious park (Map 8) with a welcome landscape of trees and open lawn. It's perfect for picnics, strolls and just about any sport that doesn't require retrieving balls over walls. Best of all, it's free. Take some time to visit the pond at the park's southern end, with its ever-gaping carp. The park is most beautiful in the plum and cherry blossom seasons (early March and April, respectively). It is bounded by Teramachi-dōri and Karasuma-dōri on the east and west sides, and by Imadegawa-dōri and Marutamachi-dōri on the north and south.

Kyoto Imperial Palace

The original Imperial Palace (Kyoto Gosho) was built in 794 and has, like a phoenix, undergone numerous rebirths after destruction by fires. The present building (Map 8), on a different site and smaller than the original, was constructed in 1855. Ceremonies related to the enthronement of a new emperor and other state functions are still held here.

The tour guide (see the following Reservations & Admission entry) will elaborate on the details in English while you are led for about one hour past the Shishin-den (Ceremonial Hall), Ko Gosho (Small Palace), Tsune Gosho (Regular Palace) and Oike-niwa (Pond Garden). Regrettably, it is forbidden to enter any of these buildings.

Shinsen-den is an outstanding, single storey structure thatched with a cypress-bark roof. Covered walkways connect it to the surrounding buildings. From outside, you can see a throne *(takamikura)* where the emperor sat on formal occasions. It is covered with a silk canopy, and on each side are stands to hold treasures such as swords, jewels and other imperial regalia. Just in front of the throne are two wooden *koma-inu* statues, mythical animals believed to ward off evil spirits. The palace is full of other treasures including priceless sliding screens adorned with Tosa school paintings. Though the hall initially was used as living quarters for the emperor, it was later set aside for ceremonial use only.

Foreigners are given preferential access to the palace and can obtain permission to enter in a few hours or days, while Japanese visitors (unless accompanied by a foreigner as an 'interpreter') may have to wait months. Twice-yearly, in spring and autumn, the palace grounds are chock-full when the inner sanctum is opened to the public for several days.

MASON FLORENCE

The Imperial Palace is one of Kyoto's enduring attractions and contains many treasures, including this court figurine.

Reservations & Admission This is organised by the Imperial Household Agency office (Kunaichō; ☎ 211-1215), a short walk south-east of Imadegawa station (Map 7) on the Karasuma line subway, or the Karasuma-Imadegawa bus stop. The office is inside the walled park surrounding the palace.

To make a reservation you will have to fill out an application form in person and must show your passport. Children should be accompanied by an adult over 20 years of age. Permission to tour the Imperial Palace is usually granted the same day. Guided tours in English are given at 10 am and 2 pm from Monday to Friday and at 10 am on the third Saturday of the month (except during April, May, October and November); once permission has been granted, you should arrive no later than 20 minutes before the tour time at Seisho-mon Gate. Allow extra time to find your way. Admission is free.

The agency's office is open weekdays from 8.45 am to noon and from 1 to 4 pm. This is also the place to make reservations to see Sentō Gosho Palace and the Katsura Rikyū and Shūgaku-in Rikyū imperial villas. As there is limited space for each tour at these three, you may need to work around their schedule. Reservations cannot be made from abroad.

Sentō Gosho Palace

A few hundred metres south-east of the Imperial Palace in the park is Sentō Gosho (Map 8). It was originally constructed in 1630 during the reign of Emperor Go-Mizunō as a residence for retired emperors. The palace was repeatedly destroyed by fire and reconstructed but served its purpose until a final blaze in 1854 (it was never rebuilt). Today only two structures, the Seika-tei and Yūshin-tei teahouses, remain. The magnificent gardens, laid out in 1630 by renowned landscape designer Kobori Enshū, are the main attraction.

Visitors must obtain advance permission from the Imperial Household Agency (see the previous entry) and be over 20 years old. One hour tours (in Japanese) start daily at 11 am and 1.30 pm. Admission is free.

Horino Memorial Museum

A few minutes walk south of the Imperial Palace Park is Horino Kinenkan (Map 10), an 18th century sake brewery housed in a vintage kyō-machiya (wooden townhouse). Though the original Kinshi Masamune brewery moved south to Fushimi in the 1880s, pure spring water (a key ingredient in sake brewing) continues to flow from the Momo-no-I well in the courtyard, where it has been since 1781. Much of the old architecture remains well preserved, including a fine warehouse (kura) open for viewing, and there are interesting displays on traditional sake brewing methods. Don't miss the cosy cafe serving tasters of the house sake, commendable micro-brewed beer and light meals. For a unique souvenir, you can pick up a bottle of sake and put your own artistic touch on the label.

The facilities are open from 11 am to 9 pm, closed Monday. Admission costs ¥300. It's on Sakaimachi-dōri, south of Ebisugawa-dōri.

Nijō-jō Castle

This castle (Map 9) was built in 1603 as the official residence of Tokugawa Ieyasu. The ostentatious style was intended as a demonstration of Ieyasu's prestige and to signal the demise of the emperor's power. To safeguard against treachery, Ieyasu had the interior fitted with 'nightingale' floors (intruders were detected by the squeaking boards) and concealed chambers where bodyguards could keep watch and spring out at a moment's notice. Fans of ninja movies will recognise the features immediately.

The Momoyama-era Kara-mon Gate, originally part of Hideyoshi's Fushimi-jō, features lavish, masterful woodcarving and metalwork. After passing through the gate, you enter **Ninomaru Palace**, which is divided into five buildings with numerous chambers. Access to the buildings used to depend on rank – only those of highest rank were permitted into the inner buildings.

Ōhiroma Yon-no-Ma (Fourth Chamber) has spectacular screen paintings. Also, don't miss the Ninomaru (Palace) Garden, designed by Kobori Enshū. The vast garden is composed of three separate islets spanned by stone bridges, and is meticulously kept.

The neighbouring **Honmaru Palace** dates from the mid-19th century and is only open for special viewing in autumn. After the Meiji Restoration in 1868, the castle became a detached palace of the Imperial Household and in 1939 was endowed to Kyoto city.

Admission to Ninomaru Palace and garden is ¥600, and they take about an hour to walk through. The palace is open daily from 8.45 am until last admission at 4 pm (gates close at 5 pm). It's closed from 26 December to 4 January. A detailed fact sheet in English is provided.

While you're in the neighbourhood, you might want to take a look at **Shinsen-en** (Sacred Spring) Garden (Map 9), just south of the castle (outside the walls). This forlorn garden, with its small shrines and pond, is all that remains of the original 8th century Imperial Palace, abandoned in 1227. Entry is free.

To reach the castle, take bus No 9, 12, 50, 61 or 67 to the Nijō-jō-mae stop. Alternatively, you can take the Tōzai subway to Nijōjō-mae station and walk about two minutes.

Nijō Jinya

A few minutes walk south of Nijō-jō, Nijō Jinya (Map 9) is one of Kyoto's hidden gems. Seldom seen by short-term visitors, this former merchant's home was built in the mid-1600s and served as an inn for provincial feudal lords visiting the capital. What appears to be an average Edo-period mansion, however, is no ordinary dwelling.

The house contains fire-resistant earthen walls and a warren of 24 rooms which were ingeniously designed to protect the daimyō (domain lords) against possible surprise attacks. Here you'll find hidden staircases, secret passageways and an array of counter-espionage devices. The ceiling skylight of the main room is fitted with a trap door from where samurai could pounce on intruders, and sliding doors feature alternate panels of translucent paper to expose the shadows of eavesdroppers.

One hour tours are conducted several times daily (in Japanese) and advance reservations must be made (also in Japanese – ☎ 841-0972). An English leaflet is provided, but you might consider arranging a volunteer guide through the TIC. Admission costs ¥1000.

Mibu-dera Temple

Mibu-dera (Map 9) was founded in 991 and belongs to the Risshū school. In the late Edo period, it became a training centre for samurai. Mibu-dera houses tombs of pro-shōgunate Shinsen-gumi members, who fought bloody street battles resisting the forces that succeeded in restoring the emperor in 1868. Except for an unusual stupa covered in Jizō statues, visually the temple is of limited interest. It is, however, definitely worth visiting during Mibu Kyōgen performances in late April, or the Setsubun celebrations in early February (see the Festivals boxed text in the Facts for the Visitor chapter).

The temple is a five minute walk south-west of Ōmiya station on the Hankyū Kyoto line. Admission is free.

Kodai Yūzen-en Gallery

This building (Map 9) is devoted to Kyoto's traditional Yūzen fabric dyeing, created in the 17th century by painter Miyazaki Yūzen. It houses the Yūzen Art Museum, displaying an impressive collection of antique kimono, paintings, scrolls, dyeing patterns and tools. There is a film shown in English about the Yūzen dyeing process and, of course, a shop selling Yūzen dyed goods. On the top floor you can catch a glimpse of fabric artists at work and even stencil-dye your own handkerchief (see the Activities section later in this chapter for details).

It is open daily from 9 am to 5 pm; admission costs ¥500. From Kyoto station take the No 9 bus (terminal B-1) to the Horikawa-Matsubara stop and walk two minutes west on Takatsuji-dōri; or walk eight minutes

south-east from Ōmiya station on the Hankyū Kyoto line.

Yūzen Cultural Hall (Kyoto Yūzen Bunka Kaikan; Map 5) has a museum dedicated to the craft (open from 9 am to 5 pm, closed Sunday, admission ¥350); it's a five minute walk east of Nishikyōgoku station on the Hankyū Kyoto line.

Museum of Kyoto

Housed in and behind the former Bank of Japan, a classic brick Meiji-period building, this outstanding museum (Map 10) features much more than paintings on the wall. There are models of ancient Kyoto, audiovisual presentations and a gallery dedicated to Kyoto's film industry. On the 1st floor, the Roji Tempō is a reconstructed Edo-period merchant area showing 10 types of exterior lattice work (some of the shops sell souvenirs and serve local dishes as well).

The museum has English-speaking volunteer tour guides available. The entrance is on Takakura-dōri, just north of Sanjō-dōri. The museum is open from 10 am to 8.30 pm, closed the third Wednesday of each month. Admission costs ¥500.

Ponto-chō

Once the city's red-light district, Ponto-chō (Map 10) is a traditional centre for dining and night entertainment in a narrow street running between the Kamo-gawa River and Kiyamachi-dōri. It's a pleasant place for a stroll if you want to observe Japanese nightlife. Many of the restaurants and tea-houses which have verandas over the river can be difficult to get into, but a number of reasonably priced, accessible places can be found on Pontochō-dōri (see the Places to Eat chapter). The geisha teahouses usually control admittance of foreigners with a policy of introductions from Japanese persons only and astronomical charges. Many of the bars also function along similar lines, though this seems to be changing.

Ponto-chō is a great place to spot geisha and apprentice geisha *(maiko)* making their way between appointments, especially on weekend evenings at the Shijō-dōri end of the street. Incidentally, Ponto-chō was originally designed by the Portuguese in the Edo period.

EASTERN KYOTO

The eastern part of Kyoto, *raku-tō*, notably the Higashiyama (Eastern Mountains) District, merits top priority for its fine temples, peaceful walks and the traditional ambience of Gion. It is a long, narrow area sandwiched between the Kamo-gawa and eastern hills, stretching north-south, and an ideal area for touring on foot.

The following descriptions of places to see in eastern Kyoto begin with sights in the southern Higashiyama area; the sights in the northern area begin with the Okazaki Park Area section. Allow at least a full day to cover the sights in the southern section, and another full day for those in the north.

Southern Higashiyama Area

Sanjūsangen-dō Temple The original temple, called Rengeō-in, was built in 1164 at the request of the retired Emperor Go-shirakawa. After it burnt to the ground in 1249, a faithful copy (Map 6) was constructed in 1266.

The temple's name refers to the 33 *san-jūsan* (bays) between the pillars of this long, narrow building which houses 1001 wooden statues of Kannon (the Buddhist goddess of mercy). The chief image, the 100 armed Senju Kannon, was carved by the celebrated sculptor Tankei in 1254. It is flanked on either side by 500 smaller Kannon images, neatly lined in rows.

There are an awful lot of arms, but if you are picky and think the 1000 armed statues don't have the required number, you should remember to calculate according to the nifty Buddhist mathematical formula, which holds that 40 arms are the equivalent of 1000 because each saves 25 worlds.

At the back of the hall are 28 guardian statues in a great variety of expressive poses. The gallery at the western side of the hall is famous for the annual Tōshi-ya Festival,

---

Night Walk Through the Floating World
Time: two hours
Distance: about 2km
Major Sights: Traditional entertainment districts, classic architecture, contemporary nightlife (all sights are on Map 10)

The traditional entertainment areas of Gion and Ponto-chō make for an excellent evening stroll. Begin your walk on the steps of the main gate into Yasaka-jinja (beautifully lit at night). Cross west on the southern side of Shijō-dōri and, just after passing the Gion Hotel, turn left. Wind through the narrow alleys of *ryōtei* restaurants and teahouses, finally working your way out to **Hanami-kōji**.

Heading north on Hanami-kōji, cross Shijō-dōri and go west (left) for about 20m before turning right on to Kiri-dōshi; continue north until you cross the small Tatsumi-bashi Bridge. This is the lovely and well preserved **Shinbashi District**, which features some of Kyoto's finest traditional architecture.

At the split in the road by the small **Tatsumi Shrine**, you can go up the left fork or the right (or better yet make a loop) and see a charming group of exclusive teahouses and traditional shops. From this area, work your way out to the neon lights of **Nawate-dōri** (note the gangster-types in black Mercedes with dark-tinted windows!). Continue north to Sanjō-dōri and cross the bridge west.

Just after you've reached the other side of the Sanjō bridge, turn left and soon the road becomes a dead end; turn right here and after a few steps veer left into **Ponto-chō**. From here it's a leisurely 500m stroll south back to Shijō-dōri. This narrow road is pleasantly void of motor traffic and full of restaurants, bars and ancient teahouses. Keep your eyes (and ears) open for geisha and their maiko apprentices in elegant kimono and tall click-clacking wooden sandals *(pokkuri)*.

When you reach the southern end of Ponto-chō at Shijō-dōri, turn right. In about 20m you'll hit bustling **Kiyamachi-dōri**. Turn right here to soak up a bit of Kyoto's modern 'floating world'. There are endless bars and restaurants and packs of young Japanese out on the town (invariably one in the group will be vomiting on the sidewalk due to alcohol overindulgence and being tenderly comforted by friends). ■

held on 15 January, when archers shoot arrows the length of the hall. The ceremony dates to the Edo period, when an annual contest was held to see how many arrows could be shot from the southern to the northern end in 24 hours. The all-time record was set in 1686, when an archer successfully landed over 8000 arrows at the northern end.

The temple is open from 8 am to 5 pm (1 April to 15 November) and 9 am to 4 pm (16 November to 31 March). Admission is ¥500 and an explanatory leaflet in English is supplied. Photography is forbidden in the main hall.

The temple is a 15 minute walk east of Kyoto station, or you can take bus No 206 or 208 and get off at the Sanjūsangen-dō-mae stop. It's also very close to Keihan Shichijō station, from which you walk east up Shichijō-dōri.

Kyoto National Museum The Kyoto National Museum (Map 6) was founded in 1895 as an imperial repository for art and treasures from local temples and shrines. It is housed in two buildings opposite Sanjūsangen-dō. There are 17 excellent rooms with displays of over 1000 artworks, historical artefacts and handicrafts. The fine arts collection is especially highly rated, holding some 230 items that have been classified as National Treasures or Important Cultural Properties.

Admission costs ¥420 but note that a separate charge is made for special exhibitions. It's open daily from 9 am to 4.30 pm and is closed on Monday.

Chishaku-in Temple Chishaku-in (Map 6) was built on the ruins of Shōun-ji Temple in the early Edo period by Toyotomi Hideyoshi to enshrine his deceased eldest son. The gardens on the east side of the temple are notable, particularly in May when the azaleas are in full bloom. The Shūzōko Hall houses Momoyama-era paintings from the Tōhaku Hasegawa school; these include the famed *Sakura-zu* (The Cherry Tree) and *Kaede-zu* (The Maple Tree).

The temple is open from 9 am to 4.30 pm,

and admission costs ¥350. It's a five minute walk east of Sanjūsangen-dō.

Kawai Kanjirō Memorial Hall This museum (Map 6) was once the self-designed home and workshop of one of Japan's most famous potters, Kawai Kanjirō (1890-1966). The 1937 house is built in rural style and contains examples of his work, his collection of folk art and ceramics, and his workshop and kiln.

The museum is open daily from 10 am to 5 pm. It's closed Monday and from 10 to 20 August and 24 December to 7 January. Despite the steep admission cost (¥900), most come away satisfied. The museum is a 10 minute walk north of the Kyoto National Museum, or you can take bus No 206 or 207 from Kyoto station and get off at the Uma-machi stop. The museum is near the intersection of Gojō-dōri and Higashiōji-dōri.

Rokuharamitsu-ji Temple An important Buddhist pilgrimage stop, this temple (Map 10) was founded in 963 by Kūya Shōnin who carved an image of an 11 headed Kannon and installed it in the temple in the hope of stopping a plague which was ravishing Kyoto at the time.

The temple itself is unremarkable but the treasure house at the rear contains a rare collection of 15 fantastic statues; the most intriguing is a standing likeness of Kūya, staff in hand and prayer gong draped around his neck, with a string of tiny figurines parading from his gums. Legend holds that while praying one day, these manifestations of the Buddha suddenly ambled out of his mouth.

Entry to the treasure house is ¥500. It's open from 8 am to 5 pm. Walk about seven minutes north from Kawai Kanjirō Memorial Hall.

Kiyomizu-dera Temple This temple (Map 6) was first built in 798 and devoted to Jūichimen, an 11 headed Kannon. The present buildings – built under order of Iemitsu, the third Tokugawa shōgun – are reconstructions dating from 1633. As an affiliate of the Hossō school, which originated in Nara, the temple has successfully survived the many

Southern Higashiyama Walking Tour

Time: half-day to a full day
Distance: about 5km
Major Sights: Kiyomizu-dera Temple, Kōdai-ji Temple, Yasaka-jinja Shrine (sights are on Maps 6 & 10)

One of the most enjoyable strolls around the backstreets and temples of Kyoto follows a winding route between Kiyomizu-dera (Map 6 & 10) and Maruyama-kōen Park (Map 10). The walk begins near the Gojō-zaka slope (Maps 6 & 10), but those with strong legs or pack-it-all-in-at-once ambition could start at **Sanjūsangen-dō Temple** (Map 6), with stops at the Kyoto National Museum and Kawai Kanjirō's house, making it a full-day excursion.

Start your walk after a look at the pottery shops on the Gojō-zaka slope, near the north-western corner of Gojō-dōri and Higashiōji-dōri. Cross north and head uphill until you reach the first fork in the road; bear right and continue up to **Kiyomizu-dera** (Map 10). When you reach the top, the temple entrance will be on your left; but take a short detour uphill to the right for an amazing view of the neighbouring cemetery before heading toward the temple.

After touring Kiyomizu-dera, exit down the **Kiyomizu-zaka slope**, the steep approach to the temple known as Teapot Lane(Chawan-zaka). It is lined with shops selling Kyoto handicrafts (notably Kiyomizu-yaki pottery), local snacks and souvenirs. Shopkeepers hand out samples of *yatsuhashi*, a type of local dumpling filled with a sweet bean paste. After about 200m, you'll see a small street on your right down a flight of steps. This is **Sannen-zaka**, lined with old wooden houses and traditional shops and restaurants. There are also pleasant teahouses with gardens – it's a good place to relax over a bowl of steaming noodles.

Halfway down Sannen-zaka, the road bears sharp left. Follow it a short distance, then go right down a flight of steps into **Ninen-zaka**, another street lined with historic houses, shops and teahouses. At the end of Ninen-zaka zigzag left, then right and continue north for five minutes to reach the entrance of **Kōdai-ji** (Map 10), on the right up a long flight of stairs. Just before this entrance you can detour into **Ishibei-kōji** on your left – perhaps the most beautiful street in Kyoto, though it's actually a cobbled alley lined on both sides with elegant, traditional Japanese inns and restaurants.

Exit Kōdai-ji the way you came and walk to the 'T' in the road; turn right here and zigzag right and left into **Maruyama-kōen**, a pleasant spot to take a rest. From the park, head west into the grounds of **Yasaka-jinja** (Map 10). From here you can exit west to Shijō-dōri, or head back through the park and north toward **Chion-in** and **Shōren-in** temples (both Map 10). From either it's about a 10 minute walk back to the bright lights of Shijō-dōri. ■

intrigues of Kyoto Buddhist schools through the centuries and is now one of the most famous landmarks of the city. This, unfortunately, makes it a prime target for bus loads of Japanese tourists, particularly during cherry blossom season. Some travellers are also put off by the rather mercantile air of the temple – stalls selling good luck charms, fortunes and all manner of souvenirs. If you find this bothersome, head to some of the quieter temples further north.

The main hall has a huge veranda which juts out over the hillside, deftly supported by 139 wooden, 15m-high pillars. The terrace commands an excellent view over the city centre and inspired the Japanese saying 'Kiyomizu no butai kara tobioriru', which likens jumping from the Kiyomizu-dera veranda to going out on a limb.

Just below this hall is the Otowa-no-taki Waterfall, where visitors drink or bathe in sacred waters which are believed to have therapeutic properties (and also to improve school test results). Dotted around the precincts are other halls and shrines. South of the main hall is Koyasu-no-tō, a three storey pagoda housing a statue of the goddess responsible for the safe delivery of babies (which explains the frequent visits by pregnant women). At the Jishu-jinja Shrine, north of the main hall, visitors try to ensure success in love by closing their eyes and walking about 18m between a pair of stones – if you miss the stone, your desire for love won't be fulfilled!

Admission to the temple costs ¥300, and it's open from 6 am to 6 pm. To get there from Kyoto station take bus No 206 and get off at either the Kiyomizu-michi or Gojō-zaka stops. Plod up the hill for 10 minutes to reach the temple.

Kōdai-ji Temple Kōdai-ji (Map 10) was founded in 1605 by Kita-no-Mandokoro in memory of her late husband, Toyotomi Hideyoshi. The extensive grounds include gardens designed by Kobori Enshū, teahouses designed by the renowned master of tea ceremony, Sen no Rikyū, and a lovely little grove of bamboo trees.

The temple was only recently opened to the public and is worth taking a stroll through. It's open from 9 am to 4.30 pm (4 pm from November to March) and admission costs ¥500. An explanatory leaflet in English is provided.

Just before you reach the temple you can't help but notice the **Ryōzen Kannon**, an enormous seated Bodhisattva statue perched at the foot of a hill. It is a recent creation, dating from 1955, commemorating Japanese who died fighting in WWII. There is a small war memorial on the grounds including files with the names of more than 48,000 foreign soldiers who perished in Japanese territories during the war, and bottled dirt from military graveyards from around the world. Unless you're a war enthusiast, you might just opt to grab a quick snapshot from outside the entrance gate and save the ¥200 entry.

Maruyama-kōen Park This park (Map 10) is a favourite of locals and visitors alike as a place to escape the bustle of the city centre and amble around the gardens, ponds, souvenir shops and restaurants. Peaceful paths meander through the trees and carp glide through the waters of a small pond in the centre of the park.

For two weeks in April, when the park's cherry trees come into bloom, the calm atmosphere of the park is shattered by hordes of drunken revellers having cherry viewing parties *(hanami)* under the trees. The centrepiece is a massive shidare-zakura cherry tree – one of the most beautiful sights in Kyoto, particularly when lit up from below at night. For those who don't mind crowds, this is a good place to observe the Japanese at their most uninhibited. The best advice is to arrive early and claim a good spot high on the east side of the park from where you can safely peer down on the mayhem below.

Yasaka-jinja Shrine This colourful shrine (Map 10) is down the hill from Maruyama-kōen. It's considered the guardian shrine of the neighbouring Gion area and is endearingly referred to as 'Gion-san'. The present buildings, with the exception of the older, two storey west gate, date from 1654. The granite *torii* (entrance gate) on the south side was erected in 1666 and stands 9.5m high, making it one of the largest in Japan. The roof of the main shrine is covered with cypress shingles. Among the treasures here are a pair of carved wooden koma-inu, mythological animals attributed to the renowned sculptor Unkei.

This shrine is particularly popular as a spot for *hatsu-mōde*, the first shrine visit of the new year. If you don't mind a stampede, come here around midnight on New Year's Eve or any of the following days. Surviving the crush is proof that you're blessed by the gods! Yasaka-jinja also sponsors Kyoto's biggest festival, Gion Matsuri.

Chion-in Temple Chion-in (Map 10) was built by the monk Genchi in 1234 on the site where his mentor, Hōnen, had taught and eventually fasted to death. Today it is still the headquarters of the Jōdo school, which was founded by Hōnen, and it's a hive of religious activity. For visitors with a taste for the grand and glorious, this temple is sure to satisfy.

The oldest of the present buildings date from the 17th century. The two storey Sanmon Gate at the main entrance is the largest in Japan, and prepares the visitor for the massive scale of the temple. The immense main hall contains an image of Hōnen and is connected with the Dai Hōjō Hall by a 'nightingale' floor.

After visiting the main hall, with its fantastic gold altar, you can walk around the back of the same building to see the temple's gardens. On the way, you'll pass a darkened hall with a small statue of Amida Buddha on display – glowing eerily in the darkness. It makes a nice contrast to the splendour of the main hall.

The Daishōrō belfry houses a bell cast in 1633, measuring 2.7m in diameter and weighing almost 80 tonnes – the largest in Japan. The combined muscle power of 17 monks is required to make the bell budge for a ceremony held here to ring in the new year.

The temple is open from 9 am to 4.30 pm (March to November), to 4 pm (December to February); admission costs ¥400. The temple is near the north-eastern corner of Maruyama-kōen. From Kyoto station take bus No 206 and get off at the Chion-in-mae stop, or walk east from the Keihan line Sanjō or Shijō stations.

Shōren-in Temple Shōren-in (Map 10) is hard to miss, with its giant camphor trees growing just outside the walls. This temple, commonly called Awata Palace after the road it faces, was originally the residence of the chief abbot of the Tendai school. Founded in 1150, the present building dates from 1895 but the main hall has sliding screens with paintings from the 16th and 17th centuries. Often overlooked by the crowds which descend on other Higashiyama area temples, this is a pleasant place to sit and think while gazing out over one of Kyoto's finest landscape gardens.

Admission to the temple costs ¥500, and it's open from 9 am to 5 pm. An explanatory leaflet in English is provided. The temple is a five minute walk north of Chion-in.

Gion District Gion (Map 10) is the famous entertainment and geisha quarters on the eastern bank of the Kamo-gawa. While Gion's true origins were in teahouses catering to weary visitors to Yasaka-jinja, by the mid-18th century the area was Kyoto's largest pleasure district. Despite the looming modern architecture, congested traffic and contemporary nightlife establishments which have cut a swathe through its historical beauty, there are still some places left in

Gion for an enjoyable walk (see the Night Walk Through the Floating World boxed text in this chapter).

Hanami-kōji runs north to south and bisects Shijō-dōri. The southern section is lined with 17th century, traditional restaurants and teahouses, many of which are exclusive establishments for geisha entertainment. At the south end you reach **Gion Corner** and next door **Gion Kōbu Kaburenjō Theatre** (for details on these two places, see the Entertainment chapter).

If you walk from Shijō-dōri along the northern section of Hanami-kōji, you will reach **Shinbashi-dōri.**

For more historic buildings in a beautiful waterside setting, wander down **Shirakawa Minami-dōri,** which is roughly parallel with, and one block south of, the western section of Shinmonzen-dōri.

Kennin-ji Temple Tucked in the heart of Gion, this temple (Map 10) belongs to the Rinzai school. Founded in 1202 by the priest Eisai after returning from China, Kennin-ji holds the distinction of being Kyoto's first Zen temple. With the exception of Chokushimon Gate, all the original structures were destroyed by fire. The temple is famed for its 17th century paintings by Tawaraya Sōtatsu depicting the gods of wind and thunder. Kennin-ji is open from 10 am to 4 pm and entry costs ¥500.

Also on the grounds, **Ryōsoku-in Temple** is known for its garden with springs and ponds, but a visit here usually requires advance reservation (☎ 561-3216) of a few days if they're busy. You may get in on the same day if things are quiet.

Northern Higashiyama Area
Okazaki Park Area Okazaki Park (Map 10) runs along beside the Biwa-ko Sosui Canal leading from Lake Biwa-ko and contains several attractions.

The **National Museum of Modern Art** (Map 10) is renowned for its Japanese ceramics and paintings. There is an excellent permanent collection, including many pottery pieces by Kawai Kanjirō. Exhibits are

Geisha & Maiko

Of all the stereotypical images one associates with Kyoto and traditional Japan, perhaps the most endearing is that of the kimono-clad *geisha*. Although their numbers are ever-decreasing, geisha (*geiko* in the Kyoto dialect) and *maiko* (apprentice geisha) can still be seen in the Gion District (Map 10), especially after dusk.

They cater to the wealthy behind the closed doors of the exclusive teahouses and restaurants which dot the backstreets between the Kamo-gawa River and Yasaka-jinja Shrine. A true geisha is well versed in an array of visual and performing arts, including playing the three stringed *shamisen*, singing old teahouse ballads and traditional dancing.

With the exception of public performances at annual festivals or dance presentations, geisha and maiko perform only for select customers. It is virtually impossible to enter a Gion teahouse and witness a performance without the introduction of an established patron. The teahouses are typically managed by a retired geisha. Their atmosphere is intimate and subdued, with traditional tatami serving rooms.

An evening in a Gion teahouse begins with an exquisite *kaiseki* dinner. Form, not volume, is the operative word here, as former Russian premier Nikita Khrushchev once discovered. A famous Gion story goes that after he had eaten the entire meal, Khrushchev turned to his Japanese hosts and remarked that the appetisers were great and that he was looking forward to the main course!

After dinner, the geisha or maiko enter the room one by one. The introduction ceremony is elaborate and each will give a short speech in pure Kyoto dialect, laced with witty comments, before saying her name. After everyone claps, she goes around the room handing out her perfumed business card.

A shamisen performance, followed by a traditional fan dance, is often given, and all the while the geisha and maiko pour drinks, light cigarettes and engage in charming banter. Some maiko are very young, in their mid-teens, and have the same interests as teenage girls everywhere. It is, to say the least, an unusual experience to talk about Tom Cruise with a woman in an elaborate kimono and a white painted face.

To answer the most frequent question, *no*, geisha are not prostitutes, at least not in the typical sense of the word. Some geisha, once they retire at 50 or so and decide to open their own teahouse, do get financial backing from a well-to-do client (with whom they may be intimately involved). The patron has to be wealthy, as one maiko may charge up to US$1000, and geisha even more, for an evening's entertainment.

The personalities of geisha and maiko reflect the personality of the towns they perform in, and in the case of Kyoto both are known for their artistry and sophistication. Maiko often enter the care of an older geisha at age 16 (upon completing compulsory education). Depending on her abilities, a maiko may or may not be promoted to a geisha.

Although their exact number is something of a mystery, some media reports have said there may now be less than 20 fully fledged geisha living in Kyoto today, and perhaps only 100 maiko. The rigorous, disciplined lifestyle, the long apprenticeship, and a wider choice of career alternatives have reduced the number of women wishing to enter the profession. Still, given the large number of contemporary 'snack bars' with their doting hostesses who perform chores similar to that of geisha, it appears the tradition has been adapted to modern tastes.

For those who may wonder how they might appear as a maiko, you can live out your fantasy at one of the numerous Kyoto studios that dress up tourists for the occasion. See the Activities section in this chapter for details. ■

MASON FLORENCE

Though the number of geisha and maiko in Kyoto is dwindling, they can still be seen, particularly in the Gion District.

changed on a regular basis (check with the TIC or *Kansai Time Out* for details). Admission costs ¥420 and it's open from 9.30 am to 5 pm, closed Monday.

The **Kyoto Municipal Museum of Art** (Map 10) organises several major exhibitions a year; admission varies with each show, and it's open from 10 am to 5 pm, closed Monday. For an interesting break from temple gazing, pop into the **Kyoto Museum of Traditional Crafts** (Map 10) with exhibitions, demonstrations and sales of Kyoto handicrafts. It's in the basement of the Kyoto International Exhibition Hall. Admission is free, and it's open from 10 am to 6 pm, closed Monday.

Another nearby museum of limited interest is the **Lake Biwa Aqueduct Museum** (Map 10) dedicated in 1989 for the 100th anniversary of the building of the canal. It's open from 9 am to 5 pm, closed Monday; admission is free.

Finally, there is always the **Kyoto Municipal Zoo** (Kyoto-shi Dōbutsu-en). The zoo (Map 10) is home to about 1000 animals, and is famed for its gardens and groves of cherry trees. It's open from 9 am to 5 pm, closed Monday; admission is ¥500.

Heian-jingū Shrine Heian-jingū (Map 10) was built in 1895 to commemorate the 1100th anniversary of the founding of Kyoto. The shrine buildings are gaudy replicas, reduced to a two-thirds scale, of the Imperial Court Palace of the Heian period.

The spacious garden, with its large pond and Chinese-inspired bridge, is also meant to represent gardens popular in the Heian period. It is well known for its wisteria, irises and weeping cherry trees. About 500m in front of the shrine is a massive steel torii. Although it appears to be entirely separate, this is actually considered the main entrance to the shrine itself.

Two major events, Jidai Matsuri (22 October) and Takigi Nō (1 to 2 June), are held here. Entry to the shrine precincts is free, but admission to the garden costs ¥600. The shrine is open from 8.30 am to 5.30 pm (15 March to 31 August) though closing time can be an hour earlier the rest of the year.

Take bus No 5 from Kyoto station or Keihan Sanjō station and get off at the Jingū-michi stop, or walk up from Higashiyama Sanjō station; alternatively, walk 10 minutes north from the Tōzai subway line Higashiyama station.

Murin-an Villa Murin-an (Map 10) was the elegant villa of prominent statesman Yamagata Aritomo (1838-1922) and the site of a pivotal 1902 political conference as Japan was heading into the Russo-Japanese War.

Built in 1896, the grounds contain well preserved wooden buildings including a fine Japanese tearoom. The western-style annex is characteristic of Meiji-period architecture and the serene garden features small streams which draw water from the Biwa-ko Sosui Canal. For ¥300 you can savour a bowl of frothy *matcha* (green powdered tea) while viewing the 'borrowed scenery' backdrop of the Higashiyama mountains.

Murin-an is open from 9 am to 5 pm daily; entry costs ¥350.

Nanzen-ji Temple This is one of the most pleasant temples (Map 10) in Kyoto, with its expansive grounds and numerous subtemples *(tatchū)*. It began as a retirement villa for Emperor Kameyama but was dedicated as a Zen temple on his death in 1291. Civil war in the 15th century destroyed most of the temple; the present buildings date from the 17th century. It operates now as the headquarters of the Rinzai school.

At the entrance to the temple stands the massive 1628 San-mon Gate, its ceiling adorned with Tosa and Kanō school murals of birds and angels. Steps lead up to the 2nd storey (¥300 entry) which has a fine view over the city. Beyond the gate is the *hōjō* (abbot's) hall with impressive screens painted with a vivid depiction of tigers. A good look reveals that the artist never actually saw a tiger but relied on accounts received from China and India. The effect is that of 'tiger-dog'.

Within the precincts of the same building, the Leaping Tiger Garden is a classic Zen garden well worth a look. While you're in the hōjō, you can enjoy a cup of tea while sitting on *tatami* (straw mats) gazing at a small waterfall (¥400; ask at the reception desk). This is an inexpensive way to get a quick taste of the tea ceremony in pleasant surroundings.

Perhaps the best part of Nanzen-ji is overlooked by most visitors: a small shrine hidden in a forested hollow behind the main precinct. To get there, walk up to the red-brick aqueduct that is in front of Nanzen-in Subtemple. Follow the road that runs parallel to the aqueduct up into the hills, past a small subtemple on your left. Follow the path into the woods, past several brightly coloured torii until you reach a waterfall in a beautiful mountain glen. Here, pilgrims pray while standing under the waterfall, sometimes in the dead of winter. Hiking trails lead off in all directions from this point; by going due north, you'll eventually arrive at the top of Mt Daimonji-yama (two hours) and east you'll get to Yamashina (also about two hours).

Admission to the temple costs ¥400, though most of the grounds can be explored for free. It's open from 8.30 am to 5 pm. A brief explanatory leaflet in English is provided. The temple is a 10 minute walk south-east of Heian-jingū; from Kyoto station, or Sanjō station on the Keihan line, take bus No 5 and get off at the Eikan-dō-mae stop.

Dotted around the grounds of Nanzen-ji are several subtemples which are often skipped by the crowds and consequently easier to enjoy.

Nanzen-in Subtemple This subtemple (Map 10) is on your right when facing the hōjō hall – follow the path under the aqueduct. It has an attractive garden designed around a heart-shaped pond. This garden is best in the morning or around noon, when sunlight shines directly into the pond and illuminates the colourful carp. Admission costs ¥350.

Tenju-an Temple This temple (Map 10) stands at the side of San-mon, a four minute walk west of Nanzen-in. Constructed in

---

Northern Higashiyama Walking Tour

Time: full day
Distance: about 6km
Major Sights: Heian-jingū Shrine, Nanzen-ji Temple, Path of Philosophy, Ginkaku-ji Temple (sights are on Maps 8 &10)

The northern half of the Higashiyama area ranks high for its religious monuments, museums and strolling along the contemplative Path of Philosophy. An easy landmark to begin this walk is the massive orange *torii* (shrine gate) in the **Okazaki Park area**, leading to **Heian-jingū** (Map 10). There are several places of varied interest in the park area, including a handful of museums and the city zoo. The main attraction, however, is Heian-jingū, a scaled-down replica of the original imperial palace.

A slight detour north-west will bring you to the **Budō Center** (Map 10), Japan's oldest *dōjō* (martial arts training centre), where you can observe martial arts being practised. Also nearby is the **Kyoto Handicraft Center** (Map 10), a one-stop shopping emporium for Japanese souvenirs.

Head back south-east to **Nanzen-ji**, with a possible stop at the **Murin-an Villa** or the **Kyoto International Community House** (both Map 10). From Nanzen-ji, the walk becomes interesting. After exploring the temple, head north toward the **Nomura Museum** and **Eikan-dō Temple** (both Map 10). A short walk north from Eikan-dō, turn right and this will lead you to the southern end of the **Path of Philosophy** (Tetsugaku-no-michi).

Follow the quiet, cherry tree-lined canal – a nice break spot for *matcha* (green powdered tea) is **Kanō Shōju-an Teahouse** (Map 10) – and after about 15 minutes make a small detour east to the serene **Hōnen-in** (Map 8). From here, return to the canal and continue north on the final stretch to **Ginkaku-ji** (Map 8), the famed Silver Pavilion. If you are still feeling energetic, make the praiseworthy hike up to **Daimonji-yama** (Map 6) to view a gorgeous sunset and one of the best panoramic views of the city (see the Mt Daimonji-yama Climb boxed text in this chapter). ■

1337, Tenju-an has a splendid garden and a great collection of carp in its pond. A detailed leaflet in English is provided. Admission costs ¥300.

Konchi-in Temple When leaving Tenju-an, turn left and continue for 100m – Konchi-in (Map 10) is down a small side street on the left. The stylish gardens fashioned by Kobori Enshū are the main attraction. Admission costs ¥400. It's open from 8.30 am to 5 pm (March to November), but closes half an hour earlier the rest of the year.

Nomura Museum Nomura Museum (Map 10) is a 10 minute walk north of Nanzen-ji. Exhibits include scrolls, paintings, tea ceremony implements and ceramics which were bequeathed by business magnate Nomura Tokushiki. It's open from 10 am to 4 pm, closed Monday. Admission is ¥600.

Eikan-dō Temple Eikan-dō (Map 10), also known as Zenrin-ji, is made interesting by its varied architecture, its gardens and works of art. One of Kyoto's best spots for viewing the autumn colours, the temple was founded in 855 by the priest Shinshō, but the name was changed to Eikan-dō in the 11th century to honour the philanthropic priest Eikan.

The best approach is to follow the arrows and wander slowly along the covered walkways connecting the halls and gardens.

In the Amida-dō Hall at the southern end of the complex is a famous statue of Mikaeri Amida (Buddha Glancing Backwards).

There are various legends about this statue. One version maintains that Eikan was doing a dance in honour of Amida Buddha when the statue stepped down and joined in. When Eikan stopped in amazement, the Buddha looked over his shoulder and told him to keep on jiving. A more prosaic version holds that the Buddha looked back over his shoulder to admonish a monk who was lax in chanting his sutras.

On the right of this statue, there's an image of a bald priest with a superb expression of intense concentration.

From Amida-dō, head north to the end of the curving covered walkway (garyūrō). Change into the sandals provided, then climb the steep steps up the mountainside to the Tahō-tō Pagoda, from where there's a fine view across the city.

The temple is open from 9 am to 5 pm, and admission costs ¥500. An explanatory leaflet in English and a map are provided.

Path of Philosophy Tetsugaku-no-michi (Path of Philosophy; Maps 8 & 10) has been a favourite with contemplative strollers since noted 20th century philosopher Nishida Kitarō is said to have meandered along the path 'lost in thought'. Follow the traffic-free route along a canal lined with cherry trees which come into spectacular bloom in April. It only takes 30 minutes to follow the walk, which starts at Nyakuōji Bridge (Map 10), near Eikan-dō, and leads to Ginkaku-ji Temple. During the day be prepared for crowds; a night stroll will definitely be quieter.

Hōnen-in Temple This temple (Map 8) was founded in 1680 to honour the priest Hōnen. This is a lovely, secluded temple with carefully raked gardens set back in the woods. The temple buildings include a small gallery where frequent exhibitions featuring local and international artists are held.

Entry is free. It's open from 7 am to 4 pm. Hōnen-in is a 12 minute walk from Ginkaku-ji, on a side street just east of the Path of Philosophy. Cross the bridge over the canal and follow the road uphill through the bamboo groves.

Ginkaku-ji Temple One of Kyoto's most breathtaking sites, Ginkaku-ji (Map 8) is definitely worth seeing; unfortunately it is usually swamped with bus loads of visitors jamming the narrow pathways. Also known as Jishō-ji, the temple belongs to the Shōkokuji school of the Rinzai school.

In 1482, shōgun Ashikaga Yoshimasa constructed a villa here which he used as a genteel retreat from the turmoil of civil war. Although its name translates as 'Silver Temple', the scheme to completely cover the building in silver leaf was never carried out. After Yoshimasa's death, it was converted to a temple.

The approach to the main gate runs between tall hedges before turning sharply into the extensive grounds. Walkways lead through the gardens laid out by painter and garden designer Sōami. The gardens include meticulously raked cones of white sand *(kōgetsudai)* designed to reflect moonlight and enhance the beauty of the garden at night.

In addition to the Buddha image in the main hall, the Tōgudō (residence of Yoshimasa) houses an effigy of Yoshimasa dressed in monk's garb. The tiny tearoom here is said to be the oldest in Japan (closed to the public).

Admission to the temple costs ¥500, and it's open from 8.30 am to 5 pm (15 March to 30 November) and from 9 am to 4.30 pm the rest of the year. An explanatory leaflet in English is provided. From Kyoto station or Keihan Sanjō station, take bus No 5 and get off at the Ginkaku-ji-mae stop. From Keihan Demachiyanagi station or Keihan Shijō station, take bus No 203 to the same stop.

NORTHERN & NORTH-EASTERN KYOTO

The area north of Imadegawa-dōri, *rakuhoku*, provides scope for exploration of rural valleys and mountainous regions said to be the haunts of evil spirits. Kitayama-dōri, Kyoto's answer to Madison Avenue, is lined with boutiques, chic restaurants and galleries. It is an excellent area to get a taste for some of the city's modern architecture.

Several worthwhile sights lie within the fork of the Kamo-gawa. These include the ancient sister shrines of Shimogamo-jinja and Kamigamo-jinja, and the sprawling Botanical Gardens. In the far north-eastern region are the Shūgaku-in Rikyū Imperial Villa and several secluded temples, as well as the chance to head up Mt Hiei-zan and wander through Enryaku-ji Temple's vast precincts. The area north-west of the upper Kamo-gawa is home to the Zen complex of Daitoku-ji Temple, Kinkaku-ji Temple (Golden Pavilion) and Ryōan-ji Temple (with Japan's most famous rock garden).

Mt Daimonji-yama Climb
Time: two hours (round trip)
Distance: about 5km
Major Sights: nature, site of the main Gozan Okuribi bonfire, panoramic view over Kyoto (sights are on Maps 6 & 8)

Directly behind Ginkaku-ji Temple (Map 8), **Mt Daimonji-yama** (Map 6) is the main site of the momentous Daimonji Gozan Okuribi fire festival. From almost anywhere in town the Chinese character for great *(dai)* is visible in the middle of a bare patch on the face of this mountain. Every year on 16 August, this character is set ablaze to guide the spirits of the dead on their journey home. The view of Kyoto from the top is unparalleled.

Take bus No 5 to the Ginkaku-ji-michi stop and walk up to **Ginkaku-ji**. Here you have the option of visiting the temple or starting the hike immediately. To find the trailhead, turn left just in front of the temple and head north for about 50m toward a stone torii. Just before the torii, turn right up the hill.

The trail proper starts just after a small parking lot on the right with a barn where horses are kept. It's a broad avenue through the trees. A few minutes walking brings you to a red banner hanging over the trail (warning of forest fire danger). Soon after this you must cross a bridge to the right, then continue up a smaller, switchback trail. When the trail reaches a saddle not far from the top, go to the left. You'll climb a long flight of steps (and see the pulley system used for transporting wood for the bonfire) before coming out in the middle of the bald patch. The sunset from here is great, but bring a torch (flashlight) for the way down.

If you are interested in a longer hike, walk to the top of the ridge and head down the trail to the right. The path forks in several places, but if you continue on you *will* come out somewhere in civilisation. One of the routes leads to **Hōnen-in Temple** (Map 8) and another to the southern end of the Path of Philosophy near **Eikan-dō Temple** (Map 10). As the limited signposting is written in Japanese only, be prepared to get lost. ∎

In the far north, the twin valleys of Kurama and Kibune, as well as Ōhara, make pleasant day trips, providing a feeling of being deep in the country without the necessity of long travel.

Ōhara could be combined with an excursion to Mt Hiei-zan and Enryaku-ji, or Shūgaku-in Rikyū.

Shisen-dō Temple

Shisen-dō (House of Poet-Hermits; Map 4) was built in 1641 by Ishikawa Jōzan, a scholar of Chinese classics and a landscape architect who wanted a place to retire to. Formerly a samurai, Jōzan abandoned his warrior status after a rift with Tokugawa Ieyasu and became a recluse here until his death in 1672 at the age of 90.

The hermitage is noted for its display of poems and portraits of 36 ancient Chinese poets, which are found in the Shisen-no-ma Room. The *karesansui* (waterless pond) white-sand garden is lined with azaleas, which are said to represent islands in the sea. The garden also reflects Jōzan's distinct taste for a Chinese flair. It's a tranquil place to relax.

Water flows from a small waterfall to the *shishi-odoshi*, or *sōzu*, a device designed to scare away wild boar and deer. It's made from a bamboo pipe into which water slowly trickles in, fills up and swings down to empty. On the upswing to its original position, the bamboo strikes a stone with a rhythmic 'thwack' – just loud enough to interrupt your snooze – before starting to refill.

Admission to Shisen-dō costs ¥500, and

Kyoto's Contemporary Architecture

Kyoto is deservedly famous for its wealth of traditional buildings, no matter how difficult they are becoming to find. A large number of contemporary architectural masterpieces also lie within the city limits, and although modern architecture is anathema to preservationists, such buildings are not wholly out of place in a city that has been the most progressive and innovative in Japanese history.

A tour should begin on **Kitayama-dōri** (Map 4), the northern edge of the city proper. Originally developed by overenthusiastic investors during the 'bubble economy' years of the late 1980s, Kitayama-dōri's boutiques are hardly bustling. Yet the street does contain some of the stranger architectural sights in town.

Coming out of the Karasuma line Kitayama subway exit, interesting buildings are only a minute's walk in every direction. To the south is the **Kyoto Concert Hall** (Map 4) by Isozaki Arata, a leading light in contemporary Japanese architecture. It's a stylish combination of old and new that doesn't resort to historical pastiche. The spiral ramp in the lobby is worth a look, a space entirely devoid of colour – just nuanced shades of grey. Its elegant restraint is very Kyoto, very *shibui*. If you have time (and money) for a concert, the acoustics are superb.

To the north-east of the subway exit, you can't miss the **Syntax building** (Map 4) by Takamatsu Shin. Takamatsu is Kyoto's local architectural star, with projects all over Japan, offices in Europe and even appearances in TV commercials. Inside, Syntax is just a collection of expensive shops, but outside it is typical, inimitable Takamatsu: concrete monumentality articulated in robotic stone and steel. Directly opposite is **Ining '23** (Map 4), another Takamatsu work of similar ilk.

About 100m west of the subway exit is the world-renowned Osaka architect Andō Tadao's **Garden of Fine Art** (Map 4; ¥100 entry fee), a concrete stroll garden dug into the ground. A series of ramps descends three or four storeys into a magical, sunlit space surrounded by waterfalls. On display is a peculiar series of giant reproductions of famous western artworks.

A few minutes walk west, past the entrance to the Kyoto Botanical Gardens and on the north side of Kitayama-dōri, is another Andō work: a small collection of boutiques called **B-Lock** (Map 4). It's a good example of Andō's interest in the juxtaposition of pure geometric forms and the play of natural light, all executed in unadorned concrete. A little further along is Takamatsu's **WEEK building** (Map 4), a collage in concrete and steel housing a collection of small boutiques.

One city block south on Kitaōji-dōri (take the subway or walk through the botanical gardens), on the corner opposite Daitoku-ji Temple, is the small but expensive Japanese restaurant **Wakuden** (Map 7), designed by local architect Kishi Warō. Built with modern materials in traditional detail, it's a very

an English leaflet is provided; it's open from 9 am to 5 pm. It's a five minute walk from the Ichijōji-sagarimatsu-mae bus stop on the No 5 route.

With time to spare, venture further up the road to explore the secluded **Tanuki-dani Fudō-in Temple** (Map 4).

Manshu-in Temple

About 30 minutes walk north of Shisen-dō you'll reach the stately gate of Manshu-in (Map 4), a popular retreat of former emperors and a great escape from the crowds. This temple was originally founded by Saichō on Mt Hiei-zan, but was relocated here at the beginning of the Edo period by Ryōshōhō, the son of Prince Hachijōnomiya Tomohito (who built Katsura Rikyū).

The graceful temple architecture is often compared with Katsura Rikyū for its detailed woodwork and rare works of art like sliding *fusuma-e* doors painted by Kanō Eitoku, a famed artist of the Momoyama era. The karesansui garden by Kobori Enshū features a sea of gravel intended to symbolise the flow of a waterfall, and stone islands representing cranes and turtles.

The temple is open from 9 am to 5 pm, and admission costs ¥500; a leaflet in English is provided.

Shūgaku-in Rikyū Imperial Villa

Unfolding at the foot of Mt Hiei-zan, this villa (Map 4), or detached palace, was begun in the 1650s by Emperor Go-Mizunō following his abdication; work was continued after his death in 1680 by his daughter Akenomiya. It was designed as a lavish summer

---

successful hybrid of old and new. Twenty minutes walk east on Kitaōji-dōri, almost to the intersection of Shirakawa-dōri, British architect David Chipperfield has designed **TAK** (Map 8), one of the more elegant car showrooms in Kyoto.

Over in Nishijin (the garment district) you'll find a Takamatsu triptych: Origin **I, II and III** (Map 7). The complex is a factory and showroom for *obi*, the wide sashes worn around kimono. Despite the bizarre forms, the three buildings sit quite comfortably among their traditional neighbours. Apparently fascinated by the surgical precision of obi manufacture, Takamatsu decorated the top of the tower with giant, shiny knife blades.

Back in the centre of town, you'll find Andō's much celebrated **TIME'S building** (Map 10) on the corner of Sanjō-dōri and Kiyamachi-dōri. It's a long concrete box with a barrel-vaulted roof and a beautiful little plaza facing onto the narrow canal beside it (one of the few outdoor public spaces in the city centre). The neighbouring cherry trees are brilliant in April. A one minute walk south on Kiyamachi-dōri is Takamatsu's **Cella building** (Map 10), a black stone cylindrical tower of karaoke rooms.

Across the river is Gion, Kyoto's traditional entertainment district and home to unsurpassed clashes between old and new, and the city's most extreme architectural indulgences. Unfortunately, little of it is very good; just a mishmash of mediocre buildings trying to out-weird one another. The highlights are a couple of Takamatsu's, and several buildings by another local architect Wakabayashi Hiroyuki. One is memorably named **Gion Freak** (Map 10).

Gion is certainly fun to wander around, especially by night – the buildings are at their best when covered in luminous neon. During the day, make sure you visit the **Shinbashi District** (Map 10), with two of Kyoto's best preserved historic streets. And step into the **Nexus building** (Map 10), where you'll discover that a tiny traditional exterior conceals a cavernous modern bar and restaurant.

If you're heading down to Uji (Map 2), you can further broaden your contemporary architectural tour at a couple of stops along the way. Right next to Momoyama-Minamiguchi station on the Keihan Uji line is Takamatsu Shin's infamous **Ark dental clinic** (Map 3). All chimneys and portholes, it resembles a train. Further along the line, near Mimurodo station, you'll find architect Umebāyashi Katsu's **Organ building** (Map 2). It's an office that seems to be growing like an enormous aluminium plant!

Finally, love it or hate it, you can't avoid Hara Hiroshi's **Kyoto station building** (Map 11). The outcome of an international architectural design competition several years ago, the station is hypermodern, a big chunk of city compressed into a single building. It's fantastically out of scale in Kyoto, although it does handle admirably the huge volume of people flowing in and out.

See the Books section in the Facts for the Visitor chapter for information on a couple of books detailing Kyoto's contemporary architecture. ■

retreat for the imperial family. The villa grounds are divided into three enormous garden areas on a hillside – lower, middle and upper. Each has superb tea ceremony houses; the upper, **Kami-no-chaya** and lower, **Shimo-no-chaya**, were completed in 1659, and the middle teahouse, **Naka-no-chaya**, was completed in 1682. The gardens' reputation rests on their ponds, pathways and impressive use of 'borrowed scenery' in the form of the surrounding hills. The view from the Rinun-tei Teahouse in Kami-no-chaya is particularly impressive.

One-hour tours (in Japanese) start at 9, 10 and 11 am, and 1.30 and 3 pm; try to arrive early. A basic leaflet in English is provided and more detailed literature is on sale in the tour waiting room.

Admission is free, but you must make reservations through the Imperial Household Agency – usually several weeks in advance (see the earlier Kyoto Imperial Palace section for details).

From Kyoto station, take bus No 5 and get off at the Shūgaku-in Rikyū-michi stop. The trip takes about an hour. From the bus stop (or from Manshu-in) it's a 15 minute walk to the villa. You can also take the Eiden Eizan line from Demachiyanagi station to the Shūgaku-in stop and walk east for about 25 minutes toward the mountains.

Mt Hiei-zan & Enryaku-ji Temple

A visit to the 848m-high Mt Hiei-zan (Map 2) and the vast Enryaku-ji complex (Map 2) is a good way to spend half a day hiking, poking around temples and enjoying the atmosphere of a key site in Japanese history.

Enryaku-ji was founded in 788 by Saichō, also known as Dengyō-daishi, the priest who established the Tenzai school. This school did not receive imperial recognition until 1823, after Saichō's death. But from the 8th century the temple grew in power; at its height it possessed some 3000 buildings and an army of thousands of *sōhei*, or warrior monks. In 1571, Oda Nobunaga saw the temple's power as a threat to his aims to unify the nation and he destroyed most of the buildings, along with the monks inside.

Today only three pagodas and 120 minor temples remain.

The complex is divided into three sections – Tōtō, Saitō and Yokawa. **Tōtō** (Eastern Pagoda section) contains the Kompon Chū-dō (Primary Central Hall), which is the most important building in the complex. The flames on the three Dharma (Wheel of the Law, in Sanskrit) lamps in front of the altar have been kept lit for over 1200 years. The Daikō-dō (Great Lecture Hall) displays life-size wooden statues of the founders of various Buddhist schools. Admission to Tōtō costs ¥400. It's open from 8.30 am to 4.30 pm (April to November) and from 9 am to 4 pm the rest of the year. A leaflet in English is provided. This part is heavily geared to group access, with large expanses of asphalt for parking.

Saitō (Western Pagoda section) contains

MASON FLORENCE

Enryaku-ji Temple, magnificently situated on Mt Hiei-zan, makes an excellent half-day trip out of the city centre.

the Shaka-dō Hall, which dates from 1595 and houses a rare Buddha sculpture of the Shaka Nyorai. Saitō, with its stone paths winding through forests of tall trees, temples shrouded in mist and the sound of distant gongs, is the most atmospheric part of the temple. Hold onto your ticket from the Tōtō section, as you may need to show it here.

Yokawa is of minimal interest and a 4km bus ride away from the Saitō area. The Chū-dō (Central Hall) here was originally built in 848. It was destroyed by fire several times and has undergone repeated reconstruction (the most recent in 1971). If you plan to visit this area as well as Tōtō and Saitō, allow a full day for in-depth exploration.

Getting There & Away You can reach Mt Hiei-zan and Enryaku-ji by either train or bus. The most interesting way is the train/cable car/ropeway route described below. If you're in a hurry or would like to save money, the best way is a direct bus from Keihan Sanjō or Kyoto stations.

Train Take the Keihan line north to the last stop, Demachiyanagi, and change to the Yase-yūen/Hiei-bound Eiden Eizan line train (be careful not to board the Kurama-bound train which leaves from the same platform). At Yase-yūen (¥260; the last stop), board the cable car (nine minutes, ¥530) and then the ropeway (three minutes, ¥300) to the peak, from where you can walk down to the temples.

Enryaku-ji is also accessible from Sakamoto on the Lake Biwa-ko side of the mountain (the cable car costs ¥840).

Bus Kyoto bus Nos 17 and 18 run from Kyoto station to Ōhara in about 50 minutes. Be careful to board a tan-coloured Kyoto bus, not a green Kyoto city bus of the same number. Get off before Ōhara at the Yase-yūen bus stop. From there it's a short walk to the cable car station (departures every half-hour) where you can ascend the mountain in two stages. A combined ticket (one way) for both sections costs ¥820. The lookout at the top cable-car station has fine views across Lake Biwa-ko, though skip it if the weather is dull; entry costs ¥300.

From Keihan Sanjō station in central Kyoto, you can take Kyoto bus No 16 toward Ōhara and get off at the Yase-yūen bus stop.

From Kyoto and Keihan Sanjō stations, there are direct buses to Enryaku-ji and Mt Hiei-zan which take about 70 and 50 minutes respectively (both cost ¥800). Check with the TIC for current schedules.

Takara-ga-ike Park
This expansive park (Map 4) is an excellent place for a stroll or picnic in natural surroundings. Far from the throngs in the city centre, it is a popular place for birdwatching and has spacious gardens. It is a 1.8km loop around the main pond where rowing boats can be hired for ¥1000 per hour.

In the north-east of the park, the monstrous **Kyoto International Conference Hall** is an unfortunate attempt at replicating Japan's traditional *gasshō zukuri* (a wooden style) in concrete. Behind the conference hall, the **Hosho-an Teahouse** (designed by Soshitsu Sen, Grand Tea Master XV of the Urasenke school) is worth a look.

The park is best reached by the Tōzai subway line to the Kokusai-kaikan stop. Entry is free.

Entsū-ji Temple
Emperor Reigen built this remote temple (Map 4) in 1678 on the ruins of Emperor Go-Mizunō's villa. The picturesque garden, with some 40 carefully arranged rocks, is bordered by a manicured hedge of sananqua trees; there are fantastic views of Mt Hiei-zan from here. The temple is open from 10 am to 4 pm; entry costs ¥400. In an effort to keep the place quiet, no photography, children or tour guides are permitted. Take Kyoto bus No 45 from Kyoto station (50 minutes, ¥340); get off at the Entsū-ji-michi stop and walk 10 minutes west.

Kamigamo-jinja Shrine
Kamigamo-jinja (Map 4) is one of Japan's oldest shrines and predates the founding of Kyoto. Established in 679, it is dedicated to

Raijin, the god of thunder, and is one of Kyoto's 17 UNESCO World Cultural Heritage Sites. The present buildings (over 40 in all), including the impressive Haiden Hall, are exact reproductions of the originals, dating from the 17th to 19th century. The shrine is entered from a long approach through two torii. The two large conical white-sand mounds in front of Hosodono Hall are said to represent mountains sculpted for gods to descend upon.

From Kyoto station take bus No 9 and get off at Miso-no-bashi stop (40 minutes). Entry to the grounds and shrine are free.

Kyoto Botanical Gardens

This vast area (Map 4) opened in 1914 occupies 240,000 sq metres, and features 12,000 plants, flowers and trees. It is pleasant to stroll through the rose, cherry and herb gardens or see the rows of camphor trees and the large tropical greenhouse. It's open year-round from 9 am to 4 pm, and admission costs ¥200 (it's another ¥200 to enter the greenhouse). The gardens are just west of the Tōzai line Kitayama subway station.

Garden of Fine Art

Don't expect to find any moss at this sunken 'garden' (Map 4). Actually not a garden at all, it is an ultramodern structure by famed Japanese architect Andō Takao, exhibiting giant ceramic reproductions of masterpieces by such favourites as Monet, Van Gogh and, most memorably, Leonardo da Vinci's *The Last Supper*. It's open daily from 9 am to 4.30 pm. Entry costs ¥100 (persons over 60 get in free with ID). It's just south of the Kitayama subway station.

Shimogamo-jinja Shrine

Shimogamo-jinja (Map 8) dates from the 8th century and is a UNESCO World Cultural Heritage Site. It is nestled in the fork of the converging Kamo-gawa and Takano-gawa rivers, and is approached along a shady path through the lovely Tadasu-no-mori Forest. This wooded area is said to be a place where lies cannot be concealed and is considered a prime location to sort out disputes. The shrine is dedicated to the god of harvest; traditionally, pure water was drawn from the nearby rivers for purification and agricultural ceremonies. The hondō dates from 1863 and, like the Haiden Hall at its sister shrine, Kamigamo-jinja, is an excellent example of *nagare*-style shrine architecture.

The grounds are open from 6 am to 6 pm. Entry to the precincts is free, but there is a ¥500 charge to enter the Ōidono, the shrine's national treasure house. Take bus No 205 from Kyoto station and get off at the Shimogamo-jinja-mae stop.

NORTH-WESTERN KYOTO

The north-western part of Kyoto is predominantly residential, but there are a number of superb, secluded temples with tranquil gardens. For Zen fans, visits to Daitoku-ji and Ryōan-ji temples are recommended. Kinkaku-ji is another major attraction. The Japan National Tourist Organisation (JNTO) leaflet on walks covers part of this area, but most of the walk is along unremarkable city streets.

Shōkoku-ji Temple

Shōkoku-ji (Map 8), the headquarters of the Rinzai Shōkoku-ji school, sits in an ancient pine grove north of Dōshisha University. It was established in 1392 by the third Ashikaga shōgun, Yoshimitsu. The original buildings were almost totally destroyed during the civil wars in the 15th century. Inside the vast compound, the **Jōtenkaku Museum** (¥600) houses treasures from Kinkaku-ji and Ginkaku-ji.

The museum is open from 10 am to 5 pm (last entry at 4.30 pm). Entry to the grounds is free. The temple is a five minute walk north-east of the Karasuma line Imadegawa subway station.

Urasenke Foundation

Anyone interested in tea ceremony should make their first stop at the Urasenke Chadō Research Center (Map 7). Urasenke is also Japan's largest tea school, and hosts hundreds of students annually who come from

国宝三十三間堂

National Treasure
SANJU-SANGEN-DO

Twenty-eight Guardian Deities of Kannon

The twenty-eight images placed in a straight line in front of the 1001 Kannon statues are guardian deities which protect the Buddhist deity Kannon as well as pious Buddhists who believe in Kannon. Many of these deities, whose mythic images are expressed in a vivid manner, have their origin in ancient India. Technically these statues are made in an assembled construction method. Arms and heads were carved separately, then joined together, coated with lacquer, and finished by coloring.

Daibenkudoku-ten

The Temple Fair "Yanagi-no-Okaji" and Archery

The Yanagi-no-Okaji temple fair held in January is one of the largest events of Sanju-sangen-do. The fair is believed to be effective in preventing headaches. An archery competition is held in a traditional style all day long in the western garden. Many illustrated votive tablets in the temple record the history of this archery competition. Every year 20-year-old lady archers, who celebrate the Coming-of-Age Day in beautiful traditional dresses, participate in the competition.

Archery

Sanju-sangen-do

The official name of Sanju-sangen-do is Rengeo-in temple, and the structure is registered as a National Treasure by the Japanese government. It was established by the powerful warrior-politician Taira-no-Kiyomori in 1164. The original temple building was lost in a fire, but the building was reconstructed in 1266. That structure has remained unchanged for 700 years since then with four great renovations during that period. The long temple hall, which is about 120 meters long, is made in the Wayo (Japanese) style architecture. As there are thirty-three spaces between the columns, this temple came to be called "Sanju-sangen-do" (a hall with thirty-three spaces between columns). Other noteworthy objects in this temple are the roofed earthen fence and the South Gate, which are registered as Important Cultural Properties. They are noted in connection with Regent Toyotomi Hideyoshi and reflect the aesthetics of the 16th century.

The Thousand Images of Kannon

The principal images of Sanju-sangen-do temple are the 1001 statues of the Buddhist deity, Juichimen-senju-sengen Kanzeon, which is often called by the simplified name, "Kannon". One thousand standing statues of Kannon (Important Cultural Properties) and one gigantic seated statue (National Treasure), placed at the center of the standing statues, are housed in the temple hall. The statues are made of Japanese cypress. Among the standing statues, 124 were made in the 12th century when this temple was founded, and the remaining 876 were made in the 13th century when the temple was renovated.

Senju-Kannon figure No. 550

Statues of Thunder God and Wind God

The powerful and dynamic statues of the Thunder God and the Wind God are placed at either side of the temple hall on raised pedestals of cloud shape. The images of these gods derived from people's fear of and gratitude for nature in the old days. People worshipped them as deities who controlled rain and wind, and brought about good harvests. These statues are representative masterpiece sculptures of the Kamakura period (12th-14th centuries).

Fujin(Wind God)

branch schools worldwide to further their studies in 'the way of tea'.

The gallery on the 1st and 2nd floors holds quarterly exhibitions on tea-related arts (open from 9.30 am to 4.30 pm – you must enter by 4 pm; it's closed Monday); call to if there is a show being held during your stay. The entrance fee (¥800) includes a bowl of matcha and a sweet.

The Konnichi-an library here has more than 50,000 books (about 100 in English), plus videos on tea which can be viewed. It's open from 10 am to 4 pm (3 pm on Saturday), closed Sunday and public holidays; admission is free.

For more information contact Urasenke's Office of International Affairs *(kokusai kyoku)* (☎ 431-3111). The centre is a 10 minute walk north of the Horikawa-dōri and Imadegawa-dōri intersection.

Nishijin Textile Center

In the heart of the Nishijin textile district, this centre (Map 7) is a good place to observe the weaving of fabrics used in kimono and their ornamental belts *(obi)*. There are also displays of completed fabrics and kimono. It's on the south-west corner of the Horikawa-dōri and Imadegawa-dōri intersection, and is open daily from 9 am to 5 pm; admission is free (with a ¥600 charge for certain special kimono displays). To get there, take bus No 9 from Kyoto station to the Horikawa-Imadegawa stop; otherwise walk for 10 minutes west of the Karasuma line Imadegawa subway station.

Orinasu-kan

This museum (Map 7) is housed in a Nishijin weaving factory. It has impressive exhibits of Nishijin textiles and the Susamei-sha building (recently restored) next door is also open to the public and worth a look. With advance reservations, traditional weaving workshops can be attended (see the Activities section later in this chapter). It is open from 10 am to 4 pm, closed Monday. Entry costs ¥500.

Kitano-Tenman-gū Shrine

Commonly known as Kitano Tenjin, this shrine (Map 4) was established in 947 to honour Sugawara Michizane (845-903), a noted Heian-era statesman and scholar.

Sugawara had been defied by his political adversary, Fujiwara Tokihira, and exiled to Kyūshū to live out his life in secluded desolation. Following his death in 903, calamitous earthquakes and thunderstorms shook Kyoto, and the Imperial Palace was repeatedly struck by lightning. Fearing that Sugawara, reincarnated as Raijin had returned from beyond to avenge his rivals, the shrine was established and dedicated to him.

The present buildings were built in 1607 by Toyotomi Hideyori, and the grounds contain an extensive grove of plum and apricot trees *(baika)*, said to have been Sugawara's favourite fruits.

Unless you are trying to avoid crowds, the best time to visit is for the Tenjin-san Market fair held here on the 25th of each month. Those held in December and January are particularly colourful.

There's no charge for admission to the shrine, and it's open from 5.30 am to 5.30 pm. From Kyoto station, take bus No 50 or 101 and get off at the Kitano-Tenmangū-mae stop. From Keihan Sanjō station, take bus No 10 to the same stop.

Daitoku-ji Temple

The precincts of this temple (Map 4), headquarters of the Rinzai Daitoku-ji school, contain an extensive complex of 24 subtemples, three of which are mentioned below, but eight are actually open to the public. If you want an intensive look at Zen culture, this is the place to visit, but be prepared for temples which are thriving business enterprises and often choked with visitors.

Daitoku-ji is on the eastern side of the grounds. It was founded in 1319, burnt down in the next century and rebuilt in the 16th century. The 1589 San-mon Gate contains a self-carved statue of its erector, the famous tea master Sen no Rikyū, on the 2nd storey. According to some sources, Toyotomi

Hideyoshi was so enraged when he discovered he had been demeaning himself by walking under Rikyū's effigy that he forced the master to commit *seppuku* (ritual suicide) in 1591.

The temple bus stop is Daitoku-ji-mae. Convenient buses from Kyoto station are No 205 and 206. It's also not a far walk west of Kitaōji subway station on the Karasuma line.

Daisen-in Subtemple The masterpiece Zen garden in this subtemple (Map 4) is an elegant example of 17th century karesansui style, and ranks with the revered rock garden at Ryōan-ji. Here the trees, rocks and sand are said to represent and express a spectacle of nature, from waterfalls and valleys to mountain lakes. It's worth a look – that is, of course, if you can make any progress through the crowds.

Admission costs ¥400, and it is open from 9 am to 5 pm.

Kōtō-in Subtemple This subtemple (Map 7) in the western part of the grounds is slightly less swarming with visitors than Daisen-in. Surrounded by lovely maples and bamboo, the moss garden viewed from the temple veranda is superb.

Admission costs ¥300, and it is open from 9 am to 4.30 pm.

Zuihō-in Subtemple Zuihō-in (Map 7) enshrines the 16th century Christian daimyō, Ōtomo Sōrin. In the early 1960s, a landscape architect named Shigemori Misuzu rearranged the stones in its rock garden into the shape of a crucifix! Admission costs ¥300, and it is open from 9 am to 5 pm.

Kinkaku-ji Temple

Kinkaku-ji (Map 4), the famed 'Golden Temple', is one of Japan's best known sights. Also known as Rokuon-ji, it belongs to the Shōkokuji school. The original building was constructed in 1397 as a retirement villa for shōgun Ashikaga Yoshimitsu. His son, complying with father's wishes, converted it into a temple.

The three storey pavilion is covered in bright gold leaf and features a bronze phoenix on top of the roof. The mirror-like reflection of the temple in the Kyō-ko Pond is extremely photogenic, especially when the maples are ablaze in autumn. In 1950, a young monk consummated his obsession with the temple by burning it to the ground. The monk's story is fictionalised in Mishima Yukio's *The Golden Pavilion*.

In 1955, a full reconstruction was completed which exactly followed the original design, but the gold-foil covering was extended to the lower floors. The temple may not be to everyone's taste (the tremendous crowds just about obscure the view anyway), but it is still an impressive feat.

The temple is open from 9 am to 5 pm, and admission costs ¥400. To get there from Kyoto station, take bus No 205 or 101 and get off at the Kinkaku-ji-michi stop; bus No 59 also stops close to the temple.

Ryōan-ji Temple

This temple (Map 3) belongs to the Rinzai school and was founded in 1450.

The main attraction is the garden arranged in the karesansui style. An oblong of sand with an austere collection of 15 carefully placed rocks, apparently adrift in a sea of sand, is enclosed by an earthen wall. The designer, who remains unknown, provided no explanation.

Although many historians believe it was arranged during the Muromachi period by Sōami, some contend that it is a much later product of the Edo period. It is Japan's most famous *hira-niwa* (a flat garden void of hills or ponds), and reveals the stunning simplicity and harmony of the principles of Zen meditation.

The viewing platform for the garden can become packed solid, but the other parts of the temple grounds are also interesting and less of a target for the crowds. Among these, Kyoyo-chi Pond is perhaps the most beautiful, particularly in autumn.

Try to come as early in the day as possible. Admission costs ¥400, and the temple is open from 8 am to 5 pm (8.30 am to 4.30 pm from December to February). From Keihan

Sanjō station take bus No 59, or walk from Kinkaku-ji for about 15 minutes.

Ninna-ji Temple

Ninna-ji (Map 3) was built in 888 and is the head temple of the Omuro branch of the Shingon school. Originally there were more than 60 structures; the present temple buildings, including a five storey pagoda, date from the 17th century. The extensive grounds keep a peculiar grove of short-trunk, multipetal cherry trees called Omuro-no-Sakura, which draw large crowds in April.

The temple is open from 9 am to 4 pm; admission costs ¥400, though you can stroll some of the grounds for free. Separate entrance fees are charged for the kondō and *reihōkan* (treasure house), which is only open for the first two weeks of October. To get there, take bus No 59 from Keihan Sanjō station and get off at the Omuro Ninna-ji stop which is opposite the entrance gate. From Kyoto station take bus No 26.

Takagamine Area

In the far north-west area of Takagamine (Map 4) there are several interesting, less visited temples worth exploring.

Kōetsu-ji Temple This temple (Map 4) dates from 1651 and was once the hermitage of Honami Kōestu, a celebrated Edo-period artisan. After his death the villa was reconstructed as a temple and dedicated to him. The grounds contain seven tea ceremony houses and a notable fence called *kōtsu-gaki*, made with slats of interwoven bamboo. The temple is open from 8 am to 5 pm; admission costs ¥300.

From Kyoto station, take bus No 6 to the Takagamine-genkō-an-mae bus stop (40 minutes) and walk three minutes west.

A short walk north-east of Kōetsu-ji, two other small temples worth a visit are **Genkō-an** (Map 4) and **Jōshō-ji** (Map 4); both are open from 9 am to 5 pm and charge ¥300 admission.

Shōden-ji Temple Shōden-ji (Map 4) is approached up a long flight of stone steps

through a thick grove of trees. It was founded south of its current location in 1268, but shortly after was destroyed in a fire and was established in 1282 on the present site. Of interest here are the wooden ceiling boards of the Chi Tenjō (Blood Ceiling), once flooring in the corridor of Fushimi-jō, where 1200 people committed ritual suicide following the surrender of the castle in 1600.

It's open from 9 am to 5 pm; admission costs ¥300. Take bus No 9 from Kyoto station and get off at the Jinkō-in-mae stop, then walk 15 minutes north-east. Near the bus stop, **Jinkō-in Temple** (free entry) is of limited interest, but on the 21st of each month exhibits a rare self-carved statue of 9th century priest Kūkai; brace yourself for the swarms of geriatric bus tour groups.

ŌHARA & KURAMA-KIBUNE

Ōhara

Since ancient times Ōhara (Map 2), a quiet farming town about 10km north of Kyoto, has been regarded as a holy site by followers of the Jōdo school. The region provides a glimpse of old rural Japan, along with the picturesque Sanzen-in Temple, Jakkō-in Convent and several other fine temples. It's most popular in autumn, when the maple leaves change colour and the mountain views are spectacular. From late October to mid-November avoid this area on weekends as it will be packed. For details on hands-on papermaking or wool dyeing in Ōhara, see the Activities section later in this chapter.

From Kyoto station, Kyoto bus Nos 17 and 18 run to Ōhara. The ride takes about an hour and costs ¥580. From Keihan Sanjō station, take Kyoto bus No 16 or 17 (45 minutes, ¥490). Be careful to board a tan-coloured Kyoto bus, not a green Kyoto city bus of the same number. Allow at least half a day for a visit, possibly combined with an excursion to Mt Hiei-zan and Enryaku-ji (see the earlier Northern & North-Eastern Kyoto section).

Sanzen-in Temple Founded in 784 by the priest Saichō, Sanzen-in (Map 2) belongs to the Tendai school. Saichō, considered one of the great patriarchs of Buddhism in Japan, also founded Enryaku-ji. The temple's Yūsei-en Garden is one of the most often photographed sights in Japan, and rightly so. Take some time to sit on the steps of the Shin-den Hall and admire the garden's beauty. Then head off to Ōjō-gokuraku-in Hall (Temple of Rebirth in Paradise) to see the impressive Amitabha trinity, a large Amida image flanked by attendants Kannon and Seishi (god of wisdom). After this, walk up to the hydrangea garden at the back of the temple where, in late spring and summer, you can walk among hectares of blooming hydrangea.

To get to Sanzen-in, follow the signs west from Ōhara's main bus stop up the hill past a long arcade of souvenir stalls. The entrance is on your left as you crest the hill. The temple is open from 8.30 am to 4.30 pm from March to November, and it closes half an hour earlier the rest of the year. Admission costs ¥550, and an English leaflet is provided.

A short walk uphill from Sanzen-in, is **Raigō-in Temple** (Map 2; entry ¥300), the place where Shōmyō Buddhist chanting originated (these entranced chants are said to have had a profound influence on traditional Japanese folk music or *minyō*). Each Sunday from 1 pm, you can come and see the monks chanting here.

If you feel like a short hike after leaving the temple, continue up the hill to see the oddly named **Soundless Waterfall** (Otonashi-no-taki). Though in fact it sounds like any other waterfall, its resonance is believed to have inspired Shōmyō Buddhist chanting.

Jikkō-in Temple Only about 50m north of Sanzen-in, this small temple (Map 2) is often praised for its lovely garden and *fudan-zakura* cherry tree which blossoms between October and March.

It's open from 9 am to 4.30 pm; entry costs ¥500.

Shōrin-in Temple This temple (Map 2; admission ¥200) is worth a look, if only

through its admission gate, to admire the thatched roof of the main hall.

Hōsen-in Temple This temple (Map 2) is just down the path west of Shōrin-in's entry gate. The main tatami room offers a view of a bamboo garden and the surrounding mountains, framed like a painting by the beams and posts of the building. There is also a fantastic 700-year-old pine tree in the garden. The blood-stained Chi Tenjō ceiling boards came from Fushimi-jō. It's open from 9 am to 5 pm; entry costs ¥500.

Jakkō-in Convent The history of Jakkō-in (Map 2) is exceedingly tragic – bring a supply of hankies. The actual founding date of the convent is subject to some debate (somewhere between the 6th and 11th centuries), but it acquired fame as the nunnery which harboured Kenrei Mon-in, a lady of the Taira clan. In 1185, the Taira were soundly defeated in a sea battle with the Minamoto clan at Dan-no-ura. With the entire Taira clan slaughtered or drowned, Kenrei Mon-in threw herself into the waves with her son Antoku, the infant emperor; she was fished out – the only member of the clan to survive.

She was returned to Kyoto, where she became a nun living in a bare hut until it collapsed during an earthquake. Kenrei Mon-in was accepted into Jakkō-in Temple and stayed there, immersed in prayer and sorrowful memories, until her death 27 years later. Her tomb is enshrined high on the hill behind the temple.

The convent itself is quite plain, its real beauty coming from the maple glade in which it is set. Unfortunately, like many Japanese temples, the tranquillity of the place is shattered periodically by announcements, in this case a version of Kenrei Mon-in's tragic tale read in a melodramatic voice.

Jakkō-in is open from 9 am to 5 pm, and admission costs ¥500. Perhaps it's best to climb up to the entrance gate and look from there, as the admission price is quite steep

A more traditonal style of transport still used by the police of Kyoto.

MASON FLORENCE

MASON FLORENCE

MARTIN MOOS

MASON FLORENCE

MARTIN MOOS

A	B
C	E
D	

The many aspects of contemporary architecture in the Kansai region:
A: The massive Kyoto station building. B: Ceramic reproductions of Modernist icons grace the Garden of Fine Art. C: Stairways you may encounter on the outside of a building, Osaka. D: The hyper-modern at play: Andō Takao's Garden of Fine Art. E: Osaka's Umeda Sky Building, designed to resemble a garden floating in the sky.

considering the small size of the convent. It lies to the west of Ōhara. Walk out of the bus station up the road to the traffic lights, then follow the small road to the left; the temple is at the top of a steep flight of stone steps.

Kurama & Kibune

Only 30 minutes north of Kyoto on the Eiden Kurama train line, Kurama and Kibune (Map 2) are a pair of tranquil valleys long favoured by Kyotoites as places to escape the crowds and stresses of the city below. Since ancient times, Mt Kurama has been feared as the haunt of evil spirits. Kurama's main attractions are its mountain temple and *onsen* (hot-spring bath). Kibune, over the ridge, is a cluster of *ryokan* (traditional inns) overlooking a mountain river. Kibune is best enjoyed in summer, when the ryokan serve dinner on platforms built over the rushing waters of Kibune-gawa River, providing welcome relief from the summer heat.

The two valleys lend themselves to being explored together. In winter, you can start from Kibune, walk 30 minutes over the ridge, visit Kurama-dera Temple, then soak in the onsen before heading back to Kyoto. In summer, the reverse route is best: start from Kurama, walk up to the temple, then down the other side to Kibune to enjoy a meal suspended above the cool river. If you happen to be in Kyoto on the night of 22 October, be sure not to miss the exciting Kurama-no-himatsuri Fire Festival.

To get to Kurama and Kibune, take the Eiden Eizan line from Kyoto's Demachiyanagi station. For Kibune, get off at the second last stop, Kibuneguchi, take a right out of the station and walk about 20 minutes up the hill. For Kurama, go to the last stop, Kurama, and walk straight out of the station. Both destinations cost ¥410.

Kurama-dera Temple In 770 the monk Gantei left Nara's Toshōdai-ji Temple in search of a wilderness sanctuary in which to meditate. Wandering in the hills north of Kyoto, he came across a white horse which led him to the valley known today as Kurama. After seeing a vision of the deity Bishamon-ten, guardian of the northern quarter of the Buddhist heaven, he established Kurama-dera (Map 2) just below the peak of Mt Kurama. This temple is said to be the place where Minamoto-no-Yoshitsune of the mighty Genji family underwent spiritual training with a long-nosed and winged Tengu goblin. Originally belonging to the Tendai school, since 1949 Kurama has been independent, describing its own brand of Buddhism as Kurama-kyō.

The entrance to the temple is just up the hill from Kurama station. Admission is ¥200, and it's open every day from 9 am to 4.30 pm. A tram goes to the top for ¥100, or you can hike up in about 30 minutes (follow the main path past the tram station). The trail is worth taking if it's not too hot, as it winds through a forest of towering old-growth cedar. At the top, there is a courtyard dominated by the honden. Behind the honden a trail leads off to the mountain's peak.

At the top, those who want to continue to Kibune can take the trail down the other side. It's a 1.2km, 30 minute hike from the honden to the valley floor of Kibune. On the way down are two mountain shrines which make pleasant rest stops.

Kurama Onsen Kurama Onsen (Map 2), one of the few onsen within easy reach of Kyoto, is a great way to relax after a hike. The outdoor bath, with a fine view of Mt Kurama, costs ¥1100. For ¥2500, you get use of the indoor bath as well, but even with a sauna and locker thrown in, it's difficult to imagine why you would opt for the indoor bath. For both baths, buy a ticket from the machine outside the door of the main building (instructions are in Japanese and English). The onsen is open daily from 10 am to 9 pm.

To get to Kurama Onsen, walk straight out of Kurama station and continue up the hill past the entrance to Kurama-dera. The onsen is about 10 minutes walk on the right. There's also a free shuttle bus which runs between the station and the onsen which leaves about every 30 minutes.

MASON FLORENCE

A long soak in Kurama Onsen is a pleasurable finale to the hike across from Kibune.

Kibune Kibune's main attractions are its river dining platforms, which are open from 1 June to the end of September. In addition to these, all the ryokan in the valley are open year-round and are a romantic escape for travellers willing to pay mid-range to top-end ryokan prices.

Halfway up the valley, **Kibune-jinja Shrine** (Map 2) is worth a quick look, particularly if you can ignore the plastic horse statue at its entrance. The shrine predates the 8th century founding of Kyoto. It was established to worship the god of water and has been long revered by farmers and sake brewers. Admission is free.

From Kibune you can hike over the mountain to Kurama-dera (see the Kurama section above); the trail starts halfway up the valley on the east side. Many prefer to start the day in Kibune, have lunch on the river and, following the hike over to Kurama, enjoy the hot-spring baths at Kurama Onsen.

WESTERN KYOTO

Kyoto's western region, *raku-sai*, is famed for its beautiful natural scenery and tranquil atmosphere, and holds a predominant place in Kyoto history. Arashiyama (literally, Stormy Mountain) flourished in the 8th century as a romantic playground for Heian-era emperors, war lords and aristocrats who built lavish villas and Buddhist temples. Nearby Sagano was the *monzen machi* (town in front of a temple/shrine gate) of the Atago-jinja Shrine and the lovely walk between

Arashiyama and Sagano's Toriimoto District is one of Kyoto's best.

In Uzumasa stands Kyoto's oldest temple, Kōryū-ji, and the Tōei Uzumasa Eiga Mura (Movie Village) theme park is popular, especially with families and film buffs.

Myōshin-ji Temple

Myōshin-ji (Map 5), a vast complex dating to 1342, belongs to the Rinzai school. There are 47 subtemples, but only a few are open to the public.

From the north gate, follow the broad stone avenue flanked by rows of temples to the southern part of the complex. The ceiling of the *hattō* (lecture hall) features Tanyū Kanō's unnerving painting *Unryūzu* (Dragon Glaring in Eight Directions). Admission costs ¥400 and it's open from 9.10 am to 3.40 pm, closed for one hour at lunch. The north gate of Myōshin-ji is an easy 10 minute walk south of Ninna-ji, or you can take bus No 10 from Keihan Sanjō station to the Myōshin-ji-mae stop and walk two minutes north.

Taizō-in Temple

This temple (Map 5) is in the south-western corner of the grounds. The karesansui garden depicting a waterfall and islands is worth a visit. Admission costs ¥400, and it's open from 9 am to 5 pm.

Tōei Uzumasa Movie Village

In the Uzumasa area, Tōei Uzumasa Eiga Mura (Movie Village; Map 5) is an entertaining way to spend a couple of hours between temples and shrines. As goofy as this place can seem, it does give an idea of what Kyoto must have looked like before the advent of concrete. The sets portray typical Edo-period street scenes (shown to the folks at home, snapshots from here appear convincingly 'old Kyoto').

Spend a bit of time strolling about the theme park and you'll stand a good chance of peering onto the set of a movie or TV drama being filmed. There are actors and actresses milling about in all kinds of traditional costume. Producers are occasionally scouting for foreign extras to play roles of early European arrivals in Japan, so you may want to bring along your CV – you never know. If there's no part for you, you can always pay to dress up as a samurai warrior or geisha for the photo opportunity.

Eiga Mura is open from 9 am to 4.30 pm (1 March to 30 November), and from 9.30 am to 3.30 pm (1 December through February). Admission is ¥2000 (ages six to 18 ¥1100; kids under six ¥900). Eiga Mura is a short walk from Uzumasa station on the JR San-in Main (Sagano) line or the Keifuku Arashiyama line.

Kōryū-ji Temple

Kōryū-ji (Map 5), one of the oldest temples in Japan, was founded in 622 to honour Prince Shōtoku, who was an enthusiastic promoter of Buddhism.

The hattō to the right of the main gate houses a magnificent trio of 9th century statues: Buddha, flanked by manifestations of Kannon. The reihōkan contains numerous fine Buddhist statues including the Naki Miroku (Crying Miroku) and the renowned Miroku Bosatsu which is extraordinarily expressive. A national upset occurred in 1960 when an enraptured university student embraced the statue in a fit of passion and inadvertently snapped off its little finger.

The temple is open from 9 am to 5 pm (4.30 pm from December to the end of February), and admission costs ¥600. Take bus No 11 from Keihan Sanjō station, get off at the Ukyō-ku Sogō-chōsha-mae stop and walk north. The temple is also close to Uzumasa station on the Keifuku Arashiyama line.

Hozu-gawa River Trip

The Hozu-gawa River ride (Map 12) is a great way to enjoy the beauty of Kyoto's western mountains without any strain on the legs. With long bamboo poles, boatmen steer flat-bottom boats down the Hozu-gawa from Kameoka (Map 1), in through steep forested mountain canyons before arriving at Arashiyama. Between 10 March and 30 November, there are seven trips (from 9 am to 3.30 pm) daily. During winter, the number of trips is reduced to four a day and the boats

are heated. There are no boat trips from 29 December to 4 January.

The ride lasts two hours and covers 16km through occasional sections of choppy water – a scenic jaunt with minimal danger. The scenery is especially breathtaking during cherry blossom season in April and maple foliage season *(momiji)* in autumn.

The price is ¥3900 per person. The boats depart from a dock which is eight minutes walk from Kameoka station. Kameoka is accessible by rail from Kyoto station or Nijō station on the JR San-in Main (Sagano) line. The TIC provides an English leaflet and timetable for rail connections. The fare from Kyoto to Kameoka is ¥400 one way by regular train (don't spend the extra for the express, as it makes little difference in travel time). A more colourful means of reaching Kameoka is by the nostalgic (and touristic) Romantic Train Sagano (¥600), but this entails getting out to western Kyoto to board. The tracks for the Romantic Train hug the river bank from Torokko Saga station, just beside JR Saga Arashiyama station, or from Torokko Arashiyama station, a short walk north of Ōkōchi-sansō Villa.

Takao District

This is a secluded district tucked far away in the north-western part of Kyoto. It is famed for autumn foliage and the temples of Jingo-ji, Saimyō-ji and Kōzan-ji.

Jingo-ji (Map 2) is the best of the three. This mountain temple sits at the top of a long flight of stairs which stretch from the Kiyotaki-gawa River to the temple's main gate. The kondō is the most impressive of the temple's structures, located roughly in the middle of the grounds at the top of another flight of stairs. After visiting the kondō, head in the opposite direction along a wooded path to an open area overlooking the valley. Don't be surprised if you see people tossing small disks over the railing into the chasm below. These are *kawarakenage*, light clay disks which people throw in order to rid themselves of their bad karma. Be careful: it's addictive, and at ¥100 for two it can get expensive (you can buy the disks at a nearby stall). The trick is to flick the disks very gently, convex side up, like a Frisbee. When you get it right, they sail all the way down the valley – taking all that bad karma with them (and don't worry, they're biodegradable).

To reach Jingo-ji, take bus No 8 from Keihan Sanjō station to the last stop, Takao, allowing one hour for the ride. The hourly JR bus also takes about an hour to reach the Takao stop from Kyoto station. The other two temples are within easy walking distance of the bus stop, **Saimyō-ji** (Map 2)

Arashiyama/Sagano Walking Tour
Time: full day
Distance: about 3km
Major Sights: Temples, shrines, gardens, bamboo forests (all sights are on Map 12)

Once you've arrived in Arashiyama and had a look at the sights on the south side of the Togetsu-kyō Bridge, cross to the north side of the bridge and begin your walk here.

See the famed Zen garden at **Tenryū-ji Temple** and exit the temple from the north side. After a quick look at **Nonomiya-jinja Shrine** and its black torii (alluded to in *The Tale of Genji*), head to the gardens at **Ōkōchi-sansō Villa**, a 10 minute walk through bamboo groves west of Tenryū-ji.

If you continue north from Ōkōchi-sansō, the narrow road soon passes stone steps on your left leading up to the pleasant grounds of **Jōjakkō-ji Temple**. A few minutes further brings you to **Rakushisha**, a charming poet's hut; continuing north-west from here you'll reach **Nison-in Temple**, in an attractive setting on the wooded hillside.

Five minutes from Nison-in, **Giō-ji** and **Takiguchi-dera** are two other secluded temples appearing in *The Tale of Genji*. Returning to the main path, climb the slope up to **Adashino Nembutsu-ji Temple** to see the thousands of stone Buddhas in the grounds. From here it is a short climb past a few of Sagano's remaining thatched-roof houses to the huge orange **Torii-moto**.

From here, tired legs can catch a Kyoto bus (No 72) from the Toriimoto bus stop back to Arashiyama (it continues to Kyoto station). If you're still ready for more temples, head back down the slope and take your first left toward **Seiryō-ji** and **Daikaku-ji**; from here take Kyoto bus No 71 or 81, or city bus No 28, back to Kyoto station from the Daikakuji bus stop. ■

---

being the better of the two (five minutes north of Jingo-ji). To get to the temple, first walk down to the river then look for the steps on the other side.

Arashiyama-Sagano District

Tucked into the western hills of Kyoto, Arashiyama and Sagano (Map 12) are both worth visiting if you feel like strolling in pleasant natural surroundings and visiting temples tucked inside bamboo groves. The area makes a nice full-day excursion and is good for an overnight in a traditional inn. There is also good hiking nearby and bicycle rental shops (¥600 for three hours, ¥1000 for the day) near the stations, but it's more enjoyable to cover the relatively short distances between sights on foot.

Note that this area is wildly popular with Japanese tourists and can be packed, particularly in the cherry blossom and maple leaf seasons. To avoid the crowds, go early on a weekday or head to some of the more offbeat spots. Upon arrival here, you may wonder why the Japanese make such a fuss about this place; it's not very beautiful around the stations, particularly with all the tacky shops and vending machines nearby. The best advice is to head north immediately to the quieter regions of Sagano (see the Arashiyama/Sagano Walking Tour boxed text on this page for directions on heading north).

Bus No 28 links Kyoto station with Arashiyama. Bus No 11 connects Keihan Sanjō station with Arashiyama. The best rail connection is the ride from Shijō-Ōmiya station on the Keifuku-Arashiyama line to Arashiyama station (20 minutes). You can also take the JR San-in Main (Sagano) line from Kyoto station or Nijō station and get off at JR Saga Arashiyama station (be careful to take the local train, as the express does not stop in Arashiyama). Arashiyama is the disembarking point for the Hozu-gawa River ride (see the previous section), hands-down the most interesting way to reach the area.

Togetsu-kyō Bridge Togetsu-kyō (Map 12) is the dominant landmark in Arashiyama and just a few minutes on foot from either the

Kiyotaki-gawa River Hike

Time: about two hours
Distance: about 5km
Major Sights: Jingo-ji Temple, Kiyotaki-gawa River, Hozu-gawa River (all sights are on Map 2)

This is one of the most beautiful hikes in the Kyoto area, especially in autumn, when the maples set the hills ablaze with colour. Start from Jingo-ji Temple (see the Takao District section in this chapter for transport details). The trail begins at the bottom of the steps leading up to the temple and follows the Kiyotaki-gawa south (downstream). After about an hour of riverside walking you'll get to the small hamlet of **Kiyotaki**, with its quaint riverside inns and restaurants. Just before the town, there is a trail junction which can be confusing; the trail leaves the riverside for a while and comes to a junction on a hillside. At this spot, head uphill back toward the river, not further into the woods. After passing through the town, cross a bridge and continue downstream. The trail continues to hug the river and passes some excellent, crystal-clear swimming holes.

After another 30 minutes or so you'll come up to a road. Turn right, walk through the tunnel and continue along this road for another 30 minutes to reach JR Hozukyō station. Below the bridge the riverside is a popular summer picnic and swimming spot – bring a bathing suit and picnic basket and join the fun. From Hozukyō station you can catch a local train back to Kyoto (20 minutes, ¥240). ∎

Keifuku line or Hankyū line Arashiyama stations. The original crossing first existed about 100m upriver from the present bridge, first constructed in 1606. On 13 April *jūsan-mairi*, an important rite of passage for local children aged 13, takes place here. Boys and girls (many in kimono), after paying respects at Hōrin-ji Temple and receiving a blessing for wisdom, cross the bridge under strict parental order not to look back toward the temple until they've reached the northern side of the bridge. Not heeding this instruction is believed to bring bad luck for life!

From July to mid-September, this is a good spot to watch *ukai* (cormorant fishing) in the evening. If you want to get close to the action, you can pay ¥1700 to join a passenger boat. The TIC can provide a leaflet and further

details (see also the Cormorant Fishing boxed text in this chapter).

Hōrin-ji Temple This temple (Map 12) was originally founded in 713 by the priest Gyōki. There are 80 steps up the hondō, where in 829 Dōshō, a disciple of maverick monk Kūkai, installed a large Jizō statue and named the temple Hōrin-ji. Hōrin-ji is renowned for the jūsan-mairi ceremony. The temple is close to the southern end of Togetsu-kyō. Admission is free.

Iwatayama Monkey Park Home to some 200 Japanese monkeys of all sizes and ages, this nature park (Map 12) is a joy. Though it is common to spot wild monkeys in the nearby mountains, here you can encounter them at a sensationally close distance and enjoy watching the playful creatures frolic about. It makes for an excellent photo opportunity, not only of the monkeys but of the panoramic view over Kyoto. The primate population here has been closely watched and studied by scientists and animal advocates since the 1950s. Refreshingly, it is the animals who are free to roam while the humans who feed them are caged in an office!

There are a few rules to remember:

Do not feed the monkeys
    (as the sign reads, 'Please don't show them any food!').
Do not touch the monkeys
    (unless you've had a very potent rabies shot lately).
Do not stare into their eyes
    (remember *Planet of the Apes*?).

You enter the park near the south side of Togetsu-kyō, through the orange torii of Ichitani-jinja Shrine. Reaching the monkeys involves a moderate hike uphill. The park is open daily from 9 am to 5 pm (15 March to 15 November), and closes at 4 pm in winter. Adult entry is ¥500 (young children ¥150).

Daihikaku Senkō-ji Temple A short walk up the south bank of the river, Daihikaku-

Cormorant Fishing

Ukai (cormorant fishing) is mentioned in Japanese historical documents as early as the 8th century. It is still common in Gifu and Kyoto prefectures, although it's largely a tourist attraction these days. The cormorants and the crew splash about; the passengers have a fun time drinking and eating.

The season lasts from May to September. The best times for fishing are moonless nights when the fish are more easily attracted to the glare of a fire in a metal basket suspended from the bow of the boat. Fishing trips are cancelled during and after heavy rain.

The cormorants, up to a dozen, sit on the boat attached to long leashes. In the water, a small metal ring at the base of their necks stops them from guzzling down their catch. After filling their gullets with fish, they are hauled on board and made to disgorge the contents. Each boat usually has a crew of four to handle the birds, the boat and the fire.

On moonless nights cormorant fishing *(ukai)* is conducted in the Arashiyama area.

The cormorant catch is usually *ayu*, a type of river trout much prized by the Japanese. A nifty cormorant can catch several dozen fish in a night. After completing their night's work, the cormorants are loaded into bamboo baskets in strictly observed order of seniority – cormorants are very conscious of social ranking and will protest if this is not respected (life expectancy for a cormorant is between 15 and 20 years, so they probably do have a point). ■

Senkō-ji (Map 12) is a seldom visited and very pleasant hillside temple with a fine view over Kyoto. It was originally constructed from 1596 to 1615 and was dedicated to the hundreds of people who died working to widen the Ōi-gawa River in the 17th century. Daihi means compassion or sympathy, and the temple name refers to 'pulling out the pain'. The temple enshrines an impressive statue of the monk Raidō (which made a recent trip to be exhibited in Texas) – check out the lifelike eyes. It's open from 9 am to 5 pm, and admission costs ¥400.

Tenryū-ji Temple Tenryū-ji (Map 12) is one of the major temples of the Rinzai school. It was built in 1339 on the former site of Emperor Go-Daigo's villa after a priest had dreamt of a dragon rising from the nearby river. The dream was interpreted as a sign that the emperor's spirit was uneasy, and the temple was constructed as appeasement – hence the name *tenryū* (heavenly dragon). The present buildings date from 1900, but the main attraction is the 14th century Zen garden.

Tenryū-ji is a popular place to sample Zen vegetarian cuisine *(shōjin ryōri)* – see the Western Kyoto section in the Places to Eat chapter. Admission costs ¥500, and it's open from 8.30 am to 5.30 pm (April to October), to 5 pm the rest of the year.

Ōkōchi-sansō Villa This is the lavish home (Map 12) of Ōkōchi Denjirō, a famous actor in samurai films. The extensive gardens allow fine views over the city and are open to visitors. The villa is open daily from 9 am to 5 pm; admission costs a hefty ¥900 (including tea and cake).

Jōjakkō-ji Temple This temple (Map 12) sits atop a moss-covered knoll, and is famed for its brilliant maples and thatched-roof Niō-mon Gate. The hondō was constructed in the 16th century from wood brought from Fushimi-jō. It is open from 9 am to 5 pm, and admission costs ¥200.

Rakushisha Rakushisha (Map 12) was the hut of Mukai Kyorai, the best known disciple of illustrious haiku poet Bashō. Literally, the house of fallen persimmons, legend holds that Kyorai dubbed the house Rakushisha after waking one morning after a storm to find the persimmons (he had planned to sell) from the garden's trees scattered on the ground.

An informative English leaflet is provided. It is open from 9 am to 5 pm, and the modest ¥150 entry fee makes it worth taking a look.

Nison-in Temple This temple is a popular spot with maple-watchers. Nison-in (Map 12) was originally built in the 9th century by Emperor Saga. It houses two important Kamakura-era Buddha statues side by side (Shaka on the right and Amida on the left). The temple features lacquered 'nightingale' floors. It is open from 9 am to 4 pm; entry costs ¥500.

Giō-ji Temple This quiet temple (Map 12) was named for the Heian-era *shirabyōshi* (traditional dancer) Giō. Giō, aged 21, committed herself here as a nun after her romance with Taira-no-Kiyomori, the mighty commander of the Heike clan. She was usurped by a fellow entertainer Hotoke Gozen (who later deserted Kiyomori to join Giō at the temple). Enshrined in the main hall are five wooden statues: these are Giō, Hotoke Gozen, Kiyomori, and Giō's mother and sister (who were also nuns at the temple).

It's open from 9 am to 5 pm; entry costs ¥300.

Takiguchi-dera Temple The history of this temple (Map 12) reads like a *Romeo and Juliet* saga. Takiguchi-dera was founded by Heian-era nobleman Takiguchi Nyūdō, who entered the priesthood after being forbidden by his father to marry his peasant consort Yokobue. One day Yokobue came to the temple with her flute to serenade Takiguchi, but was again refused by him; she wrote a farewell love sonnet on a stone (in her own blood) before throwing herself into the river to perish. The stone remains at the temple.

The temple is open from 9 am to 5 pm; entry costs ¥300.

Adashino Nembutsu-ji Temple This rather unusual temple (Map 12) is where the aban-

doned bones of paupers and destitutes without next of kin were gathered. More than 8000 stone images are crammed into the temple grounds, dedicated to the repose of their spirits. These thousands of abandoned souls are remembered each year with candles here in the Sentō Kuyō ceremony held on the evenings of 23 and 24 August. The temple is open from 9 am to 4.30 pm; admission is ¥500.

Seiryō-ji Temple This temple (Map 12) was established in 986 on the site of Seika-kan, the lavish villa of Genji family military commander Minamoto-no-Tōru (the inspiration for the main character in the *The Tale of Genji*). The Shaka-dō Hall houses a rare, 10th century Chinese Buddha statue carved from cherry wood. This life-size sculpture can be viewed by request (and with a donation of ¥1000, which includes a private chant and drumming by a resident monk).

Seiryō-ji is open from 9 am to 4 pm, and admission costs ¥300.

Daikaku-ji Temple Daikaku-ji (Map 12) is 25 minutes walk north-east of Nison-in. It was built in the 9th century as a palace for Emperor Saga, who converted it into a temple. The present buildings date from the 16th century, but are still palatial in style with some impressive paintings. The large Osawa-no-ike Pond was once used by the emperor for boating and is a popular spot for viewing the harvest moon.

The temple is open from 9 am to 5 pm, and admission costs ¥500. Close to the temple entrance are separate terminals for Kyoto-shi (Kyoto City) buses (No 28 goes to Kyoto station) and Kyoto buses (No 71 goes to Kyoto station and No 61 to Keihan Sanjō station).

SOUTH-WESTERN KYOTO
Katsura Rikyū Imperial Villa
This villa (Map 5) is considered one of the finest examples of Japanese architecture. It was built in 1624 for the emperor's brother, Prince Toshihito. Every conceivable detail of the villa, the teahouses, the large pond with

islets and the surrounding garden has been given meticulous attention.

Tours (in Japanese) start at 10 and 11 am, and 2 and 3 pm, and last about 40 minutes. You should be there 20 minutes beforehand. An explanatory video is shown in the waiting room and a leaflet is provided in English. Admission is free, but you *must* make reservations through the Imperial Household Agency (see the Kyoto Imperial Palace section earlier in this chapter for details) and often several weeks in advance. Visitors must be over 20 years of age. At the time this book went to press, photography was not allowed on the grounds, but this may change with time.

To get to the villa from Kyoto station, take bus No 33 and get off at the Katsura Rikyū-mae stop, which is a five minute walk from the villa. The easiest access from the city centre is to take a Hankyū Kyoto line train from Hankyū Kawaramachi station to Hankyū Katsura station, which is a 15 minute walk from the villa.

Saihō-ji Temple

The main attraction at this temple (Map 3) is the heart-shaped garden, designed in 1339 by Musō Kokushi. The garden is famous for its luxuriant mossy growth – hence the temple's other name, 'Koke-dera' (Moss Temple). Visiting the temple is recommended only if you have time and patience to follow the reservation rules. If you don't, visit nearby Jizō-in Temple to get a taste of the atmosphere of Saihō-ji without the expense or fuss.

Reservations Reservations are the only way you can visit. This is to avoid the overwhelming crowds which used to swamp the place (and consequently pulverise the moss) when reservations were not required.

Send a postcard at least one week before the date you require and include details of your name, number of visitors, address in Japan, occupation, age (you must be over 18) and desired date (a choice of alternative dates is preferred). The address is Saihō-ji Temple, 56 Kamigaya-chō, Matsuo, Nishikyō-ku,

Kyoto. Enclose a prestamped postcard for a reply to your Japanese address. You might find it convenient to buy an *ōfuku-hagaki* (send and return postcard set) at any post office.

You should arrive at the time and on the date supplied by the temple office. After paying your ¥3000 'donation', you spend up to 90 minutes copying or chanting sutras, or doing Zen meditation, before finally being guided around the garden for 90 minutes.

Take city bus No 28 from Kyoto station to the Matsuo-taisha-mae stop and walk 15 minutes south-west, or from Keihan Sanjō station, take Kyoto bus No 63 to Koke-dera (last stop) and walk two minutes.

Matsuo Taisha Shrine

Founded in 701, Matsuo Taisha (Map 3) is one of Kyoto's oldest shrines and enshrines the deity of water. Since the Muromachi period sake brewing families have worshipped the god (hence the large stacks of sake barrels). Pure spring water, designated 'one of the 100 best in Japan', spews from the mouth of the *kame-no-ido* (turtle well) statue here.

Admission to the lovely inner gardens costs ¥500. Take bus No 28 from Kyoto station to the Matsuo-taisha-mae stop.

Jizō-in Temple

This delightful little temple (Map 3) could be

MASON FLORENCE

Jizō, the protector of children and travellers, is often offered a hat or scarf in return.

called the 'poor man's Saihō-ji'. It's only a few minutes walk south of Saihō-ji in the same atmospheric bamboo groves. While the temple does not boast any spectacular buildings or treasures, it has a nice moss garden and is almost completely ignored by tourists, making it a great place to sit and contemplate. Admission is ¥400. For directions see the earlier Saihō-ji Temple section (be careful not to mistake Jizō-in for the temple with the same name in the Takao area).

SOUTHERN KYOTO

The district to the south of Kyoto, *raku-nan*, is today mostly devoted to industry, most notably Fushimi's famed sake breweries. Its location on the Uji-gawa River made it a perfect location for sake production, as fresh, high-quality rice was readily available from the fields of neighbouring Shiga Prefecture and the final product could be easily loaded onto boats for export downriver to Osaka.

A large majority of the area has been swallowed up by highways and factories, but there are a number of places which make a pleasant half-day or day trip. Geographically separate from the centre of Kyoto, this region escaped many of the fires which have devastated Kyoto throughout its history, leaving several ancient structures intact.

Tōfuku-ji Temple and Fushimi-Inari Taisha Shrine are especially worth a visit, as is the Chinese-influenced Mampuku-ji Temple. To the south-east, Daigo-ji Temple is in rural surroundings and offers scope for some gentle hiking to complement the area's architectural splendours.

Tōfuku-ji Temple

Founded in 1236 by the priest Enni, Tōfuku-ji (Map 3) now belongs to the Rinzai school. Since this temple was intended to compare with Tōdai-ji and Kōfuku-ji temples in Nara, it was given a name combining characters each of these.

Despite the destruction of many of the buildings by fire, this is still considered one of the five main Zen temples in Kyoto. The huge San-mon Gate is the oldest Zen main

gate in Japan. Also old are the *tōsu* (lavatory) and *yokushitsu* (bathroom), dating from the 14th century. The present complex includes 24 subtemples; at one time there were 53.

The hōjō was reconstructed in 1890. The gardens, laid out in 1938, are worth a visit. As you approach the northern gardens, you cross a stream over Tsūten-kyō (Bridge to Heaven), which is a pleasant, leafy spot – the foliage is renowned for its autumn colour. The northern garden has stones and moss neatly arranged in a chequerboard pattern.

The nearby **Reiun-in Subtemple** receives few visitors to its attractive garden.

Admission costs ¥300 for the main temple; admission to the subtemples is about the same. Opening hours are from 9 am to 4 pm. English leaflets are provided.

To reach Tōfuku-ji by train, you can either take a JR train on the Nara line or a train from Keihan Sanjō station on the Keihan main line. Get off at Tōfukuji station and walk east up the hill toward the mountains. Bus No 208 also runs from Kyoto station via Tōfuku-ji. Get off at the Tōfuku-ji-mae stop.

Fushimi-Inari Taisha Shrine

This intriguing shrine (Map 3) was dedicated to the gods of rice and sake by the Hata family in the 8th century. As the role of agriculture diminished, deities were enrolled to ensure prosperity in business. Nowadays, the shrine is one of Japan's most popular, and is the head shrine for some 40,000 Inari shrines scattered the length and breadth of the country.

The entire complex, consisting of five shrines, sprawls across the wooded slopes of Mt Inari. A pathway wanders 4km up the mountain and is lined with hundreds of red torii. There are also dozens of stone foxes. The fox is considered the messenger of Inari, the god of cereals, and the stone foxes, too, are often referred to as Inari. On an incidental note, the Japanese traditionally see the fox as a sacred, somewhat mysterious figure capable of 'possessing' humans – the favoured point of entry is under the fingernails. The key often seen in the fox's mouth is for the rice granary.

The walk around the upper precincts of the shrine is a pleasant day hike. It also makes for a very eerie stroll in the late afternoon and early evening, when the various graveyards and miniature shrines along the path take on a mysterious air. It's best to go with a friend at this time.

On 1 April, there is a festival at 11 am which features displays of flower arranging. On 8 April, there's a Sangyō-sai festival with offerings and dances to ensure prosperity for national industry. During the first few days in January, thousands of festive believers pray at the shrine.

Local delicacies sold on the approach streets include barbecued sparrow and *inari-sushi*, which is fried tofu wrapped around sweetened sushi – commonly believed to be the favourite food of the fox.

To get to the shrine from Kyoto station, take a JR Nara line train to Inari station. From Sanjō station on the Keihan main line, get off at Fushimi-Inari station. There is no admission charge for the shrine.

Daigo-ji Temple

Daigo-ji (Map 2) was founded in 874 by the priest Shobo who gave it the name of Daigo (which means the ultimate essence of milk). This refers to the five periods of Buddha's teaching, which were often compared to the five forms of milk prepared in India – the highest form is called 'daigo' in Japanese.

The temple was expanded into a vast complex on two levels, Shimo Daigo (lower) and Kami Daigo (upper). During the 15th century, those buildings on the lower level were destroyed, with the sole exception of the five storey pagoda. Built in 951, this pagoda is lovingly pointed out as the oldest of its kind in Japan and the oldest existing building in Kyoto.

In the late 16th century, Hideyoshi took a fancy to Daigo-ji and ordered extensive rebuilding. It is now one of the main temples of the Shingon school. To explore Daigo-ji thoroughly and at a leisurely pace, mixing hiking with temple viewing, you will need at least half a day.

To get there, take bus Higashi 9 and get off at the Daigo-Sampo-in-mae stop.

Sampō-in Temple

This was founded as a subtemple (Map 2) in 1115, but received a total revamp under Hideyoshi's orders in 1598. It is now a fine example of the amazing opulence of that period. The Kanō paintings and the garden are special features.

The garden is jam-packed with about 800 stones – the Japanese mania for stones goes back a long way. The most famous stone here is Fujito-no-ishi, which is linked to deception, death and a fabulous price that was spurned; it's even the subject of a nō play, *Fujito*. Admission to Sampō-in costs ¥500. It's open from 9 am to 5 pm (March to October) and closes one hour earlier the rest of the year.

Hōju-in Treasure House

This (Map 2) is close to Sampō-in, but is only open to the public from 1 April to 25 May and 1 October to 25 November. Despite the steep admission fee of ¥700, it really should not be missed if you happen to be there at the right time. The display of sculptures, scrolls, screens, miniature shrines and calligraphy is superb.

Climb to Mt Daigo-yama

From Sampō-in, walk up the large avenue of cherry trees, through Niō-mon Gate and past the pagoda. From there you can continue for a pleasant climb through the upper part of Mt Daigo-yama (Map 2), browsing through temples and shrines on the way. Allow 50 minutes to reach the top.

Mampuku-ji Temple

Mampuku-ji (Map 2) was established as a Zen temple in 1661 by the Chinese priest Ingen. It is a rare example in Japan of a Zen temple built in the pure Chinese style of the Ming dynasty. The temple follows the Ōbaku school, which is linked to the mainstream Rinzai school but incorporates a wide range of esoteric Buddhist practices.

Admission costs ¥400, and it's open from 9 am to 4.30 pm. The temple is a short walk from the two railway stations (Nara line and

Keihan Uji line) at Ōbaku (Map 2) – about 30 minutes by rail from Kyoto.

Gekkeikan Sake Okura Museum

The town of Fushimi (Map 3) just south of Kyoto is home to 37 sake breweries, the largest of which is Gekkeikan, the world's leading producer of sake. Although most of the sake is now made in a modern facility in Osaka, a limited amount of handmade sake is still made in a Meiji-era *kura* (warehouse) here in Fushimi.

This is a worthwhile journey; the museum here houses a collection of artefacts and memorabilia tracing the 350 year history of Gekkeikan and the sake brewing process. Giant murals depicting traditional methods of brewing adorn the walls and there is the chance to taste (and of course buy) some of the local brew. After you see the museum, take a walk around the pleasant canal behind the photogenic buildings.

The brewery museum is open from 9.30 am to 4.30 pm, closed Monday. Admission is ¥300. If you are travelling with a tour group larger than 20 people and call two weeks in advance (☎ 623-2001), you can arrange a guided English tour of the brewery. Otherwise, ask at the TIC about joining a tour given in Japanese. To get there, you need to take a Keihan line local train to Fushimi Momoyama station and walk five minutes south-west.

Kizakura Kappa Country

A short walk from its competitor Gekkeikan, Kizakura (Map 3) is another sake brewery worth a look while you're in the neighbourhood. The vast complex houses both sake and beer breweries, courtyard gardens and a small gallery dedicated to the mythical (and sneaky) creature, Kappa. The restaurant/bar is an appealing option for a bite to eat or a freshly brewed ale (see the Southern Kyoto section in the Places to Eat chapter).

Teradaya Inn & Museum

Famed as the inn of choice for rebel samurai Sakamoto Ryōma (1834-67), today Teradaya (Map 3) functions as a museum by day and a ryokan by night (see the Southern Kyoto section in the Places to Stay chapter). Fans of Ryōma faithfully make the pilgrimage here to see the room where he slept.

MASON FLORENCE

The Gekkeikan brewery south of Kyoto is the world's foremost producer of sake.

THINGS TO SEE & DO

It's open daily from 10 am to 4 pm; admission costs ¥400.

Fushimi Momoyama-jō Castle

Toyotomi Hideyoshi's Fushimi-jō (Map 3) was completely destroyed during the Sekigahara war in 1600, then reconstructed by Tokugawa Ieyasu, but by 1623 was abandoned. The present buildings are all modern replicas from the 1960s, and the air of the castle has given way to Disney-envy. Unless you are travelling with kids and fancy visiting the on-site Castle Land (Kasuru-rando) amusement park, you can safely give this place a miss. It is open daily from 9.30 am to 5 pm. Admission costs ¥800.

If you want to visit a respectable castle, make the day trip to Himeji or Hikone (see the Excursions chapter).

UJI

Uji (Map 2) is a small city south of Kyoto. Historically rich in Heian-period culture, its main claims to fame are Byōdō-in and Ujigami-jinja Shrine (both UNESCO World Cultural Heritage Sites) and tea cultivation. The Uji-bashi Bridge, originally all wood and the oldest of its kind in Japan (it is now constructed of concrete and wood), has been the scene of many bitter clashes in previous centuries, though traffic jams seem to dominate nowadays.

Between 17 June and 31 August, ukai trips are organised in the evening around 7 pm on the river near Byōdō-in. Prices start at ¥1800 per person. The TIC has a leaflet with up-to-date information on booking. For more details on ukai, see the Cormorant Fishing boxed text in the Arashiyama-Sagano District section earlier.

Uji can be reached by rail in about 40 minutes from Kyoto on the Keihan Uji or JR Nara lines.

Byōdō-in Temple

This temple (Map 2) was converted from a Fujiwara villa into a Buddhist temple in 1052. The Phoenix Hall (Hōō-dō), more properly known as the Amida-dō, was built in 1053 and is the only original building

remaining. The phoenix was a popular mythical bird in China and was revered by the Japanese as a protector of Buddha. The architecture of the building resembles the shape of the bird, and there are two bronze phoenixes perched opposite each other on the roof. The building was originally intended to represent Amida's heavenly palace in the Pure Land. This building is one of the few extant examples of Heian-period architecture, and its graceful lines make you wish that far more had survived the wars and fires which plagued Kyoto's past.

Inside the hall is the famous statue of Amida and 52 Bosatsu (Bodhisattvas) dating from the 11th century and attributed to the priest-sculptor, Jōchō.

The temple, complete with its reflection in a pond, is a major attraction in Japan and draws huge crowds. For a preview without the masses, take a look at the 10 yen coin. Admission costs ¥400, and it's open from 8.30 am to 5 pm (March to November) and from 9 am to 4 pm the rest of the year. Leaflets in English are provided.

Nearby, **Hōmotsukan Treasure House** contains the original temple bell and door paintings, and the original phoenix roof adornments. Admission costs ¥300. It is only open from 1 April to 31 May and from 15 September to 23 November. Opening hours are from 9 am to 4 pm; allow about an hour to wander through the grounds. A brief leaflet is supplied in English.

The approach street to the complex is lined with souvenir shops, many of which roast local tea outside. A small packet of the tea is popular as a souvenir or gift.

Uji Tea

Just beside the TIC, on the river bank behind Byōdō-in, is the delightful **Taihō-an Teahouse** (Map 2). From 10 am to 4 pm daily the friendly staff conduct a 30 minute tea ceremony (unless you've got knee trouble, ask for the tatami room). Casual dress is fine here and no reservations are necessary. Buy tickets (¥500) at the TIC next door. Taihō-an is closed from 21 December to 14 January.

Another worthwhile stop for a taste of

Uji's famed green tea is **Tsūen**. Japan's oldest surviving tea shop, it has been in the Tsūen family for more than 830 years. The present building, near Uji-bashi, dates from 1672 and is full of interesting antiques. You can try fresh matcha here for ¥530 including a sweet. It's open daily from 9 am to 5 pm.

Ujigami-jinja Shrine

Ujigami-jinja (Map 2) holds the distinction of being Japan's oldest shrine (and the least visited of Kyoto's 17 UNESCO World Heritage Sites). According to ancient records, Uji-no-waki-Iratsuko, a 5th century prince, tragically sacrificed his own life to conclude the matter of whether he or his brother would succeed the imperial throne; needless to say his brother, Emperor Nintoku, won the dispute. The main building was dedicated to the twosome and their father Emperor Ōjin, and enshrines the tombs of the trio.

The shrine is across the river from Byōdō-in and a short walk uphill. It's open from 9 am to 4.30 pm and entry costs ¥100.

ACTIVITIES

There are an infinite number of things to do in Kyoto (besides visiting temples and shrines). In addition to shopping, hiking and people-watching, there are several places to get hands-on experience in traditional arts and crafts including tea ceremony, Japanese *washi* paper, textiles, ceramics and calligraphy.

Tea Ceremony

At Urasenke Chadō Research Center (Map 7; see the Northern Kyoto section for details), it is possible to view a 20 minute tea making procedure *(temae)* during the Urasenke Foundation's quarterly art exhibitions. Here you can sample a bowl of matcha and a sweet (included in the ¥800 cost to visit to the centre's gallery).

Another spot offering a casual bowl of tea is Kanō Shōju-an (Map 10), a pleasant teahouse near Eikan-dō. The cost is ¥1000 for tea and a sweet. It's open from 10 am to 4.30 pm, closed Wednesday (open daily during the high season in April and November).

You might also try the teahouses at the Miyako Hotel (Map 10), near Keage station on the Keihan Keishin line, open daily from 10 am to 7 pm (no reservations necessary), or Kyoto International Community House (Map 10; ☎ 752-3512), open Tuesday from 2 pm (call in the morning to reserve). The cost of one session is around ¥1000.

The Taihō-an Teahouse (Map 2) in Uji is possibly the cheapest place in the world to experience authentic tea ceremony (¥500). See the Uji section for details.

continued on page 147

The Great Outdoors

Two of Kyoto's greatest assets are its proximity to the mountains and the abundance of nature trails. In addition to the two excellent hikes listed in this chapter, there are endless possibilities; knowing where and how to go, and finding people to join you, however, can often prove harder than the hikes themselves. Luckily, there is a myriad of groups in the Kansai area which organise outdoor events. Check in *Kansai Time Out* for current listings, or contact the groups below.

Japan Environmental Exchange (JEE) plans fun monthly hikes in the Kyoto area (a ¥500 donation goes toward the group's activities); call Nakano Shigeru on ☎ 771-9764. The Kyoto Nature Classroom is another ecofriendly choice with intriguing educational nature outings once a month (¥500 fee); call Mr Itakura (☎ 080-467-8723).

The Kansai Ramblers runs hikes throughout the Kinki region on the second Sunday of each month; call Mr Fukunishi (☎ 0729-88-0600). The International Outdoor Club (IOC) of Kansai organises hiking, cycling, running and weekend trips (see *Kansai Time Out* for contacts). Serious cyclists can join the all-day Sunday road rides organised by the Takenaka bike shop (☎ 256-4863).

For avid rock climbers, the Kansai Climbers Club keeps a database of climbers in the area to hook up with or learn about good routes in the region (email: vetrimatt@aol.com).

Finally, for beer-guzzling runners, the Kyoto Hash House Harriers has regular runs in Kyoto; call Mitch (☎ 0775-44-4551). ∎

THE WAY OF TEA

MASON FLORENCE

Chadō, the way of tea (also called tea ceremony or *chanoyu* – literally, hot water for tea), is one of Japan's pre-eminent traditional arts; it is, however, far more than a simple tea party. Chadō's roots go back over 1000 years, and in no place in the world has the ritual surrounding the beverage reached such artistic, cultural and spiritual levels as it has in Japan.

The Japanese have long been known to assimilate ideas from other countries, and perhaps nothing demonstrates this more than tea, which has evolved from its original use as a medicinal drink. Though difficult for many (including the Japanese) to fully comprehend, the preparation and serving ritual are as important as drinking the tea itself. The associated art, architecture, gardens and implements are integral to the ceremony. Tea ceremony also requires a deep spiritual discipline and strict etiquette.

Tea is alive and well in Japan today, especially in Kyoto, a major centre of tea production and consumption. Hundreds of Japanese and overseas visitors come to Kyoto every year to study the way of tea. For these, tea perhaps represents a chance to sneak away from the hustle and bustle of modern Japan into the other-worldly atmosphere of the tearoom.

History of Tea in Japan

Below: Sen no Rikyū (1522-91), Japan's greatest tea master, perfected tea ceremony into a pure art form. He had a lasting influence on all aspects of chadō, including its architecture, gardens and utensils. He was also the tea master of shōguns Oda Nobunaga and Toyotomi Hideyoshi.

Tea has been used in Japan since the 8th century. During the Nara period its medicinal properties were used by meditating Buddhist monks to promote alertness. At the time, however, tea was scarce, and a luxury even for the nobility. Powdered green tea *(matcha)* was first introduced to Japan from China in the 12th century by visiting Japanese monks who brought back with them a knowledge of Zen Buddhism, together with tea seeds. Thus, early on, tea became intricately linked to the principles and spirit of Zen.

By the 13th century, tea had begun to be actively harvested in Japan, most notably at Uji, south of Kyoto, which today remains one of the country's most famous tea making regions. Tea gradually gained in popularity, especially among the warriors who drank it to help them in their training. By the 14th century, tea had developed into a highly elaborate and expensive pursuit of the aristocracy.

The turning point for tea ceremony took place in the 16th century with Sen no Rikyū (1522-91). Regarded as Japan's greatest tea master, he turned tea ceremony into an unpretentious art. For the first time, using simple implements made from such things as bamboo that echoed the irregularities of nature, tea ceremony was within reach of the general populace.

The grandson of Sen no Rikyū divided the family estate among his three sons, who formed the main Senke (*ke* means family) schools: Ura, Omote and Mushakōji. All are based in Kyoto, the largest being Urasenke, headed by Sen no Soshitsu, its 15th grand tea master and a direct descendent of Sen no Rikyū. Sen no Soshitsu has been largely responsible for popularising tea ceremony around the world.

Philosophy of Tea Ceremony

For the Japanese, tea ceremony is not an everyday event but a very special and occasional encounter. The preparation and drinking of tea is conducted in pursuit of *wabi*, to achieve a simple and pure state of mind (see the Wabi-Sabi boxed text in the Facts about Kyoto chapter). The encounter between guest and host in tea ceremony is all-important. It requires the participants to be in the moment and at full concentration. The exact encounter can never be repeated, hence the saying, *ichi-go-ichi-e* (roughly, one chance in a lifetime). This can be likened to the Latin phrase, *carpe diem*, meaning seize the day.

Besides its spiritual aspects, tea ceremony is also a tangible sensory experience. It allows the guest to harmonise with the natural surroundings and other guests, to hear the delicate sounds of the whisk, to feel the uneven touch of the bowl and so on. Many novices find the proceedings fatiguing and connoisseurs maintain that full appreciation takes years of training and reflection.

Overview of Tea Ceremony

Every tea ceremony serves up a bowl of matcha, which is very healthy and high in vitamin C and caffeine. Matcha has a frothy texture, and the flavour depends greatly on the quality and freshness of the powder, and the temperature and acidity of the water. There are two types of matcha: a light batch called *usucha* (or thin tea), which the host prepares in a separate bowl for each guest, and *koicha* (or thick tea), which the guests share from the same bowl.

One foreign visitor likened the bitter flavour of matcha to 'fresh cut grass'. For most, it is an acquired taste. However, it is not for the flavour that most attend tea ceremony, but for the rituals of the ceremony itself.

Before tea ceremony begins everything must be prepared by the host.

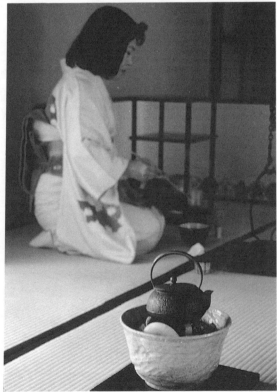

Left: Dressed in kimono, the host prepares tea for the guests. In the fore-ground a teapot is heated over a brazier.

MASON FLORENCE

MASON FLORENCE

Above: A selection of fresh wagashi (sweets), designed to off-set the strong, bitter tase of matcha.

This includes shading the windows to create the right lighting, decorating the alcove *(tokonoma)* with a hanging scroll *(kakejiku)* and flower arrangement, preparing the fire for the kettle and watering the outside path on which the guests will walk.

Though tea ceremony can involve many people meeting at a festival or temple, it typically includes five people or less gathering in an authentic tearoom. This tea gathering *(chaji)* usually lasts for about four hours, while the shorter, less formal version *(chakai)* can take under 30 minutes. During a chaji, the guests may also be served food *(cha-kaiseki)*. This elegant meal is light and takes the form of many small selections on a tray. The goodies include miso soup, rice, boiled and pickled vegetables, fish, seafood and sake. There is a specific order to how the food is served and eaten.

There are various styles of tea ceremony, from *ryūrei* (usually performed at small black-lacquered tables, with shoes on) to highly formalised events in exquisite tatami tearooms. Another significantly different convention is the Chinese-style *sencha*, which is practised at Mampuku-ji Temple in southeastern Kyoto.

Procedure of Tea Ceremony

Naturally, foreigners are not expected to display perfect tea manners and in fact most, Japanese (in particular the young) do not know all the rules. Still, it helps to know some general guidelines (the list is endless and varies from school to school). The following apply to a more formal setting.

In general, keep it clean, polite and simple. Arrive early and dress well. Most importantly, wear clean white socks (no bare feet); even if you find some *wabi-sabi* in the imperfect 'beauty' of a toe sticking out of a tear in your sock, it is likely your host will have a different interpretation. You should not wear any jewellery or perfume, as they interfere with the rustic ambience of the room.

After you enter the tearoom, sit quietly and formally with your lower legs tucked together under your thighs, a position known as *(seiza)*. The host will come out, greet the guests and begin preparing the tea. This starts by purifying the tea container *(natsume)* and tea scoop *(chashaku)* with a cloth.

Right: A display of cha-kaiseki, a light meal including miso soup, pickled vegetables and fish, which is presented at full tea ceremony. The food will be served and eaten in a particular order.

COURTESY OF TANKOSHA

While the tea is being prepared, guests can ask questions about objects in the tearoom, but bear in mind that silence is important for the atmosphere. Next the host will scoop powdered green tea into a ceramic bowl, add hot water, and finally the combination of tea and water is whisked into a thick froth.

Before being served tea, each guest is given sweets on paper. These can be freshly made or dried, and the design, shape and colour depend on the season. Before eating anything, always say 'o-saki ni' (literally, 'before you') to the person following you, with a slight bow to show humbleness and politeness.

When the host has finally finished purifying, scooping and whisking, the tea will be presented to the guest. This moment is considered the most important. The tea will be placed in front of you, and before drinking it you should say 'o-saki ni' again, and also say to the host 'otemae chōdai itashimasu' (literally, 'I humbly receive it'). Grasp the tea cup with your right hand and place it onto the palm of your left hand. Rotate the bowl clockwise to avoid drinking from the front. You can study the bowl and ask questions after returning it to the host.

Tea ceremony is not as complex or regimented as it sounds and you will not be ejected from the room if you forget to rotate the bowl or can't muster up the subtle yet audible slurp typically produced with the last sip. Tea ceremony is meant to be enjoyed, and much of the pleasure is in the ritual itself (something like enjoying 'nouvelle cuisine' at an elaborate table setting).

MASON FLORENCE

Above: The ro, a sunken hearth, is an essential part of winter tea ceremony (in summer, a brazier is more commonly used).

Teahouses & Gardens

The traditional setting for tea ceremony is a thatched teahouse *(chashitsu)* within a landscaped garden. These sparsely decorated wooden houses, or huts, are intentionally simple. Frequently the workmanship exceeds that of the best palaces and temples, and to build one today, with all the fine mounting, fixtures and cabinetwork, is extremely expensive.

Guests usually approach a teahouse by walking from a separate waiting

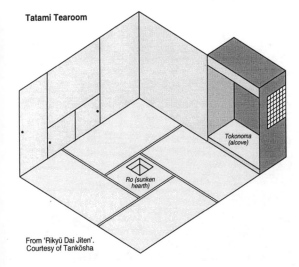

Tatami Tearoom

Tokonoma (alcove)

Ro (sunken hearth)

From 'Rikyū Dai Jiten'.
Courtesy of Tankōsha

room through the garden along a stone path *(roji)*. Along this path is a stone water basin *(tsukubai)* where guests can wash and purify their hands. Inside, rooms have walls made of wood and earth with paper windows. Rooms vary in size, though the traditional 4.5 tatami (straw mat) room is commonly considered best for chadō. The tearoom has specific areas for host and guest; the host's mat is where the utensils are placed and the tea is prepared *(temaeza)*. Some rooms contain a fire pit sunk into the floor for use in colder months.

Utensils

The various implements used are simple and handcrafted from natural materials, works of art in themselves. They include:

Mizusashi	–	jar of fresh cold water
Kama	–	metal kettle for boiling water and the stand on which it sits
Furo	–	brazier for summer; or *ro* (a sunken hearth) for winter
Kensui	–	metal pot reserved for waste water that is used to clean implements
Hishaku	–	bamboo ladle used to pour water
Natsume	–	lacquerware container for matcha powder
Chashaku	–	tea scoop
Chasen	–	bamboo whisk

Recommended Reading

There are countless books in English on chadō. The Urasenke Foundation publishes a variety of books as well as the English-language periodical *Chanoyu Quarterly – Tea & the Arts of Japan*.

The Tea Ceremony by father and son tea masters Tanaka Senō & Tanaka Sendō provides an exhaustive treatment of tea ceremony with photos and diagrams. A simple philosophical treatment of the subject is *The Book of Tea* by Okakura Kakuzō. Okakura (1862-1913) wrote the book in 1906 while living in the USA.

For information on where to experience or study tea ceremony in Kyoto, see the Activities section in this chapter.

Right: This teahouse at Kōdai-ji Temple was designed by Sen no Rikyū. Below: The utensils of tea ceremony are an art form in themselves. Pictured are ceramic drinking bowls (top); and a water pot, a tea scoop and bamboo whisk (bottom).

MASON FLORENCE

MASON FLORENCE

MASON FLORENCE

continued from page 141

Traditional Crafts

Bamboo Craft Takemata Nakagawa Takezai-ten (Map 10; ☎ 231-3968) offers hands-on bamboo craft workshops (minimum three people) where you can learn to weave a small *shikai-nami-kago* basket (¥3500; it takes about two hours). There are sessions from 9 am and 1 pm, except Sunday. Reservations are necessary at least a few days in advance.

It's about a five minute walk north of the Tōzai line Shiyakusho-mae subway station, on Gokomachi-dōri (between Nijō-dōri and Ebisugawa-dōri).

Braiding Kyoto's most famed braid maker, Adachi Kumihimo-kan (Map 7; ☎ 432-4111), has a gallery of fine items on display. Here you can weave your own braid on wooden hand looms. The cost is ¥5000 and it takes about two hours. Delicately woven *kyō-kumihimo* (Kyoto-style braidwork) was developed in the Heian period for fastening kimono, but gradually spread to other ornamental applications. Today the braid is again most commonly used as *obi-jime* (the tie for kimono sashes). Adachi is open from 9 am to 4 pm, closed on the second, third and fourth Saturday of the month, on Sunday and on holidays. Reservations are necessary.

Take the Karasuma line subway to Maru-tamachi station; from exit 2, walk north to the second traffic light and turn left onto Demizu-dōri (Adachi is on the south side of the street).

Calligraphy The Shōhō-in Temple (Map 9; ☎ 811-7768) is a great place to try your hand at copying Buddhist scriptures *(sutra)*. In the peaceful surroundings of the temple, you'll be provided with brushes and all the materials necessary to trace or create your own masterpiece. The cost is a modest ¥500 and it takes about two hours. Times are flexible, but reservations are required two days in advance. Temple lodging is also available at Shōhō-in (see the Shukubō section in the Places to Stay chapter).

Take bus No 6 or 206 to the Ōmiya-Matsubara stop and walk five minutes west or take the Hankyū Kyoto line to Ōmiya and walk eight minutes south-west. For English inquiries you can call Ms Katō on ☎ 030-947-4520.

Dolls In about four hours at Honke Katsura (Map 10; ☎ 221-6998) you can learn to paint the face on and assemble a handcrafted *kyō-ningyō* doll. The cost is ¥11,000. Honke Katsura is open from 10 am to 6 pm, closed the third Wednesday of the month. Reservations are necessary. It's on Takakura-dōri, south of Sanjō-dōri.

Ai-zome Dyeing In the Nishijin area, Aizen-Kōbō (Map 7; ☎ 441-0355) dyes beautiful indigo-blue *ai-zome* fabrics in a charming kyō-machiya. You can observe and try your hand at tie-dyeing a handkerchief (¥2000) or scarf (¥5000) in about an hour. It's open daily from 9.30 am to 5 pm; reservations should be made a few days in advance.

To get there, take the Karasuma line subway to Imadegawa-dōri and then catch a westbound bus (No 201, 203 or 59) to the Imadegawa-Ōmiya stop. The shop is a short walk south-west; look for the white *noren* curtain in front of the house.

Vegetable Dyeing In the rural Ōhara area, Ōhara Kōbō (Map 2; ☎ 744-3138) offers a chance to dye fabrics using vivid plant and vegetable dyes *(kusaki-zome)*. The time and cost depend on the item; choose from a handkerchief (¥500), scarf (¥3000) or plain woollen yarn (enough to knit one sweater; ¥8000); if you bring your own wool to dye, the cost is ¥5000. It's open from 10 am to 5 pm, closed Wednesday. Advance reservations are required, and the process takes from about two to four hours. See the Ōhara entry in the Ōhara & Kurama-Kibune section for transport details.

Yūzen Dyeing At the Kodai Yūzen-en Gallery (Map 9; ☎ 823-0500) there are facilities to experience Yūzen stencil-dyeing in about 40 minutes. You can choose from a various items to dye, such as a handkerchief (¥1050) or necktie (¥4200); there is also a ¥500 entry fee to the museum.

Offering similar activities is the Yūzen Cultural Hall, called Kyoto Yūzen Bunka Kaikan (Map 5; ☎ 311-0025). In about 20 minutes you can stencil-dye a hankie (¥450 to ¥800) or try hand painting (¥2100); there is also a ¥350 entry charge to the museum. The workshop closes for one hour at lunch (noon to 1 pm) and you must arrive by 4 pm to begin.

See the Central Kyoto section earlier in this chapter for the locations of these places.

Flower Arrangement Some schools provide instruction in English, and on the second and fourth Friday of each month the Kyoto International Community House (see the Cultural Demonstrations entry later in this chapter) holds free ikebana classes conducted by volunteers.

While there are no classes available for short-term visitors, the prominent Ikenobō Society of Floral Art (☎ 231-4922; fax 255-3568), adjacent to Rokkaku-dō Temple on Karasuma-dōri south of Oike-dōri (Map 9), can be helpful. The institution has a 500 year history in flower arranging, and students come from its branch schools around the world to further their studies. Periodically exhibits and events are held, and if you call in advance it may be possible to observe classes. There is also a museum (open from 9 am to 5 pm, Monday to Friday, admission free) on the 3rd floor of the building displaying items such as scrolls, flower containers and teaching manuscripts.

Another worthwhile contact is the Kyoto chapter of Ikebana International (☎ 722-7882), which can provide information and introductions to local teachers.

Handwoven Textiles Orinasu-kan (Map 7; ☎ 431-0020) in the Nishijin District offers traditional weaving workshops. The cost is ¥5000 for a three hour course (plus ¥500 entry fee to the museum) and you can take home your own handmade fabric. It is open from 10 am to 4 pm, closed Monday. Reservations are required five days in advance.

To get there, take the Karasuma line subway to Imadegawa-dōri and then a west-bound bus (No 201, 203 or 59) to the Imadegawa-Jōfukuji stop and walk about 200m north.

Lacquerware Hyōkan-dō (Map 10; ☎ 561-6377) has workshops in making *ikkan-bari* lacquerware; this process involves fixing washi onto a bamboo tray and coating it with persimmon juice. The 2½ hour class costs ¥5000 (to make a dustpan-shaped tray and a small basket). It's open from 9 am to 5 pm, closed Sunday and holidays. Call a few days in advance for reservations (three person minimum).

From Kyoto station, take bus No 206 (terminal A-2) and get off at the Kiyomizu-michi stop (the four storey Hyōkan-dō is just across the street).

For a quicker and more orthodox lacquerware option, stop by the small tent set up beside the teahouse at Tō-ji (Map 6). You can learn to hand painting on black lacquerware in about 20 minutes (a plate with a bamboo stand, dish or address book is ¥1000; a soup bowl or coffee cup is ¥1500). It's open daily from 9 am to 3 pm (in winter on weekends only).

Metalwork *Kyō-zōgan* is a damascene technique of laying fine metals onto figures engraved on brass and can be tried at Amita-honten (Map 10; ☎ 761-7000), just beside the Kyoto Handicraft Center on Maruta-machi-dōri. The cost of making a small pendant is ¥3500 and it takes about an hour (it will be sent to you one week later). Amita-honten is open from 10 am to 6 pm daily.

Paper Fans At Kyōsen-dō (Map 11; ☎ 371-4145), a 10 minute walk north-east of Kyoto station, you can learn to design your own *kyō-sensu* paper fan in about 90 minutes. The cost is ¥2000 and reservations are necessary at least one day in advance. There are daily sessions at 9 and 10.30 am and 1 and 3 pm. Your fan will be sent to you one month later; six weeks for overseas deliveries (postage should be prepaid).

Papermaking Rakushi-kan (☎ 251-0078) offers papermaking workshops on Thursday, Friday and Saturday, with sessions at 1, 2, 3 and 4 pm. The one hour course costs from ¥1000 for making sheets of washi, business cards or post cards. Reservations should be made a week in advance. The workshop is on the south side of Takoyakushi-dōri (Map 9), west of Muromachi-dōri.

Motoshiro Washi (Map 2; ☎ 744-3388), near Sanzen-in in Ōhara, is another good spot for making washi; the cost is ¥500 to make one sheet, and it takes about 30 minutes. You can pick up the dried paper after about an hour, so try to plan your visit before lunch or visiting the area temples. Reservations are suggested at least one day in advance (minimum two people).

Pottery Near the Gojō-zaka slope at Nishimura Koken (Map 6; ☎ 561-3552), you can throw a tea cup (¥3000) or tea ceremony bowl (¥5000). The process takes between one and two hours. Finished ceramics will be sent to you about two months later (postage costs are extra and pottery cannot be shipped abroad). It is open from 9 am to 6 pm daily. Reservations should be made a few days in advance (minimum two people).

It is an eight minute walk north of the Kyoto National Museum, or from Kyoto station take bus No 206 or 207 (terminal A2) to the Umamachi stop and walk one minute north-west.

At Kotobuki Tōshun (Map 6; ☎ 581-7195), in the Kiyomizu-zaka pottery village (over the mountain from Kiyomizu-dera), you can try glazing *(e-tsuke)* on premade ceramics (a tea cup for ¥1300, coffee mug or small flower vase for ¥2200). It is open daily from 9 am to 5 pm (arrive by 4 pm), closed Sunday and holidays between December and February. The glazing takes about 30 minutes and reservations are not necessary. Ceramics will be sent to you about one month later (postage must be prepaid).

Take a train to the Keishin Yamashina station and walk south 50m to catch the No 29 Keihan bus (bound for Ōyake) to the Kiyomizu-danchi stop (10 minutes). The studio is just in front of the bus stop.

Maiko Costume
Not exactly a traditional 'craft', the costumes of Kyoto's doll-like maiko are a work of art. If you were ever wondering how *you* might look as one of these highly trained entertainers, Kyoto has numerous outfits in town offering the chance. Maika (Map 10; ☎ 551-1661) is one in the Gion District where you will be dressed up to live out your maiko fantasy. Prices begin at ¥6700 for the basic treatment, which includes full make-up and formal kimono (studio photos cost ¥500 a take and you can have stickers made from these). If you don't mind spending some extra yen, it's possible to head out in costume for a stroll through Gion (and be stared at like never before!).

Maika is open from 10 am to 4 pm weekdays, and from 9 am to 5 pm on Saturday, Sunday and holidays. The process takes about an hour. Call to reserve at least one day in advance.

Cultural Demonstrations
Kyoto International Community House (KICH; Map 10) offers an intriguing variety of introductory courses in Japanese culture which are open to all for observation (free) and participation (¥1000). See the Flower Arranging entry for details on free ikebana classes; inquire here also about Japanese-language and calligraphy classes.

The basic demonstration schedule is as follows, but check to confirm the times and reserve a place:

The Way of Tea (tea ceremony)
    Tuesday from 2 to 4 pm
Introduction to Nō (nō drama)
    Thursday from 10 am to noon
The Koto (a Japanese string instrument)
    Wednesday from 2 to 4 pm
Introduction to Sencha (Chinese-style tea ceremony)
    Thursday from 2 to 4 pm

Call ☎ 752-3512 to register (English-speakers are on hand). KICH is in eastern Kyoto, south-west of Nanzen-ji. Take the Tōzai line subway to the Keage subway stop, or bus Higashi 9 from Keihan Sanjō station to the

Keage stop, and walk five minutes north-west (downhill) along the canal.

Zen Meditation

Several of Kyoto's Zen temples offer public *zazen* (seated meditation) where you can discover what the 'mystery' of Zen is all about.

Though these temples welcome visitors to participate, bear in mind that zazen is not held for the benefit of tourists and may not always live up to the perfect image of bald monks in robes. In fact, both physically and mentally it is much harder than you might imagine. Still, for many, a session of zazen can be an eye-opening encounter.

As there is very little English spoken at most temples, it helps to know Japanese, or have someone with you who does. Enlightenment, unfortunately, does not always come for free; some temples will require a donation. Reservations are generally not required, but you may want to call to confirm the schedule before setting your alarm clock. Most temples do not offer public zazen during the busy Obon season in August, or over the New Year holiday.

It's possible to practice Zen meditation at the following temples:

Daisen-in
    (Map 4; ☎ 491-8346) in the Daitoku-ji complex; 24th of each month from 4.30 to 5.30 pm; ¥1000
Genkō-an Temple
    (Map 4; ☎ 492-1858) in the Takagamine area (north-western Kyoto); first and third Sunday from 7 to 8.30 am; zazen and asa-gayu breakfast; registration fee ¥1000, then ¥500 per month
Ichiyō-in Temple
    (☎ 491-7571) offers a day-long Zen experience on the third Sunday of each month from 9 am to 5 pm; zazen, lectures, cooking and cleaning; one-time registration fee ¥1500, then ¥2000 per day
Kennin-ji
    (Map 10; ☎ 561-0190) in the Gion District; second Sunday from 9 to 10 am; free entry
Nanzen-in
    (Map 10; ☎ 771-0365) within the grounds of Nanzen-ji; second and fourth Sunday from 6.30 to 7.30 am; free entry
Shōkoku-ji
    (Map 8; ☎ 231-0301) north of Dōshisha University; second and fourth Sunday from 9 to 11 am; ¥100

For a more immersed experience, the Hōsen-ji Zen Center in Kameoka (Map 1) on the western outskirts of Kyoto offers overnight lodging and intensive Zen training from one night to the rest of your life. The retreat is an excellent place to learn about Zen and they are accustomed to foreign guests. Day begins at 5 am – lights out at 10 pm. The cost including meals and accommodation is ¥3000 per day, or ¥70,000 monthly. The centre is a 15 minute walk from Umahori station on the JR San-in Main (Sagano) line. Apply by sending your name, address, date of arrival and length of stay by mail, fax or email. Then just show up; no confirmation will be sent to you. For more information, contact the centre (☎/fax (81) 0771-24-0378) at: 52 Naka-jō, Yamamoto Shinochō, Kameoka-shi, Kyoto 621-0825. Its Web site is at www.zen.or.jp/kyotozen/ and its email address is kyotozen @zen.or.jp.

Vipassana Meditation Retreat

If you're looking for some spiritual awakening and Zen is not your thing, consider learning the 'art of living' on a 10 day mental training course at the Japan Vipassana Meditation Center. Born in India and preserved in Myanmar (Burma), Vipassana means 'to see things as they really are'.

About 90 minutes by train in the mountains north-west of Kyoto, it is one of more than 50 such centres worldwide and conducts sessions in both Japanese and English. Though based on the teachings of Buddha, the practice is a nondenominational, scientific approach to self-understanding. The intensive course is also designed as a practical tool for people to better deal with the complexities of daily life.

Despite the prospect of spending nine full days in silence, the retreat comes recommended by many. There is no charge to take part, though donations are happily accepted.

For more information or dates on upcoming sessions, write to: Japan Vipassana Meditation Center, Aza Hatta, Mizucho-chō, Funai-gun, Kyoto 622-03. Its email address is: jvipa@mbox.kyoto-inet.or.jp, or visit its Web site (www.dhamma.org/).

Kyoto Connection

In Pico Iyer's *The Lady and the Monk*, he describes a gathering where a 'ragtag group of bohos' holds forth late into the night with poetry and song. This was not a figment of his imagination. Iyer was referring to an evening at the Kyoto Connection, which since 1986 has been one of Kyoto's premier artistic meeting points.

On the last Saturday of each month (except August and December), organisers host an informal event bringing together diverse performers and an international audience for an evening of music, dance, comedy, poetry and any form of creative expression. Entertainers range from first-time amateurs to semiprofessionals. It's always a memorable event and a great way to be exposed to an exceedingly creative side of Kyoto.

The 'connection' is open to the public and, with at least a few days notice, anybody can get a slot on stage. There is a modest entry fee of ¥500 to cover the rental of the venue and doors open at 8 pm. It takes place at Teatro Marron (Map 4; ☎ 491-5971), on the 2nd storey of the Asakura building (above Le 5 Mars French restaurant) on Ueno-kaidō north of Kitayama-dōri. Take bus No 46 from Shijō-Kawaramachi station, get off at the Ushikawa bus stop and walk one minute

north. For more information, or to perform, call Ken Rodgers (☎ 712-7129).

Baths

After a day spent marching from temple to temple, nothing feels better than a good hot bath. Kyoto is full of *sentō* (public baths), ranging from small neighbourhood baths with one or two tubs to massive complexes offering saunas, mineral baths and even electric baths. Both of the following are worth a visit and could even double as an evening's entertainment.

Funaoka Onsen This old bath (Map 7) on Kuramaguchi-dōri boasts an outdoor bath and sauna, as well as some museum-quality woodcarvings in the changing room (apparently carved during Japan's invasion of Manchuria). It's open from 3 pm to 1 am, closed Tuesday. Admission is ¥320. To find it, head west on Kuramaguchi-dōri, where it intersects with the Horikawa-dōri intersection. It's on the left not far past the Lawson convenience store. Look for the large rocks out the front.

Shomen-yu This place (Map 11) is perhaps the mother of all sentō. Three storeys high, with an outdoor bath on the roof, this is your

---

The Japanese Bath

The Japanese bath *(o-furo)* is a ritual which has to be learned at an early stage of your visit and, like so many other things in Japan, is initially confusing but quickly becomes second nature. The all-important rule for using a Japanese bath is that you wash *outside* the bath tub and use the bath itself purely for soaking. Getting into a bath unwashed, or equally dreadful, without rinsing all the soap off your body, would be a major error.

Bathing is done in the evening, before or after dinner; a pre-breakfast bath is thought of as distinctly strange. In a traditional inn *(ryokan)* there's no possibility of missing bath-time – you will be clearly told when to bathe lest you not be washed in time for dinner. In a ryokan or a public bath *(sentō)*, the bathing facilities will either be communal (but sex-segregated) or there will be smaller facilities for families or couples.

Take off your *yukata* (dressing gown) or clothes in the anteroom to the bath and place them in the baskets provided. The bathroom has taps, plastic tubs (wooden ones in very traditional places) and stools along the wall. Draw up a stool to a set of taps and fill the tub from the taps or use the tub to scoop some water out of the bath itself. Sit on the stool and soap yourself. Rinse thoroughly so there's no soap or shampoo left on you, then you are ready to climb into the bath. Soak as long as you can stand the heat, then leave the bath, rinse yourself again, dry off and don your yukata. ■

chance to try riding an elevator naked (if you haven't already had the pleasure). Everything is on a grand scale here, including the sauna, which boasts a TV and room for 20. Men, don't be surprised if you spot some *yakuza* (gangsters) among the bathers (recognisable by their tattoos). It's open from 1.30 pm to 1 am, except Sunday, when it opens at 9 am (closed Tuesday). Admission is ¥320. It's south of Gojō-dōri about 300m east of the Kamogawa. Look for the sign in English and Japanese.

Sports

Baseball The local Kansai team is the Hanshin Tigers, which has not won a championship since the mid-80s. The Tigers play at Koshien Kyujō Stadium, which is in Nishinomiya (about halfway between Osaka and Kōbe).

Martial Arts There is not much in Kyoto for the short-term visitor as far as martial arts goes. Contact the TIC if you are interested.

Places to Stay

Kyoto has a wide range of accommodation to suit all budgets, from the finest traditional inns *(ryokan)* to youth hostels, private lodgings *(minshuku)*, guesthouses (or 'gaijin houses') and temple lodgings *(shukubō)*. Bear in mind that several of the cheaper places are further out of town and prices at some inns can nearly double in the high season (during April cherry blossom season, and autumn foliage season from late October to late November).

Credit cards (in particular Visa, Master-Card, American Express) are accepted at most hotels, but don't expect to pay with plastic at any of the budget places. At traditional inns, the higher the price, the better the chances of using a credit card.

GUESTHOUSES

Most of Kyoto's guesthouses are a casual affair and, unlike the youth hostels, are curfew-free. Shared bathrooms are common and there are usually cooking facilities. What many of these gaijin houses lack in service, they make up for in price.

For short stays, expect to pay between ¥1500 and ¥2000 per night for a dorm bed, or between ¥2500 and ¥5000 for a private room. Most gaijin houses offer reduced rates if you ask for weekly or monthly terms. Tax is usually included in the room price.

RYOKAN & MINSHUKU

A night in a traditional Japanese inn is a highlight for many visitors to Kyoto. Most offer the chance to encounter Kyoto's classical wooden architecture and native lifestyles, and to sample some fine *wa-shoku* (Japanese-style) cuisine. In most cases, the rates will include one or two meals.

Lower-price minshuku and ryokan typically charge between ¥4000 to ¥6000 per person per night and in the mid-range you can expect to pay from ¥8000 to about ¥15,000. Higher-end ryokan rates go from around ¥16,000 to more than ¥50,000 per night. Reservations should always be made (and well in advance for topnotch ryokan).

HOTELS

Though less atmospheric than traditional inns, most hotels have the advantage of modern conveniences, services like dry-cleaning, and have English-speakers on hand. Some offer both Japanese and western-style rooms, so you can get the best of both worlds. Room rates at basic 'business hotels' average around ¥5000.

TEMPLES

Shukubō, or temple lodgings, are usually in peaceful surroundings with spartan tatami rooms, optional attendance at early morning prayer sessions and an early evening curfew. Nightly rates hover at around ¥4000 per person (most with breakfast included), and guests usually use public baths near the temples.

A number of shukubō in Kyoto are hesitant to take foreigners who cannot speak Japanese, though those listed in this chapter have English-speakers on hand and are used to having non-Japanese guests. At the TIC you can also pick up a copy of a handout entitled *Shukubōs in Kyoto*, which has a comprehensive list of local temple lodgings.

WHERE TO STAY

You can save time traversing the city if you organise your accommodation around the areas that interest you. While many prefer to be central for easy access to sights in any direction, there are also advantages to staying in less populated parts of town (such as peace and quiet). The eastern Higashi-yama area is popular, as it is near temples and the mountains yet also close enough to the city centre. As far as costs go, there is a wide range of choices throughout the city and in most areas you can find something to suit your budget.

The TIC (Map 11) offers advice, accommodation lists and can help with reservations at its Welcome Inn counter. Or try the Kyoto Minshuku Reservation Center (Map 11; ☎ 351-4547), which has a comprehensive listing of local minshuku and can help locate inns and make reservations in other parts of Japan. The office is a short walk north-east of the TIC and is open daily from 9 am to 5 pm.

To help with planning, the following listings have been sorted according to type, location and price.

PLACES TO STAY – BUDGET
Camping

Though there is little in the way of facilities, it is possible to camp in some of the wooded areas surrounding the city. One of the best places is along the Kiyotaki-gawa River between Kiyotaki and Hozukyō (Map 2) – see the Kiyotaki River Hike boxed text in the Things to See & Do chapter for transport details. The river is crystal-clear and runs through picturesque mountains. You can camp by the river and use nearby trains or buses for the 30 minute trip into Kyoto. For bathing there is the river, or public baths in Kyoto. This is a pleasant, realistic option from early April to late October.

Hostels

Higashiyama Youth Hostel (Map 10; ☎ 761-8135) is a spiffy hostel and an excellent base for the sights in the eastern mountains. For a

---

Staying at a Ryokan

On arrival at a *ryokan* (traditional inn), you leave your shoes at the entrance, don a pair of slippers and are shown by a maid to your room, which has a *tatami* (reed mat) floor. Slippers are taken off before entering tatami rooms. Instead of using numbers, rooms are named after auspicious flowers, plants or trees.

The room will contain an alcove *(tokonoma)*, probably decorated with a flower display or a calligraphy scroll. One side of the room will have a cupboard with sliding doors for the bedding; the other side will have sliding screens covered with rice paper, and may open onto a veranda with a garden view.

The room maid then serves tea with a sweet on a low table surrounded by cushions *(zabuton)* in the centre of the room. At the same time you are asked to sign the register. A tray is provided with a towel, gown *(yukata)* and belt *(obi)*, which you put on before taking your bath. Remember to wear the left side over the right – the reverse order is used for dressing the dead. In colder weather, there will also be an outer jacket *(tanzen)*. Your clothes can be put in a closet or left on a hanger.

Dressed in your yukata, you will be shown to the bath *(o-furo)*. At some ryokan, there are rooms with private baths but the communal ones are often designed with 'natural' pools or a window looking out onto a garden. Bathing is communal, but sexes are segregated. Make sure you can differentiate between the bathroom signs for men 男 and women 女 – though ryokan used to catering for foreigners will often have signs in English. Many inns will have family bathrooms for couples or families.

Dressed in your yukata after your bath, you return to your room where the maid will have laid out dinner – in some ryokan, dinner is provided in a separate room but you still wear your yukata for dining. Dinner usually includes standard dishes such as miso soup, pickles *(tsukemono)*, vegetables in vinegar *(sunomono)*, hors d'oeuvres *(zensai)*, fish either grilled or raw *(sashimi)*, and perhaps tempura and a stew. There will also be bowls for rice, dips and sauces. Depending on the price, these meals can be flamboyant displays of local cuisine or refined arrangements of *kaiseki* (a cuisine that obeys strict rules of form and etiquette for every detail of the meal and setting).

After dinner, while you are pottering around or strolling in the garden, the maid will clear the dishes and prepare your bedding. A mattress *(futon)* is placed on the tatami floor and a quilt put on top. In colder weather, you can also add a blanket *(mōfu)*.

In the morning, the maid will knock to make sure you are awake and then come in to put away the bedding before serving breakfast – sometimes this is served in a separate room. Breakfast usually consists of pickles, dried seaweed *(nori)*, raw egg, dried fish, miso soup and rice. It can take a while for foreign stomachs to accept this novel fare early in the morning.

The Japanese tendency is to make the procedure at a ryokan seem rather rarefied for foreign comprehension and some ryokan are wary of accepting foreign guests. However, once you've grasped the basics, it really isn't that hard to fit in. ■

dorm bed and two meals, the charge is ¥4000 (nonmembers add ¥500). Private rooms cost from ¥5000 per person (including two meals). Bicycle rental costs ¥1000 per day. This hostel is very regimented but if you're the kind of person who likes being in bed by 9.30 pm this might be just your ticket. Meals are not a highlight, so you might prefer to skip them and find something more interesting in the city centre. To get there, take bus No 5 from Kyoto station (terminal A1) to the Higashiyama-sanjō-mae stop (20 minutes). If you're in the Sanjō station area, you can walk to the hostel in 15 minutes.

Utano Youth Hostel (Map 3; ☎ 462-2288) is friendly, well organised and makes a convenient base for the sights of north-western Kyoto. Like the Higashiyama Youth Hostel, everything is ordered: 10 pm curfew, 10.30 pm lights-out and 6.30 am wakey-wakey. The men's bath is a large jacuzzi. There's an international phone just outside the front door. The buffet breakfast is good value for ¥500. If you want to skip the hostel supper (¥850), turn left along the main road to find several coffee shops offering cheap set meals (teishoku). Rates are ¥2800, with or without membership. There's a meeting room with bilingual TV news, but for many travellers, fond memories are reserved for the heated toilet seats! You can ask at the hostel about discount bus tickets and entry tickets to Ryōan-ji Temple and Eiga Mura (Movie Village). To get to the hostel take bus No 26 from Kyoto station (bus terminal C1) to the Yūsu-Hosuteru-mae stop. The ride takes about 50 minutes.

Kitayama Youth Hostel (Map 3; ☎ 492-5345) charges ¥2800 for a dorm bed (for nonmembers add ¥1000). Breakfast costs ¥530 and dinner ¥840. This hostel is a superb place from which to visit the rural area of Takagamine with its fine, secluded temples such as Kōetsu-ji (Map 4), Jōshō-ji (Map 4) and Shōden-ji (Map 4).

Take bus No 6 from Kyoto station (bus terminal B4) to the Genkō-an-mae stop (about 30 minutes). Walk west past a school, turn right and continue up the hill to the hostel (five minutes on foot).

Guesthouses
West of Kyoto Station
Tani Guest House (Map 6; ☎ 681-7437, 671-2627) provides a dorm bed for ¥2000 and singles/doubles for ¥2500/4500. Monthly rates are ¥35,000 to ¥55,000. This is not connected with the management of the other Tani lodgings. To get there, take the JR line to Nishiōji station (five minutes), then walk for 10 minutes south.

Central Kyoto A celebrated gaijin house, *Uno House* (Map 10; ☎ 231-7763) offers you the dubious privilege of a really grungy accommodation experience. The attraction is the price and the absence of youth hostel regimentation. Dorm beds start at ¥1650, and private rooms range from ¥2250 (tiny singles) to ¥5200.

Take bus No 205 or Toku 17 from Kyoto station (bus terminal A3) to the Kawaramachi-marutamachi-mae stop (about 20 minutes). Perhaps easier, take the Karasuma line subway, get off at the Marutamachi stop and walk east for 10 minutes.

Higher standards prevail at *Tani House Annexe* (Map 10; ☎ 211-5637), but it doesn't have dorm accommodation. It has doubles with bath and air-con for ¥6500 and triples for ¥8000. Take bus No 5 from Kyoto station (bus terminal A1) to the Kawaramachi-sanjō-mae stop (about 20 minutes).

One other place worth checking out is *Tōji-An Guest House* (Map 6; ☎ 691-7017). It's around 10 minutes walk west of Kyoto station, and has dorm accommodation for ¥2060. There's no curfew here but it's often full with long-termers.

Eastern Kyoto *ISE Dorm* (Map 10; ☎ 771-0566) provides basic accommodation (42 rooms) for ¥2800 per day or from ¥35,000 to ¥56,000 per month. Facilities include phone, fridge, air-con, shower and washing machine. The place is noisy and dirty but there is usually a room available and arrangements for a stay can be made very quickly. By all means, take a look at the place before you check in. Take bus No 206 from Kyoto station (bus terminal A2) to the Kumano-jinja-mae stop. The office is down a very small alley, so ask for directions once you get into the general area.

Northern Kyoto *Aoi-Sō Inn* (Map 7; ☎ 431-0788) has dorm beds for ¥1200, singles from ¥1500, and doubles/triples from ¥3000/4500. It's a quiet place with no evening curfew, and a coin laundry and kitchen are available. The inn is a five minute walk north-west of the Karasuma line subway Kuramaguchi station (exit No 2), between the Kyoto Hospital buildings.

Tani House (Map 7; ☎ 492-5489) is an old favourite for both short-term and long-term visitors on a tight budget. There is a certain charm to this fine old house with its warren of rooms, jovial owners and quiet location next to Daitoku-ji Temple. Costs per night are ¥1700 for a space on the floor in a tatami room and ¥4200 to ¥4600 for a double private room. There's no curfew and free tea and coffee are provided. Take the 45 minute ride on bus No 206 from Kyoto station (bus terminal B4) and get off at the Kenkun-jinja-mae stop.

Greenpeace Inn Kyoto (Map 4; ☎ 791-9890) is popular with foreigners and has a friendly English-speaking staff (though it requires a minimum stay of three nights). Dorm beds are ¥4500 for three nights, ¥9400 per week, and singles/doubles are ¥7000/8400 or ¥15,000/17,500 per week. Per-month prices are ¥26,000 for dorm beds, and ¥42,000/46,000 for singles/doubles. Cooking and laundry facilities are available, as well as bilingual TV and English newspapers. Greenpeace is three minutes on foot west of the Karasuma line Matsugasaki subway station.

Takaya (Map 7; ☎ 431-5213) provides private rooms at ¥4000 per day or from ¥50,000 for one month. Take the Karasuma line subway to Imadegawa station and walk south.

Hotels
Kyoto Station Area Near Kyoto station are several 'business hotels', but don't expect much English to be spoken. *Kyōmai Inn* (Map 11; ☎ 371-3390) has Japanese-style rooms for ¥4600 per person, and the *Kyoto*

White Hotel (Map 11; ☎ 351-5511) also has singles/doubles costing ¥4600/7200.

Eastern Kyoto If you've never tried a night in one of Japan's unique 'capsule' hotels, here's your chance. *Amenity* (Map 10; ☎ 525-3900), conveniently close to Kiyomizu-dera Temple, has single capsules for ¥3600 (men only) and ¥9000 (twin capsule). Take bus No 206 from Kyoto station (terminal A2) and get off at the Kiyomizu-michi bus stop.

PLACES TO STAY – MID-RANGE
Ryokan & Minshuku
Kyoto Station Area & Central Kyoto The following five hotels are all members of the Japanese Inn Group.

Ryokan Hiraiwa (Map 11; ☎ 351-6748) is used to receiving foreigners and offers basic tatami rooms. It is close to both central and eastern Kyoto. Rates per person cost from ¥4000 (coffee and toast breakfasts are ¥320 or Japanese style is ¥1050). Facilities include bilingual TV, air-con and coin laundry. It is a 15 minute walk from Kyoto station.

Ryokan Kyōka (Map 11; ☎ 371-2709) has 10 spacious, Japanese style rooms costing ¥4200 per person. It's about eight minutes on foot from Kyoto station, close to Higashi Hongan-ji Temple.

At *Matsubaya Ryokan* (Map 11; ☎ 351-4268) per-person rates are ¥4500; triples cost ¥12,600. Western breakfasts are ¥300 and Japanese style ¥1000. This ryokan is also close to Higashi Hongan-ji.

Ryokan Murakamiya (Map 11; ☎ 371-1260) is seven minutes walk from Kyoto station. It costs ¥4000 per person (no meals are served).

Riverside Takase (Map 11; ☎ 351-7920) has singles/doubles for ¥3400/6500, triples for ¥9000. Take bus No 205 from Kyoto station (bus terminal A3) and get off at the third stop, Kawaramachi Shōmen, or walk two minutes from Keihan Shijō station.

Pension Station Kyoto (Map 11; ☎ 882-6200) is a member of the Welcome Inn Group and a quiet place. Per-person rates are ¥4200; breakfast is ¥800 and good dinners are served for ¥2000. Some rooms are available with baths for a slightly higher price. The pension is an eight minute walk from Kyoto station.

Yuhara Ryokan (Map 11; ☎ 371-9583) has a family atmosphere and a riverside location popular with foreigners. The price per person is ¥4000; no meals are served. It's a 15 minute walk from Kyoto station.

Ryokan Hinomoto (Map 10; ☎ 351-4563) is another member of the Japanese Inn Group, with a position right in the centre of the city's nightlife action. It's a small place that is a favourite with many frequent visitors to Kyoto. The price per person is ¥4000 without meals. Take bus No 17 or 205 from Kyoto station (bus terminal A3) and get off at the Kawaramachi-matsubara-mae stop.

Unassuming from the outside, the popular *Hirota Guest House* (Map 10; ☎ 221-2474; fax 221-2627) is a pleasant Japanese-style inn in an old sake brewery. Its cheerful English-speaking owner, Ms Hirota, is a former tour guide and a valuable source of information. Per-person rates begin at ¥5000 (tasty Japanese breakfasts cost ¥1000). The inn is on Nijō-dōri, about eight minutes walk north-east of Oike station on the Karasuma line subway, or north-west of the Shiyakusho-mae subway station on the Tōzai line.

Eastern Kyoto *Ryokan Mishima* (*Mishima Shrine;* Map 6; ☎ 551-0033) operates as part of a Shintō shrine and is a member of the Japanese Inn Group. Cost per person is ¥4000; no meals are served. On request, you can fulfil your photographic fantasy by dressing up in Shintō robes. Take bus No 206 (eastbound) from Kyoto station (bus terminal A2) to the Higashiyama-umamachi-mae stop.

Ryokan Ōtō (Map 11; ☎ 541-7803) is a member of the Japanese Inn Group, has a riverside location and charges ¥4000 per person. Breakfasts start at ¥700 and dinners from ¥1500. You can get there via bus No 206 or 208 from Kyoto station (bus terminal A2) to the Shichijō-Ōhashi bus stop.

Not far from Kiyomizu-dera, *Ryokan Seiki* (Map 6; ☎ 551-4911) is yet another member of the Japanese Inn Group and has singles for

¥4500, doubles for ¥8000 and triples from ¥11,000. It's 15 minutes from Kyoto station (bus terminal A2) by a No 206 bus; get off at the Gojō-zaka bus stop.

Three Sisters Inn (*Rakutō-sō;* Map 10; ☎ 761-6336) is a popular ryokan with foreigners. Singles go from ¥4900 to ¥12,800, doubles from ¥9800 to ¥16,000. Take bus No 5 from Kyoto station and get off at the Dobutsu-en-mae stop – the inn is just to the north of Heian-jingū. The *Three Sisters Annexe* (☎ 761-6333) close by has singles for ¥10,000, doubles for ¥18,000 and triples for ¥24,000. Both the inn and the annexe serve a ¥700 breakfast and fancy dinners from ¥4500.

Uemura (Map 10; ☎ 561-0377) is a beautiful little ryokan near Kiyomizu-dera that is at ease with foreign guests. Per-person prices are ¥9000 with breakfast. Book well in advance as there are only three rooms. It's on Ishibeikōji-dōri, a quaint cobblestone alley. Take bus No 206 to the Higashiyama-yasui bus stop.

Iwanami (Map 10; ☎ 561-7135) is a pleasant, old-fashioned ryokan with a faithful following of foreign guests. It's right in the heart of Gion on a quiet side street. Book well in advance. Prices start at ¥9500 per person including breakfast. Take bus No 206 to the Chion-mae stop.

Another cosy Gion ryokan, *Gion Fukuzumi* (Map 10; ☎ 541-5181) charges ¥15,000 per person including two meals. It has cheerful English-speaking staff and a glorious rooftop bath with views. It's on Shinbashi-dōri, west of Higashiōji-dōri.

Northern Kyoto *Ryokan Rakucho* (Map 4; ☎ 721-2174) is a member of the Japanese Inn Group. Prices for singles/doubles are ¥4500/8000. No meals are served here. The quickest way to get there is to take the Karasuma line subway to Kitaōji station, walk east across the Kamo-gawa River and turn north at the post office. To get there by bus, take bus No 205 from Kyoto station (bus terminal A3) and get off at the Furitsu-daigaku-mae stop.

PLACES TO STAY

Ōhara *Ōhara Sansō* (Map 2; ☎ 744-2227) is a pleasant inn just down the road from Jakkō-in Temple with a soothing outdoor bath. It costs ¥8000 per person, including two meals.

Further down from the temple, *Ryosō Chatani* (Map 2; ☎ 744-2952) has rates starting from ¥6500 per person, including meals, and is part of the Welcome Inn Group (reservations can be made at the TIC).

Western Kyoto *Minshuku Arashiyama* (Map 12; ☎ 861-4398) charges ¥7000 with two meals. A little Japanese will go a long way here. It is a short walk from Rokuōin station on the Keifuku Arashiyama line.

Pension Arashiyama (Map 3; ☎ 881-2294) has mostly western-style singles/doubles for ¥4200/8400; triples cost ¥12,000. An American breakfast is available for ¥800. To get there, take the 30 minute ride on Kyoto bus No 71, 72 or 73 and get off at the Arisugawa-mae stop.

Pension Sagano (Map 5; ☎ 881-2310) is in a brick building about 10 minutes walk from the Toei Movie Village in Uzumasa. Costs are from ¥5500, including two meals.

Southern Kyoto Despite an 8 pm curfew and inconvenient location, Japanese history buffs may enjoy a night at *Teradaya* (Map 3; ☎ 622-0243), the inn where Japan's revolutionary hero Sakamoto Ryōma put up when visiting Kyoto. The per-person cost is ¥7000 with breakfast.

Hotels
Central Kyoto In general, hotels work out slightly more expensive than staying in a ryokan and have far less character. Still, they are generally a lot more flexible about the hours you keep and are not without certain advantages. The following are some of the more reasonably priced business hotels in central Kyoto:

Hokke Club Kyoto
(Map 11; ☎ 361-1251) singles from ¥5500 to ¥9000, twins from ¥11,000; opposite Kyoto station

Karasuma Kyoto Hotel
(Map 9; ☎ 371-0111) singles from ¥8800, twins from ¥16,000, doubles from ¥20,000; next to Shijō subway station
Kyoto Central Inn
(Map 10; ☎ 211-1666) singles/twins from ¥7000/11,000; next to Kawaramachi station
Kyoto Dai-Ichi Hotel
(Map 11; ☎ 661-8800) singles/twins from ¥6800/13,500; 10 minutes walk slightly south-west of Kyoto station
Kyoto Dai-San Tower Hotel
(Map 11; ☎ 343-3111) singles from ¥6000 to ¥9500, twins from ¥11,000, doubles from ¥15,000; five minutes walk from Kyoto station

Eastern Kyoto *Kyoto Traveller's Inn* (Map 10; ☎ 771-0225) is a business hotel very close to Heian-jingū, offering both western and Japanese-style rooms. Prices for singles/twins start at ¥5500/10,000. There's no curfew and the Green Box restaurant on the 1st floor is open until 10 pm. Take bus No 5 from Kyoto station to the Dōbutsu-en-mae stop and walk north.

Pension Higashiyama (Map 10; ☎ 882-1181) is a member of the Japanese Inn Group. It's a modern construction by the waterside and convenient for sights in Higashiyama. Singles/doubles are ¥4200/8400; triples cost ¥12,000. For a break from Japanese-style breakfasts, you could try the American breakfast (¥800). To get there, take bus No 206 from Kyoto station (bus terminal A2) for an 18 minute ride to the Chioin-mae stop.

PLACES TO STAY – TOP END
Ryokan
Top-end ryokan accommodation in Kyoto is, as you might expect, very expensive. Listed here are some of the ryokan that occasionally have foreign guests.

Central Kyoto *Kinmata* (Map 10; ☎ 221-1039) commenced operations early in the last century and this is reflected in the original decor, interior gardens and *hinoki* (cypress) bathroom. Rooms cost from ¥25,000 to ¥30,000 per person, including two meals. It's in the centre of town, close to Nishiki-kōji Market – if you can afford to stay here, the cost of a taxi will be a financial pinprick.

PLACES TO STAY

The Tawaraya ryokan in central Kyoto is several centuries old and provides classic (and classy) traditional inn accommodation.

Temple. Prices per person for a room and two meals range from ¥18,000 to ¥40,000.

Kurama & Kibune For an overnight stay in Kurama, *Kurama Onsen* (Map 2; ☎ 741-2131) is a perfect option for bath-lovers. Guests have unlimited use of the indoor and outdoor hot-spring tubs and per-person rates start at ¥15,000, including two meals.

The exquisite traditional inns in the small village of Kibune are famed for their riverside location and make a delightful escape from the city. They are renowned for fine seasonal cuisine, most notably 'above-river dining' *(kawa-doko-ryōri)* – see the Places to Eat chapter for details.

Ryokan Ugenta, in Kibune (Map 2; ☎ 741-2146), is an attractive old inn with a wonderful stone bath tub. Per-person rates are from ¥20,000, including two gourmet meals.

Kibune Fujiya (Map 2; ☎ 741-2501), just below the Kibune-jinja Shrine torii, has ratesfrom ¥20,000, including meals.

Hiroya (Map 2; ☎ 741-2401), just across from Kibune-jinja, costs from ¥24,000 in winter (with a kaiseki or *botan-nabe* dinner) and in summer from ¥30,000 (serving kawa-doko-ryōri).

Ōhara A stone's throw from Sanzen-in Temple, *Seryō* (Map 2; ☎ 744-2301) is a charming inn built in the *gasshō-zukuri* style (with a steeply pitched roof designed to keep snow from accumulating). The friendly owner can speak some English. Per-person rates range from ¥13,000 to ¥20,000, with two meals.

Western Kyoto Also known as Arashiyama Onsen, *Rankyō-kan* (Map 12; ☎ 871-0001) sits in a secluded area on the south bank of the Oi-gawa River in Arashiyama. It is a classical Japanese-style inn with manicured gardens, hot-spring baths and river views from most rooms. Per-person rates begin at ¥18,000. The restaurant here (serving exquisite kaiseki-ryōri) is open to the public (see the Places to Eat chapter). Walk five minutes up the riverside path or, better still, call ahead

Hiiragiya (Map 10; ☎ 221-1136) is another elegant ryokan, favoured by celebrities from around the world. Reservations are essential. For a room and two meals, per-person costs range from ¥25,000 to ¥90,000. Close by, the *Hiiragiya Annexe* (☎ 231-0151) also offers topnotch ryokan service and surroundings but at slightly more affordable rates. Per-person costs start at ¥15,000, with two meals.

Tawaraya (Map 10; ☎ 211-5566) has been operating for over three centuries and is classed as one of the finest places to stay in the world. Guests at this ryokan have included the imperial family and overseas royalty. It is a classic in every sense. Reservations are essential, preferably many months ahead. Per-person costs range from ¥35,000 to ¥75,000.

Eastern Kyoto *Yachiyo* (Map 10; ☎ 771-4148) is an elegant ryokan close to Nanzen-ji

and be chauffeured by private boat from the Togetsu-kyō Bridge!

On the busier north side of Togetsu-kyō, there are several fine inns. *Arashiyama Benkei* (Map 12; ☎ 872-3355) charges ¥20,000, including two elegant meals – it's about 150m upriver from the bridge. *Hotel Ran-tei* (Map 12; ☎ 371-1119) has spacious gardens and both Japanese and western-style rooms from ¥16,000 to ¥35,000.

Hotels

Central Kyoto The upmarket ryokan experience is not for everyone, and if you want a hotel with full amenities, there are a number of high-class places in the central district.

Holiday Inn Kyoto
(Map 8; ☎ 721-3131) singles from ¥10,000, doubles from ¥14,000, twins from ¥18,500; free shuttle bus from south exit of Kyoto station
Hotel Fujita Kyoto
(Map 10; ☎ 222-1511) singles from ¥9800 to ¥15,000, twins from ¥16,000 to ¥28,000, doubles from ¥23,000 to ¥27,000; five minutes walk from the Tōzai line Shiyakusho-mae subway station
Hotel Granvia Kyoto
(Map 11; ☎ 344-8888) singles from ¥16,000, doubles/twins from ¥18,000/¥20,000; inside the west end of the Kyoto station building
International Hotel Kyoto
(Map 9; ☎ 222-1111) singles from ¥9000 to ¥13,000, twins from ¥16,000 to ¥25,000, doubles ¥23,000; 15 minutes by taxi from Kyoto station
Kyoto Century Hotel
(Map 11; ☎ 351-0111) singles ¥14,000, doubles from ¥18,000, twins from ¥22,000; five minutes walk from Kyoto station
Kyoto Hotel
(Map 10; ☎ 211-5111) singles/twins/doubles from ¥16,000/25,000/31,000; it's above the Shiyakusho-mae station on the Tōzai line subway
Kyoto New Hankyū Hotel
(Map 11; ☎ 343-5300) singles from ¥12,000 to ¥14,000, twins from ¥17,000 to ¥33,000, doubles from ¥22,000 to ¥26,000; two minutes walk from Kyoto station
Kyoto Tokyū Hotel
(Map 11; ☎ 341-2411) singles from ¥14,000, twins/doubles from ¥24,000; five minutes by taxi from Kyoto station, near the Gojō-dōri and Horikawa-dōri intersection

Rihga Royal Hotel Kyoto
(Map 11; ☎ 341-2311) singles from ¥12,000 to ¥17,000, doubles from ¥21,000 to ¥30,000; 10 minutes walk from Kyoto station

Eastern Kyoto *Miyako Hotel* (Map 10; ☎ 771-7111) is a famed, western-style hotel perched on the hills and a classic choice for visiting foreign dignitaries. The hotel surroundings stretch over 6.4 hectares of wooded hillside and landscaped gardens. Singles start from ¥15,000 and doubles range from ¥23,000 to ¥48,000. It's closest to Keage station on the Keihan line.

OTHER ACCOMMODATION
Shukubō (Temple Lodging)
Myōren-ji Temple (Map 7; ☎ 451-3527) charges ¥3500 (no meals are served). Take bus No 9 from Kyoto station (bus terminal B1) to the Horikawa-Teranouchi-mae stop. This pleasant temple is used to dealing with foreign guests.

Shōhō-in Temple (Map 9; ☎ 811-7768) charges ¥5000 with breakfast. Take bus No 6 or 206 to the Ōmiya-Matsubara stop and walk five minutes; or take the Hankyū Kyoto line to Ōmiya and walk eight minutes south. To inquire in English, call Ms Katō (☎ 030-947-4520).

Hiden-in Temple (Map 6; ☎ 561-8781) charges ¥4500 with breakfast. Take bus No 208 to the Sennyuji-michi-mae stop; another approach is to take the JR Nara line to Tōfukuji station.

Gesshin-in Temple (Map 10; ☎ 541-8088) charges ¥3500 with breakfast. Take bus No 18 to the Higashiyama-yasui stop and walk five minutes east. Unmarried couples are not permitted to stay.

Women-Only Accommodation
Rokuō-in Temple (Map 3; ☎ 861-1645) provides temple lodgings for women only – it's in western Kyoto, close to Rokuōin station on the Keifuku Arashiyama line. The per-person price is ¥4500, including breakfast.

There are several reasonable women-only hotels suitable for touring Kyoto's eastern Higashiyama area. Housed in a stately, late

A	B
C	D	E
F	G

A and B: Night scenes on Kyoto's Kiyamachi-dōri, bordering the traditional centre for night entertainment near the Kamo-gawa River. C, D, E : Traditional food still sells at Nishiki-kōji's speciality market, which is aptly known as 'Kyoto's Kitchen'. F: Mt Daimonji-yama ablaze during the August Daimon-ji Gozan Okuribi fire festival. G: Neon signs after dark on Kyoto streets.

The screen-like lattice work of a *kyō-machiya* townhouse is relatively open to everyone. Following Confucian principles, the further inside the house you progress, the more honoured and intimate the space – and the guest – become.

Meiji-era guesthouse, *Lady's Hotel Chōraku-kan* (Map 10; ☎ 561-0001) is central, near Maruyama-kōen Park and has per-person room-only rates from ¥4500. *Lady's Inn Sakata* (Map 10; ☎ 541-2108), near the Ninen-zaka slope, has singles/doubles for ¥6500/11,000. A basic breakfast costs ¥500.

Lady's Inn Higashiyama (☎ 751-1427), south of Heian-jingū (Map 10), charges from ¥4300 per person and does not offer meals.

Lady's Hotel Nishijin (Map 7; ☎ 415-1010), in the Nishijin garment district, has per-person rates from ¥4000. Take bus No 9 from Kyoto station (bus terminal B1) to the Horikawa-Teranouchi-mae stop.

Arashiyama Lady's Hotel (Map 12; ☎ 882-0955) is just beside the Keifuku Arashiyama station. It has Japanese and western-style rooms with per-person rates from ¥3500 (without meals).

For long-term accommodation (minimum three months) the *YWCA* (Map 7; ☎ 431-0351) offers monthly rates from ¥27,000 (room only) to ¥35,000 (with kitchen and bathroom). It is a short walk west of the Imperial Palace Park.

Places to Eat

Eating is half the fun of being in Japan and visitors to Kyoto will soon discover this. The adventurous eater will be delighted to find that Japanese food is far more than just the sushi, tempura and sukiyaki for which it is best known in other countries. Kyoto offers an astonishing range of eateries, from dirt-cheap noodle joints to the finest of haute Japanese cuisine, and it could be perfectly possible to spend a month here and dine at a different speciality restaurant each night.

Kyotoites have also heartily embraced foreign cuisine and Kyoto features a legion of restaurants representing the ever changing Japanese diet. Beyond the conspicuous glut of fast-food restaurants, there are countless places serving up local variations on everything from tacos and pasta to authentic couscous!

Luckily, however, Kyoto presents ample opportunity to sample some of Japan's truly authentic cuisine, although some may baulk at charging into a restaurant where both the language and menu are likely to be incomprehensible. The best way to get over this fear is to familiarise yourself with the main types of Japanese restaurants, so that you have some idea of what's on offer and how to order it. The Japanese will go to extraordinary lengths to understand what you want and help you to order.

The how-tos of eating Japanese food are often not what foreign visitors are used to, and for many it takes a little time to acclimatise. It's OK to lift the bowl to your face (not vice versa) and yes, even to slurp! This is the way Japanese food was designed to be eaten, and you'll do best by simply copying those around you.

When eating Japanese fare, there are some things you can definitely expect. Lots of rice, always tea, plus pickled vegetables and miso soup served with most meals. Of course you'll also want to brush up on your chopsticks skills.

Many of the restaurants listed in this chapter have English menus available, and in the ones which do not, it is worth doing your best in sign language. Top-end places which appear with telephone numbers are an indication that you should call in advance to make reservations, in particular for dinner; not only are these eateries vastly popular, but in many cases the food entails special preparation. Staff at most hotels and inns can assist with the call.

Many Japanese restaurants are speciality shops serving just one type of cuisine. This naturally makes for delicious eating, but does limit your choice. The following will introduce the main types of Japanese restaurants, along with the most common dishes served. With a little courage and effort you will soon discover that Kyoto is a gourmet paradise where good food is taken seriously.

KYOTO STATION AREA

The area around Kyoto station is awash with restaurants. On the upper floors of the station complex are an array of somewhat over-priced Japanese-style eateries, as well as a full range of fast-food joints – just head up the grand staircase. There are also several restaurants on the south side of the station, near the entrance to the *shinkansen* (bullet train) and Kintestu tracks, and also in the station's Porta underground arcade.

North of the station, try *Chūgoku Chūbō Yamucha-no-mise Kyūraku* (Map 11) for tasty dim sum. It's just across the street from the TIC and is open from noon to 3 pm and 5 to 11 pm. You can also find a number of reasonable places in the basement of the Kyoto Tower building.

East of the station near the railway tracks are two of the areas best rāmen shops (right next door to each other). *Dai Ichi Asahi* (Map 11) is open from 5.30 am to 2 am, closed Thursday; *Shinpuku Saikan* (Map 11) is open from 7 am to 11 pm, closed Wednesday. The hours it keeps are an indicator of its popularity.

continued on page 177

RESTAURANTS

Customarily eateries hang a cloth banner *(noren)* on a bamboo rod in front of their doors bearing the name of the restaurant. Noren also indicate that the shop is open for business (they are taken down at closing time).

This section outlines the types of eating establishments you will come across in Kyoto, from the most basic noodle shops to elegant *ryōtei* restaurants, and the kinds of food they serve, plus tips, such as how to order your meal. The following entries describe the varieties of Japanese food, and information on eating and drinking etiquette.

Shokudō 食堂

A *shokudō*, or eating place, is an inexpensive, all-round eatery with plastic food models in the window. Most serve both Japanese *(washoku)* and western *(yōshoku)* cuisine, both à la carte and as set meals *(teishoku)*. These combo sets typically include a main dish of meat or fish, a bowl of rice, miso (soybean paste) soup, shredded cabbage and a few Japanese pickles called *tsukemono*. In addition, most shokudō serve a fairly standard selection of *donburi* (rice dishes) and *menrui* (noodle dishes). What many lack in culinary creativity or ambience, they make up for in speed and cost (most meals are under ¥1000). Some of the more common dishes are:

Rice Dishes

katsu-don	カツ丼	a bowl of rice topped with a fried pork cutlet
oyako-don	親子丼	a bowl of rice topped with egg and chicken
niku-don	肉丼	a bowl of rice topped with thin slices of cooked beef
ten-don	天丼	a bowl of rice topped with tempura shrimp and vegetables

Noodle Dishes

Add 'soba' (thin, brown, buckwheat noodles) or 'udon' (thick, white, wheat noodles) to the following when ordering:

kake	かけ	plain noodles in broth
kitsune	きつね	noodles with fried tofu
tempura	天ぷら	noodles with tempura shrimp
tsukimi	月見	noodles with raw egg on top

Izakaya 居酒屋

An *izakaya* is the Japanese equivalent of a pub. They offer a wide selection of food, a hearty atmosphere and, of course, plenty of beer and sake. You have the choice of sitting at the counter, at a table or on a tatami floor. Food is usually ordered a bit at a time, and you choose from a selection of typical Japanese foods such as *yakitori*, *sashimi* and grilled fish, as well as creative interpretations of western foods like French fries and beef stew.

Izakaya can be easily spotted by their rustic facades and red lanterns *(chōchin)* outside their doors. Since izakaya food is casual drinking fare, it is usually fairly inexpensive. Depending on how much you drink, you can expect to get away with ¥2500 to ¥4500 per person.

In addition to the following dishes, see the Yakitori and Sushi & Sashimi entries in the following Food Section.

Pickled plums – served with almost every meal, the ubiquitous umeboshi has been appreciated by the Japanese for its health-giving properties for hundreds of years.

agedashi-dōfu	揚げだし豆腐	deep-fried tofu in a fish stock soup
jaga-batā	ジャガバター	baked potatoes with butter
niku-jaga	肉じゃが	beef and potato stew

shio-yaki-zakana	塩焼魚	a whole fish grilled with salt
yaki-onigiri	焼きおにぎり	a triangle of grilled rice with yakitori sauce
poteto furai	ポテトフライ	French fries
chiizu-age	チーズ揚げ	deep-fried cheese
hiya-yakko	冷奴	a cold block of tofu with soy sauce and scallions
tsuna sarada	ツナサラダ	tuna salad over cabbage
yaki-soba	焼きそば	fried noodles with meat and vegetables
kata yaki-soba	固焼きそば	hard fried noodles with meat and vegetables
sashimi mori-awase	刺身盛りあわせ	a selection of sliced sashimi

Robatayaki 炉端焼

Similar to an izakaya, a *robatayaki* is a rustic drinking restaurant serving a wide variety of foods grilled over charcoal. The name means hearthside cooking, and every effort is made to re-create the atmosphere of an old country house – which was always centred around a large hearth, or *irori*. Eating at a robatayaki is a feast for the eyes as well as the taste buds: you sit around a counter with the food spread out in front of you on a layer of ice, behind which is a large charcoal grill. You don't need a word of Japanese to order, just point at whatever looks good. The chef will grill your selection, then pass it to you on a long wooden paddle – grab your food quickly before he snatches it back. Some of the best robatayaki chefs are real performers and make a show of cooking the food and serving customers.

The fare at a robatayaki is largely the same as at an izakaya. They have

Eating in a Japanese Restaurant

When you enter a restaurant in Japan, you'll be greeted with a hearty *'Irasshaimase!'* ('Welcome!'). In all but the most casual places the waiter will next ask you *'Nan-mei sama?'* ('How many people?'). Answer with your fingers, which is what the Japanese do. You will then be led to a table, a place at the counter or a *tatami* (straw mat) room.

At this point you will be given an *oshibori* (hot towel), a cup of tea and a menu. The oshibori is for cleaning your hands (and while actually considered bad form, many Japanese men fancy wiping their faces with these as well). When you're done with it, just roll or fold it up and leave it next to your place. Now comes the hard part: ordering. If you don't read Japanese, you can use the romanised translations in this book to help you, or direct the waiter's attention to the Japanese script. If this doesn't work, there are two phrases which may help: *'O-susume wa nan desu ka?'* ('What do you recommend?') and *'O-makase shimasu'* ('Please decide for me'). If you're still having problems, you can try pointing at other diners' food or, if the restaurant has them, dragging the waiter outside to point at the plastic food models in the window.

When you've finished eating, you can ask for the bill by saying *'O-kanjō kudasai'*. Remember that there is no tipping in Japan and tea is free of charge. Usually you will be given a bill to take to the cashier at the front of the restaurant. At more upmarket places, the host of the party will discreetly excuse themself to pay before the group leaves. Unlike in the west, don't leave cash on the table by way of payment. Only the bigger and more international places take credit cards, so cash is always the surer option.

When leaving, it is polite to say to the restaurant staff, *'Gochisō-sama deshita'* which means 'It was a real feast'. ■

menus, but no one uses them – just point and eat. The drink of choice is beer or sake. Expect to spend about ¥3000 per head. Less common than izayaka, robatayaki usually have rustic wooden facades modelled on traditional Japanese farmhouses.

Yatai 屋台

Though a relative rarity in Kyoto, you may stumble across a *yatai*, simply an outdoor version of an izakaya serving things like yakitori and noodle dishes. These hawker stalls are typically set up in empty lots between buildings and are only open in the evening. The emphasis is on a quick bite and a glass of beer, and yatai are not really places to linger (or you may be ushered out by waiting customers). Like izakaya, yatai can be spotted by red lanterns hanging outside the stalls. Perhaps more common than traditional yatai today are a kind of mobile yatai which operate out of small vans cruising the city streets and typically selling rāmen noodles.

Meshiya & Nomiya 飯や／飲み屋

Meshiya and *nomiya* are narrow, tiny spots usually with just a counter or a few small tables. They mostly cater to *salarymen* (office workers) and as their names suggest (meshiya means food place and nomiya means drink place), they are casual 'at home' places for a little after-work food, drink and a bit of conversation. Both are similar in fare and price to an izakaya or robatayaki, but without the rustic atmosphere (decorations are usually limited to an Asahi Beer Girl poster). Many meishiya and nomiya are found tucked away in narrow alleys around larger train stations and in entertainment areas.

Kissaten 喫茶店

Kissaten are Japanese coffee shops, mostly serving basic coffees, teas and sometimes simple cakes or pastries. Many kissaten also serve a reasonable lunch special *(sābisu ranchi* or *ranchi setto)*, but the food tends to be fairly basic.

Coffee at a kissaten is often seen as overpriced by foreign visitors. Largely the coffee is expensive because, in part, you are renting a place to sit and relax without the pressure of having to make room for the next customer.

Mukokuseki 無国籍

Mukokuseki restaurants, literally, no nationality restaurants, are places which bypass the single culinary theme of French, Italian or Vietnamese by offering borderless menus with a wide mix of food from Japan and all over the world.

Ryōtei 料亭

Ryōtei are as 'Japanese' (and expensive) as restaurants get. They are high-class, traditional-style eateries serving Japanese haute cuisine, in particular elaborate *kaiseki-ryōri* courses. Most tend to be exclusive and many only cater to those with an introduction.

The food is typically served by kimono-clad waitresses *(nakai-san)* in private tatami rooms *(zashiki)*. These rooms are often overlooking a private, tranquil garden, in Kyoto's case, a river. Occasionally, those eating at one of Kyoto's ryōtei will employ *geisha* or *maiko* in full costume to join their meal, providing conversation and entertainment.

The decor at ryōtei is pure Japanese, both inside and out. As many ryōtei are in old Japanese-style homes, the customers get the feeling they are guests in a private home. The exterior facade may have a traditional wooden gate *(mon)* and a path of stones leading into the building. Note the small cone-shaped lumps of salt (called *morijio*) that many ryōtei place on the ground outside either side of the entrance; a 'welcome' sign to customers and a symbol of purity and prosperity.

Soybeans (daizu) – the nutritious base for an endless variety of Japanese foods – soy sauce, miso, tofu and the smelly nattō.

FOOD

Kyō-ryōri 京料理

Kyō-ryōri, or Kyoto cuisine, is a style of cooking which evolved out of Kyoto's landlocked location and age-old customs of the imperial court. The preparation of dishes makes ingenious use of fresh seasonal vegetables and emphasises subtle flavours, revealing the natural flavour of the ingredients. Kyō-ryōri is selected according to the mood and hues of the ever-changing seasons, and the presentation and atmosphere are as important as the flavour.

Kaiseki 懐石

Kaiseki is the pinnacle of Japanese cuisine, where ingredients, preparation, setting and presentation come together to create a dining experience quite unlike any other. Born as an adjunct to tea ceremony, kaiseki is a largely vegetarian affair (though fish is often served). One usually eats kaiseki in the private room of a traditional ryōtei. The meal is served in several small courses, giving one the opportunity to admire the plates and bowls which are carefully chosen to complement the food and seasons. Rice is eaten last (usually with an assortment of pickles) and the drink of choice is sake or beer.

Kaiseki features a wide range of Japanese dishes, and great attention is given to service and overall presentation. As you might expect, it's a very expensive experience. A modest kaiseki course might cost ¥6000 per person, and a full spread is ¥10,000 to ¥15,000. At the most exclusive establishments, such as those serving *yūsoku-ryōri* (kaiseki in the style of ancient court banquets), you can easily shell out up to ¥50,000 a head (if you are deemed fit to make a reservation). For lesser mortals with punier budgets, many restaurants do a lunchtime kaiseki *bentō* (boxed lunch) containing a sample of their dinner fare from around ¥2000, or a 'mini-kaiseki' course for about ¥4000.

O-bentō *(boxed lunch) – sold in tiny street takeaways, bustling department stores and on station platforms, the bentō serves as a handy, cheap and nutritious meal of rice, seafood, meat and vegetables.*

Unfortunately for foreigners, kaiseki restaurants can be intimidating places to enter. If possible, bring along a Japanese friend or ask a Japanese friend to call ahead and make arrangements. There is usually only one set course, but some places offer a choice of three courses – *take* (regular), *matsu* (special) and *ume* (extra-special). Other variations on kaiseki include *cha-kaiseki*, an elegant, light meal served as a prelude to tea ceremony.

Shōjin-ryōri 精進料理

Another style of cooking for which Kyoto is renowned is *shōjin-ryōri*. This is a vegetarian cuisine (no meat, fish, eggs or dairy products are used), which was introduced from China along with Buddhism and is now available in special restaurants usually connected with temples. As it is a style of cooking that has its origins in Buddhist asceticism, don't expect a hearty affair – great attention is given to presentation and dishes tend to be small.

Typically the meal will include a variety of fresh vegetables such as boiled *daikon* (radishes). Tofu also plays a prominent role in the menu. For a meal of this type, several Kyoto temples offer lunch courses from around ¥3000. Most shōjin-ryōri restaurants require reservations a few days in advance and in some cases a minimum of four people.

Eating Etiquette

When it comes to eating in Japan, there are a number of implicit rules but they're fairly easy to remember. If you're worried about putting your foot in it, relax – the Japanese almost expect foreigners to make fools of themselves in formal situations and are unlikely to be offended as long as you follow the rules of politeness standard in your own country.

Among the more important eating 'rules' are those regarding chopsticks. Sticking them upright in your rice is very bad form – that's how rice is offered to the dead! It's also bad form to pass food from your chopsticks to someone else's – another Buddhist funeral rite which involves passing the remains of the cremated deceased among members of the family using chopsticks.

It's worth remembering that a lot of effort has gone into the preparation of the food so don't pour soy sauce all over it (especially the rice) and don't mix it up with your chopsticks. Also, if possible, eat everything you are given. And don't forget to slurp your noodles!

When eating with other people, especially when you're a guest, it is polite to say *'Itadakimasu'* (literally, 'I will receive') before digging in. This is as close as the Japanese come to saying grace. Similarly, at the end of the meal you should thank your host by saying *'Gochisō-sama deshita'*.

When drinking with Japanese remember that it is impolite to fill your own glass; fill that of the person next to you and wait for them to reciprocate. Filling your own glass amounts to admitting to everyone at the table that you're an alcoholic. It is polite to raise your glass a little off the table while it is being filled. Once everyone's glass has been filled, the usual starting signal is a chorus of *'kampai'* which means 'cheers!'. Constant topping up means a bottomless glass – just put your hand over your glass if you've had enough.

There is also a definite etiquette to bill-paying. If someone invites you to eat or drink with them, they will be paying. Even among groups eating together it is unusual for bills to be split. The exception to this is found among young people and close friends and is called *warikan* (each person paying their own share). Generally, at the end of the meal something of a struggle will ensue to see who gets the privilege of paying. It is polite to at least make an effort to pay – it is extremely unlikely that your Japanese 'hosts' will acquiesce. ∎

Another variation on shōjin-ryōri is the Chinese-influenced *fucha-ryōri*, and there are a handful of places in Kyoto to sample this fare.

Tofu-ryōri 豆腐料理

Kyoto is famed for its tofu (soybean curd); there are numerous tofu makers *(tofu-ya-san)* scattered throughout the city and a legion of exquisite *yudōfu* (boiled tofu) restaurants – many are concentrated along the road into Nanzen-ji Temple and in the Arashiyama area. One typical Kyoto tofu byproduct is called *yuba*, sheets of the chewy thin film which settles on the surface of vats of simmering soy milk.

Okonomiyaki お好み焼

The name means cook what you like, and an *okonomiyaki* restaurant provides you with an inexpensive opportunity to do just that. Sometimes described as Japanese pizza or pancake, the resemblance is in form only. At an okonomiyaki restaurant, you sit around a *teppan* (iron hotplate) armed with a spatula and chopsticks to cook your choice of meat, seafood and vegetables in a cabbage and vegetable batter.

Some places will do most of the cooking and bring the nearly finished product over to your hotplate for you to season with bonito flakes *(katsuo bushi)*, soy sauce *(shōyu)*, parsley, Japanese Worcestershire-style sauce and mayonnaise. Cheaper places will simply hand you a bowl of ingredients and expect you to cook it yourself. If this happens, don't panic. First, mix the batter and filling thoroughly, then place it on the hot grill, flattening it into a pancake shape. After five minutes or so, use the spatula to flip it and cook for another five minutes. Then dig in.

Most okonomiyaki places also serve *yaki-soba* (fried noodles) and *yasai-itame* (stir-fried vegetables). All of this is washed down with mugs of draught beer. One final word: don't worry too much about preparation of the food – as a foreigner you'll be expected to be inept and the waiter will keep a sharp eye on you to make sure no real disasters occur.

mikkusu okonomiyaki	ミックス お好み焼き	mixed fillings of seafood, meat and vegetables
modan-yaki	モダン焼き	okonomiyaki with fried egg
gyū okonomiyaki	牛お好み焼き	beef okonomiyaki
yasai okonomiyaki	野菜お好み焼き	vegetable okonomiyaki
negi okonomiyaki	ネギお好み焼き	thin okonomiyaki with scallions

Yakitori 焼き鳥

Yakitori means skewers of grilled chicken, a popular after-work meal. Yakitori is not so much a full meal as it is an accompaniment for beer and sake. At a yakitori restaurant, you sit around a counter with the other patrons and watch the chef grill your selections over charcoal. The best way to eat here is to order a few skewers of several varieties, then order seconds of those you really like.

In summer, the beverage of choice at a yakitori restaurant is beer or cold sake, while in winter it is hot sake. A few drinks and enough skewers to fill you should cost from ¥3000 to ¥4000 per person. Yakitori restaurants are usually small places, often near railway stations, and are best identified by a red lantern outside and the smell of grilling chicken.

Daikon *radish – a tasty vegetable commonly used in non-meat dishes. Freshly grated, it adds a tangy taste to the dipping sauces served with* tempura *and* soba *noodles.*

yakitori	焼き鳥	plain, grilled white meat
hasami/negima	はさみ／ねぎま	pieces of white meat alternating with leek
sasami	ささみ	skinless chicken breast pieces
kawa	かわ	chicken skin
tsukune	つくね	chicken meat balls
gyū-niku	牛肉	pieces of beef
rebā	レバ	chicken livers
tebasaki	手羽先	chicken wings

Yakitori – *skewers of grilled chicken, and* tsukune *meatballs, can be bought from pushcarts, used as a stomach liner for a night of sake drinking, or admired for their thoughtful presentation in an elegant restaurant.*

shiitake	しいたけ	Japanese mushrooms
piiman	ピーマン	small, green peppers
tama-negi	たまねぎ	round, white onions
yaki-onigiri	焼きおにぎり	a triangle of rice grilled with yakitori sauce

Sushi & Sashimi 寿司／刺身

There are two main types of *sushi: nigiri-zushi* (served on a small bed of rice – the most common variety) and *maki-zushi* (served in a seaweed roll). Lesser known varieties include *chirashi-zushi* (a layer of rice covered with egg and fish toppings), *oshi-zushi* (fish pressed in a mould over rice) and *inari-zushi* (rice in a pocket of sweet, fried tofu). Whatever kind of sushi you try, it will be served with lightly vinegared rice. In the case of nigiri-zushi and maki-zushi, it will contain a bit of *wasabi* (spicy green horseradish). *Sashimi* is simply sushi without the rice; slices of raw fish with a shredded daikon garnish.

Sushi is not difficult to order. If you sit at the counter of a sushi restaurant, you can simply point at what you want, as most of the selections are visible in a refrigerated glass case between you and the sushi chef. You can also order à la carte from the menu. When ordering, you usually order *ichi-nin mae* (one portion), which usually means two pieces of sushi. Be careful since the price on the menu will be that of only one piece. If ordering à la carte is too daunting, you can order an assortment plate of nigiri-zushi called a *mori-awase*. This will be one of three grades: *futsū nigiri* (regular nigiri), *jō nigiri* (special nigiri) and *toku-jō nigiri* (extra-special nigiri). The difference is in the type of fish used. Most mori-awase contain six or seven pieces of sushi.

Before popping the sushi into your mouth, dip it fish-side down in shōyu (soy sauce) which you pour from a small decanter into a low dish specially provided for the purpose. If you're no good at using chopsticks, don't worry, as sushi is one of the few foods in Japan that is perfectly acceptable to eat with your hands. Slices of pickled ginger *(gari)* will also be served to help refresh the palate. The beverage of choice with sushi is beer or sake (usually hot in the winter and cold in the summer), with a cup of green tea at the end of the meal.

Be warned that a good sushi restaurant can cost upwards of ¥10,000, while an average place will cost about ¥3000 to ¥5000 per person. One way to sample the joy of sushi on the cheap is to try a *kaiten-zushi* restaurant, where the sushi is served on a conveyor belt which runs around an oval counter. Here you simply reach up and grab whatever looks good (which certainly takes the pain out of ordering). You're charged according to how many plates of sushi you've eaten. Plates are colour-coded according to their price and the cost is written either somewhere on the plate itself or on a sign on the wall. You can usually fill yourself up in one of these places for ¥1000 to ¥2000.

ama-ebi	甘海老	sweet shrimp
awabi	あわび	abalone
ebi	海老	prawn or shrimp
hamachi	はまち	yellowtail
ika	いか	squid
ikura	イクラ	salmon roe
kai-bashira	貝柱	scallop
kani	かに	crab
katsuo	かつお	bonito
maguro	まぐろ	tuna
tai	鯛	sea bream
tamago	たまご	sweetened egg
toro	とろ	the choicest cut of fatty tuna belly, very expensive
unagi	うなぎ	eel with a sweet sauce
uni	うに	sea urchin roe

Sukiyaki & Shabu-shabu すき焼／しゃぶしゃぶ

Restaurants usually specialise in both these dishes. Popular in the west, *sukiyaki* is a favourite of most foreign visitors to Japan. When made with high-quality beef, like Kōbe beef, it is a sublime experience. Sukiyaki consists of thin slices of beef cooked in a broth of soy sauce, sugar and sake, and is accompanied by a variety of vegetables and tofu. After cooking, all the ingredients are dipped in raw egg (the heat of the ingredients tends to lightly cook the egg) before being eaten.

Shabu-shabu consists of thin slices of beef and vegetables cooked by swirling the ingredients in a light broth, then dipping them in a variety of special sesame seed and citrus-based sauces. Both of these dishes are prepared in a pot over a fire at your private table, but you needn't fret about preparation – the waiter or waitress will usually help you get started and then keep a close watch as you proceed. The key is to take your time and add the ingredients a little at a time, savouring the flavours as you go.

Sukiyaki and shabu-shabu restaurants usually have a traditional Japan-

Sukiyaki – *prepared in a pot over a fire at your table and dipped in various sauces, this provides a novel dining experience.*

GLENN BEANLAND

ese decor and sometimes a picture of a cow to help you recognise them. Ordering is not difficult. Simply say 'sukiyaki' or 'shabu-shabu' and indicate how many people's worth of food is required. Expect to pay between ¥3000 to ¥10,000 per person.

Tempura 天ぷら

One of the most famous of all Japanese foods, *tempura* is not actually Japanese at all, but was borrowed from Portuguese traders in the 16th century. Since then, the Japanese have transformed it into something uniquely their own. Good tempura is portions of fish, prawns and vegetables cooked in fluffy, nongreasy batter.

When you sit down in a tempura restaurant, you will be given a small bowl filled with a light-brown sauce *(ten-tsuyu)* and a plate of grated daikon, which you mix into the sauce. Dip each piece of tempura into this sauce before eating it.

While it's possible to order à la carte, most diners choose to order a *teishoku*, which includes rice, miso soup and Japanese pickles. Some tempura restaurants also offer courses of tempura which include different numbers of tempura pieces.

Expect to pay between ¥2000 and ¥10,000 for a full tempura meal.

Rāmen ラーメン

The Japanese imported this dish from China and put their own spin on it to make what is one of the world's most delicious fast foods. *Rāmen* dishes are big bowls of noodles in a meat broth served with a variety of toppings, such as sliced pork, bean sprouts and leeks. In some restaurants, particularly in Kansai, you may be asked if you'd prefer *kotteri* (thick) or *assari* (thin) soup. Other than this, ordering is simple: just sidle up to the counter and say 'rāmen', or ask for any of the other choices usually on offer (see the list below). Expect to pay between ¥500 and ¥900 for a bowl. Since rāmen is originally Chinese food, some rāmen restaurants also serve *chāhan* or *yaki-meshi* (fried rice), *gyōza* (dumplings) and *kara-age* (deep-fried chicken pieces).

Rāmen restaurants are easily distinguished by their long counters lined with customers hunched over steaming bowls. You can also hear a rāmen shop – it is considered polite to slurp the noodles, and aficionados claim that slurping brings out the full flavour of the broth.

rāmen	ラーメン	standard issue, the cheapest item on the menu – soup and noodles with a sprinkling of meat and vegetables
chāshū-men	チャーシュー麺	rāmen topped with slices of roasted pork
wantan-men	ワンタン麺	rāmen with meat dumplings
miso-rāmen	みそラーメン	rāmen with miso-flavoured broth
chānpon-men	ちゃんぽん麺	Nagasaki-style rāmen with assorted vegetables and meat in the broth

Soba & Udon そば／うどん

Soba and *udon* are Japan's answer to Chinese-style rāmen. Soba are thin, brown, buckwheat noodles, while udon are thick, white, wheat noodles. Most Japanese noodle shops serve both soba and udon prepared in a variety of ways. Noodles are usually served in a bowl containing a light, bonito-flavoured broth, but you can also order them served cold and piled on a bamboo screen with a cold broth for dipping. By far the most popular type of cold noodles is *zaru soba*, which is served with bits of seaweed *(nori)* on top. If you order these noodles, you'll receive a small plate of wasabi and sliced scallions – put these into the cup of broth and eat the noodles by

Wasabi *(horseradish)* – the fresh wasabi root, grown in clear mountain streams, is grated into a paste and served as a fiery seasoning with cool dishes like sushi.

Zaru soba noodles – to sample one of Kyoto's most traditional foods, try a fortifying bowl of these cold, freshly made buckwheat noodles.

dipping them in this mixture. At the end of your meal, the waiter may give you some hot broth to mix with the leftover sauce which you drink like a kind of tea. As with rāmen, you should feel free to slurp as loudly as you please.

Soba and udon places are usually quite cheap, but some fancy places can be significantly more expensive (the decor is a good indication of the price).

Add 'soba' or 'udon' to the following four dishes when ordering:

kake	かけ	plain noodles in broth
kitsune	きつね	noodles with slices of fried tofu
tempura	天ぷら	noodles with tempura shrimp
tsukimi	月見	noodles with raw egg on top (literally, moon viewing)
zaru soba	ざるそば	cold noodles with seaweed strips served on a bamboo tray

Unagi うなぎ

Unagi is Japanese for eel, an expensive and popular delicacy in Japan. Even if you can't stand the creature back home, you owe it to yourself to try unagi at least once while in Japan. It's cooked over hot coals and brushed with a rich sauce made from shōyu and sake. Full unagi dinners can be quite expensive, but many unagi restaurants offer unagi bentō and lunch sets for around ¥1500. Most unagi restaurants display plastic models of their unagi sets in the front windows and have barrels of live eels to entice passers-by.

unagi teishoku	うなぎ定食	full-set unagi meal with rice, grilled eel, eel-liver soup and pickles
unadon	うな丼	grilled eel over a bowl of rice
unajū	うな重	grilled eel over a flat tray of rice (larger than unadon)
kabayaki	蒲焼き	skewers of grilled eel without rice

Nabemono 鍋物

A *nabe* is a large cooking pot and the term *nabemono* refers to any of a variety of dishes cooked in these pots. Like sukiyaki and shabu-shabu, nabemono are cooked at your table on a small gas burner or a clay *hibachi* (small barbecue). Eating nabemono is a participatory experience, with each diner putting in ingredients from trays of prepared, raw food. The most famous nabemono is called *chanko-nabe*, the high-calorie stew eaten by sumō wrestlers during training. Chanko-nabe restaurants are often run by retired sumō wrestlers and the walls of such restaurants are usually festooned with sumō arcana.

Since nabemono are filling and hot, they are usually eaten in winter. They are also popular as banquet and party dishes since the eating of a nabe dish is a very communal experience. It is difficult to pick out a nabe restaurant – the best way is to ask a Japanese friend for a recommendation.

chanko-nabe	ちゃんこ鍋	sumō wrestler's stew of meat and vegetables
botan-nabe	ぼたん鍋	wild boar stew with vegetables
yose-nabe	寄せ鍋	seafood and chicken stew with vegetables

Tonkatsu トンカツ

Although it's held in low esteem abroad, the Japanese have figured out a way to prepare pork that rivals the best steak. *Tonkatsu* is a deep-fried breaded pork cutlet served with a special sauce, usually as part of a set meal *(tonkatsu teishoku)*. Even if you shy away from pork at home, you ought to try this dish once while you're here – you'll probably be pleasantly surprised.

Tonkatsu is served both at speciality restaurants and at shokudō. Naturally, the best tonkatsu is to be found at the speciality places, where a full set will cost from ¥1500 to ¥2500. When ordering, you can choose between *rōsu*, a fatter cut of pork and *hire*, a leaner cut.

tonkatsu teishoku	とんかつ定食	a full set meal of tonkatsu, rice, miso soup and shredded cabbage
minchi katsu	ミンチカツ	minced pork cutlet
kushikatsu	串カツ	deep-fried pork and vegetables on skewers

Kushiage & Kushikatsu 串アゲ／串カツ

Dieters beware, this is the fried food to beat all fried foods. *Kushiage* and *kushikatsu* are deep-fried skewers of meat, seafood and vegetables eaten as an accompaniment to beer. Kushi means skewer, and if it can be fitted onto a skewer, it's probably on the menu. Cabbage is often eaten with the meal to ease the guilt of eating all that grease.

You order kushiage and kushikatsu by the skewer (one skewer is *ippon*, but you can always use your fingers to indicate the number). Like yakitori, this food is popular with after-work salarymen (office workers) and students, and is therefore fairly inexpensive, though upmarket places exist. Expect to pay from ¥2000 to ¥5000 for a full meal and a couple of beers. Not particularly distinctive in appearance, the best way to find a kushiage and kushikatsu place is to ask a Japanese friend.

ebi	えび	shrimp
ika	いか	squid
renkon	レンコン	lotus root
tama-negi	たまねぎ	white onion
gyū-niku	牛肉	beef pieces
shiitake	しいたけ	Japanese mushrooms
ginnan	銀杏	ginkgo nuts
imo	いも	potato

Lotus root (renkon) – appreciated for its firm and crisp texture, slices of this root are often added to pots of steaming nabe or deep-fried as tempura.

DRINKS

TONY WHEELER

Alcohol

Drinking is the glue that holds Japanese society together. It is practised by almost every adult, male or female, and by a good number of teenagers (alcohol is sold from vending machines, and underage drinking is not nearly as frowned upon as in the west). Going out for a few rounds after work with co-workers is both the joy and bane of the Japanese salaryman's life. After a few drinks, Japanese workers feel secure enough to vent their frustrations and speak their minds, confident that all will be forgiven by the time they arrive at the office in the morning. Occasionally, Japanese drinking crosses the boundary between good-natured fun and ugly inebriation, as anyone who has been in a public park during cherry blossom season can attest.

Beer Introduced at the end of the last century, beer *(biiru)* is now the favourite tipple of the Japanese. The quality is generally excellent, and the most popular type is the light lager, although recently some breweries have been experimenting with darker brews. The major breweries are Kirin, Asahi, Sapporo and Suntory. Beer is dispensed everywhere, from vending machines to beer halls and even in some temple lodgings. A standard can of beer from a vending machine is about ¥250, although some of the monstrous cans cost over ¥1000. At bars, beer starts at ¥500 and climbs upwards depending on the establishment. Draught beer *(nama biiru)* is widely available, as are imported beers.

Sake Rice wine has been brewed for centuries in Japan. Once restricted to imperial brewers, it was later produced at temples and shrines across the country. In recent years, consumption of beer has overtaken that of sake, but it's still a standard item in homes, restaurants and drinking places. Large casks of sake are often seen piled up as offerings outside temples and shrines, and it plays an important part in most celebrations and festivals.

There are several major types of sake, including *nigori* (cloudy), *nama* (unrefined) and regular, clear sake. Of these, the clear sake is by far the most common, and is generally divided into *karakuchi* (dry) and *amakuchi* (sweet). Apart from the national brewing giants, there are thousands of provincial brewers producing local brews called *jizake*.

Sake is served *atsukan* (warm) and *reishū* (cold), the former being more popular in winter. When you order sake, it will usually be served in a small flask called a *tokkuri*. These come in two sizes, so you should specify whether you want an *ichigo* (small) or a *nigo* (large). From these flasks, you

Sake *barrels – these casks are often left at temples or shrines as offerings to the* kami *(gods) to watch over the rice harvest. Sake making was once a communal affair, with the entire village involved. After WWII, rice shortages required that pure alcohol be mixed with rice mash to increase yields of drink. Nearly all sake is produced this way today.*

TONY WHEELER

pour the sake into small ceramic cups called *o-choko* or *sakazuki*. Another way to sample sake is to drink it from a small wooden box called a *masu*.

However you drink it, with a 17% alcohol content, sake is likely to go right to your head, particularly the warm stuff. After a few bouts with sake, you'll come to understand why the Japanese drink it in such small cups.

Shōchū For those looking for a quick and cheap escape from their sorrows, *shōchū* is the answer. It's a distilled spirit with an alcohol content of about 30%, which has been resurrected from low esteem (it was used as a disinfectant in the Edo period) to the status of a trendy drink. You can drink it as *oyu-wari* (with hot water) or as *chūhai* (a highball with fruit-flavoured soda). A 720ml bottle sells for about ¥600, which makes it a relatively cheap option compared to other spirits.

Wine, Imported Drinks & Whisky Japanese wines are available from areas such as Nagano, Hokkaidō and the Tamba region north-west of Kyoto. Imported wines are often stocked by large liquor stores or department stores in the cities. Bargain bottles are usually available for under ¥1000.

Prices of imported spirits have been coming down in recent years, and discount liquor stores have been popping up everywhere. Whisky is available at most drinking establishments, and is usually drunk *mizu-wari* (with water and ice) or *onzarokku* (on the rocks). Local brands, such as Suntory, are sensibly priced, while more expensive foreign labels are popular as gifts.

Most other imported spirits can be had at drinking establishments in Japan. Bars with a large foreign clientele, including hotel bars, can usually mix anything at your request.

Drinking Places What you pay for your drink depends on where you drink and, in the case of some bars, with whom you drink. As a rule, hostess bars are the most expensive places (up to ¥10,000 per drink), followed by upmarket traditional Japanese bars, hotel bars, beer halls and casual pubs. If you are not sure about a place, ask about prices and cover charges before sitting down. As a rule, if you are served a small snack with your first round, you'll be paying a cover charge (usually a few hundred yen, but sometimes much more).

Izakaya and *yakitori-ya* are cheap places for beer, sake and food in a casual atmosphere resembling that of a pub. *Aka-chōchin*, which display a red lantern outside the premises, are similar pubs for the working man (less popular with women) – down-to-earth in price and decor. All Japanese cities have a few informal pubs with reasonable prices. Such places are popular with young Japanese and resident foreigners, who usually refer them as gaijin bars. In summer, rooftop beer gardens are popular spots to cool off and check the view. Beer halls are affordable and popular places to swill your beer in a faux-German atmosphere.

The 'snack' bars which are found in their hundreds, jammed into tiny rooms of large buildings, are used by their customers as a type of club – if you drop in unexpectedly, the reception may be cool. Hostess bars are inevitably expensive, often exorbitant and, without an introduction, best avoided. They cater mainly to those entertaining on business accounts. Hostesses pamper customers with compliments or lend a sympathetic ear to their problems. The best way to visit is in the company of a Japanese friend who knows the routine.

Japan, of course, is also where *karaoke* got its beginnings. If you've never sung in a karaoke bar, it's worth a try at least once. The uninitiated usually find that a few stiff drinks beforehand helps. Customers sing to the accompaniment of taped music and, as the evening wears on, voices get progressively more ragged. Sobbing, mournful *enka* (folk ballads) are the norm, although more and more western hits are finding their way into karaoke 'menus'. If you visit a karaoke place with a Japanese friend, it's unlikely that you'll escape without singing at least one song – a version of 'Yesterday' or 'My Way' will usually satisfy the crowd.

Nonalcoholic Drinks

Most of the drinks you're used to at home will be available in Japan, with a few colourfully named additions like Pocari Sweat and Calpis Water. One convenient aspect of Japan is the presence of drink machines on virtually every street corner, and for ¥110 refreshment is rarely more than a few steps away.

Coffee & Tea Coffee *(kōhii)* tends to be expensive in Japan, costing between ¥350 and ¥500 a cup, with some places charging up to ¥1000. A cheap alternative is some of the newer chains of coffee restaurants like Doutor or donut shops like Mr Donut (which offers free refills). An even cheaper alternative is a can of coffee, hot or cold, from a vending machine. Although unpleasantly sweet, at ¥110 the price is hard to beat.

When ordering coffee at a coffee shop, you'll be asked whether you like it *hotto* (hot) or *aisu* (cold). Black tea also comes hot or cold, with *miruku* (milk) or *remon* (lemon). A good way to start a day of sightseeing in Japan is with a *mōningu setto* (morning set) of tea or coffee, toast and eggs, which costs around ¥450. The following are some of the more common drinks available in *kissaten* (Japanese coffee shops).

kōhii	コーヒー	regular coffee
burendo kōhii	ブレンドコーヒー	blended coffee, fairly strong
american kōhii	アメリカンコーヒー	weak coffee
kōcha	紅茶	black, British-style tea
kafe ōre	カフェオーレ	café au lait, hot or cold
orenji jūsu	オレンジジュース	orange juice

Japanese Tea Unlike the black tea which westerners are familiar with, Japanese tea is green and contains a lot of vitamin C and caffeine. The powdered form used in tea ceremony is called *matcha* and is drunk after being whipped into a frothy consistency. The more common form is leafy green tea *(o-cha)*, which is drunk after being steeped in a pot. While *sencha* is one popular variety of green tea, most restaurants will serve a free cup of brownish tea called *bancha*. In summer a cold beverage called *mugicha* (roasted barley tea) is served in private homes.

Although not particularly popular in the west, Japanese tea is very healthy and refreshing, and is said by some to prevent cancer. Most department stores carry a wide selection of Japanese teas.

SWEETS

Although most restaurants don't serve dessert (plates of sliced fruit are usually served at the end of a meal in Japan), there is no lack of sweets in Japan. Most sweets (known generically as *wagashi*) are sold in speciality stores for you to eat at home. Many of the more delicate-looking ones are made to balance the strong, bitter taste of matcha.

Although pleasant to look at, some westerners find Japanese sweets unappealing – perhaps because many of them contain a sweet, red-bean paste called *anko*. This unusual filling turns up in even the most innocuous looking pastries. But don't let anyone make up your mind for you: try a Japanese sweet for yourself. Who knows, you may be a member of that small minority of foreigners who really love them.

With such a wide variety of sweets, it's difficult to specify names. However, you'll probably find many variations on the anko-covered-by-glutinous rice theme *(mochi)*. Another sweet to look out for is the *yōkan* – a sweet, bean jelly slice. For confectionery aficiondos, however, Kyoto is undisputedly the place to be.

Sweet shops are easy to spot; they usually have open fronts with their wares laid out in wooden trays to entice passers-by. Buying sweets is simple – just point at what you want and indicate with your fingers how many you'd like.

Lemon peel – this is a refreshing and popular addition to black tea drunk in kissaten *(coffee shops).*

continued from page 162

If you're feeling noodled-out, *Yamamoto Manbo* (Map 11), just across the street, serves good okonomiyaki.

If you're visiting Tō-ji Temple, there are a few good eateries in the area. *Red Pepper* (Map 11) serves fresh 'oriented Italian cuisine' and has good lunch courses starting from ¥800. It's just east of Tō-ji, on the south side of Kujō-dōri, and is open for lunch from 11.30 am to 2 pm and dinner from 5 to 9.30 pm, closed Wednesday.

CENTRAL KYOTO

Central Kyoto, in particular the Kawaramachi area, has the highest concentration of restaurants in the city. There's a wide range of both international and Japanese eateries in all price ranges.

Budget

For a delicious, filling lunch of noodles or donburi (rice served with a variety of toppings) try *Toroku* (Map 9). Its tannin donburi (rice with egg and beef) is a good choice for ¥850, as is kitsune soba (fried tofu with noodles) for ¥550. It's open for lunch from 11.30 am to 2.30 pm and dinner from 5 to 8 pm, closed Saturday evening and Sunday.

Near Sukaraza theatre, *Kane-yo* (Map 10) is a good lunch place to try grilled eel (unagi). You can sit downstairs with a nice view of the waterfall or upstairs on the *tatami* (straw mats). The ¥800 kane-yo donburi set is great value. It's open daily from 11.30 am to 3 pm. Look for the barrels of live eels outside and the wooden facade.

North of Shijō-dōri, tucked away in the narrow streets between Kawaramachi-dōri and Kiyamachi-dōri, there are couple of classic combination bar-and-restaurants serving cheap food and drink to start the evening. *A-Bar* (Map 10) is an izakaya with a log-cabin interior. There's a big menu to choose from and everything's cheap. The staff here are famous for opening beer bottles with chopsticks. It's a little tough to find – look for the small black and white sign at the top of a flight of steps just past Ōsho Chinese restaurant. For a slightly less rambunctious

atmosphere, *Zappa* (Map 10) is a cosy little place which is said to come recommended by David Bowie. The friendly owner, Hiroko-san, serves up savoury South-East Asian fare and a few Japanese tidbits for good measure. Prices are reasonable and the music is groovy (but no Frank Zappa?). It's open from 6 pm to midnight, closed Sunday. Equally as hard to find as A-Bar, it's down a narrow alley between Kiyamachi-dōri and Kawaramachi-dōri; turn south at the wooden *torii* (Shintō gate).

If you've never tried fast food-style automatic sushi, don't miss *Musashi Sushi* (Map 10), at the Sanjō-dōri and Kawaramachi-dōri intersection. At this place, you sit as a parade of sushi goes sliding by on multicoloured plates. The price of each item is written on the plate itself – red plates are ¥100, orange ¥190 and green ¥290. About ¥1500 is enough to fill you. It's open daily from 11 am to 9.30 pm. Look for the mini-sushi conveyor belt in the window.

Further west on Sanjō-dōri, diagonally across from the Nakagyō post office, *Biotei* (Map 9) is a favourite of Kyoto health food nuts. Best for lunch, it serves a daily set of Japanese vegetarian/whole food for ¥850 (the occasional bit of meat is offered as an option, but you'll be asked your preference). Lunch is from 11 am to 2 pm and dinner from 5 to 8.30 pm (open till midnight); closed Sunday and Monday.

A little out of the way, but good value, *Obanzai* (Map 9) serves a fantastic buffet-style, all-you-can-eat health food lunch for ¥840 (¥1050 on weekends) and dinner for ¥2100. Most of the vegetables are organically grown, a rarity in this country. It's open daily from 11 am to 9 pm.

North of Oike-dōri are some more interesting choices. For rāmen, try *Shin-shin-tei* (Map 10), famous for its shiro (white) miso rāmen (¥600). The place doesn't look much, but the rāmen is excellent. It's open from 10.30 am to 5 pm, closed Sunday. For good okonomiyaki, try *Okonomiyaki Mai* (Map 10); it's open from 5 to 10.30 pm, closed Saturday.

For excellent home-made udon noodles and

tempting teishoku sets try *Tengu* (Map 8), on Kawaramachi-dōri just north of Kojinguchi-dōri and east of the Imperial Palace Park. It's open from 11.30 am to 3 pm and from 5 to 9 pm, closed Sunday.

Mid-Range

Takasebune (Map 10; ☎ 561-6040) serves a fine tempura set for lunch or dinner in a classic old Japanese house behind Hankyū department store for ¥700/1500/ 2000, depending on the amount of tempura you'd like. The sashimi is also good, and there's a simple English menu. Lunch is from 1 am to 3 pm and dinner from 4.30 to 9.30 pm, closed Monday.

Nishiki-kōji Food Market

If you're interested in viewing, or perhaps purchasing, all the weird and wonderful foods required for Kyoto-style cooking *(kyō-ryōri)*, wander through Nishiki-kōji Market (Map 10). It began as a fish market in the early 1300s, and many of the shops today have been in business for centuries. Better known as 'Kyoto's Kitchen', Nishiki-kōji is a must-see, a remarkable remnant of old Kyoto smack in the centre of town.

About 150 speciality shops line the narrow 400m-long covered alley. Many specialise in the high-quality ingredients used in the elegant *kaiseki-ryōri*. The street bustles with customers shopping for fresh fish, vegetables and extremely colourful Japanese pickles *(tsukemono)*.

Nishiki-kōji is an all-sensory experience and a great place to visit on a rainy day or as a break from temple-hopping. It is particularly lively in the morning, when chefs from Kyoto's finest restaurants and inns come to hand-pick the makings for the day's special delicacy. Also, in the late afternoon, Kyotoites come to see what's fresh for dinner. At year's end, the market becomes jam-packed with shoppers searching for the best ingredients to prepare *osechi-ryōri*, traditional New Year cuisine. Many Nishiki-kōji shops sell several types of ready-to-eat foods, like kushi-katsu skewers, tempura and sweet bean-filled rice cakes.

The market runs one block north of (and parallel to) Shijō-dōri, between the shopping arcade of Shinkyōgoku and Takakura-dōri (near the rear of Daimaru department store). Most shops are open from about 10 am to 7 pm. ■

For inexpensive Italian food, *Capricciosa* (Map 10) serves authentic pasta and pizza, delivered in enormous portions. The main store is a little south of the intersection of Sanjō-dōri and Kawaramachi-dōri. It's open daily from 11.30 am to 10 pm. A further possibility is *Daniel's* (Map 10), behind Daimaru department store; you can eat well here from around ¥1500.

North of Oike-dōri, behind the Kyoto Hotel, *Merry Island* (Map 10) is a good place for coffee or a light lunch. In warm weather the front doors are opened and the place takes on the air of a sidewalk cafe. The lunch set is a good bet for ¥800. It's open daily from 11.30 am to 11 pm.

On Pontochō-dōri, the izakaya (traditional pub) *Zu Zu* (Map 10) is a fun place to eat and drink (although many of the items available aren't listed on its English menu). The best bet is to point at what other diners are eating or ask the waiter for a recommendation. The fare is sort of nouveau-Japanese – things like shrimp and tofu or chicken and plum sauce. Count on spending about ¥3000 per person.

For good sushi in lively surroundings, head to *Tomi-zushi* (Map 10) near the Shinkyōgoku shopping arcade. Here, you rub elbows with your neighbour, sit at a long marble counter and watch as some of the fastest sushi chefs in the land do their thing. One person can fill up here for about ¥4000. It's open from 5 pm to midnight, closed Thursday. Go early or wait in line.

Almost midway along Pontochō-dōri, *Kappa Zushi* (Map 10) is another popular sushi bar with fair prices and an English menu. Figure on about ¥3000 a head.

Near the Sanjō bridge, *Ganko Zushi* (Map 10) is a good place for sushi or just about anything else. It serves good lunch sets for under ¥1000 and dinners from about ¥3000 per person; open daily from 11.30 am to 10.30 pm. Look for the large display of plastic food models in the window. There is also a more upscale branch (Map 10) on Kiyamachi-dōri, north of Oike-dōri, serving nabemono and kaiseki-ryōri in elegant Japanese surroundings.

For a slightly more upmarket robatayaki

experience, *Karyō-an* (Map 10; ☎ 212-7099) makes for a pleasant dinner choice. Chefs whip up a full range of fish, meat and vegetables right before your eyes for about ¥4000 per person. It's on the 3rd floor of the Yūrika building, north of Sanjō-dōri on Kiyamachi-dōri, and is open daily from 5 to 11 pm.

For excellent kushi-katsu (skewers of fried meat and vegetables) try *Ōiwa* (Map 10; ☎ 231-7667), just south of the Fujita Hotel. Ordering is easy, just ask for the course (30 skewers) and say 'stop' when you're full (you'll only be charged for what you've eaten; the whole course is ¥5000). It's open from 5 to 10 pm, closed Wednesday.

For authentic Italian food in a charming *kyō-machiya* (traditional townhouse), try *Kyoto Al Dente* (Map 10; ☎ 221-3553). The restaurant, behind the Kyoto Hotel, serves a variety of pastas and lunch sets from ¥1200, dinners à la carte around ¥2000, and full courses from ¥4000. It's open from 11.30 am to 2.30 pm for lunch, 5.30 to 9.30 pm for dinner, and offers tea, coffee and cakes from 2.30 to 5.30 pm; closed Monday.

In a country where 'salad' usually means a tiny helping of shredded cabbage, *Sancho* (Map 10) is a blessing. Also called the 'Salad House', it serves up grilled chicken, meats and delicious salads on the side, or à la carte; look for the plastic food display in the front. It's open from 11.30 am to 9 pm. Tucked into the narrow alley behind Sancho, *Shizuka* (Map 10) is a classic little izakaya with walls absolutely covered with graffiti. It's open from 5 to 10 pm; there's no English menu.

For a light meal *Shiruko* (Map 10; ☎ 221-3250) has been serving simple Kyoto obanzai-ryōri since 1932. The restaurant features more than 10 varieties of miso soup, and the rikyū bentō (¥2600) is a bona fide work of art. Shiruko is just north-east of the Shijō-Kawaramachi intersection and is open from 11.30 am to 8.30 pm, closed Wednesday.

Tagoto (Map 10; ☎ 221-1811) is famed for its artistic bentō, notably the popular koetsu mizusashi-bentō (¥3000), a delightful assortment of fresh fish and vegetables. The tranquil atmosphere here makes it hard to believe you are smack in the middle of the city. It's open daily from 11 am to 9 pm.

For a taste of some of Kyoto's best soba noodles in traditional surroundings, head for *Misoka-an Kawamichi-ya* (Map 10; ☎ 221-2525), north of Sanjō-dōri on Fuyachō-dōri. It's been hand-making noodles for 300 years. A simple bowl of nishin soba (topped with fish) costs ¥1000, and more elaborate nabe dishes start at around ¥3800 per person. It is open from 11 am to 8 pm, closed Thursday.

Yamatomi (Map 10; ☎ 221-3268) is another jewel on Pontochō-dōri where you can try your hand with the house special, teppin-age, frying up tasty tempura on skewers in a cast-iron pot (¥2800 per person). For a lighter meal, it also serves up good oden, both à la carte (from ¥150 per piece) and in a mixed moriawase set, and 'tofu skin' yuba-ryōri from ¥500. It is open from noon to 11 pm, closed Monday.

Also on Pontochō-dōri, *Fujino-ya* (Map 10; ☎ 221-2446) has tatami rooms overlooking the Kamo-gawa River; here you can feast on tempura, okonomiyaki, yaki-soba and kushi-katsu. Prices are reasonable at around ¥2000 a head. It's open from 5 to 10 pm, closed Wednesday.

In a classic building at the west end of the Shijō bridge, *Tōkasai-kan* (Map 10) serves up Peking-style Chinese dishes inspired by the imperial cuisine of ancient China. It has great spring rolls (haru-maki) for ¥1500 and boiled dumplings (mizu-gyōza) for ¥1000. It's open from 11.30 am to 8.30 pm daily.

Fiasco (Map 7), tucked away in a narrow street behind Dōshisha University, blends the best of Italy and California. It serves excellent pastas, pizzas, salads and tempting desserts, including *real* New York cheesecake. Expect to spend about ¥1500 for a light dinner or around ¥3000 for a full spread; the daily lunch special is ¥950. Fiasco is open from 11 am to 10.30 pm, closed Wednesday.

Top End

A good place to try kaiseki cuisine is *Uzuki* (Map 10; ☎ 221-2358) on Pontochō-dōri. It's an elegant place with a great platform for riverside dining in the summer. Set kaiseki courses start at ¥5000. It's open from 5 to 11 pm, closed Wednesday.

If you are set on eating beef, *Morita-ya* (Map 10; ☎ 231-5118) is one place where you need not worry about quality control; Morita raises its own livestock. It serves excellent sukiyaki and shabu-shabu in traditional tatami rooms, some overlooking the Kamo-gawa. Expect to spend upwards of ¥8000 per person. It's on Kiyamachi-dōri about 100m north of Sanjō-dōri, and open daily from noon to 11 pm. Another sensational sukiyaki spot with similar fare, decor and prices is *Mishima-tei* (Map 10; ☎ 221-0003), south of Sanjō-dōri in the Teramachi covered arcade. It's open from 11.30 am to 11 pm, closed Wednesday.

Mukade-ya (Map 9; ☎ 256-7039), or centipede house, is in an exquisite kyō-machiya. For lunch, try the special bentō (¥3000), two rounds (five small dishes each) of delectable obanzai-style fare. Kaiseki courses start at ¥5000. Mukade-ya is open for lunch from 11 am to 2 pm and dinner from 5 to 9 pm, closed Wednesday. It's on Shinmachi-dōri, about five minutes walk north-west of the Shijō-Karasuma intersection.

For superb tempura, head for *Yoshikawa* (Map 10; ☎ 221-5544). It offers fancy table seating with lunch from ¥6000 and dinner from ¥12,000, but it's much more interesting to sit around the small counter and observe the chefs at work. Special counter-only lunches start from ¥2000, and dinners from ¥6000. Yoshikawa is on Tominokōji-dōri, just south of Oike-dōri. It's open from 11 am to 2 pm and 5 to 8 pm, closed Sunday.

Mankamerō (Map 7; ☎ 441-5020) prepares traditional Kyoto cuisine, and is well known for cha-kaiseki. Light lunches such as takekago bentō start from ¥6000. If you want to sample opulent yushoku-ryōri, plan to spend ¥30,000 per person. It's open daily from noon to 9 pm.

EASTERN KYOTO
Budget
Buttercups (Map 8) is a favourite of the local expat community and a great place for lunch, dinner or a cup of coffee. The menu is international; most of the dishes were discovered by the friendly, bilingual owner on his world travels. Try the Mexican rice for ¥580 or the vegetarian gado-gado for ¥850. For dessert, try the home-made cakes and pies. It's open from 10 am to 11 pm, closed Tuesday. Look for the plants and whiteboard menu outside.

Mid-Range
In the grounds of Chishaku-in Temple, *Chishaku-in Ikkyū-an* (Map 6; ☎ 531-0210) may be the cheapest place in town to sample simple shōjin-ryōri (lunch sets from ¥1500). It specialises in dishes made from konyaku (arum root). It's a few minutes walk east of the Kyoto National Museum; open from 11 am to 6 pm daily.

In the Higashiyama area, tucked inside the north gate of Maruyama-kōen Park, is a traditional restaurant called *Imobō Hiranoya Honten* (Map 10; ☎ 561-1603) which specialises in imobō, a dish consisting of a local type of sweet potato and dried fish. All meals are served in restful, private tatami rooms. An English menu is available, and prices for a set meal start at ¥2400. It's open daily from 10.30 am to 8 pm.

On the 4th storey of the Gion Kaikan theatre (Map 10), not far from the step leading into the Yasaka-jinja Shrine is *Ninniku-ya*. The name means garlic shop, and the place is a garlic-lovers haven, dishing out reasonably priced salads, pastas and a wide variety of appetisers. Most dishes are around ¥1000 and are best shared Chinese style. It's open daily from 5 to 10 pm (11 pm on weekends).

From Keihan Sanjō station walking east, you'll see two good choices for yakitori. The first, on the right just after the post office, is *Ichi-ban Yakitori* (Map 10), where there's an English menu and a friendly young owner to help with ordering. It's open from 5 pm to midnight, closed Sunday. Look for the yellow and red sign and the big lantern. Further up the street, on the left side just before Higashiyama-dōri, look for the red lanterns outside *Dai-kitchi Yakitori* (Map 10). The yakitori is very good and the owner is friendly. It's open daily from 5 pm to 1 am.

At both places, figure on about ¥3000 per person with beer or sake.

If you walk north of Nanzen-ji Temple for a couple of minutes along the Path of Philosophy you reach *Okutan* (☎ 771-8709), a restaurant inside the luxurious garden of Chōshō-in (at Nanzen-ji). This is a popular place which has specialised in vegetarian temple food for hundreds of years. A course of yudōfu (bean curd cooked in a pot) together with vegetable side dishes costs ¥3000. The restaurant is open from 10.30 am to 6 pm daily, except Thursday.

For an experience you won't soon forget, try *Okariba* (Map 10; ☎ 751-7790), at the east end of Marutamachi-dōri, near the Sunflower Hotel. The owner is an avid hunter and fisherman who serves much of his quarry. If it crawls, walks or swims, it's probably on the menu. The inoshishi (wild boar) barbecue is a good start. Non-meat eaters can try the fresh ayu (sweet river fish). Hoba miso is worth a try just for the presentation. More daring options include bear meat, venison, and even horse meat sashimi. Those in need of a boost can try the hebi-iri-sake (sake with snake in the bottle). It's said to increase one's stamina (after the hangover wears off). If the master likes you, you'll probably be served the house speciality – candied insects (they're not that bad). The rule here is, don't eat anything until the master himself has a bite. Figure on about ¥4000 per person. Okariba is open from 5 to 11 pm, closed Sunday.

About five minutes walk from Ginkaku-ji, and virtually opposite the Ginkaku-ji-mae bus stop, is *Omen* (Map 8), a noodle shop named after the thick, white noodles it serves in a hot broth with a selection of seven fresh vegetables. At ¥900, the standard omen set is good value and the folksy decor is charming. It's open from 11 am to 10 pm daily, except Thursday. There is another branch in the city centre on Gokomachi-dōri just north of Shijō-dōri.

Toward the west end of Nijō-dōri, on the east side of the Kamo-gawa, *Chabana* (Map 10) is a classic okonomiyaki joint. If you don't have a favourite, just ask for the mixed okonomiyaki (¥750). Good for a late-night snack, it's open daily from 5 pm to 4 am. Look for the rotating light outside.

Near the south-west corner of Okazaki Park, *Panama Joe's* (Map 10) whips up some of the best Mexican food this side of Tokyo – good tacos, burritos, nachos and authentic guacamole, plus a selection of Mexican beers and margaritas. It's open from noon to 10 pm daily.

On Marutamachi-dōri, near the Kyoto Handicraft Center, *Zac Baran* (Map 10) is a good spot for a meal (try the dry curry special) or drink. It serves a variety of spaghetti dishes, as well as a good lunch special. It's open daily from noon to 4 am. Look for the picture of the Freak Brothers near the downstairs entrance. While you're there, you may want to check out *Second House Cake Works* upstairs for good cookies and cakes.

There are two excellent natural-food restaurants on Marutamachi-dōri. On the 2nd level of the Sun Plaza supermarket on the north-east corner of Higashiōji-dōri, *Kuraisu* (Map 10) has a wholesome breakfast set for ¥480 and an excellent lunch set for ¥750. It's open from 8.30 am to 7.30 pm, closed Sunday. East from Kuraisu, near the Kamo-gawa, the tiny *Earth Kitchen Company* (Map 10) seats just two people but does a bustling business serving tasty takeaway bentō lunches for ¥700. It's open from 10.30 am to 6.30 pm (4 pm on Saturday), closed Sunday.

French food in Japan tends to be over-priced and adulterated to suit Japanese tastes. *Le Zephyr* (Map 10) is a great exception to this rule. Hidden down a narrow alley about two minutes walk north-east of Keihan Sanjō station, the friendly owner serves up hearty portions of authentic French food for very reasonable prices. Lunch sets start at ¥800 and dinners start as low as ¥1500. It's open daily from 11.30 am to 11 pm.

Top End
Aunbo (Map 10; ☎ 525-2900) is an excellent establishment to sample creative Japanese cooking in traditional Gion surroundings. The friendly chef extraordinaire, Tashima-san, speaks good English and his tasting

menu (omakase-kōsu) for ¥6000/8000/10,000 per person (depending on how much you order) is a feast for the eyes and the tastebuds. Aunbo takes reservations from 5 to 10 pm, except Sunday. The ¥2500 lunch course (noon to 2 pm) is also praiseworthy.

Minokō (Map 10) (☎ 561-0328) is another classic Gion restaurant serving lunch bentōs from ¥4500 and cha-kaiseki dinners from ¥13,000. It's open daily from 11.30 am to 2.30 pm and 5 to 8 pm.

Just south-west of the Kyoto International Community House (KICH; Map 10), *Hyōtei* (☎ 771-4116) is one of Kyoto's oldest and most picturesque traditional restaurants. In the main building, you can sample exquisite kaiseki-ryōri courses in private tearooms from ¥18,000. The house speciality, asagayu (which is only available from 1 July to 31 August; 8 to 10 am), is a variation on the traditional Japanese breakfast and features sumptuous rice gruel, seasonal vegetables, fresh fish and tofu (¥4500); from 12 December to 15 March, a similar uzura-gayu lunch special (11 am to 2 pm) features quail eggs in rice gruel (¥10,000). In the neighbouring annex, both of these specials, as well as lovely bentō lunches and tofu meals, are served from ¥3500. Stop by to pick up its English brochure for complete details.

NORTHERN KYOTO
Budget
Woodsy *Honyarado* (Map 8) is a Kyoto institution, and has one of the best lunch deals in town (a daily stew set for ¥500). Dinners start at ¥600. It's a good place to relax over coffee and read a book. It's open daily from 9.30 am to 9.30 pm.

Speakeasy (Map 4) is a foreigner's hangout in Shūgakuin, famous as the only place in town for a 'real' western breakfast. It also serves good tuna melts, tacos and burgers. It's open from 7 am to 2 am, closed Wednesday. Look for the US flag outside.

On Higashiōji-dōri, north of Okage-dōri you'll find *Didi* (Map 8), a friendly little smoke-free restaurant serving good Indian lunch/dinner sets from about ¥1000. It serves good vegetarian fare, as well as great breakfast sets of pancakes, muffins etc for ¥500.

Heading south from Didi and east on Mikage-dōri, *Hiragana-kan* (Map 8) is popular with Kyoto University students, and dishes up creative variations on chicken, fish and meat. Most entrees are around ¥800 and come with rice, salad and miso soup. The menu is only in French and Japanese, but if you're at a loss for what to order, try the tasty chicken roll katsu. It's open from 11.30 am to 9.30 pm, closed Tuesday.

Up in the Kitayama-dōri area is one of Kyoto's newest gems, *Haruya* (Map 4), an all-natural foods eatery run by Harufumi and Yumie Fujimura. This friendly young couple speak English, and serve up tasty international vegetarian food (great Indian curries) prepared with fresh seasonal vegetables. All ingredients are organic (even the wine!), and the woodsy, Japanese country-style decor is delightful. Try their daily special set from noon to 2.30 pm, or come for dinner from 6 to 9.30 pm. It's closed from Thursday morning until after lunch on Friday.

Housed in a plant-filled glass atrium on Kitayama-dōri, just across from the Botanical Gardens, *Taiyō-ga-Ippai* (Map 4), or 'lots of sunlight', lives up to its name. It serves healthy fare including organic vegetable curries, noodle dishes and several varieties of mineral water. Lunch sets are under ¥1000. In the evening the name changes, appropriately enough, to *Hoshizora-ga-Ippai*, meaning lots of stars; it's open daily from 11 am to 10 pm.

Mago's (Map 4) is a bright and airy bistro serving first-rate sandwiches on fresh French bread or croissants. Try the teriyaki chicken sandwich or the spicy curry hot dog (which are both ¥600). It's on Kitayama-dōri near Matsugasaki subway station; open from 11.30 am to midnight, closed Monday.

Further south on Kitaōji-dōri, a short walk from Daitoku-ji Temple, *Knuckles* (Map 4) is a New York-style deli with excellent sandwiches, cheesecake and bagels.

Not far from Kamigamo-jinja Shrine, *Azekura* (Map 4) is an intriguing noodle shop/gallery in a converted Edo-period sake warehouse *(kura)*. The building features huge pine and cypress beams, earthen floors and an open hearth. Handmade soba noodles are the speciality; try the five-variety goshiki set (¥1400). Azekura is open from 9 am to 5 pm, closed Monday.

Top End

Izusen (Map 4; ☎ 491-6665), in the Daiji-in Subtemple at Daitoku-ji, serves Zen vegetarian (shōjin ryōri) lunches from ¥3000 (seven selections in vermilion-coloured lacquered bowls (tepastu) fashioned after monk's alms bowls). It's open from 11 am to 4 pm, closed Thursday. There is a branch of *Izusen* (Map 7; ☎ 493-0889) just north of Kitaōji-dōri.

In front of Daitoku-ji, *Daitoku-ji Ikkyū* (Map 7; ☎ 493-0019) boasts a 500 year history and is known for its special natto (fermented soybean) sauce. Try the basic lunch bentō for ¥3500 or complete courses from ¥7000. It is open daily from noon to 6 pm.

For Chinese-style fuchya-ryōri, try *Kanga-an* (Map 8; ☎ 256-2480), not far from the Kuramaguchi subway station on the Karasuma line. It has lunch courses from ¥5000 and dinners from ¥8000. Kanga-an is open from noon to 3 pm and 5 to 8 pm.

Kiyosu (Map 8; ☎ 231-5121), on Teramachi-dōri, is a popular kaiseki-ryōri place with courses from ¥4000. For a light meal, try the delightful vegetarian sushi à la carte for ¥1000 (made with tsukemono, including pickled eggplant, daikon and cucumber over vinegared rice). It's open from 11.30 am to 1.30 pm and 5 to 10 pm, closed Monday.

ŌHARA

Just by the entry gate to Sanzen-in Temple, *Seryō-jaya* (Map 2) serves wholesome sansai ryōri (mountain vegetables), fresh river fish and tororo soba noodles topped with grated yam. It's open from 11 am to 5 pm daily.

Near Jakkō-in Temple, *Kumoi-jaya* (Map 2) serves a delectable miso-based chicken stew (nabe) for ¥2000 and has udon noodles for ¥700. It's open daily from 9 am to 4.30 pm. Further down the road from the temple, *Tamba-jaya* (Map 2) dishes up great home-

made udon – you can fill up on the inaka-teishoku set for ¥1000.

KURAMA & KIBUNE

Near the gate to Kurama-dera Temple are several places to grab lunch. *Yōshūji* (Map 2; ☎ 741-2848) serves superb shōjin ryōri in a delightful old Japanese farmhouse with an open hearth *(irori)*. The house special, a sumptuous selection of vegetarian dishes served in red lacquered bowls, is called kurama-yama shōjin zen (¥2500). Or if you just feel like a quick bite, try the uzu-soba (soba topped with mountain vegetables) for ¥1000. It's open from 10 am to 5.30 pm, closed Tuesday.

Across the road from Yōshū-ji Temple, another soba place specialising in local mountain vegetables is *Aburaya-shokudō* (Map 2). The sansai teishoku (¥1700) is a delightful selection of vegetables, rice and soba topped with grated yam. It's open daily from 9.30 am to 5.30 pm.

Shōsai-an (Map 2; ☎ 741-3232) provides the chance to see the workings of an Edo-period townhouse. It serves a sumptuous yudōfu lunch course with vegetable tempura for ¥3500. It's open from 11.30 am to 2 pm, closed Wednesday.

Visitors to Kibune from June to September should not miss the chance to cool down by dining at one of the picturesque restaurants beside the Kibune-gawa River. Known as kawa-doko-ryōri, meals are served on platforms jutting over the river as cool water flows just underneath. Most of the restaurants offer some kind of lunch special for around ¥3000, but reserve in advance and expect to spend between ¥5000 to ¥10,000 for a full kaiseki spread featuring fresh river trout (ayu). In the cold months you can dine indoors overlooking the river. The local winter speciality is wild boar stew (botan-nabe); in spring it's mountain vegetables (sansai) and in autumn prized matsutake mushrooms.

There are a handful of spots lining the river, many of which are connected to local inns (see the Places to Stay chapter). One of the more reasonably priced is *Nakayoshi* (Map 2; ☎ 741-2000), open from 11 am to 9 pm.

PLACES TO EAT

Other possibilities include *Beniya* (Map 2; ☎ 741-2041) and *Kibune Tochigiku* (Map 2; ☎ 741-2934), both open daily from 11 am to 7.30 pm.

If you don't feel like breaking the bank on a snazzy course lunch, head for *Hirobun* (Map 2). Here you can sample nagashi-somen (¥1200), thin white noodles which flow to you in globs down a split bamboo gutter; just pluck them out and slurp away. Hirobun is open daily from 11 am to 7 pm.

Another lunch spot to expand your culinary horizons is *Torii-jaya* (Map 2), just by the torii of Kibune-jinja Shrine. The speciality here is ayu-chazuke, three small river trout over a bowl of rice into which hot green tea is poured. It comes with carp sashimi and pickles for ¥1700. A chamise-bentō set is also served for ¥2500. It's open from 11.30 am to 6 pm, closed the first and third Tuesday of each month.

ARASHIYAMA-SAGANO DISTRICT

For a quick snack before heading off temple-hopping, drop by *Kushi-tei* (Map 12), a tiny stand-and-eat stall set up across from the Keifuku Arashiyama station. Grab a couple of tasty potato puffs (korokke) for ¥60 each or kushi katsu skewered pork for ¥100 a stick. Look for the line of people.

Just beside Keifuku Arashiyama station, *Gyātei* (Map 12) offers a ¥1500 all-you-can-eat lunch buffet of healthy obanzai-ryōri (over 30 dishes) from 11 am to 2.30 pm. From 5 to 10.30 pm, Gyātei turns into an izakaya, with à la carte choices from ¥500 or a full-course tasting menu for ¥3000. It's closed Monday.

For a sample of the area's acclaimed tofu, *Seizansō-do's* (Map 12) yudōfu teishoku is good value at ¥3000. The seven course meal includes a pot of fresh yudōfu and an array of tofu-based dishes displaying the creative possibilities of the soybean. As lunchtime hours can get packed here, take a number and be prepared to wait. It's open from 11.30 am to 5 pm, closed Wednesday.

On the south side of Togetsu-kyō Bridge, *Togetsu-tei* (Map 12) has great riverside views. Try the delightful take-kago bentō

basket with locally grown bamboo shoots (¥2700) or tofu-ryōri courses from ¥3500. It's open daily from 11 am to 7 pm. Keeping the same hours, *Nishiki* is another good riverside lunch option near the bridge with seasonal bentōs from ¥3000.

Upriver from Togetsu-tei, *Rankyō-kan* has a fine lunchtime bentō for ¥4000, and mini-kaiseki courses from ¥5000. It even offers a soothing Japanese bath to lunch guests (they'll supply a small towel) for ¥300. It's open from 11 am to 3 pm daily.

In the Sagano area, on the road up to Adashino Nembutsu-ji Temple, *Bokuseki* (Map 12) serves a wholesome, all-organic lunch set (¥1800). It is open from 10 am to 5 pm, closed Wednesday.

To sample shōjin ryōri, try *Shigetsu* (☎ 881-1235), in the precincts of Tenryū-ji Temple (Map 12). It has beautiful garden views and lunches from ¥3000. It's open daily from 11 am to 2 pm.

East of the Arashiyama area, just opposite the south gate of Myōshin-ji Temple (Map 5), *Ajiro* (☎ 463-0221) is another shōjin-ryōri option. Courses are served one by one in traditional tatami rooms where you eat off individual lacquered tray tables. Ajiro specialises in tofu, offering 15 different varieties that change with the seasons. Lunches begin at ¥3000 and dinners from ¥6000. It's open from 11 am to 9 pm, closed Wednesday.

SOUTHERN KYOTO

Just in front of Fushimi-Inari Taisha Shrine, *Tamaya* (Map 3; ☎ 641-0103) is a popular kaiseki restaurant with interesting lunch options: try the light tokuno makunochi set for ¥2800, or the daimyō bentō for ¥3500. It's open from 11 am to 2.30 pm for lunch, and for dinner from 5 to 7.30 pm (reservations necessary).

Another Fushimi treat is the exquisite kaiseki haunt *Uosaburō* (Map 3; ☎ 601-0061), based since 1764 in a magnificent kyō-machiya. It serves lovely hanakago bentō lunches of seasonal dishes brilliantly presented in flower-shaped baskets, from ¥4000. Dinner courses begin at ¥10,000. Uosaburō is just a few minutes on foot from

Fushimi-Momoyama station on the Keihan Main line. It's open from 11 am to 7 pm, closed on the second and fourth Wednesday of the month.

Not far from Uosaburō, more casual fare is available at the tasty-salad restaurant *Sancho* (Map 3). It's open from 11.30 am to 9 pm, closed Wednesday.

A lovely spot for vegetarian fuchya-ryōri is *Ōryū-kaku* (Map 2; ☎ 0774-32-3900) at Mampuku-ji Temple. It serves a lunch bentō for ¥3150 and full courses from ¥5000 (plus ¥500 temple entry fee). Lunch is served from 11 am to 1 pm (reserve a few days in advance).

For a great winter body warmer, try the sake-kasu rāmen noodles (¥650) at *Genya* (Map 3); the central ingredient is the sediment (kasu) left behind in the sake brewing process. It's open from 11.30 am to 8 pm, closed Thursday.

The *Kizakura Kappa Country* (Map 3) sake brewery restaurant/bar has full-course barbecue dinners from ¥2000, an all-you-can-eat lunch buffet for ¥800 (weekdays), and three shades of delicious home-brewed beer on tap. It's open daily from 11.30 am to 2 pm and 5 to 10 pm.

UJI

If you're hungry while in Uji and can't wait to get back to Kyoto, there are plenty of places for a quick lunch. *Tsūen-jaya* (Map 2), the modern annex of the old Tsūen tea shop, is on the road up to Ujigami-jinja Shrine. It serves tasty soba and sansai (mountain vegetables), as well as tempting desserts made with fresh green tea (try the matcha parfait). It's open from 10 am to 5 pm, closed Thursday.

There are also several small lunch spots on the road leading to Byōdō-in Temple. *Renge-jaya* (Map 2) has good set lunches for around ¥1500; it's open from 10 am to 4 pm, closed Wednesday.

COFFEE SHOPS

Cafe David (Map 10) is named after legendary art connoisseur David Kidd, who died in 1996 after more than 45 years in Japan. It was opened as an ongoing tribute to Kidd by lifelong partner Morimoto Yasuyoshi, who has turned the cafe into a stylish and ever changing gallery of traditional Asian art (with a touch of modernism). It serves real plunger coffee (¥500), English and herbal teas, freshly baked cheesecake, strawberry shortcake, donuts and light sandwiches. Should you meet epicure Morimoto-san, you can count on a stimulating chat (he speaks eloquent English). Cafe David is on Sanjō-dōri, across from the Museum of Kyoto. It's open from noon to 9.30 pm, closed Wednesday.

Other praiseworthy coffee shops include Kyoto's three smoke-free *Papa Jon's*. There is one near the north-west corner of the Imperial Palace Park (Map 7); another on Kitayama-dōri (Map 4), just west of Kitashirakawa-dōri; and a third in the city centre in the Shinkyōgoku covered arcade (Map 10). All three cafes are owned and run by American Charles Roche and are known for good coffee (¥400), cappuccinos and freshly baked cakes that has Roche adapted from secret family recipes (try the cheesecake for ¥500).

Another possibility in the centre of town is *Kinoshita* (Map 10), on Fuyachō-dōri, just north of Nishiki-kōji Market. It has good coffee, and offers an excellent egg and cheese toasted sandwich. Takeaway coffee is only ¥200.

The *Inoda Coffee* (Map 10) chain is a Kyoto institution, with branches scattered throughout the city centre. Though slightly overrated for the price, the old-Japan atmosphere at their main shop on Sakaimachi-dōri, south of Sanjō-dōri, is worth a try.

Cafe du Monde in Kyoto station (great for people-watching) and on Shijō-dōri (Map 9), east of Ōmiya-dōri, brings a little bit of New Orleans to Kyoto with chicory-flavoured coffee and fresh beignets (French donuts).

For a cheap fix of second-rate coffee, there is always *Doutor* (Map 10) on Shijō-dōri. You can't beat the price (¥180), but expect to be cramped and smoked-out.

TEA & SWEET SHOPS

Kagizen Yoshifusa (Map 10) on Shijō-dōri in Gion is one of Kyoto's oldest and best known okashi-ya (sweet shops). It sells a variety of traditional sweets and has a cosy tearoom upstairs where you can sample cold kuzukiri (transparent arrowroot noodles), served with a kuro-mitsu (sweet black sugar) dipping sauce. It's open from 9 am to 6 pm, closed Monday.

Bun-no-Suke-jaya (Map 10) is a classic tea shop serving amazake, a sweet fermented rice drink mixed with grated sugar. It also offers tasty warabi-mochi (rice-flour dumplings). It's near Kōdai-ji Temple and is open from 9 am to 6 pm daily.

At *Kasagi-ya* (Map 10), on the Ninen-zaka slope near Kiyomizu-dera, you can try o-hagi cakes made from sweet red beans (azuki). It's open from 11 am to 6 pm, closed Tuesday.

Since 1682, *Kagiya Masaaki* (Map 8) has been preparing a delightful Kyoto confection called tokiwagi. It's at the intersection of Imadegawa-dōri and Higashiōji; open from 9 am to 6 pm, closed Sunday.

For more than 300 years, *Kazariya* (Map 4) has been specialising in aburi-mochi (grilled rice cakes coated with soybean flower) and served with miso-dare (sweet bean paste). It's north of Daitoku-ji; open from 10 am to 5 pm, closed Wednesday.

Two other old-Kyoto sweets shops worth a peek are *Tsuruya Yoshinobu* (Map 7) on Imadegawa-dōri west of Horikawa-dōri (open every day from 9 am to 6 pm), and *Tachibana-ya* (Map 10) on Kawaramachi-dōri north of Takatsuji-dōri (open from 10 am to 7 pm, closed the second and fourth Wednesday and Sunday of the month).

Entertainment

Most of Kyoto's cultural entertainment is of an occasional nature, and you'll need to check with the Tourist Information Centre (TIC), *Kansai Time Out* or *Kyoto Visitor's Guide* to find out whether anything interesting coincides with your visit. Regular events are generally geared toward the tourist market and tend to be expensive and, naturally, somewhat touristy.

While geisha entertainment is going to be well out of the reach of all but the fabulously rich with personal introductions, Kyoto has a good variety of standard entertainment options such as bars, clubs and discos, all of which are good places to meet young Japanese.

CINEMAS

Kyoto has plenty of movie theatres, most in the Shijō-Kawaramachi area, which show popular Hollywood hit films. These arrive in Japan up to six months after their original release and usually just as they're appearing on video or airplanes in the west. This, combined with the ticket prices (usually around ¥1800), keep many foreign visitors away.

There are a few places in town that feature European and Asian films, notably *Renaissance Hall* (Map 11) near Kyoto station and the *Asahi Cinema* (Map 10) near the Sanjō-dōri and Kawaramachi-dōri intersection. One of the best deals is the free Wednesday showing of classic Japanese films at the *Japan Foundation* (Map 9) – see Useful Organisations in the Facts for the Visitor chapter.

TRADITIONAL DANCE, THEATRE & MUSIC

Gion Corner (Map 10; ☎ 561-1119) presents traditional shows every evening at 7.40 and 8.40 pm between 1 March and 29 November (except 16 August).

While you get the chance here to see snippets of tea ceremony, *koto* (zither) music, flower arrangement, *gagaku* (court music), kyōgen (ancient comic plays), *kyōmai* (Kyoto-style dance) and *bunraku* (puppet plays), you will probably be doing so with camera and video-toting tour groups, and the presentation is a little on the tacky side. On top of this, 50 minutes of entertainment for ¥2800 is a little steep by anyone's standards. That said, if this is your only opportunity to dip into Japan's traditional entertainment and you have the cash, do it by all means – many people come away very pleased with the experience.

Geisha Dances

Annually in autumn and spring, geisha and their maiko apprentices from Kyoto's five schools dress elaborately to perform a sequence of traditional dances in praise of the seasons. The cheapest tickets cost about ¥2000 (nonreserved), better seats cost between ¥3000 and ¥3800, and spending an extra ¥500 includes participation in a quick tea ceremony. The dances are fairly similar from place to place and are repeated several times a day. Dates and times vary slightly yearly, so check with the TIC.

Gion Odori
from 1 to 10 November; *Gion Kaikan Theatre* (Map 10; ☎ 561-0160), on Higashiōji-dōri (near Yasaka-jinja Shrine)
Kamogawa Odori
from 1 to 24 May and from 15 October until 7 November; *Pontochō Kaburen-jō Theatre* (Map 10; ☎ 221-2025), on Pontochō-dōri
Kitano Odori
from 15 to 25 April; *Kamihichiken Kaburen-jō Theatre* (Map 4; ☎ 461-0148), east of Kitano-Tenman-gū Shrine
Kyō Odori
from the first to the third Sunday in April; *Miyagawa-chō Kaburen-jō Theatre* (Map 10; ☎ 561-1151), east of the Kamo-gawa River between Shijō-dōri and Gojō-dōri
Miyako Odori (Cherry Blossom Dance)
throughout April; *Gion Kōbu Kaburen-jō Theatre* (Map 10; ☎ 561-1115), near Gion Corner

Kabuki

The *Minami-za Theatre* (Map 10; ☎ 561-0160) in Gion is the oldest kabuki theatre in Japan. The major event of the year is the

ENTERTAINMENT

Kao-mise Festival (1 to 26 December), which features Japan's finest kabuki actors and sees new ones begin their careers. Other performances take place infrequently. Those interested should check with the TIC. The most likely months for performances are May, June and September.

Nō

For performances of nō, the main theatres are *Kanze Kaikan Nō Theatre* (Map 10; ☎ 771-6114), *Kongō-dō Nō Stage* (Map 9; ☎ 221-3049) and *Kawamura Nō Stage* (Map 7; ☎ 451-4513). Takigi-Nō is an especially picturesque form of nō performed with lighting from blazing fires. In Kyoto, this takes place on the evenings of 1 and 2 June at *Heian-jingū Shrine* – tickets cost ¥2000 in advance (ask at the TIC for the location of ticket agencies) or pay ¥3300 at the entrance gate.

Musical Performances

Musical performances featuring the koto, *shamisen* and *shakuhachi* are held in Kyoto on an irregular basis. Performances of *bugaku* (court music and dance) are often held at Kyoto shrines during festival periods. Occasionally contemporary *butō* dance is also performed in Kyoto. Check with the TIC to see if any performances are scheduled to be held while you are in town.

CLASSICAL MUSIC

The *Kyoto Concert Hall* (Map 4; ☎ 361-6629) and *ALTI* (Kyoto Fumin Hall; Map 7; ☎ 441-1414) both hold regular performances of classical music and dance (traditional and contemporary). Ticket prices average between ¥3000 and ¥5000. Again, check with the usual sources for current schedules.

ROCK/FOLK/ACOUSTIC MUSIC

There are several options for live music, though most places vary the type of music from night to night. Call to find out what's happening at the following 'live houses'.

Two of the most atmospheric clubs, *Taku-Taku* (Map 10; ☎ 351-1321) and *Juttoku* (Map 7; ☎ 841-1691), are in old sake warehouses *(saka-gura)*. Taku-Taku is central, on

Tominokōji-dōri south of Shijō-dōri, and tends to present more major acts (the Neville Brothers, Los Lobos and Dr John have all performed here). Cover charges average between ¥1500 and ¥3500. Juttoku is on Ōmiya-dōri (north of Nijō-jō Castle) and admission is closer to the ¥1000 range.

On Teramachi-dōri just south of Shijō-dōri, *Toga-Toga* (Map 10; ☎ 361-6900) is a basement-level joint hosting a wide variety of both amateur and professional artists. *Other Side* (Map 8; ☎ 256-5259), south of Imadegawa-dōri on Kawaramachi-dōri, is a good spot to hear amateur acoustic acts (they have an open-mike night on Wednesday from 7 pm to midnight).

Finally, for the best in live country music, it's well worth the trip up north to *Honky Tonk* (Map 4; ☎ 701-8015), near the Kyoto International Conference Hall. This place is a gas; an authentic western saloon full of Japanese cowboys dressed in full garb – hats, boots and, occasionally, spurs. The friendly owner, Beau, speaks English well and is a regular performer. It closes on the early side (11 pm); call to confirm that there's a show on before making the haul out.

JAZZ

Live jazz takes place irregularly at several clubs in town. The best place to catch topnotch jazz is *Rag* (Map 10; ☎ 241-0446), on the 5th storey of the Empire building on Kiyamachi-dōri, north of Sanjō-dōri. Door charges range from about ¥1500 to ¥4000.

CLUBS & DISCOS

Yes, you can dance the night away in the cultural heart of Japan and give the temples and shrines a miss the next day while you sleep off your hangover. Most clubs charge about ¥2000 admission (with one drink).

The best place for this kind of thing is *Metro* (Map 10). It's part disco, part 'live house' and even hosts the occasional art exhibition. Metro attracts an eclectic mix of creative types and every night has a different theme, so check ahead to see what's going on (pick up a schedule in Rub-a-Dub). Some of the best gigs are Latino Connection night,

Cool-to-Cool jazz night and the Diamond Night Transvestite Cabaret; the popular Non-hetero-At-The-Metro night (also called *sutoraito jai nai* – not straight night) draws gays, lesbians and everyone in between. Weekends usually have an admission charge, while Wednesday and Thursday are usually free. It's actually inside the No 2 exit of Keihan Marutamachi station.

Another hip spot is *CK Cafe*, on the 4th storey of the Gion Kaikan building (Map 10), opposite Yasaka-jinja on Higashiyama-dōri. This place is about as close to Tokyo nightlife as you'll get in Kyoto, right down to *chapatsu* (dyed brown hair) girls in criminally short mini-skirts gyrating on the loudspeakers. The normal

admission is ¥2500 (with two drinks), but foreigners and Japanese women pay ¥1000; you must have a 'CK ticket' (free) with you to be admitted (these can usually be picked up from foreigner street vendors along Kiyamachi-dōri – just ask).

Collage (Map 10) is a tiny venue favouring acid jazz and techno. It's tucked inside a small building (2nd floor) down a narrow east-west alley, just south of the *izakaya*, A-Bar. Spacious *Lab Tribe* (Map 10) draws a younger crowd and leans toward techno and hip-hop. It's on Kawaramachi-dōri, north of Oike-dōri. Finally, *Groove* (Map 10) is an interesting option in the heart of Gion's narrow streets (amid a swathe of love hotels).

PUBS & BARS

Kyoto has an astounding variety of bars, from exclusive Gion clubs where it's possible to spend ¥100,000 in a single evening to grungy gaijin bars. Most bars are concentrated in the central Kawaramachi area. During the warmer months, rooftop beer gardens spring up throughout town and offer tempting all-you-can-eat/drink deals and great views of the surrounding mountains (see the Gardens of Beer boxed text on this page).

One of Kyoto's most popular gaijin hangouts is the *Pig & Whistle* (Map 10). Like its counterparts in Osaka, it's a British-style pub with darts, pint glasses and fish and chips. The pub's two main drawcards are Guinness on tap and its friendly bilingual manager, Ginzo. Drunken giants should watch their heads on the rowing boat suspended from the ceiling. It's on the 2nd floor of the Shobi building, opposite Keihan Sanjō station.

Less British and more American in style is *Pub Africa* (Map 10). It's not as good a place to meet people as the Pig & Whistle, mainly because the video screens showing movies tend to dominate everyone's attention, but it's still a good place for an early evening beer and something to eat. The menu is in Japanese only.

Bar, Isn't It? (Map 10), part of the chain that started in Kōbe and has swept Japan, is popular with young Japanese and foreign men desperately searching for something. It's huge,

---

Gardens of Beer

So you've strolled around wooded ponds, seen misty moss gardens and unravelled the esoteric meaning of dry rock-garden landscapes, all in Kyoto's sweltering summer heat; maybe it's time to soak up a bit of 'borrowed scenery' from the rooftop of a tall building or a platform over the Kamo-gawa River at one of Kyoto's plentiful beer gardens.

The beer garden season generally runs from mid-May to mid-September, but always check before you go. Each spot in town has a distinct view and a slightly different system; some serve beer and food à la carte, and others offer tempting all-you-can-eat and drink specials. One of the best places is the *Sunflower Hotel* (Map 10; ☎ 761-9111), which is right at the eastern end of Marutamachi-dōri. The view of the Higashiyama mountains from the roof is one of the finest in town.

Other beer gardens with great views include:

ANA Hotel (Map 9; ☎ 231-1155), just across from Nijō-jō Castle on Horikawa-dōri
Gion Hotel (Map 10; ☎ 551-2111) at the eastern end of Shijō-dōri, near Yasaka-jinja Shrine
Hotel Fujita Kyoto (Map 10; ☎ 222-1511) on Nijō-dōri, on the west bank of the Kamo-gawa
Kikusui Beer Garden (Map 10; ☎ 561-1001), across from the north-east end of the Shijō-Ōhashi Bridge
Kyoto Tower Hotel (Map 11; ☎ 361-3222), just across from Kyoto station
Tōkasai-kan Chinese Restaurant (Map 10; ☎ 221-1147) at the western end of the Shijō-Ōhashi Bridge ■

loud and often very crowded. All drinks are ¥500 and there's simple bar food for those who want to pad their stomachs.

At the northern end of Kiyamachi-dōri, *Rub-a-Dub* (Map 10) is a funky little reggae bar with a shabby tropical look and good daiquiris. It's a good place for a quiet drink on weekdays, but on Friday and Saturday nights you'll have no choice but to bop along with the crowd. Look for the stairs heading down to the basement beside the popular (but stinky) Nagahama rāmen shop. On the 2nd storey of the same building, *Picca Bar* (Map 10) is a stylish place with subdued lighting and soft Latin music. Drinks are a bit pricey and there's a ¥200 peanut charge to boot, but it's a pleasant place to be with a date.

A short stumble south of Rub-a-Dub on Kiyamachi-dōri, *Roku-han* (Map 10) is a hip after-hours pub and one of the handful of places in town that can still be packed at 7 am on a Sunday morning. All drinks are ¥600. Look for the street-level sign reading '6½'; it's on the 4th floor.

On one of the narrow east-west streets between Kiyamachi-dōri and Kawaramachi-dōri, *Sama Sama* (Map 10) is a groovy spot with cosy floor seating on cushions. It's run by long-term Kyoto residents Teddy and El, Indonesian brothers, who serve up spicy island food and cold Bintang beer. Teddy's name still lives on at his former haunt, *Teddy's* (Map 10), which features faux tropical surroundings and a great view over the Kamo-gawa. It's in the Empire building on the 7th floor.

Further down Kiyamachi-dōri, about 100m north of Shijō-dōri, *Hachimonjiya* (Map 10) is a popular haunt with local artists and takes the cake for the messiest bar in Kyoto. It is cluttered floor-to-ceiling with books, postcards and pictures by acclaimed street photographer (and bar owner) Kai-san. There is a ¥500 table charge, which includes a bit of food; drinks are reasonably priced. Take the elevator to the 3rd floor.

On a little alley off Kiyamachi-dōri, one street north of Sanjō-dōri, *Backgammon* (Map 10) is where the strange people come late at night. Check out the crow's nest drink-

ing area at the top of the ladder – if you don't want to climb down for the next round, they'll send it up to you with a special drink elevator. It's open until dawn and the lack of windows in the joint guarantees that the first light of day will be a bracing shock when you stumble out the door. In the same alley, *Scoreboard* (Map 10) is a popular sports bar with an army of wide-screen TVs and cheap bar food.

Real late-nighters might want to check out *Step-Rampo* (Map 10), a 7th floor bar overlooking Kawaramachi-dōri. This place does not really get going until around 2 am and it's been known to stay open until way past dawn, when the morning light casts a strange pall over the drunks left dangling from the bar. It's on Kawaramachi-dōri, one building north of the Hagen Daaz ice cream shop. While you're in there, you might want to poke your head into *Bar Amnesia* (Map 10) on the 5th floor.

Northern Kyoto

Near Kyoto University, *Post Coitus* (Map 8) is worth a visit, not only for its unusual name. The interior decorations are an experiment in radical minimalism, intended to make you concentrate on the drink at hand. This place has plenty to from which to choose – a real connoisseur's haven. If it's not on the drink list it probably doesn't exist. It's 150m north of the Higashiyama-dōri and Imadegawa-dōri intersection, on the east side down a small side street (turn at the Fujii paint store).

A bit further up Higashiyama-dōri and a few steps west on Mikage-dōri, the *Flying Keg* (Map 8) is an aptly named beer emporium with an enormous selection of brews from over 25 countries. It's quiet, casual, reasonably priced and has an impressive selection of wines; all-in-all a nice break from the fracas downtown.

Finally, *Mekhong* (Map 4) is an appealing option, especially if you're lodging up north. It's an atmospheric little candle-lit bar done up in South-East Asian decor. There is a ¥100 'candle charge' and ample Mekhong (Thai whisky) behind the bar. It's a 15 minute walk north-west from Kamigamo-jinja Shrine, across the Kamo-gawa.

Shopping

Kyoto offers ample opportunity to deplete your supply of yen. Whether you're hardcore souvenir hunting or simply 'window shopping', there are an infinite number of shops and markets to explore. If you are fashion-conscious, try Kyoto's legion of department stores or the chic boutiques on Kitayama-dōri and Kawaramachi-dōri. Antiques hunters should head for Shinmonzen-dōri in the Gion District, or better yet one of the city's lively monthly flea markets (see Other Markets in this chapter).

The heart of Kyoto's shopping district is around the intersection of Shijō-dōri and Kawaramachi-dōri. The blocks running north and west of here are packed with all sorts of stores selling both traditional and modern goods. Several of Kyoto's largest department stores are grouped together in this area. The 6th floor of Takashimaya is a good place for deals on pottery and kitchenware. The Teramachi and Shinkyōgoku covered shopping arcades running north of Shijō-dōri are lined with restaurants, cinemas and a mix of tacky souvenir shops (mostly catering to kids visiting on school excursions) and more traditional, upmarket stores.

Further south on Teramachi-dōri, below Shijō-dōri, is Kyoto's electronics ghetto with the full range of the latest in computers, stereos and home appliances. For camera equipment, head for the area around Sanjō-dōri on Kawaramachi-dōri. To find an impressive display of foodstuffs, check out the basements of any of the big department stores. It's difficult to believe the variety of food; shopping on display, as well as some of the prices (check out the ¥10,000 melons or the Kōbe beef, for example). In these basement food emporiums you can really get a feel for the wealth of modern Japan. A visit to Nishiki-kōji Market (Map 10) is an eye-opener (see the Nishiki-kōji Food Market boxed text in the Places to Eat chapter for details on the market).

Some of the best purchases in town are crafts native to Kyoto such as *kyō-ningyō* (dolls), *kyō-shikki* (lacquerware), *kyō-sensu* (fans) and *kyō-yaki* (ceramics). *Nishijin-ori* is a special technique of silk textile weaving and *kyō-yūzen* is a local form of silk-dyeing. *Zōgan* is a damascene technique laying pure gold and silver onto figures engraved on brass. *Old Kyoto: A Guide to Traditional Shops, Restaurants & Inns* by Diane Durston, available at Maruzen bookshop, is useful for finding unusual traditional items sold (and often produced) by elegant shops with vintage character. For a sampling of places to track down traditional crafts, see Arts & Handicrafts in this chapter.

If you want to do all your shopping under one roof, the following places offer a wide selection of Kyoto handicrafts. The Kyoto Craft Center (Map 10; ☎ 561-9660), near Maruyama-kōen Park, exhibits and sells handicrafts and is open from 11 am to 6 pm daily (except Wednesday). The Kyoto Handicraft Center (Map 10; ☎ 761-5080), just north of Heian-jingū Shrine, is a huge co-operative that exhibits, sells and demonstrates crafts. It's open from 9.30 am until 6 pm (or 5.30 pm during December, January and February). In the Shinkyōgoku arcade, Lakumi (☎ 231-2924) is a friendly spot that carries an array of reasonably priced souvenirs (it accepts both foreign currency and travellers cheques). It's open daily from 11 am to 5 pm, except Monday.

See the Business Hours section in the Facts for the Visitor chapter for locations and opening hours of department stores.

MARKETS

A definite highlight of a Kyoto visit is the colourful monthly flea markets around town. Droves of dealers set up open-air stalls to display and sell their wares – this is one of the few occasions where bargaining is the norm. Most vendors can manage a bit of English but a smile will often go as far as perfect Japanese. Of the better deals, look for antique kimono starting at around ¥500.

Tō-ji & Kitano

On the 21st of each month Kōbō-san is held at Tō-ji Temple (Map 6) to commemorate the death of Kōbō Taishi (Kūkai), who in 823 was appointed abbot of the temple. Another major market, Tenjin-san, is held on the 25th of each month at Kitano Tenman-gū Shrine (Map 4), marking the day of birth (and coincidentally the death) of the Heian-era statesman Sugawara Michizane (845-903).

For each of these huge fairs, the January (Hatsu-Kōbō and Hatsu-Tenjin) and December (Shimai-Kōbō and Shimai-Tenjin) renditions are by far the biggest and most lively. If you're looking for antiques, arrive early and prepare to bargain. There is a better selection in the morning, but vendors loosen up with prices as the market winds down.

If you aren't in Kyoto on the 21st, there is also a regular antiques fair at Tō-ji on the first Sunday of each month and a major annual fair here from 1 to 4 January.

Other Markets

Other markets are held monthly at various temples but feature household goods and handmade wares rather than antiques. On the 12th of each month there is a bazaar at Myōren-ji Temple (Map 7; ☎ 451-3527), north-west of Imadegawa-Horikawa. Potential vendors can set up shop here for ¥1000.

Again on the 15th, Tezukuri-ichi is held at Chion-in Temple (Map 10; ☎ 781-9171) with food and handmade clothes. On the 28th, there is the Omoshiroi-ichi at Kōsho-ji Temple (Map 8; ☎ 371-0075).

On the third Saturday of each month from 11 am to 2 pm, there is a flea market and general get-together of foreigners at the YWCA's thrift shop (Map 7).

ARTS & HANDICRAFTS
Ceramics

In eastern Kyoto, the paved streets of Ninen-zaka and Sannen-zaka slopes (Maps 6 & 10), close to Kiyomizu-dera Temple, are famed for crafts and antiques. Akebono, housed in

a renovated ryokan decorated with antiques, sells an impressive variety of gift items and has a great selection of local ceramics. There are also several Kiyomizu-yaki pottery shops on Gojō-zaka (Map 6), near the northwest corner of Higashiōji-Gojō, and good pickings at the Kyoto Tōjiki Kaikan (Kyoto Pottery Hall) nearby.

Textiles

There are several central kimono shops worth stopping at for a peek at the elegant fabrics. Shikunshi (Map 9; ☎ 221-0456) is in a wonderful old kyō-machiya on Shijō-dōri, east of Nishinotōin-dōri. Have a look at the small shop in the restored warehouse at the back. Kyō-kimono Plaza (Map 9; ☎ 352-2323) is another possibility; it's near the corner of Karasuma-dōri and Takatsuji-dōri.

If you're looking for Nishijin-ori fabrics, try the shop at the Nishijin Textile Center (Map 7). For kyō-yūzen fabrics, head for Erizen (Map 10; ☎ 221-1618), near Takashimaya department store on Shijō-dōri.

Dolls

Just north of Shijō-dōri, on the eastern side of Kawaramachi-dōri, Matsuya (Map 10; ☎ 221-5902) sells an impressive assortment of delicately painted kyō-ningyō. It's open from 10 am to 6 pm, except Wednesday. On Shijō-dōri, Tanakaya (Map 10; ☎ 221-1959) is another appealing option and keeps the same hours as Matsuya.

Fans

For more than 170 years, Miyawaki Baisen-an (☎ 221-0181) has been handcrafting fans for traditional dances, the tea ceremony and ornamental use. It is on Rokkaku-dōri, west of Tominōkoji-dōri (Map 10), and is open from 9 am to 5 pm daily.

On Karasuma-dōri, a short walk south of Gojō-dōri, Yamani (Map 11; ☎ 351-2622) also boasts a wide selection. It's open from 9 am to 5 pm, except Sunday and the second and third Saturday of the month.

About a 10 minute walk north-east of Kyoto station, Kyōsen-dō (Map 11; ☎ 371-4151) sells a colourful variety of paper fans;

ALL PHOTOGRAPHS BY MASON FLORENCE

A	B
C	D
E	F

Kyoto shopping scenes:
A: The monthly flea market at Kitano-Tenman-gū Shrine. B: Food stalls around Fushimi-Inari Taisha Shrine. C: Market stalls display vegetables typically used in Japanese cooking. D: A Buddhist nun shelters from the sun at Kitano-Tenman-gū. E and F: Stalls outside Sanzen-in Temple, Ōhara.

ALL PHOTOGRAPHS BY MASON FLORENCE

A	B
C	D
E	F

A: Traditional *kayabuki-yane* (thatched-roof) farmhouses, Miyama-chō.
B: Ashyu-gawa River, Miyama-chō.
C and D: Deer grazing at Nara-kōen Park and at Tōdai-ji Temple, Nara.
E: View from the Mt Hiei-zàn cable car, north-eastern Kyoto.
F: Forests of *sugu* (cedar) blanket the Kitayama mountains, Miyama-chō.

here you can see the process of assembling the fans and even paint your own. It's open from 9 am to 5 pm, closed Sunday, holidays and the second Saturday of the month.

Japanese Paper

A short walk south of the Shijō-Karasuma intersection (Map 9), House of Kajinoha/Morita Washi (☎ 341-1419) sells a fabulous variety of handmade *washi* (Japanese paper) for reasonable prices.

Rakushi-kan (☎ 251-0078), on the 1st floor of the Museum of Kyoto (Map 10), also sells a wide variety of washi goods. It's open daily from 10 am to 7.30 pm.

Kakimoto (☎ 211-3481), at 54 Tokiwagi-chō, Teramachi-dōri deals in exquisite washi (even some for use in computer printers!), is open from 9 am to 6 pm, closed Sunday.

Lacquerware

Across from Daimaru department store (Map 10) on Shijō-dōri, Asobe (☎ 211-0803) specialises in exquisite kyō-shikki. Asobe is open from 9.30 am to 6 pm, closed Wednesday. It also has a small branch on the 6th floor of Takashimaya department store (Map 10).

Wood-Block Prints

In the Teramachi arcade (Map 10) on Sanjō-dōri, Nishiharu (☎ 211-2849) is an attractive shop dealing in wood-block prints (*hanga*). All the prints are accompanied by English explanations and the owner is happy to take the time to find something you really like. It's open from 1 to 6.30 pm daily.

Further south in the same arcade, Daishodō (☎ 221-0685) also has a fine selection of wood-block prints and scrolls. It's open from 11 am to 8 pm, closed Wednesday.

Woodwork

About five minutes walk south of the Gojō-dōri and Karasuma-dōri intersection (Map 11), Enami (☎ 361-2816) deals in high-quality local *kyō-sashimono* wood wares (*mokkōhin*), from small trays to delicate implements for tea ceremony. It is open from 9 am to 5 pm, closed Sunday.

Metalwork

For a look at Kyoto's famed *kyō-zōgan* brass-work, stop in at Kawahito Hands (Map 5; ☎ 461-2773). It's open from 9 am to 5.30 pm, closed on weekends and holidays. Also, beside the Kyoto Handicraft Center, Amita-honten (Map 10; ☎ 761-7000) is open from 10 am to 6 pm daily.

OTHER ITEMS

A short walk north of the Shijō-Kawara-machi intersection, Tsujikura (Map 10; ☎ 221-4396) has a good selection of waxed-paper umbrellas and paper lanterns with traditional and modern designs. It's open from 11 am to 8.30 pm, closed Wednesday.

While you're in the Nishiki-kōji Market (Map 10), have a look in Aritsugu (☎ 221-1091), near the northern end. Here, you can find some of the best kitchen knives in the world. It's open daily from 9 am to 5.30 pm.

Ippō-dō (☎ 211-3421), a classic, old-style tea shop selling all sorts of tea, is open from 9 am to 7 pm, closed Sunday. It's north of the city hall (Map 10), near Teramachi-dōri.

Not far from Kyoto station, Kungyoku-dō (☎ 371-0162) has sold incense, herbs, spices and fine woods for four centuries. A haven for the olfactory senses, it's opposite the gate of Nishi Hongan-ji Temple (Map 11) and is open from 9 am to 7 pm, except for the first and third Sundays of the month.

Excursions

Kyoto is surrounded by many worthwhile and easily reached destinations in the Kansai District, with virtually all of them less than an hour away by train. To the south lies Nara with its temple treasures, and to the south-west is Kōbe with its modern architecture and fantastic location overlooking Osaka Bay. Other major attractions include the scenic areas of Lake Biwa-ko to the east and Miyama-chō to the north, with its delightful villages nestled in the Kitayama mountains. The centuries-old Himeji-jō Castle, west of Kyoto, should not be missed.

While all places listed in this chapter can easily be made as day trips from Kyoto, we have included information on accommodation and places to eat should you wish to stay overnight anywhere.

NARA
奈良

Nara (population 350,000) is known as the birthplace of Japanese culture, and became Japan's first permanent capital (then known as Heijō-kyō) in 710. The city acted as the eastern terminus of the legendary Silk Road, the ancient trading route between Asia and Europe, and today is the number two tourist attraction in Kansai after Kyoto.

Orientation

Like Kyoto, Nara is uninspiring at first glance, but careful inspection will reveal the rich history and hidden beauty of the city. It's small enough to make it quite possible to pack the most worthwhile sights into one full day. Those with time to spare could allow one day for the Nara-kōen Park area and a second for the sights in western and south-western Nara.

Nara retains the grid pattern of streets laid out in Chinese style during the 8th century. Nara station and Kintetsu Nara station are roughly in the middle of the city and Nara-kōen is on the east side. It's easy to cover the city centre and the major attractions in the

park on foot, though some may prefer to rent a bicycle. Other sights south-west of the city are best reached by bus.

Information

Tourist Offices The Tourist Information Centre (TIC) in Kyoto has information on Nara including a useful leaflet on local walking tours. In Nara, the best source of information is the Nara City Tourist Center (☎ 0742-22-3900), which is open from 9 am to 9 pm. It's at 23-4 Kami Sanjō-dori, on the 1st floor of the Nara Central Public Hall and just a short walk from the Nara or Kintetsu Nara stations. There are also information offices at both train stations and beside Sarusawa-no-ike Pond. Two English-speaking volunteer guide groups are YMCA Goodwill Guides (☎ 0742-45-5920) and Nara Student Guides (☎ 0742-26-4753). It's best to call ahead and, because they are volunteers, you should cover their expenses.

Books John & Phyllis Martin's *Nara: A Cultural Guide to Japan's Ancient Capital* (Tuttle, Tokyo, 1993) is a detailed guide to religious monuments throughout the city. For a more academic look, pick up a copy of *Historical Nara* by Herbert Plutschow (Japan Times, Tokyo, 1983).

Nara-kōen Park

This park is home to about 1200 deer, which in old times were considered messengers of the gods and today enjoy the status of National Treasures. They roam the park and surrounding areas in search of handouts from tourists, often descending on petrified children who have the misfortune to be carrying food. You can buy special biscuits (*shika-sembei*, ¥100) from vendors to feed the deer (don't eat them yourself).

Kōfuku-ji Temple

Kōfuku-ji was established here in 710 as the main temple for the Fujiwara family. Although the original complex had 175 buildings, fires and destruction through power struggles have left only a dozen still standing. There are two pagodas, a three storey and a five storey one, dating from 1143 and 1426 respectively.

The National Treasure Hall (Kokuhōkan) contains a variety of statues and art objects salvaged from previous structures. A descriptive leaflet is provided in English. The Kokuhōkan is open from 9 am to 4.30 pm; admission costs ¥500.

Nara National Museum

The Nara Kokuritsu Hakubutsukan is devoted to Buddhist art and has two wings. A western gallery exhibits archaeological finds and the eastern gallery has displays of sculptures, paintings and calligraphy.

Opening hours are from 9 am to 4.30 pm, closed Monday. Regular admission costs ¥420 and special exhibitions are ¥830.

Neiraku Art Museum & Isui-en Garden

The Art Museum (Neiraku Bijutsukan) displays Chinese bronzes and Korean ceramics and bronzes. The nearby garden, dating from the Meiji era, is beautifully laid out with abundant greenery and a fine view of Tōdai-ji Temple. For ¥450 you can enjoy a cup of tea on *tatami* mats overlooking the garden.

The museum is open from 10 am to 4.30 pm, closed Tuesday. Admission costs ¥600, and the same ticket allows entry into the garden.

Tōdai-ji Temple

Tōdai-ji is the largest wooden building in the world and houses the Great Buddha – one of the largest bronze images in the world. On your way into the main hall *(hondō)* you'll pass through the Nandai-mon Gate which contains two fierce-looking Niō guardians carved in the 13th century by the sculptor Unkei.

Daibutsu-den (Hall of the Great Buddha) is a reconstruction dating from 1709. The Daibutsu, however, dates to 746. Represented here is the Dainichi Buddha, the cosmic Buddha believed to give rise to all worlds and their respective historical Buddhas.

Each lotus leaf on which the Buddha sits represents one entire universe.

Over the centuries the statue took quite a beating from earthquakes and fires. The present statue was rebuilt in the Edo period and stands just over 16m high, consisting of 437 tonnes of bronze and 130kg of gold. As you circle the statue toward the back, you'll see a wooden column with a small hole at the base. Popular belief maintains that those who can squeeze through are ensured of enlightenment.

Admission to Daibutsu-den costs ¥400, and your ticket has a convenient list of the Daibutsu's vital statistics. Opening hours are as follows: November to February from 8 am to 4.30 pm, March from 8 am to 5 pm, April to September from 7.30 am to 5.30 pm and October from 7.30 am to 5 pm.

East from the entrance to Daibutsu-den, climb up a flight of stone steps, and continue to your left to reach two subtemples. From **Nigatsu-dō** there is a splendid view across Nara. The hall is open from 8 am to 4.30 pm (admission is free). A short walk south of here is **Sangatsu-dō Hall** which is the oldest building in the Tōdai-ji complex and contains a small collection of fine statues. It's open from 8 am to 4.30 pm; admission costs ¥400.

A short walk west of the entrance gate to the Daibutsu-den, you can visit the **Kaidan-in Hall**, which was used for ordination ceremonies and is famous for its clay images of the Shi Tennō (Four Heavenly Guardians). The hall is open from 8 am to 4.30 pm, and admission costs ¥400.

Kasuga Taisha Shrine

This shrine was founded in the 8th century by the Fujiwara family and completely rebuilt every 20 years according to Shintō tradition, until the end of the 19th century. The approaches to the shrine are lined with hundreds of lanterns and there are many more in the shrine itself. The Hōmotsu-den (Treasure Hall) displays Shintō ceremonial regalia and props used in *bugaku, nō* and *gagaku* performances. It's open from 9 am to 4 pm; admission costs ¥400.

EXCURSIONS

Shin-Yakushi-ji Temple

This temple, south-east of Nara, was founded by Empress Kōmyō in 747 in thanks for her husband's recovery from an eye disease. Most of the buildings were destroyed or have been reconstructed, but the present main hall dates from the 8th century. The hall contains sculptures of Yakushi Nyorai (Healing Buddha) and a set of 12 divine generals. Admission costs ¥500, and the temple is open from 9 am to 5 pm.

Organised Tours

Nara Kōtsū (☎ 0742-22-5263) has daily bus tours on a variety of routes, including two with Nara city sights only and two including more distant sights like Hōryū-ji Temple and the burial mounds around Asuka (see the Around Nara section). Prices for the all-day trips average ¥7000 for adults. Lunch at a Japanese restaurant on the route is optional.

Places to Stay

Youth Hostels The *Seishōnen Kaikan Youth Hostel* (☎ 0742-22-5540) in the northern part of town has dorm rooms for ¥2650 per person, and private double/triple rooms for ¥3850/3350 per person. The nearby *Nara*

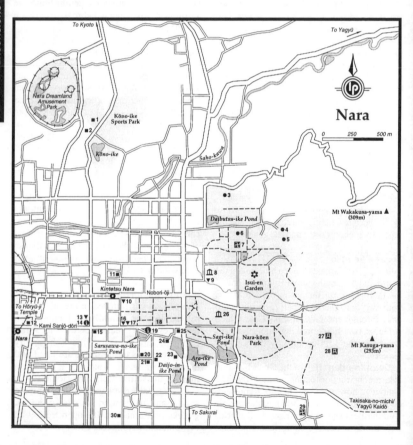

Youth Hostel (☎ 0742-22-1334) only takes guests with a hostel membership card and charges ¥3000 per person. Check with the tourist centre for bus access.

Ryokan & Minshuku *Ryokan Seikan-sō* (☎ 0742-22-2670) has wooden architecture and a pleasant garden. It's a 15 minute walk south of Kintetsu Nara station. Prices for a Japanese-style room without bath start at ¥3800 per person. *Ryokan Hakuhō* (☎ 0742-26-7891) is in the centre of town, just a five minute walk from Nara station. Prices for a Japanese-style room without bath start at ¥6500 per person. *Furuichi Ryokan* (☎ 0742-22-2440) is good value at ¥4500 (¥5000 with private bath), or ¥9000 including two meals.

One of Nara's finest inns, *Kikusuirō* (☎ 0742-23-2001), is on the south-western edge of Nara-kōen. Per person rates, including two exquisite meals, range from ¥35,000 to ¥43,000 (with private bath). No credit cards accepted.

There are some minshuku in the city centre. *Minshuku Sakigake* (☎ 0742-22-7252) is in an attractive, traditional-style building

and costs ¥4500 per person, including breakfast. *Minshuku Yamaya* (☎ 0742-24-0045) costs ¥4100 per person, with no meals.

Shukubō The Nara City Tourist Center has a list of temples offering lodgings. *Shin-Yakushi-ji Temple* (☎ 0742-22-3736) is in a quiet area near Nara-kōen. It offers lodging and breakfast from ¥4900 per person per night (plus there is the ¥500 entry fee to the temple). No dinner is served, so be sure to eat early enough to be back for the 7 pm curfew.

Hotels The *Nara Green Hotel* (☎ 0742-26-7815) has singles from ¥6400, doubles from ¥12,000. The *Nara Kokusai Hotel* (☎ 0742-26-6001), close to Nara station, has singles and twins from ¥6000 and ¥18,000. Not far from the south-western corner of Nara-kōen, the *Hotel Sunroute Nara* (☎ 0742-22-5151) has singles/doubles from ¥8000/10,000. Nearby is the rambling *Nara Hotel* (☎ 0742-26-3300), which is the city's premier hotel. It has singles from ¥14,000, and twins and doubles from ¥23,000.

EXCURSIONS

Places to Eat

Nara is especially known for the full-course delights of kaiseki cuisine, starting at about ¥5000 for a basic version. This usually includes the local delicacy called narazuke, tart vegetables pickled in sake. A good place to try simple kaiseki and narazuke is *Yamazakiya* (☎ 0742-27-3751) in the arcade just to the south of Kintetsu Nara station, where set lunches start from ¥1350.

In the same arcade, close to the northern end on the 2nd floor, is *Tsukihi-tei* (☎ 0742-23-5470) which serves simple kaiseki dishes at reasonable prices. The tenshin bentō is a very good bet at ¥1500. There are plastic food models in the window. Just downstairs, *Udon-tei* serves set noodle dishes. Sample the goshiki (five colour) teishoku lunch for ¥1350. Nearby, *Beni-e* (☎ 0742-22-9439) has good tempura from ¥2000 for both lunch and dinner.

Perhaps the best place for lunch in Nara is *Sanshū* (☎ 0742-22-2173), next to the beautiful Isui-en Garden in Nara-kōen. Guests sit on tatami enjoying the food while gazing out over the splendour of one of Nara's best gardens. Ordering is simple due to the choice of either the mugitoro gozen (without eel) for ¥1100 or the unatoro gozen (with eel) for ¥2200. Lunch is served every day except Tuesday from 11.30 am to 2 pm.

Nara has many other good restaurants; the tourist centre can help with reservations and recommendations. For picnics in Nara-kōen, *Subway* just north of the tourist centre makes perfect sandwiches.

Getting There & Away

See the Getting There & Away chapter for details on getting to/from Nara.

Getting Around

Bus Nara has an excellent bus system. Most of the area around Nara-kōen is covered by two circular bus routes (¥170 flat fare). You can easily see the main sights in the park on foot and use the bus if you are pushed for time or getting tired. There are also a variety of buses which run from central Nara to areas south of the city.

Cycling Central Nara is a convenient size for getting around by bicycle. Kintetsu Rent-a-Cycle Center (☎ 0742-24-3528) is close to

---

Kofun Burial Mounds

Though the origins of the Japanese race remain shrouded in mystery, much of what is known comes from the large, earthen burial mounds scattered throughout the archipelago. Called *kofun*, these served as tombs for members of Japan's early nobility, primarily members of the imperial household.

The practice of building kofun dates from the 3rd century, but under the growing influence of Buddhism (which practices cremation) it gradually died out by the end of the 7th century. Some of the best preserved mounds are around Nara Prefecture, where the forerunners of the present imperial family, the Yamato clan, had consolidated their power over Japan's warring factions.

Many early tombs are decorated with abstract, geometric patterns and are devoid of any human representation. Later tombs reveal influences from Chinese and Korean astrology, and feature distinctive writing and realistic wall paintings depicting the lives of the rulers. Human remains have been discovered in lacquered wooden coffins containing bronze mirrors and overlaid with elaborate gold leaf.

One of most notable mounds is the Takamatsuzuka-kofun, which contains wall paintings of figures said to symbolise the deities of the four directions. Since its startling discovery in 1972 by archaeologists in Asuka, the tomb has sparked considerable controversy over whether it dates from the 7th or 8th century. An even more significant dispute continues to boil over *who* exactly was enshrined in it.

Much of the debate centres on the issue of ancient cosmology and whether the tomb's occupant was of 'pure' Japanese imperial stock or, in fact, one of Japan's early *gaijin* (foreigners) visiting from China or Korea. At a 1997 symposium marking 25 years since the find, more than 50 possible candidates were still being considered.

For a detailed historical account, including photos of the off-limits inner tomb, surf the Internet to: www2.gol.com/users/stever/asuka.html. ■

the Nara City Tourist Center (¥900 for four hours or ¥1000 for the day).

AROUND NARA

Southern Nara Prefecture was the birthplace of imperial rule and is rich in historical sites which are accessible as day trips from Nara or Kyoto. Of particular historical interest are the kofun burial mounds which mark the graves of Japan's first emperors. There are also several isolated temples which allow you to escape the crowds which plague Nara's city centre.

The Nara City Tourist Center can provide copies of *Japan – Nara Prefecture* which gives an overall view of the prefecture, and has insets providing precise locations for other sights and temples south of the city including **Hōryū-ji** (founded in 607), one of the oldest Buddhist temples in Japan.

Asuka

Two places worth seeing in this village south of Nara are the **Takamatsuzuka-kofun** and **Ishibutai-kofun** tombs. The former is closed to the public, but it has a museum (open between 9 am and 5 pm, closed Monday; admission ¥200) with a copy of the frescos. The entire tomb is in the Chinese style of the time (T'ang), demonstrating the great degree to which early Japanese civilisation was influenced by continental culture. The stonework at Ishibutai-kofun is open to the public, but has no frescos. It is said to have housed the remains of 7th century noble, Soga no Umako, but is now totally empty. It's open from 9 am to 5 pm daily and entry is ¥200.

The **Asuka Historical Museum** has exhibits from regional digs. If you have time, take a look at **Asuka-dera Temple**, which dates from 596 and is considered the first true temple in Japan. Housed within the temple is the oldest remaining image of Buddha in Japan – after more than 1300 years of venerable existence, you'll have to excuse its decidedly tatty appearance.

Getting There & Away From Nara, take the Kintetsu Nara line to Yamato-Saidai-ji station

Takisaka-no-michi/Yagyū Kaidō Day Walk

Time: about three hours
Distance: about 8km
Major Sights: stone Buddhas, tea plantations, Shin-Yakushi-ji Temple

Traipsing around dozens of temples in quick succession can be tiring for mind and body. If you've got half a day to spare, this walk in the forested hills surrounding Nara is definitely recommended.

The Nara City Tourist Center can provide transport information and detailed Japanese maps. Ask the staff to circle a few key points on the route and write down the names in romaji, or better yet take along a volunteer guide (see the Orientation & Information section under Nara).

The **Takisaka-michi** is the old highway leading from the Yagyū area to Nara city. It is cobblestone for part of the way but most of it is a dirt path which meanders through forests passing the occasional stone Buddha and shrine. Take an early bus from boarding bay 4 opposite Kintetsu Nara station to Enjō-ji Temple. The ride takes about 30 minutes and costs ¥520. Bus Nos 100, 101 and 102 go via Enjō-ji and take another 17 minutes (and an extra ¥230) to reach Yagyū, which is another possible starting point if you want a longer walk down the Takisaka-michi.

After arriving, you can visit **Enjō-ji** or start the hike immediately. To find the trailhead, cross the road south of the temple and look for a wide path leading off into the woods. There are some confusing trail junctions but if you stick to the signs leading to Nara you should have no problem (the signs are mounted on posts with the word Nara written in Japanese as it appears at the beginning of this section). After passing through a small village you'll come to a teahouse which marks the halfway point of the hike. This is an ideal spot to stop for lunch (tea is free and *kusamochi* cakes are ¥130 each).

After the teahouse, the trail works its way downhill to a road which you must cross; after this descend a stone flight of stairs. At the bottom you'll come to a circular wooden rest house, from which you should follow the path downhill beside the stream. This is the walk's nicest section. Stick to this trail and you'll see shrines and stone Buddhas along the way. Tucked away on a side track, almost obscured by trees, is the Sunset Buddha, so named because the last rays of the sun light up its face. The trail comes out near Shin-Yakushi-ji. If you are exhausted by the time you reach the temple, the No 2 bus will take you back to the city centre. ■

and change to the Kashihara line to get to Kashihara-jingū-mae station. Two stops south from here on the Kintetsu Yoshino line is Asuka station. You can rent bicycles here and head east to explore the district's tombs, palace remains, temples, and strange stones. Manyō Rent-a-Cycle (☎ 0744-54-3500) hires out bicycles for ¥300 per hour or ¥1000 per day.

OSAKA
大阪

Osaka and Kyoto represent the poles of the Japanese experience – Kyoto a reminder of Japan's elegant past, and Osaka a bustling showcase of its present. While Kyotoites are famous across Japan for their refined manners and cool demeanour, Osakans pride themselves on their down-to-earth form and boisterous ways.

Almost bombed flat during WWII, Osaka appears to be an endless expanse of ugly concrete boxes punctuated by pachinko parlours and elevated highways. What Osaka (often called 'Japan's kitchen') offers is the chance to enjoy great food and drink in a big-city atmosphere. Osakans call this *kuidaore*, which means eat until you drop, and with thousands of restaurants lining the cramped streets, there are ample opportunities to do just that.

Information

The Osaka Tourist Association has offices with useful maps and information at several train stations: Shin-Osaka (☎ 06-305-3311), Osaka (☎ 06-345-2189), Namba (☎ 06-643-2125) and Tennō-ji (☎ 06-774-3077). All are open from 8 am to 8 pm. The Osaka office is in the south-east corner of the complex near the Midō-suji (east) exit.

Central Osaka

Osaka-jō Castle Osaka's foremost attraction is a 1931 concrete reproduction of the original. The castle's exterior underwent major renovations in 1997 and boasts an indisputable grandeur. The original castle, completed in 1583, was a display of power on the part of Toyotomi Hideyoshi. After he

achieved his goal of unifying Japan, 100,000 workers toiled for three years to construct an 'impregnable' granite castle. However, it was destroyed just 32 years later in 1615 by the armies of Tokugawa Ieyasu.

Within 10 years the castle had been rebuilt by the Tokugawa forces, but it was to suffer a further calamity when another generation of Tokugawas razed it rather than let it fall to the forces of the Meiji Restoration in 1868. The interior of today's castle houses a museum of Toyotomi Hideyoshi memorabilia as well as displays relating the history of the castle. They are of marginal interest, but the 8th floor provides an excellent view across Osaka. The castle is open from 9 am to 5 pm daily; admission is ¥500.

Ōte-mon Gate, which is the entrance to Osaka-jō-kōen Park, is about a 10 minute

---

Business as Usual

First and foremost, Osaka is a working city and Osakans have business in their blood. Where else in the world do people commonly greet each other with the question, 'Mōkari makka?' ('Are you making any money?'). Without question, Osaka is. In recent years the city has recorded a gross domestic product greater than all but eight countries in the world. This remarkable economic success has its roots deep in the history of the city, for Osaka was the merchant capital of Japan long before Tokyo was even incorporated as a city.

Aside from infinite legitimate enterprise, organised crime has long held a notorious presence here (romanticised in the west in the 1980s motion picture *Black Rain*). There have been countless Japanese TV shows and movies in which ominous *yakuza* (gangsters) visit Osaka 'bosses' and invariably end up blazing at each other in scathing *Osaka-ben* (Osaka dialect).

Still, while there may be some truth in tales of Osaka's underworld dealings, obliquely reflected in a string of recent scandals, the city continues to flaunt its economic might. In 1995 Osaka hosted the Asia-Pacific Economic Cooperation (APEC) forum and is hoping to play host to the G-8 Summit in 2000. Also, the city is already seeing signs of a gradual face-lift aimed at increasing its chances to be chosen as the site for the summer Olympic Games in 2008. ■

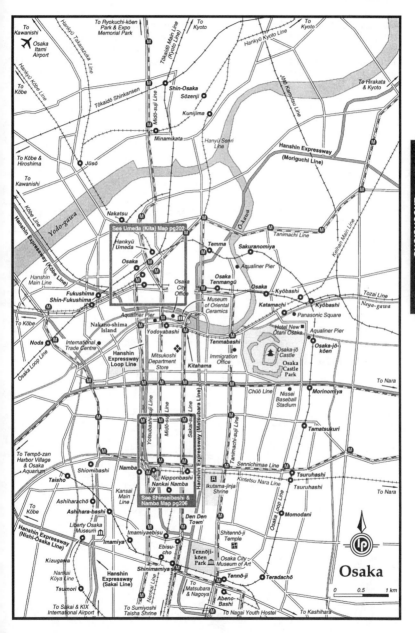

Osaka

walk north-east of Tanimachi-yonchōme station on the Chūō and Tanimachi subway lines. The castle can also be easily reached on foot from the Osaka loop line at Morinomiya or Osaka-jō-kōen stations.

Museum of Oriental Ceramics With more than 1000 exhibits, this museum has one of the finest collections of Chinese and Korean ceramics in the world. Opening hours are from 9.30 am to 5 pm daily (closed on Monday), and admission is ¥400. The museum is near Yodoyabashi station on either the Midō-suji line or the Keihan Main line.

Panasonic Square Billed as a 'Futuristic Electro-Fun Zone', Panasonic Square is a display forum for high-tech gadgetry. It's very much a hands-on experience and quite fun if you haven't already been to a similar place in Japan. Highlights include the Starforce virtual reality game and a CD jukebox that you enter and request songs from by punching in a number.

Panasonic Square is open daily from 10 am to 6 pm (admission ¥500). It's on the 2nd floor of the Twin 21 Tower building, a few minutes on foot from Kyōbashi station on the Osaka loop line or Keihan Main line.

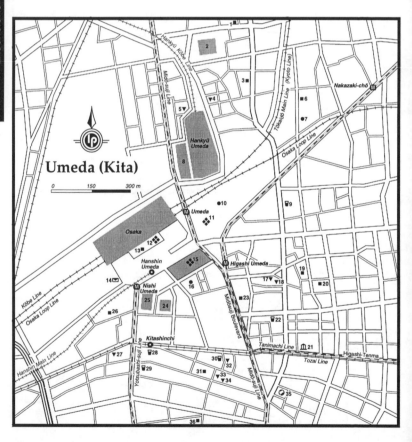

Kita-ku

There's not a whole lot to do in Kita-ku and if you've passed through the area on your arrival, that might be enough to get a feel for what the northern part of town is about.

North-west of Osaka station, the **Umeda Sky building** has twin towers joined at the top. There are two observation galleries, an outdoor one on the roof and an indoor one on the floor below (both are open from 10 am to 10.30 pm; entry costs ¥1000). You can walk to the building through an underground passage which heads due north from Osaka or Hankyū Umeda stations, or take the Osaka loop line and get off at Fukushima station.

One area worth exploring is the **Umeda Chika Centre**, a labyrinthine underground shopping/eating arcade which links Osaka station with Hankyū Umeda station.

Minami-ku

The southern (minami) part of town between the Shinsaibashi and Namba subway stations (on the Midō-suji line) is fun just to wander around, but really doesn't come into its own until night falls. All along this stretch between Midōsuji-dōri and Sakaisuji-dōri the narrow streets and colourful arcades are packed with restaurants, bars, pachinko parlours, strip clubs, cinemas and who knows what else – take a camera.

Amerika-Mura Amerika-mura, or America village, is a compact enclave of trendy shops and restaurants, with a few discreet love hotels thrown in for good measure. Highlights include colourful graffiti, the futuristic Wave complex and the general ambience, courtesy of hordes of colourful Japanese teens living out the myth of *Amerika*.

In the middle of Amerika-mura is the small 'triangle park' (all concrete) with benches. It's a good place to sit down for a while and watch the action. Amerika-mura is one or two blocks west of Midōsuji-dōri, bounded on the north by Suomachisuji-dōri and to the south by the Dōtombori-gawa River.

EXCURSIONS

UMEDA (KITA) 梅田（北）

PLACES TO STAY
1 Hotel Sunroute Umeda
  ホテルサンルート梅田
2 Hotel Hankyū International
  ホテル阪急
  インターナショナル
3 Osaka Tōkyū Hotel
  大阪東急ホテル
6 Hotel Green Plaza Osaka
  ホテルグリーン
  プラザ大阪
8 Hotel New Hankyū
  新阪急ホテル
13 Osaka Terminal Hotel
  大阪ターミナルホテル
19 Hokke Club Osaka
  法華クラブ大阪
20 Hotel Kansai
  ホテル関西
23 Umeda OS Hotel
  梅田ＯＳホテル
24 Osaka Dai-ichi Hotel
  大阪第１ホテル
25 Osaka Hilton Hotel
  大阪ヒルトン
26 Hotel Hanshin
  ホテル阪神

31 Hotel New Central
  ホテルニュー
  セントラル
36 Osaka Zen-Nikkū Hotel
  大阪全日空ホテル

PLACES TO EAT
4 Hatago
  旅篭
5 Isaribi
  漁火
17 Kamesushi
  亀寿司
18 Nawasushi
  縄寿司
27 Shabu-zen
  しゃぶ禅
32 Canopy Restaurant
  キャノピー
  レストラン
33 Maguro-tei
  まぐろ亭
34 Kani Dōraku
  かに道楽

OTHER
7 Osaka Nō Theatre
  大阪能楽会館

9 Bar, Isn't It?
  バーイズントイット
10 Hankyū Grand Building
  阪急グランドビル
11 Hankyū Department Store
  阪急デパート
12 Daimaru Department Store
  大丸デパート
14 Central Post Office
  中央郵便局
15 Hanshin Department Store
  阪神デパート
16 New Hankyū Building
  新阪急ビル
21 Umeda Gallery of Modern Art
  梅田近代美術館
22 Pig & Whistle Bar
  ビッグアンド
  ホイッスル
28 Karma Bar
  カーマ
29 Underground Bar
  アンダーグラウンド
30 Canopy Bar
  キャノピーバー
35 American Consulate
  アメリカ領事館

Osaka Human Rights Museum/Liberty Osaka This museum is dedicated to Japan's burakumin people. The burakumin were the outcasts in Japan's four-tier caste system which was officially outlawed in 1879. Though legally freed from discrimination, the group still suffers today from unfair hiring practices as well as stigmas against marrying those of burakumin ancestry. Exhibits on display document burakumin professions like slaughterhouse work, drum making and shoe repair. An English leaflet is available. The museum is open from 10 am to 5 pm, closed Monday. Admission is ¥250. Take the Osaka loop line to Ashihara-bashi station and walk south for five minutes.

Shitennō-ji Temple Shitennō-ji, founded in 593, is one of the oldest Buddhist temples in Japan, but none of the present buildings are originals. Most are the usual concrete reproductions, a notable exception being the big stone *torii* (entrance gate), quite an unusual feature for a Buddhist temple. It dates back to 1294, making it the oldest of its kind in Japan.

The temple is open from 9 am to 5 pm daily. Entry is free, and the adjoining museum costs ¥200 (it's of limited interest). It's most easily reached from Shitennōji-mae station on the Tanimachi-suji subway line. There is a lively flea market here on the 21st of each month.

About a 10 minute walk from the temple is Tennōji-kōen Park, which has a botanical garden, a zoo and a circular garden known as Keitaku-en.

Sumiyoshi Taisha Shrine This shrine is dedicated to Shintō deities associated with the sea and sea travel, in commemoration of a safe passage to Korea by a 3rd century empress. Having survived the bombing in WWII, the shrine actually has a couple of buildings that date to just 1810, even though it was founded in the early 3rd century – the buildings that can be seen today are faithful replicas of the originals. They offer a rare opportunity to see a Shintō shrine that pre-

dates the influence of Chinese Buddhist architectural styles.

The shrine is open every day from 6.30 am to 5 pm, and admission is free. It's near both Sumiyoshi-taisha station on the Nankai line and Sumiyoshi-tori-mae station on the Hankai line.

Other Attractions

Aqualiner River Cruises Sure, it's not Venice, but Osaka *does* have a few canals on which you can cruise the city, taking in the sights without any strain on the legs. There are guide tapes available on request to explain the sights. Tours depart on the hour daily from 10 am to 4 pm with additional departures at 6 and 7 pm on weekends and holidays. The fare is ¥1800 for the one hour ride. Take the Osaka loop line to Osaka-jō-kōen station and walk west toward the next bridge over from the station.

Tempō-zan Harbor Village The highlight of this bayside complex is the **Osaka Aquarium** (Kaiyū-kan). You start by taking an elevator to the top before you begin a slow descent down a walkway which winds its way around the aquarium's giant main tank. Here, a variety of sharks and other fish share their quarters with the aquarium's star attractions, two enormous whale sharks. On the other side of the walkway are displays of life found on eight different ocean levels. It's open daily from 10 am to 8 pm; entry is ¥1950.

Also in the 'village', the **Suntory Museum complex** holds an IMAX 3-D theatre and art gallery with posters and glass artwork on display. Admission to the gallery is ¥950, and it's open daily from 10 am to 8 pm. The IMAX theatre has daily showings on the hour from 11 am to 7 pm for ¥1000.

Nearby, the **Tempō-zan Contemporary Museum** has interesting displays of holographic art and optical illusions. It's open daily from 10 am to 7 pm, and costs ¥1000.

Expo Memorial Park This park is the legacy of Expo '70, and houses a few interesting attractions such as Expo Land and a Japanese garden. The impressive **National Museum of Ethnology** features artefacts and everyday items from cultures around the world. Admission is ¥400, and it is open from 10 am to 5 pm, closed Wednesday.

To get to the park, take the Midō-suji line to Senri-Chūō station and change to bus No 114 or 115 to the park. Alternatively, there is a monorail service from Senri-chūō that takes around five minutes and costs ¥220.

Sakai Nintoku Burial Mound The history of Sakai's burial mound is a lot more interesting than its present reality. Today it merely looks like, well, a big mound. In its time, however, it is thought that some 800,000 workers laboured to fashion the final resting place of 4th century Emperor Nintoku. To get to the mound, take the Hanwa line from Tennō-ji station in Osaka to Mozu station, from where it is about a five minute walk.

Open-Air Museum of Old Japanese Farmhouses There are nine restored thatch-roof farmhouses on display here in pleasant natural surroundings, each representing a different regional building style used in pre-industrial Japan. The surrounding park, Ryokuchi-kōen, is pleasant for strolling and picnics. An English pamphlet is available. Take the Midō-suji subway line to its northern terminus, Esaka station, and walk north to the park. It's open daily from 9.30 am to 5 pm (4 pm in summer). Admission is ¥410.

Places to Stay

Unless you plan to be out in the bars late, the best place to stay when visiting Osaka is Kyoto. It's less than 40 minutes away and there's a far better choice of accommodation, particularly traditional style and budget. There are, however, plenty of beds in Osaka.

Youth Hostels *Nagai Youth Hostel* (☎ 06-699-5631) near the new stadium in Nagai (Midō-suji subway line) is the nearest youth hostel to central Osaka (dorm beds ¥2500). Also on the Midō-suji subway line near Ryokuchi-kōen station is *Osaka-fu Hattori Ryokuchi Youth Hostel* (☎ 06-862-0600),

where beds are ¥2300 (dinner ¥850, breakfast ¥550).

Hotels – Mid-Range In the Minami area, the wonderfully kitsch *Hotel California* (☎ 06-243-0333) is a Japanese interpretation of the California style. Prices are from ¥8000/12,700 for singles/doubles.

South-west from here is the *Asahi Plaza Hotel Amenity Shinsaibashi* (☎ 06-212-5111), which has singles/twins from ¥7800/14,500. Continuing east is another Asahi hotel with similar rates: the *Asahi Plaza Hotel East Shinsaibashi* (☎ 06-241-1011). In Amerikamura the *Arrow Hotel* (☎ 06-211-8441) has singles/doubles/twins for ¥7200/8800/9200.

In the Osaka station area, just north of Hankyū Umeda station is the *Hotel Sunroute Umeda* (☎ 06-373-1111), where singles/doubles/twins from ¥8400/13,900/15,000. Not far south-east of here the *Hotel Green Plaza Osaka* (☎ 06-374-1515) has singles/twins/doubles from ¥7500/10,300/11,550. About five minutes south-east of Osaka station the *Umeda OS Hotel* (☎ 06-312-1271) has 208 single rooms from ¥8300; twins are from ¥11,800. About five minutes walk east of the OS is the *Hotel Kansai* (☎ 06-312-7971), a cheaper business hotel, where singles/doubles/twins start at ¥5500/7800/8000. Close by is the *Hokke Club Osaka* (☎ 06-313-3171), another cheaper option with the luxury of a noon checkout; singles/twins are from ¥5700/8800.

Hotels – Top End Osaka is brimming with upper-end accommodation. One of the most expensive hotels in town is the *Hotel Hankyū International* (☎ 06-377-2100) just north of Hankyū Umeda station. Singles here start at ¥27,000, doubles from ¥40,000 and twins from ¥42,000.

The following is a list of Osaka's major upmarket hotels:

Holiday Inn Nankai Osaka
(☎ 06-213-8281) five minutes north of Namba subway station; singles/doubles from ¥14,500/20,000

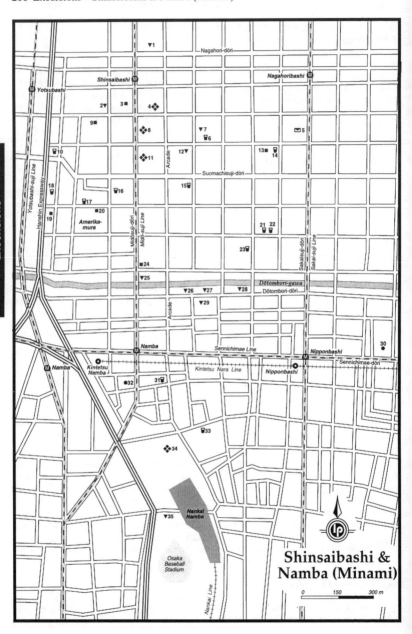

Shinsaibashi &
Namba (Minami)

Hotel Hanshin
(☎ 06-344-1661) three minutes south of Osaka station; singles/doubles/twins from ¥13,500/ 19,000/21,500

Hotel New Hankyū
(☎ 06-372-5101) next to Hankyū Umeda station; singles/twins/doubles from ¥13,000/19,000/ 24,000

Hotel New Ōtani Osaka
(☎ 06-941-1111) near Osaka-jō-kōen station on the Osaka loop line; singles/doubles/twins from ¥18,000/29,000/33,000

Hotel Nikkō Osaka
(☎ 06-244-1111) above Shinsaibashi subway station; singles/doubles from ¥17,000/ 26,500

Hyatt Regency Osaka
(☎ 06-612-1234) near Nakafutō subway station; singles/doubles from ¥20,000/ 31,000

Osaka Dai-Ichi Hotel
(☎ 06-341-4411) three minutes south of Osaka station; singles/twins/doubles from ¥12,500/ 21,000/24,500

Osaka Hilton Hotel
(☎ 06-347-7111) just south of Osaka station; singles/doubles from ¥26,000/ 32,000

Osaka Tōkyū Hotel
(☎ 06-373-2411) near Hankyū Umeda station; singles/doubles/twins from ¥10,000/19,000/ 22,000

Osaka Zen-Nikkū Hotel
(☎ 06-347-1112) 10 minutes walk south of Osaka station; singles/doubles from ¥13,000/ 24,000

Places to Eat

Kita-ku The backstreets and shopping arcades around Osaka and Hankyū Umeda stations are bursting with restaurants. Starting at the northern end of Hankyū Umeda station, you can choose from two excellent robotayaki places (robotayaki is easy to order, since all the food is laid out in front of you).

EXCURSIONS

SHINSAIBASHI & NAMBA
心斎橋／難波

PLACES TO STAY
3 Hotel Nikkō Osaka
　ホテル日航
9 Hotel California
　ホテルカリフォルニア
13 Asahi Plaza Hotel East Shinsaibashi
　朝日プラザホテル
19 Asahi Plaza Hotel Amenity Shinsaibashi
　朝日プラザホテル
　アメニティー心斎橋
20 Arrow Hotel
　アローホテル
24 Holiday Inn Nankai Osaka
　ホリデーイン南海

PLACES TO EAT
1 Field of Farms
　フィールドオブ
　ファームス
2 Wakamatsu
　若松
7 Nishiya
　にし家
12 Vlado's; Chico-n-Charlie's; Capricciosa
　ブラドス／チコ＝ン＝
　チャーリース／
　カプリチョーザ

25 Shabu-zen
　しゃぶ禅
26 Zuboraya
　づぼらや
27 Kani Dōraku
　かに道楽
28 Sawasdee
　サワディー
29 Kuidaore
　くいだおれ
35 Hard Rock Cafe
　ハードロックカフェ

OTHER
4 Sogō Department Store
　そごうデパート
5 Minami Post Office
　ミナミ郵便局
6 Diva
　ディバ
8 Daimaru Department Store
　大丸デパート
10 Vinyl
　ヴァイナル
11 Daimaru Department Store Annex
　大丸デパート
　アネックス

14 Murphy's
　マーフィーズ
15 Pig & Whistle
　ピッグアンド
　ホイッスル
16 Uncle Steven's
　アンクル
　スティーブンス
17 Grand Cafe
　グランドカフェ
18 Someplace Else
　サムプレースエルス
21 Vino
　ビノ
22 Nell's
　ネルス
23 Bar's Bar
　バーズバー
30 National Bunraku Theatre
　国立文楽劇場
31 Southside Blues & Co
　サウスサイドブルース
32 Shin Kabukiza Theatre
　新歌舞伎座
33 Karapara
　カラパラ
34 Takashimaya Department Store
　高島屋デパート

Isaribi (☎ 06-373-2969) is downstairs at the north-west end of the station. Everything here is ¥300 except beer, which is ¥600. On the other side of the station just down a little side street, *Hatago* (☎ 06-373-3440) has a warm, country feel. Both places are open daily from 5 to 11.15 pm.

A short walk east from Hanshin department store, *Nawasushi* (☎ 06-312-9891) offers good sushi and is open from 3 pm to midnight. Just down the street, *Kamesushi* (☎ 06-312-3862) offers similar fare in slightly more spacious digs and its hours are the same as Nawasushi's.

In one of the narrow streets just south of the Osaka Ekimae Dai-San building, *Kani Dōraku* (☎ 06-344-5091) serves anything to do with crab, with sets going from about ¥3000. It's open daily from 11 am to 11 pm. Look for the giant crab out the front.

Nearby *Maguro-tei* (☎ 06-452-5863) is a modern, noisy, automatic sushi place which has an all-you-can-eat special on weekday evenings from 5 pm and all day on Sunday (¥1500 for men and ¥1000 for women). It's open daily from 11 am to 4 am (for those late-night sushi cravings).

For delicious shabu-shabu, try *Shabu-zen* (☎ 06-343-0250) on the 10th floor of the AX building, not far from the Osaka Hilton. It serves sets from ¥3300. Lunch is served from 11 am to 2 pm and dinner from 5 to 11 pm.

In the Osaka Hilton, just across from the reception desk, *The In Place* serves a curry buffet for ¥1700, including salad and dessert, daily from 11.30 am to 2.30 pm. Downstairs on level B2, *Victoria Station* (☎ 06-347-7470) has a good salad bar and steak menu starting at ¥1500.

Minami-ku The place to eat in Minami is the restaurant-packed street of Dōtombori-dōri. You can't miss *Kuidaore* (☎ 06-211-5300), as it has a lively mechanical clown posted outside its doors, attracting the attention of potential customers by beating a drum. The restaurant has eight floors serving almost every kind of Japanese food, and windows featuring a huge range of plastic replicas. It's open daily from 11 am to 10 pm.

Nearby is a restaurant that sports a huge mechanical crab, called *Kani Dōraku* (☎ 06-211-8975) and specialising in crab dishes (mostly ¥3000 and up). It's open daily from 11 am to 11 pm.

Wakamatsu (☎ 06-245-5150), tucked in on the narrow street just behind the Nikkō Hotel, is a cosy little dig serving excellent home-cooked food from tempura to spicy chilli and has a wide selection of sake. It's open evenings from 6.30 to 11.30 pm, except Sunday.

Zuboraya (☎ 06-211-0181) is the place to go if you've worked up the nerve to try fugu (Japanese puffer fish). A standard set of fugu prepared a variety of ways goes for ¥6000 – about the cheapest fugu set anywhere. It's open daily from 11 am to 11.30 pm.

Sawasdee (☎ 06-212-2301) is a small Thai restaurant with friendly staff and great food. Open from 11.30 am to 10 pm (closed Monday) it's on the 2nd floor of the Shibata building, not far from Kani Doraku.

Across the river on Midōsuji-dōri, on the 6th floor of the Gurukas building, *Shabu-zen* (☎ 06-213-2935) serves excellent shabu in an elegant setting. Courses start at ¥3000. It's open daily from 11 am to 11 pm.

For delicious steaks, head to *Vlado's* (☎ 06-244-4129), run by a staff of Australian expats. The lunchtime steak sets are good value. In the same building, try *Chico-n-Charlie's* (☎ 06-243-6025) for good Mexican food, or *Capricciosa* (☎ 06-243-6020) for cheap, plentiful Italian food.

Not far north of Vlado's, *Nishiya* (☎ 06-241-9221) serves Osaka udon noodles and a variety of hearty nabe (iron pot) dishes for reasonable prices. It's open daily from 11 am to 10 pm.

On the northern side of Nagahori-dōri, *Field of Farms* (☎ 06-253-0500) is a must for lovers of vegetarian cooking. It serves a buffet-style lunch for ¥900 and has an extensive menu for dinner.

Osaka also has a branch of the *Hard Rock Cafe* (☎ 06-646-1470), with drinks and American-style eats. On weekdays it's open from 11 am to 11 pm, weekends till 3 am. From Monday to Thursday there is an excellent happy hour from 4 to 7 pm. It's south of Nankai Namba station.

Entertainment

Traditional Check the *National Bunraku Theatre* (☎ 06-212-1122) for *bunraku* (Japanese puppet shows). *Osaka Nō Theatre* (☎ 06-373-1726), a five minute walk east of Osaka station, holds nō shows about four times a month, some of which are free. There are also five *manzai* (comic dialogue) theatres around the city with something going on most nights. It's possible, if your timing is right, to take in some *rakugo* (comic monologue) performances held in small theatres in Osaka.

Unfortunately, none of these places has regularly scheduled shows. The best thing is to check with the TIC about current shows, check the listings in the *Meet Osaka* guide or look in *Kansai Time Out*.

If you happen to be in town during March, you might catch the Osaka sumō *basho*, one of Japan's six yearly sumō wrestling tournaments; tickets start at around ¥3000. Again, contact the TIC for exact dates and ticket information.

Bars & Clubs A big Japanese city with a large foreign community, such as Osaka, is bound to have a lively nightlife – and it does. In the Kita area, check out *Underground* for its ¥300 weekday happy hour from 6 to 9 pm and occasional live music. It's in a basement not far from the Osaka Hilton. Look for the British Underground sign outside.

Nearby, *Karma* is also popular, and a short walk east on the same street brings you to *Canopy*, which serves drinks and food until dawn.

Walking north toward the station you'll find the *Pig & Whistle*, a British-style pub which serves good fish & chips and imported beer (there is another branch in Minami). A few minutes walk east of Hankyū department store brings you to *Bar, Isn't It?*, a large bar popular with the young, after-work crowd.

For more intense late-night action, head south to the Minami District, particularly the backstreets of Shinsaibashi and Amerika-mura. The futuristic *Karapara* is a good place to start your pub crawl. At the opposite end of the spectrum, *Southside Blues & Co* is a good place to enjoy blues music in a mellow atmosphere. There's also a grill for those who want to combine dinner and a drink.

North of the Dōtombori-gawa River, *Vino* and *Nell's* offer two intriguing options. A few blocks north *Murphy's* is an Irish pub and on the same block is *Diva*, a karaoke place specialising in English songs (look hard for the sign written in English at street level outside; Diva is on the 6th floor). A good place to hide from dawn is *Bar's Bar*, a classic hole-in-the-wall hidden down a small alley just north of the river.

For something a little more trendy, head across Midōsuji-dōri to Amerika-mura. *Uncle Steven's* is a Tex-Mex bar good for spicy food, music and beer. *Grand Cafe* is a spacious place which occasionally offers live music. *Someplace Else*, in a basement just across from the little 'park' in Amerika-mura, is very popular with expats and gets pretty wild late at night.

A block north of Someplace Else on the same street, *Vinyl* is a good bar with 60s mod decor and an interesting clientele.

Things to Buy

There are major department stores in both the Kita and Minami areas. For cheaper, more interesting shopping, check out Amerika-mura in Minami. For electronics, head to Den Den Town (Nipponbashi), an area of shops almost exclusively devoted to electronic goods. To avoid sales tax, check if the store has a 'Tax Free' sign outside and bring your passport. Take the Sakai-suji subway line to Ebisu-chō station and exit at the No 1 or 2 exit. Most stores are closed Wednesday.

Getting There & Away

There are frequent limousine buses between Itami airport and various parts of Osaka. Buses run to/from Shin-Osaka station every 15 minutes from 8 am to 9.30 pm and cost ¥500. The trip takes around 25 minutes.

EXCURSIONS

Buses run at about the same frequency to/from Osaka and Namba stations (half an hour, ¥680).

To Kansai International Airport (KIX) there are a variety of routes from Osaka. Limousine buses leave to/from Shin-Osaka, Osaka Umeda, Kyōbashi, Tenmabashi, OCAT Namba, Uehonmachi, Tennō-ji and Nanko (Cosmo Square) stations. The fare is ¥1300 for most routes, and the journeys take an average of 50 minutes depending on traffic conditions.

By train, the fastest way to and from the airport is the private Nankai express Rapid, which departs from Namba station on the Midō-suji subway line. The ride takes 30 minutes and costs ¥1410. The JR limited airport express Haruka operates between the airport and Shin-Osaka (45 minutes, ¥2990) and Tennō-ji (30 minutes, ¥2280). Regular JR expresses called Kanku Kaisoku also operate between the airport and Osaka station (66 minutes, ¥1210), Kyōbashi (75 minutes, ¥1210), Tennō-ji (45 minutes, ¥1080) and Namba (61 minutes, ¥1080).

See also the Getting There & Away chapter for details on rail transport to Osaka.

Getting Around
Osaka has a vast subway network and the Osaka loop line *(kanjō-sen)* that circles the city. In fact, there should be no need to use any other form of transport while you are in Osaka unless you stay out late and miss the last train.

KŌBE
神戸

Several years have passed since the disastrous earthquake of 17 January 1995 struck Kōbe, levelling whole neighbourhoods and killing more than 6000 people. Though some evidence of the disaster is still visible, mostly in construction sites dotted around the city, it's mainly business as usual in this pleasant city by the bay. In spite of all the damage wrought by the quake, Kōbe remains one of Japan's most attractive cities, owing largely to its location perched on hills overlooking the sea.

In many ways Kōbe can be likened to Nagasaki (on the island of Kyūshū in western Japan). Both cities are ports, have Chinese communities and in the late 19th century were settled by European traders. Both the Chinese and the European influences linger, and can be found in the city's diverse restaurants and architectural styles.

Information
There is an information counter in Shin-Kōbe station (☎ 078-241-9550), and another west of Sannomiya station (☎ 078-322-0220), across from Sogō department store. Both counters can assist with accommodation bookings.

Kitano-chō
Kitano-chō is the area where most of Kōbe's foreign architecture can be found (some homes double as museums). As in Nagasaki, the western-style homes may be of limited appeal to westerners, but it's a very pleasant area to stroll around. There are also a number of places of religious worship – a Russian Orthodox church, a mosque, a synagogue and a Catholic church. This area gets *very* busy with Japanese tourists on weekends.

Kōbe Municipal Museum
Kōbe Municipal Museum has a collection of so-called Namban (literally, Southern Barbarian) art and occasional special exhibits. Namban art is a school of painting that developed under the influence of early Jesuit missionaries in Japan, many of whom taught western painting techniques to Japanese students. Entry to the museum is ¥200, and it's open from 10 am to 4.30 pm, closed Monday.

Kōbe Phoenix Plaza
This recently built hall is both an earthquake museum and a clearing house of information for Kōbe citizens affected by the quake. There is a wide variety of displays documenting the earthquake and the fires which swept the city in its wake and the city's continuing efforts at reconstruction. It's open daily from 10 am to 7 pm and entry is free. It's just south of the main tourist information

KŌBE　神戸

PLACES TO STAY
1 Shin-Kōbe Oriental Hotel
新神戸オリエンタル
ホテル
4 Green Hill Hotel Kōbe
グリーヒルホテル神戸
5 Green Hill Urban Hotel
グリーヒルアーバ
ホテル
20 Kōbe Plaza Hotel
神戸プラザホテル

PLACES TO EAT
6 Wang Thai
ワンタイ
7 Marrakech
マラケシュ

8 Ju Ju
樹樹
9 Cookhouse Un Deux
Trois
クックハウス
アンドゥトゥワ
10 Abait Faim
アバイトファーム
14 Ikariya
いかりや
15 Omoni
おもに

OTHER
2 OPA Shopping
Centre & Hub
OPAショッピング
センター

3 Wantage Books
ワンタゲブックス
11 Korean Consulate
大韓民国領事館
12 Rub-a-Dub Reggae
Bar
ラブダブバー
13 Bar, Isn't It?
バーイズントイット
16 Tourist Information Office
観光案内所
17 Kōbe Phoenix Plaza
神戸フェニックス
プラザ
18 Sogō Department Store
そごうデパート
19 Polo Dog
ポロドッグ

EXCURSIONS

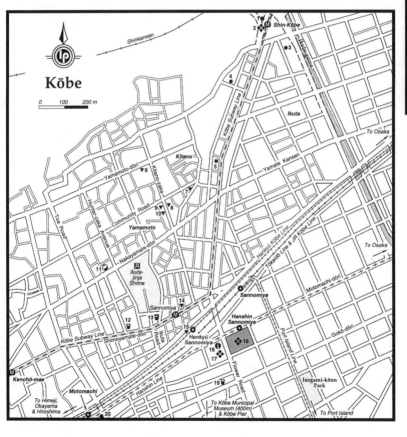

office near Sannomiya station. Look for the new glass building.

Chinatown
Known as Nankinmachi by locals, Kōbe's Chinatown is no rival for Chinatowns elsewhere, but is a good place for a stroll and a quick bite to eat. The best bets are not the full-course, sit-down meals offered by nearly all the restaurants, but the small delicacies that are served out the front for takeaway. Nankinmachi is easy enough to find – starting from Motomachi station, walk south on Koikawasuji-dōri for a few blocks until you see the Chinese-style gate at the entrance to the street.

Mt Rokkō-san
At 931m, it's a pleasant trip by cable car to the top (¥560). To get there, take bus No 25 from Rokkō station on the Hankyū line. Get off the bus at the Rokkō cable car station. You can continue onwards on the Arima cable car (¥700). This is also a good area for hiking; some people take the cable car up and then hike down. Further up are great views of Kōbe Harbour.

Cruises
From 11 February to 25 December, cruises depart daily from Kōbe's Naka pier. These usually last a couple of hours and cost ¥3150. Possibilities include the Akashi Bay cruise (and a look at the Akashi-Kaikyō Bridge, the world's longest suspension bridge), a cruise around the new Kansai airport project and an evening Osaka Bay cruise. Dinner cruises are also available with a variety of menus. For more information ring Luminous Kankō (☎ 078-333-8414).

Places to Stay
Youth Hostels The *Kōbe Tarumi Youth Hostel* (☎ 078-707-2133) has dormitory beds for ¥2800, single rooms from ¥4000 to ¥5000 and twins for ¥4500 per person. Breakfast is available for ¥500, dinner for ¥800. Unfortunately, it's a little out of town. Take a San-in line train from Kōbe station and get off after six stops at Tarumi station.

The hostel is an eight minute walk east along the road that runs parallel to the south side of the railway tracks.

Hotels The *Green Hill Urban Hotel* (☎ 078-222-1221) is in the Sannomiya area about 10 minutes walk to the north (equidistant between Shin-Kōbe and Sannomiya stations). It charges ¥6500/11,500 for singles/twins.

The *Green Hill Hotel Kōbe* (☎ 078-222-0909) is further up the hill and down a side street. It has slightly bigger rooms at ¥8300/14,600.

Another option is the *Kōbe Plaza Hotel* (☎ 078-332-1141), about five minutes walk west of Sannomiya station, behind Motomachi station. Singles range from ¥7200 to ¥8200, twins from ¥13,500 to ¥15,000.

In the top end, you could try *Shin-Kōbe Oriental Hotel* (☎ 078-291-1121), not far from Shin-Kōbe station. Singles range from ¥13,000 to ¥22,000, with doubles costing from ¥23,000 to ¥33,000.

Near the waterfront, about 10 minutes walk south of Motomachi station, *Hotel Ōkura Kōbe* (☎ 078-333-011) has singles/doubles from ¥14,000/24,000. About 10 minutes walk south of here, *Kōbe Harbourland New Ōtani* (☎ 078-360-1111) has singles from ¥10,000 to ¥16,000, twins are from ¥26,000 to ¥35,000, and doubles are from ¥30,000 to ¥45,000.

Places to Eat
Kōbe is teeming with restaurants, and the best advice is to wander around the southern part of the Kitano-chō area.

For Kōbe beef, *Ikariya* is your best bet. It's only a short walk north of Sannomiya station; there's a menu in English with set meals from ¥10,000.

For more economical fare, take a stroll up Kitano-zaka. Here you'll find *Abait Faim*, a good Italian restaurant with reasonable prices. A few doors up the road is *Cookhouse Un Deux Trois*, a French restaurant with courses from ¥3000. On the other side of the road look out for *Ju Ju* (it means tree tree), a very upmarket Chinese restaurant.

The Sri Lankan restaurant *Court Lodge* is

Kōbe Beef

Kōbe has long been known for its culinary attractions, and topping the list is its beef. Meat-eaters agree that the savoury local steaks are hard to beat and for the price they should be. At many of the better restaurants, Kōbe beef can cost up to ¥40,000 a plate!

This exorbitant cost has its roots in not just the chef's preparation but in the unconventional lifestyle of the cows. Mostly raised in the countryside of Hyōgo Prefecture, these lovable but ill-fated creatures receive daily massage and a diet consisting of none other than fat-encouraging beer! Such royal treatment, many say, is what gives the delectable Kōbe beef its tenderness. ■

a great place for lunch or dinner, and other favourites include *Wang Thai* for Thai food and *Marrakech* for superb, if pricey, Moroccan food.

Down by Sannomiya station there is authentic Korean cuisine in a warm atmosphere at *Omoni*, under the tracks on the north side of the station.

For Chinese food, the natural choice is Nankinmachi (Chinatown), just south of Motomachi station. For a light lunch, you can choose from any of the restaurants serving takeaway dumplings and other delicacies from stands in front of the stores.

Entertainment

Kōbe has a large number of bars. A few minutes walk south of Sannomiya station, *Polo Dog* serves cheap drinks and light pub food, and has live acoustic music on weekends. Across from Shin-Kōbe station, on the 2nd floor of the OPA shopping centre, *Hub* is a popular British-style pub. *Bar, Isn't It?* is like its counterparts in Osaka and Kyoto – loud, lively and cheap. In addition to these, a walk around the small streets north of Sannomiya station will turn up any number of small bars, karaoke rooms and clubs.

Getting There & Away

See the Getting There & Away chapter for details on getting to/from Kōbe.

Getting Around

Kōbe is small enough to negotiate on foot, most of the sights being within 30 minutes walk of the main train stations. A subway line connects Shin-Kōbe station with Sannomiya station (¥160). There is also a city loop bus service which makes a circle tour of most of the city's sightseeing spots (¥250 per ride, ¥650 for an all-day pass).

HIMEJI
姫路

If you see no other castles in Japan, you should at least visit Himeji-jō, unanimously acclaimed as the most splendid Japanese castle still standing. It is also known as Shirasagi (White Egret) a title which derives from the castle's stately white form.

Himeji can easily be visited as a day trip from Kyoto. A couple of hours at the castle, plus the 10 to 15 minute walk from the station, is all the time you really need. Other attractions worth lingering for are Himeji's history museum and a trip up to Engyō-ji Temple on Mt Shosha-zan.

There's a tourist information counter (☎ 0792-85-3792) at the station (exit the north central gate and turn left). Between 10 am and 3 pm friendly English-speaking staff are on duty and can help with hotel/ryokan reservations.

Himeji-jō Castle

Himeji-jō is the most magnificent of the handful of Japanese castles which survive in their original (nonconcrete) form. Although there have been fortifications in Himeji since 1333, today's castle was built in 1580 by Toyotomi Hideyoshi and enlarged some 30 years later by Ikeda Terumasa. Ikeda was awarded the castle by Tokugawa Ieyasu when the latter's forces defeated the Toyotomi armies. In the following centuries the castle was home to 48 successive lords.

The castle has a five storey main *donjon* and three smaller donjons, and the entire structure is surrounded by moats and defensive walls punctuated with rectangular, circular and triangular openings for firing guns and shooting arrows at attackers. The

EXCURSIONS

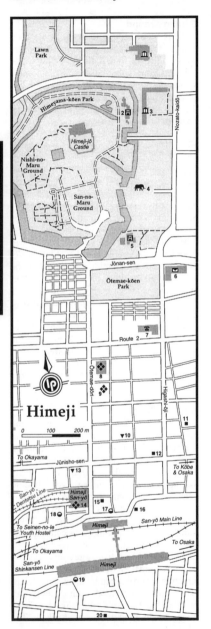

HIMEJI 姫路

PLACES TO STAY
11 Hotel Tsubota
ホテルつぼた
12 Washington Hotel
ワシントンホテル
15 Hotel Sunroute New
Himeji
ホテルサンルート
ニュー姫路
16 Hotel Sunroute Himeji
ホテルサンルート姫路
20 Hotel Himeji Plaza
ホテル姫路プラザ

PLACES TO EAT
10 Fukutei Restaurant
ふく亭
13 Toridoru Restaurant/Bar
トリドル

SHRINES
2 Himeji Shrine
姫路神社
5 Gokoku Shrine
護国神社

OTHER
1 Hyōgo Prefectural
Museum of History
兵庫県立歴史博物館
3 Art Museum
姫路市立美術館
4 Himeji City Zoo
姫路市立動物園
6 Himeji Post Office
姫路郵便局
7 Telephone Office (NTT)
8 Daiei Department Store
ダイエー
9 Yamatoyashiki
Department Store
ヤマトヤシキ
14 Sanyō Department
Store
サンヨーデパート
17 City Bus Terminal
市バスターミナル
18 Shinki Bus Terminal
神姫バスターミナル
19 City South Bus
Terminal
市バス南ターミナル

walls of the donjon also feature *ishiotoshi*, special openings that allowed defenders to pour boiling water or oil onto anyone who made it past the defensive slits.

Ask at the tourist information counter at the station or the castle reception desk about English-speaking guides. The guide service is free and highly recommended. It's best to call the castle (☎ 0792-85-1146) ahead of time to make an appointment. The castle is open from 9 am to 6 pm (last entry 5 pm) in summer; it closes an hour earlier in winter. It takes about 1½ hours to follow the arrow-marked route around the castle. Entry costs ¥500.

Hyōgo Prefectural Museum of History

This well laid out museum has good displays on Himeji-jō and other castles around Japan and, indeed, the world. At 11 am, and 2 and 3.30 pm you can even try on a suit of samurai armour or a kimono.

The museum is a five minute walk north of the castle. It's open from 10 am to 5 pm daily, except Monday; admission is ¥200.

Mt Shosha-zan & Engyō-ji Temple

Around 8km north-east of Himeji station is the beautiful Engyō-ji complex on Mt Shosha-zan. Take your time to explore the temple grounds, which continue up the mountain from the cable car stop.

To get there, take a No 6 or 8 bus from Himeji station (¥260). The trip takes around 25 minutes. Get off at Shosha-zan and board the cable car (¥500 one way, ¥900 return) to the top. Entry to the temple area is ¥300, and the cable car operates every 15 minutes between 8.30 am and 6 pm.

Places to Stay

There *are* some places to stay in Himeji but, in general, visiting Himeji as a day trip is a far better option. The information counter at the station has listings of lodgings and can help with directions and reservations.

Seinen-no-Ie Youth Hostel (☎ 0792-93-2716) costs ¥900 for a bed in the dorm room or ¥1200 on tatami mats (no meals). Temple lodging is available at Engyō-ji (☎ 0792-66-3240) for ¥5000 with meals.

Places to Eat

There is a *food court* in the underground mall at Himeji station with several bakeries, if you want to take food along for picnics around the castle.

On the way to the castle, a good place to try Japanese kaiseki cuisine at a reasonable price is *Fukutei* (☎ 0792-23-0981). It serves a mini-kaiseki lunch for ¥1600 from 11 am to 2 pm every day, except Thursday. Kaiseki dinners, served from 6 to 9.30 pm, start at ¥5000.

If you're sticking around after dark, stop by *Toridoru* (☎ 0792-83-1832), a lively restaurant/bar just a short walk from the station. It attracts an eclectic and boisterous crowd, and has good and reasonably priced food and drinks. It's open daily from 5 to 11 pm.

Getting There & Away

The best way to Himeji is by the JR *shin-kaisoku* (limited express) train. To/from Kyoto it costs ¥2210 and takes two hours. To/from Osaka it costs ¥1420 and takes 90 minutes. To/from Kōbe it costs ¥930 and takes one hour. You can save a little money by taking the private Hankyū line from any of these places, but you'll have to change trains at least once and spend more time travelling. It's also possible to travel to/from Himeji by *shinkansen* (bullet train).

LAKE BIWA-KO
琵琶湖

Biwa-ko is Japan's largest lake (235km in circumference). The lake takes its name from its shape, resembling a *biwa* (traditional Japanese lute), and is thought to have been created by the same mammoth earthquake which sprouted Japan's beloved Mt Fuji.

The basin dominates Shiga Prefecture and has a number of attractions easily visited as day trips from Kyoto. Summer water sports are popular, and there are also several sightseeing cruises on the lake. From atop Mt Hiei-zan and Enryaku-ji Temple (see the Northern & North-Eastern Kyoto section in the Things to See & Do chapter) there are excellent views over the lake.

The Kyoto TIC has more detailed information on transport, sights and events in this region. Cycling is an excellent way to explore the region. There are youth hostels dotted around the lake at Ōmi-hachiman (☎ 0748-32-2938), Ōtsu (☎ 077-522-8009), Makino (☎ 0740-28-0051), Yasu (☎ 077-587-2201) and Wani (☎ 077-594-4203).

Ōtsu Area

Ōtsu (population 260,000), on Biwa-ko's south-west shore, developed from a 7th century imperial residence (the city was capital of Japan for a brief five years) into a lake port and major post station on the Tōkaidō Highway between eastern and western Japan. It is now the capital of Shiga Prefecture. Ōtsu has a number of praiseworthy spots and makes an interesting area to combine with a visit to Enryaku-ji Temple on Mt Hiei-zan.

The Ōtsu Matsuri Festival takes place on 9 and 10 October at Tenson-jinja Shrine, near Ōtsu station. On 8 August there is a magnificent fireworks display near Hama-Ōtsu.

The tourist information office (☎ 077-522-3830) at Ōtsu station is open from 8.45 am to 5 pm daily. Some English is spoken, and it has an excellent map of the area.

Mii-dera Temple Mii-dera, formally known as Onjō-ji Temple, is a short walk from Keihan Hama-Ōtsu station. The temple, founded in the late 7th century, is the headquarters of the Tendai-jimon school of Buddhism. It started its days as a branch of Enryaku-ji, but later the two fell into conflict and Mii-dera was repeatedly razed by Enryaku-ji's warrior monks. Of the original 850 buildings in the vast compound, about 60 remain today.

Mii-dera is famous for its treasures, including two great temple bells, Mii-no-banshō (Evening Bell of Mii) and Benkei-no-hikigane (Bell Dragged by Benkei). The latter, according to local folklore, was single-handedly hauled up Mt Hiei-zan by the renowned monk Benkei.

The temple is open from 8 am to 5 pm; admission costs ¥450.

Hiyoshi-taisha Shrine Hiyoshi-taisha is dedicated to the gods of the 108 shrines scattered among its expansive grounds. The shrine has close to 4000 branches throughout Japan, and is said to safeguard nearby Enryaku-ji. On display here are the *mikoshi* (portable shrines) which had to be carried into ancient Kyoto by the monks of Mt Hiei-zan whenever they wished to make demands of the emperor. Since it would have been gross sacrilege to harm the sacred shrines, this tactic of taking the shrines hostage proved highly effective. During the Sannō-sai Festival from 12 to 15 April, these mikoshi are released for fighting festivals at the shrine on the 13th, and a procession through the streets of Sakamoto and on boats on the 14th.

The shrine is a 10 minute walk from Sakamoto station on the Keihan Ishiyama-Sakamoto line. It's open from 9 am to 5.30 pm, and admission costs ¥300.

Ishiyama-dera Temple Founded in the 8th century by Rōben (a distinguished monk from Nara's Tōdai-ji), this temple now belongs to the Shingon school. Its name (literally, stony mountain) derives from the scenery of beautiful rocks in the area. This temple is also prized for its Tōdai-mon Gate, Tsukimi-tei moon viewing pavilion, and Tahō-tō Pagoda. Attached to the *hondō* (main hall) is the Genji-no-ma room, which is renowned as the place where Lady Murasaki wrote the classic *The Tale of Genji*.

The temple is open from 8 am to 5.15 pm (4.45 pm in winter); admission costs ¥400. It's a short walk from Ishiyama-dera station on the Keihan Ishiyama-Sakamoto line.

Lake Biwa Museum Biwa-ko Hakubutsu-kan (☎ 077-568-4811) is a new, high-tech museum housing an extraordinary freshwater aquarium where you can get a close look at the lake's marine life. There are also exhibits on the region's prehistoric creatures and life in traditional farmhouses. It is open

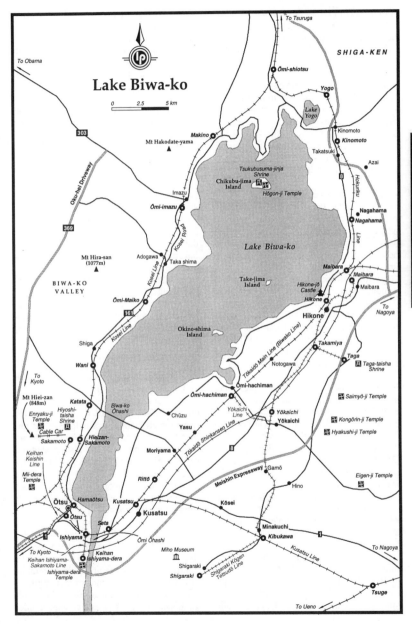

Lake Biwa-ko

from 9.30 am to 4.30 pm (except Monday) and entry is ¥500. To reach the museum, take the Tōkaidō line to Kusatsu station and then a Karasuma-hantō-bound bus (20 minutes, ¥420).

Miho Museum The Miho Museum (☎ 0748-82-3411) may be Japan's most uncanny museum and makes for an interesting, if costly and time-consuming, excursion. Owned and operated by Shinji Shumei-kai, an art-revering Shintō-based religious group, the building's modernistic conception is the brainchild of illustrious architect IM Pei.

Built deep into the side a mountain, it took six years and a cost of more than US$200 million to complete! The museum houses an outstanding collection of priceless, world-class art and artefacts from Japan and around the world, from majestic Persian carpets to rare Egyptian statues.

It is open from 10 am to 5 pm (closed Monday) but *only* operates during irregular exhibitions (check with the Kyoto TIC). Travel to Ishiyama station on the Tōkaidō line; from there buses (50 minutes, ¥800) leave twice-daily on weekdays at 9.10 and 11.55 am, and five times daily on Saturday and Sunday. Admission costs ¥1000.

Places to Stay There are several interesting lodging options in the Ōtsu vicinity. If you are willing to wake with the monks for 6.30 am chanting, try the youth hostel at *Saikyō-ji Temple* (☎ 077-578-0013), about eight minutes by bus from Sakamoto station. Costs are ¥2500 (nonmembers ¥3800) per person; meals are charged separately: ¥500 breakfast, ¥850 dinner.

Slightly more upscale temple lodging can be found at *Enman-in Temple* (☎ 077-522-3690), in the Mii-dera complex. Per-person rates are ¥12,000, including sumptuous *shōjin ryōri* vegetarian meals.

If you're craving a taste of home-baked rural atmosphere, head for *Meson* (☎ 0775-96-1657; email meson@skyblue.ocn.ne.jp), a charming, western-style retreat run by American Sandy Paolini and her husband

Nobu. Per-person rates including gourmet meals range from ¥13,000 to ¥25,000 (for a palatial log cabin with private jacuzzi!). Pick-up service is provided for the 30 minute ride from Ōmi-Maiko station on the Kosei line (about a 30 minute ride from Kyoto station).

Getting There & Away To Ōtsu from Kyoto you can either take the Tōkaidō line from Kyoto station to Ōtsu station (10 minutes, ¥190), or the Keihan Tōzai line from Keihan-Sanjō station to Hama-Ōtsu station (25 minutes, ¥390).

Sakamoto is the main access point from Lake Biwa-ko to Enryaku-ji on Mt Hiei-zan, and can be reached by cable car from the temple area in about 10 minutes (¥840). From Kyoto station take the Kosei line (on the western side of the lake) to Hiei-zan Sakamoto station (15 minutes, ¥320). If you take the Keihan line, change trains at Hama-Ōtsu station to the Sakamoto-bound local (40 minutes, ¥520).

To reach Ishiyama-dera via the Keihan line, change trains at Hama-Ōtsu and take the Ishiyama-dera-bound local to the final stop (40 minutes, ¥520).

Hikone

Hikone (population 99,000), on the east side of Lake Biwa-ko, is of special interest to visitors for its castle. The tourist information office (☎ 0749-22-5540), on your left as you leave the JR station, has helpful maps and literature. The *Street Map & Guide to Hikone* has a map on one side and a suggested one day bicycle tour of Hikone's sights on the reverse. The castle is straight up the street from the station – about 10 minutes on foot. There's another tourist office just before you enter the castle grounds.

Hikone-jō Castle The castle was completed in 1622 by the Ii family who ruled as *daimyō* (feudal domain lords) over Hikone. It is rightly considered one of the finest remaining castles in Japan – much of it is original – and there is a great view across the lake from the upper storeys. The castle is surrounded by more than 1000 cherry trees, making it a popular spot for spring *hanami* (cherry blossom viewing) activities.

Next to the main gate of the castle is Hikone-jō Castle Museum. Items on display came from the Ii family, and include armour, nō costumes, pottery and calligraphy. Admission to the museum costs ¥500, and it's open from 9 am to 4 pm.

The beautiful **Genkyū-en Garden** is below the castle. Buy yourself a bag of fish food for ¥20 at the gate and copy the other visitors who save the bloated carp the effort of movement by lobbing morsels straight into their blubbery lips.

Admission to the castle costs ¥500 and includes entry to Genkyū-en. The castle is open from 8.30 am to 5 pm (4.30 pm in winter).

Other Attractions If you have more time in Hikone, you can follow the cycling route in the *Street Map & Guide to Hikone*. The route passes through the old town to the west of the castle, then south-west via Ichiba (Market Street) to **Kawaramachi**. There you can take a look at a candle-maker's shop and then cross to the other side of the Seri River.

From here, you can cross the town and see a couple of Zen temples in the south-east. The more interesting of these is **Ryōtan-ji**, which has a fine garden. Admission to the temple is ¥300, and it's open from 9 am to 5 pm (4 pm in winter).

Getting There & Away Hikone is only one hour (¥1150) from Kyoto on the Tōkaidō line.

MIYAMA-CHŌ
美山町

Nestled in the northern Kitayama mountains between Kyoto and the Sea of Japan is Miyama-chō (population 5000), a delightful place to explore a charming piece of rural Japan.

The 'town' is composed of several village clusters spread over a vast area. These picturesque hamlets are home to an abundance of traditional *kayabuki-yane* (thatched-roof)

farmhouses thatched with a thick roof of long *susuki* (pampas grass) reeds. The Japanese countryside was once covered with such homes, though in recent years a frightful number of these magnificent structures have been abandoned and razed, in favour of modern conveniences.

Miyama-chō has become a popular home for artists, and is also gaining attention from outdoor enthusiasts for its excellent hiking, camping and kayaking on the Yura-gawa River. Travelling by car to Miyama-chō can be done as a day trip from Kyoto, but it makes a much nicer overnight trip.

At Kyoto station, the Kyoto Tourism Federation (see Tourist Offices in the Facts for the Visitor chapter) can provide information (mostly in Japanese) on Miyama-chō and surrounding areas. The English-language *Map Kyoto* is a useful road map of the greater Kyoto Prefecture area and lists some of the places below.

Kitamura

Miyama-chō's star attraction is Kitamura, or North Village, a small hamlet boasting a cluster of some 50 thatched-roof farmhouses. In 1994 the village was designated a national preservation site, and the local government has been generously subsidising the exorbitant cost of rethatching the roofs (the average cost is ¥6,000,000 – more than US$40,000!).

Stop in at the **Minzoku Shiryō-kan**, a 'history and folk' museum in one of the village's farmhouses (open 9 am to 4 pm, closed Monday; admission ¥200). Across the road, *Kitamura* serves good noodles and light food from 10 am to 5 pm, every day except Wednesday.

Miyama Kayabuki Art Museum

About 20 minutes drive west of Kitamura, the Miyama Kayabuki Bijutsukan is a traditional Japanese kite *(tako-age)* museum which is housed in a recently restored thatched-roof farmhouse. On display is a fascinating collection of hand-painted kites made by museum owner Mr Ono. Included in the ¥600 admission fee is entry to the neighbouring building, which displays vivid still-life paintings by Mrs Ono.

The museum is open between April and November from 10 am to 5 pm, closed Thursday. If you are arriving during the winter months, call ahead (in Japanese) and it should be possible to arrange a visit.

Ashyū

The quiet village of Ashyū sits on the far eastern edge of Miyama-chō and is the access point to one of Japan's most sensational natural forests. From here you can set off to hike and camp in 4200 hectares of virgin forest safeguarded under the administration of Kyoto University's Department of Agriculture (its 99 year lease ends in 2020).

Serious hikers should pick up a copy of Shōbunsha's *Kitayama 2* map (Japanese only, ¥700) in Kyoto, with detailed trails and topography of the area. The folks at the university research centre in the village may also be able to provide advice. Before setting out, you must fill out a short form and drop it in a box at the trailhead (include your name, address and how long you expect to be out).

Places to Stay

There are a number of interesting places to stay (all with per-person rates), though it is best to make advance reservations; do not expect many people to speak English.

In Kitamura try the recently rethatched *Matabe* (☎ 0771-77-0258) with per-person rates from ¥7500, including two meals. *Kajika-sō* (☎ 0771-77-0014) is a large, outdoorsy complex about five minutes by car east of Kitamura (on the way to Ashyū), with rates from ¥7000, including meals.

At *Morishige* (☎ 0771-75-1086), about

seven minutes driving time west from Kitamura, guests dine by an open fire pit *(irori)* in a 130-year-old house (¥7500 with two meals). On the road to Ōno Dam, *Miyama Heimat Youth Hostel* (☎ 0771-75-0997) costs ¥5000 with two meals (nonmembers add ¥1000).

In the village of Ashyū, a few minutes on foot from the forest trailhead, is the basic *Yama-no-Ie* (☎ 0771-77-0290) costing ¥2000 (cooking facilities available).

Getting There & Away

Miyama-chō is about 50km due north of Kyoto over a series of mountain passes. As there are no train lines passing through Miyama, it is best reached by road. There is infrequent bus service taking about three hours (¥2280; check with the TIC for routes and times), though you are far better off arranging private transport (about 1½ hours by car).

The best road to Miyama-chō is Rte 162 (Shūzan-kaidō), though there is a lovely (but time-consuming) alternative route via Kurama in the north of Kyoto and over the Hanase-tōgei Pass. Serious cyclists should be able to reach the area via either route by pedalling for about five arduous hours.

Another possibility is a train (by the San-in line) to Wachi station (about two hours, ¥2460) and continuing by bus into Miyama, but this can take much time waiting and getting from place to place. Likewise for getting around, if you are without private transport, you must depend on very infrequent buses, as the distances between areas are far too long to do on foot (driving from the Ōno Dam at Miyama's western edge to Ashyū in the far east takes about an hour).

Language

Visitors to Kyoto shouldn't have too many language problems. Lots of people speak English, and there are quite a few English signs. The main issue is the writing system, which uses three different scripts. The most difficult of these is *kanji*, the ideographic script developed by the Chinese. Some 2000 kanji are in daily use.

If you want to get into the written language before arriving, it would make more sense to learn *hiragana* and *katakana*. There are 48 characters in each, the former being used for native Japanese words and for verb endings, and the latter for foreign loan words such as *kōhii* (coffee) and *kēki* (cake).

The *romaji* used in this book follows the Hepburn system of romanisation/translitera-tion, with macrons (bars over vowels) used to indicate long vowels. Most place names use both romaji and English – the romaji suffix is usually separated from the proper name by a hyphen and followed by its English translation, eg Kōdai-ji Temple (*ji* is the romaji word for temple).

Happily, Japanese is not tonal and pronun-ciation is fairly easy to master.

Traditionally, only close friends and chil-dren call each other by their first names, so a new Japanese acquaintance will normally just tell you their surname. Surnames come before given names, not after as in the west (although the names of famous Japanese are usually westernised in English texts.) When addressing a person, follow their surname

---

Kyoto Dialect

Kyoto's distinctive dialect, Kyoto-ben or Kyō-no-kotoba, is one of the city's most distinguishing traits. While the language overlaps in many areas with the Kansai dialect Kansai-ben, which is spoken in Osaka, Kōbe, Nara and other parts of the region, Kyoto-ben has a personality and sound all its own.

In marked contrast to the grittier, straight-talking business jargon of Osaka, Kyoto-ben has a softer, melodic intonation. This, combined with the peculiar, cultured refinement of Kyotoites, produces a kind of speech comparable to that of a Louisiana southern belle.

Part of the mystery of Kyoto-ben lies in the indirect nature of the language and the elusive way in which Kyotoites interact with one another. Even when becoming emotional, they are notorious among Japanese for concealing their true feelings. A smiling face in Kyoto could be sincerely joyful, or concealing bitterness or contempt. Kyotoites always seem to sound placid, and arguing in Kyoto-ben is considerably more difficult than in standard Japanese.

Though the Tokyo dialect Kantō-ben has become the national standard, it wasn't always. Kyoto-ben has ancient, imperial roots and as the city was the capital for over 1000 years, it was appropriate that the Kyoto way of speaking was dominant in Japan. Today, though many elderly and people in traditional Kyoto industries, as well as geisha and maiko of the Gion entertainment district, still speak 'pure' Kyoto-ben, the old dialect has become significantly diluted with modern Japanese.

There are several Kyoto-ben phrases you are likely to hear, such as ōkini for thank you and the word -hen (not really a word at all, but a negative ending for verb stems). Though these can be heard all over the Kansai region, phrases like okoshiyasu, meaning welcome, and kannin, expressing apology, are unique to Kyoto. Kyotoites also frequently use san not only as an honorific for people, which is how most Japanese use it, but also for objects. People in Kyoto can tack on a san to glorify everything from temples and shrines to fried tofu (o-age-san)! They are also known for repeating adjectives twice, hence 'it's cold' (samui desu) would be said as 'it's cold-cold' (samui-samui). You could find yourself saying 'I'm tired-tired' (shindoi-shindoi) at the end of a long day in Kyoto!

Anyone interested in general Kansai-ben should pick up a copy of Peter Tse's Kansai Japanese, or Kinki Japanese by Palter & Horiuchi. Both are good introductions to the local dialect. More specific to the Kyoto tongue, Kyō no meisho to Kyō kotoba by Kimura Kyōzō is an amusing presentation of Kyoto-ben, combining dialogues with short stories about famous sightseeing spots around the city. ■

with *san*, equivalent to Mr, Mrs, Miss or Ms, eg Ms Suzuki becomes *Suzuki san*.

The following Japanese phrases should cover most everyday situations, but for a more comprehensive guide, get Lonely Planet's *Japanese phrasebook* or *Japanese audio pack*.

Pronunciation

a	as in 'father'
e	as in 'get'
i	as in 'hit'
o	as in 'lot'
u	as in 'put'

Vowels that have a bar (macron) over them (ā, ē, ō, ū) are pronounced the same as standard vowels except that the sound is held twice as long.

The vowel **u** is not always pronounced, eg when it occurs between **k** and **s** (eg *gakusei*, 'student', sounds like *gaksei*), and in the verb endings *-desu* and *-masu* (for example, *ii desu*, 'It's good', sounds like *ii des*).

Consonants are generally pronounced as in English, with these exceptions:

f	purse the lips and blow lightly
g	as the 'g' in 'goal' at the start of a word; as the 'ng' in 'sing' in the middle of a word
r	more like an 'l' than an 'r'

Greetings & Civilities

Good morning.
ohayō gozaimasu
おはようございます。
Good afternoon.
konnichi wa
こんにちは。
Good evening.
konban wa
こんばんは。
How are you?
o-genki desu ka?
お元気ですか。

Fine. (appropriate response)
ē, okagesamade
ええ、おかげさまで。
Goodbye.
sayōnara
さようなら。
See you later.
dewa, mata
では、また。
Excuse me.
sumimasen
すみません。
I'm sorry.
gomen nasai/sumimasen
ごめんなさい／すみません。
Excuse me. (when entering a room)
o-jama shimasu/shitsurei shimasu
おじゃまします／失礼します。
Thank you.
arigatō gozaimasu
ありがとうございます。
It's a pleasure.
dō itashimashite
どういたしまして。
No, thank you.
iie, kekkō desu
いいえ、結構です。
Thanks for having me.
(when leaving)
o-sewa ni narimashita
お世話になりました。
Please. (when offering something)
dōzo
どうぞ。
Please. (when asking for something)
onegai shimasu
お願いします。
OK.
daijōbu (desu)/ōke
大丈夫（です）／オーケー。
Yes.
hai
はい。
No.
iie
いいえ。
No. (for indicating disagreement)
chigaimasu
ちがいます。

No. (for indicating disagreement;
  less emphatic)
  chotto chigaimasu
  ちょっとちがいます。

Small Talk

Do you understand (English/Japanese)?
  *(ei-go)/(nihon-go)
  wa wakarimasu ka?*
  （英語）／（日本語）
    はわかりますか。
I don't understand.
  wakarimasen
  わかりません。
Please say it again more slowly.
  mō ichidō, yukkuri itte kudasai
  もう一度、ゆっくり言ってく
    ださい。
What is this called?
  kore wa nan to iimasu ka?
  これは何といいますか。
My name is ...
  watashi wa ... desu
  私は、 ... です。
What's your name?
  o-namae wa nan desu ka?
  お名前はなんですか。
This is Mr/Mrs/Ms (Smith).
  kochira wa (Sumisu) san desu
  こちらは（スミス）
    さんです。
Pleased to meet you.
  dōzo yoroshiku
  どうぞよろしく。
Pleased to meet you too
  *hajimemashite, kochira koso dōzo
  yoroshiku*
  はじめまして、
    こちらこそどうぞよろしく。
Sorry to keep you waiting.
  taihen o-matase shimashita
  大変お待たせしました。
It's been a long time since I last
  saw you.
  o-hisashi buri desu
  お久しぶりです。
Please (also) give my regards to
  Mr/Mrs/Ms Suzuki.

  *Suzuki san ni (mo) yoroshiku
  o-tsutae kudasai*
  鈴木さんに（も）
    よろしくお伝えください。
It's up to you. (when asked to make
  a choice)
  o-makase shimasu
  おまかせします。
Is it OK to take a photo?
  shashin o totte mo ii desu ka?
  写真を撮ってもいいですか。

Requests

Please give me this/that.
  (kore)/(sore) o kudasai
  （これ）／（それ）をください。
Please give me a (cup of tea).
  (o-cha) o kudasai
  （お茶）をください。
Please wait (a while).
  (shōshō) o-machi kudasai
  （少々）お待ちください。
Please show me (the ticket).
  (kippu o) misete kudasai
  （切符を）見せてください。

Getting Around

I want to go to ...
  ... ni ikitai desu
  ... に行きたいです。
Where is the ... ?
  ... wa dochira desu ka?
  ... はどちらですか。
How much is the fare to ...?
  ... made ikura desu ka?
  ... までいくらですか。
Does this (train, bus, etc) go to ...?
  kore wa ... e ikimasu ka?
  これは ... へ行き
    ますか。
Is the next station ...?
  tsugi no eki wa ... desu ka?
  次の駅は ... ですか。
Please tell me when we get to ...
  ... ni tsuitara oshiete kudasai
  ... に着いたら教え
    てください。
Where is the ... exit?
  ... deguchi wa doko desu ka?
  ... 出口はどこですか。

How far is it to walk?
aruite dono kurai kakarimasu ka?
歩いてどのくらいかか
りますか。
Where is this address please?
kono jūsho wa doko desu ka?
この住所はどこですか。
Could you write down the address
for me?
jūsho o kaite itadakemasen ka?
住所を書いていただけ
ませんか。
east/west/north/south
higashi/nishi/kita/minami
東／西／北／南

Accommodation
I'd like a ... (hotel/inn).
*... (hoteru)/(ryokan)
o sagashiteimasu*
・・・　（ホテル）／（旅館）
を探しています。
Do you have any vacancies?
aita heya wa arimasu ka?
空いた部屋はありますか。
I don't have a reservation
yoyaku wa shiteimasen
予約はしていません。
a single room
shinguru rūmu
シングルルーム
a double room
daburu rūmu
ダブルルーム
a Japanese-style room
washitsu
和室
a room with a bath
basu tsuki no heya
バス付きの部屋

Food
Do you have an English menu?
eigo no menyū wa arimasu ka?
英語のメニュー
はありますか。
I'm a vegetarian.
*watashi wa bejitarian
desu*
私はベジタリアンです。

Do you have any vegetarian meals?
*bejitarian no ryōri wa
arimasu ka?*
ベジタリアンの料理は
ありますか。
I'd like the set menu please.
setto menyū o o-negai shimasu
セット・メニュー
をお願いします。
What do you recommend?
o-susume wa nan desu ka?
お勧めは何ですか。
Please bring the bill.
o-kanjō onegai shimasu
お勘定お願いします。

Shopping
How much is this?
kore wa ikura desu ka?
これはいくらですか。
It's too expensive.
taka-sugimasu
高すぎます。
I'll take this one.
kore o itadakimasu
これを頂きます。
Can I have a receipt?
ryōshūsho o itadakemasen ka?
領収書をいただけませんか。
I'm just looking.
miteiru dake desu
見ているだけです。

Numbers

0	*zero/rei*	○
1	*ichi*	一
2	*ni*	二
3	*san*	三
4	*yon/shi*	四
5	*go*	五
6	*roku*	六
7	*nana/shichi*	七
8	*hachi*	八
9	*kyū/ku*	九
10	*jū*	十
11	*jūichi*	十一
12	*jūni*	十二
13	*jūsan*	十三
14	*jūyon*	十四
20	*nijū*	二十

21	*nijūichi*	二十一
30	*sanjū*	三十
100	*hyaku*	百
200	*nihyaku*	二百
1000	*sen*	千
5000	*gosen*	五千
10,000	*ichiman*	一万
20,000	*niman*	二万
100,000	*jūman*	十万
one million	*hyakuman*	百万

Health

How do you feel?
kibun wa ikaga desu ka?
気分はいかがですか。
I don't feel well.
kibun ga warui desu
気分が悪いです。
It hurts here.
koko ga itai desu
ここが痛いです。
I have asthma.
watashi wa zensoku-mochi desu
私は喘息持ちです。
I have diarrhoea.
geri o shiteimasu
下痢をしています。

I have a toothache.
ha ga itamimasu
歯が痛みます。
I'm allergic to antibiotics/penicillin.
*kōsei busshitsu/penishirin ni
arerugii ga arimasu*
抗生物質／ペニシリン
にアレルギーがあります。
I need a doctor.
o-isha san ni mite moraitai desu
お医者さんにみて
もらいたいです。

Emergencies

Help me!
tasukete!
助けて。
Watch out!
ki o tsukete!
気をつけて。
Call the police!
keisatsu o yonde kudasai!
警察を呼んでください。
Call a doctor!
isha o yonde kudasai!
医者を呼んでください。

Glossary

ageya – traditional entertainment banquet halls which flourished during the Edo period
aka-chōchin – red-lantern bar; working man's pub with snack food like *yakitori*
Amida – Buddha of the Western Paradise

bashi – bridge (also *hashi*)
basho – *sumō* wrestling tournament
ben – dialect, as in Kyoto-ben or Osaka-ben
bentō – boxed lunch or dinner, usually of rice, fish or meat and vegetables
bijutsukan – art museum
biwa – Japanese version of a lute
bonkei – art of miniaturising whole landscapes
bonsai – art of cultivating miniature trees by careful pruning of the branches and roots
bonshō – temple bell
bosatsu – a *bodhisattva*, or Buddha attendant, assisting others attain enlightenment
bunraku – classical puppet theatre using life-size puppets to enact dramas similar to those of *kabuki*
bushidō – way of the warrior; esoteric ethos of the *samurai* class
butsu – Buddha statue

carp – see *koi*
chadō – tea ceremony, or the way of tea (also pronounced *sadō*)
chaji – small, intimate tea gathering usually lasting several hours; a *chakai* is a less formal, abbreviated version lasting 20 or 30 minutes
chaniwa – tea garden
chanoyu – tea ceremony; see also *chadō*
chasen – bamboo whisk used for preparing powdered green tea
chashaku – tea scoop (typically made from bamboo)
chashitsu – traditional tearoom
chizu – map

dai – great; large
daimyō – regional lords under the *shōgun*
deguchi – exit, as at a railway station

densha – train
depāto – department store
dōri – street (also *tōri*)

eki – railway station
ekiben – *bentō* lunch boxes sold at railway stations
ema – small votive plaques hung in shrine sanctuaries as petitions to resident deities
en – garden (also *niwa*)

fugu – poisonous blowfish or pufferfish, elevated to haute cuisine with a bite
furo – brazier used in tea ceremony in summer; a *ro*, or sunken hearth, is used in winter
futon – cushion-like mattress that is rolled up and stored away during the day
futsū – literally, ordinary; a basic stopping-at-all-stations train service

gagaku – music of the imperial court
gaijin – the usual term for a foreigner; the contracted form of *gaikokujin* (literally, outside country person)
gawa – river (also *kawa*)
geiko – Kyoto dialect for *geisha*
geisha – not a prostitute but a 'refined person'; a woman versed in the arts and other cultivated pursuits who entertains guests
genkan – foyer area where shoes are exchanged for slippers before entering the interior of a building
geta – traditional wooden sandals
gochisō-sama – after meals expression of thanks
goju-no-tō – a five storey pagoda

haiden – hall of worship in a shrine
haiku – 17 syllable poem
hakubutsukan – museum
hanami – cherry blossom viewing
hanko – personal stamp or seal used to authenticate documents; carries the same weight as a signature in the west
hashi – chopsticks

higashi – east

hiragana – phonetic syllabary used to write Japanese words

hishaku – bamboo water ladle used in tea ceremony

honden – main building of a shrine

hondō – main building of a temple

ichiba – market

ike – pond

ikebana – art of flower arranging

irori – open hearth found in traditional Japanese houses

itadakimasu – literally, I will receive; this is a before meals expression

izakaya – Japanese version of a pub; beer, sake and lots of snacks available in a rustic, boisterous setting

ji – temple; *see also* tera

jinja – shrine (also jingū, or *gū*)

jitensha – bicycle

Jizō – guardian *bosatsu* of children and travellers

jō – castle (also *shiro*)

kabuki – form of Japanese theatre drawing on popular tales and characterised by elaborate costumes, stylised acting and the use of male actors for all roles

kaiseki – elegant, Buddhist-inspired meal, called *cha-kaiseki* when served as part of tea ceremony

kaisha – a company or firm

kaisoku – rapid train

kakejiku – painted or calligraphy scroll typically hung in the alcove of a *tatami* room

kama – metal kettle for boiling water in tea ceremony

kami – Shintō gods or spirits associated with natural phenomena

kamikaze – literally, wind of the gods; originally the typhoon that sank Kublai Khan's 13th century invasion fleet and the name adopted by Japanese suicide bombers in the waning days of WWII

kampai – cheers, as in a drinking toast

kan – building/hall

kana – the two Japanese syllabaries *(hiragana* and *katakana)* used to supplement *kanji* in the Japanese writing system

kanji – literally, Chinese writing; Chinese ideographic script used for writing Japanese

Kannon – The Buddhist goddess of mercy (also *Guanyin* in Chinese, *Avalokiteshvara* in Sanskrit and a large camera company in Japanese)

kannushi – chief Shintō priest

karaoke – a now famous export where revellers sing along to taped music minus the vocals

karesansui – dry-landscaped rock garden

katakana – phonetic syllabary used to write foreign words, among other things

katamichi – one way ticket

katana – Japanese sword

keitai denwa – mobile phone

kendō – the way of the sword; fencing technique based on the two handed samurai sword

kensui – metal pot used to clean implements in tea ceremony

kimono – traditional outer garment similar to a robe

kissaten – Japanese coffee shop

kita – north

ko – lake (also *mizu-umi*)

kōban – local police box; a common sight in urban Japan

kōen – park

koi – carp; considered a brave, tenacious fish; *koinobori* windsocks are flown in honour of sons whom it is hoped will inherit these virtues

koicha – thick green tea; as compared to the lighter *usucha*, thin green tea

kokuminshukusha – an inexpensive form of accommodation found in rural Japan; literally, peoples' lodges

kokutetsu – Japan Railways (JR); literally, national line

koma-inu – dog-like guardian stone statues found in pairs at the entrance to Shintō shrines

kondō – see *hondō*

kotatsu – heated table with quilt or cover to keep the lower body warm in the winter

koto – 13 stringed zither-like instrument

kyōgen – drama typically performed as

comic relief between *nō* plays, or as separate events

kyō-machiya – see *machiya*

kyūkō – ordinary express train (faster than *futsū*, stopping only at certain stations)

machiya – traditional wooden houses, in Kyoto called *kyō-machiya*

maiko – apprentice *geisha*

manga – Japanese comic books or magazines

matcha – powdered green tea used in tea ceremony

matsuri – festival

meishi – business card; very important in Japan

miko – shrine maidens

mikoshi – portable shrines carried around by phalanxes of sweaty half-naked *salarymen* during festivals

minami – south

minshuku – Japanese equivalent of a B&B; family-run budget accommodation usually found in rural Japan

minyō – Japanese folk music

Miroku – the Buddha of the Future

mizusashi – ceramic water jar used for tea ceremony

mizu-shōbai – see *water trade*

momiji – Japanese maple trees; *momiji-gari* refers to the viewing of the changing autumn colours *(kōyō)* of trees

mon – temple gate

morning service – *mōningu sābisu*; a light breakfast served by coffee shops until around 10 am; usually a doorstep slice of bread, a boiled egg, and jam and butter

natsume – lacquerware container holding *matcha* powdered tea

Nihon or **Nippon** – Japanese word for Japan; literally, Source of the Sun

nihonjinron – the controversial 'uniqueness of being Japanese' concept

ningyō – Japanese doll

niō – temple guardians

nishi – west

nō – classical Japanese mask drama performed on a bare stage

nomiya – traditional Japanese pub; see also *izakaya*

noren – door curtain for restaurants, usually with the name of the establishment

obi – sash or belt worn with *kimono*

obon – mid-August festivals and ceremonies for deceased ancestors

o-bōsan – Buddhist priest

ofuku – return ticket

o-furo – traditional Japanese bath

o-jiisan – elderly man; grandfather

o-jisan – middle-aged man; uncle

okiya – old-style *geisha* quarters

OL – stands for Office Lady; female employee of a large firm; usually a clerical worker

o-mamori – good luck talismans sold at shrines

o-mikuji – paper fortunes drawn from a bamboo or metal stick and tied to tree branches at Shintō shrines

o-miyage – souvenir; an obligatory purchase on any trip for Japanese

oni – a devil

onsen – mineral hot spring with bathing areas and accommodation

origami – art of paper folding

pachinko – vertical pinball game which is a Japanese craze (estimated to take in ¥6 trillion a year) and a major source of tax evasion, *yakuza* funds and noise

pink salon – seedy hostess bars; pink is the Japanese equivalent of blue, as in pornography and the like

puriipeido kādo – literally, prepaid card; a magnetically coded card for a given sum of money which can then be spent on telephone calls, railway tickets and so on

Raijin – god of thunder

rakugo – performances of stand-up comedy or long tales; a traditional art that is dying out

robotayaki – *yakitori* and the like, served in a boisterous, homey, rustic atmosphere; see also *izakaya*

roji – stone walking path in a Japanese garden

romaji – roman script, as used in English

ryokan – traditional Japanese inn
ryōtei – traditional-style, high-class restaurants; *kaiseki* is typical fare
ryūrei – a style of tea ceremony usually performed at small tables

sabi – a poetic ideal finding beauty and pleasure in imperfection; often used in conjunction with *wabi*
sakura – cherry blossoms
salaryman – male employee of a large firm
sama – even more respectful than *san*
samurai – Japan's traditional warrior class
san – a respectful suffix applied to personal names; similar to Mr, Mrs or Ms but more widely used
sanshō – Japanese three-spice powder
seiza – formal sitting position (on knees with legs tucked under the body)
sembei – soy-flavoured crispy rice crackers often sold in tourist areas
sen – line, usually railway line
sencha – a Chinese-style tea ceremony; also a variety of green tea
sensei – teacher, but also anyone worthy of respect
sensu – folding paper fan
sentō – public bath
setto – set meal; see also *teishoku*
Shaka – the historical Buddha (Sanskrit: Shakyamuni)
shakuhachi – wooden flute-like instrument
shamisen – a three stringed, banjo-like instrument
shibui – an aesthetic atmosphere of restrained elegance
shidare-zakura – a weeping cherry tree (also *atarashii*)
shin – new
shinkansen – bullet train (literally, new trunk line)
Shintō – the indigenous Japanese religion
shodō – Japanese calligraphy; literally, the way of writing
shōgun – military ruler of pre-Meiji Japan
shokudo – Japanese-style cafeteria/cheap restaurant
shukubō – temple lodging
soba – traditional buckwheat noodles

sumi-e – black ink-brush paintings
sumō – Shintō-derived sport where two immovable objects in ritual diapers collide in a ring

taiko – traditional Japanese drums
tako – traditional Japanese kite
tatami – tightly woven floor matting on which shoes should not be worn
tatchu – subtemples within large temple precincts
tengu – long-nosed goblin
teishoku – a set meal in a restaurant (usually lunch)
tera – temple (also *dera,* or *ji*)
tokkyū – limited express train; faster than ordinary express *(kyūkō)*
torii – entrance gate to a Shintō shrine
tsukubai – stone water basin in gardens for washing hands before tea ceremony

ukiyo-e – wood-block prints; literally, pictures of the floating world
uranai – palm-reading

wabi – a Zen-inspired aesthetic of rustic simplicity
wagashi – traditional Japanese sweets that are served with tea
waka – 31 syllable poem
warikan – custom of sharing the bill (among good friends)
wasabi – spicy Japanese horseradish
washi – Japanese paper
water trade – the world of bars, entertainment and sex for sale

yakitori – grilled chicken on a stick
yakuza – Japanese mafia
yukata – like a dressing gown, worn for lounging after a bath; standard issue at *ryokan* and some budget business hotels

zōgan – damascene ware

ACRONYMS

IDC – International Digital Communication
ITJ – International Telecom Japan
JEE – Japan Environmental Exchange

JETRO – Japan External Trade Organization
JNTO – Japan National Tourist Organization
JR – Japan Railways
JTB – Japan Travel Bureau
KDD – Kokusai Denshin Denwa
KIX – Kansai International Airport
LDP – Liberal Democratic Party

MIPRO – Manufactured Imports Promotion Organization
MITI – Ministry of International Trade & Industry
NHK – Japan Broadcasting Corporation
NTT – Nippon Telegraph & Telephone Corporation

Index

LONELY PLANET PRODUCTS

Lonely Planet is known worldwide for publishing practical, reliable and no-nonsense travel information in our guides and on our web site. The Lonely Planet list covers just about every accessible part of the world. Currently there are nine series: *travel guides, shoestring guides, walking guides, city guides, phrasebooks, audio packs, travel atlases, Journeys – a unique collection of travel writing and Pisces Books - diving and snorkeling guides.*

EUROPE

Amsterdam • Austria • Baltic States phrasebook • Berlin • Britain • Canary Islands• Central Europe on a shoestring • Central Europe phrasebook • Czech & Slovak Republics • Denmark • Dublin • Eastern Europe on a shoestring • Eastern Europe phrasebook • Estonia, Latvia & Lithuania • Finland • France • French phrasebook • Germany • German phrasebook • Greece • Greek phrasebook • Hungary • Iceland, Greenland & the Faroe Islands • Ireland • Italian phrasebook • Italy • Lisbon • London • Mediterranean Europe on a shoestring • Mediterranean Europe phrasebook • Paris • Poland • Portugal • Portugal travel atlas • Prague • Romania & Moldova • Russia, Ukraine & Belarus • Russian phrasebook • Scandinavian & Baltic Europe on a shoestring • Scandinavian Europe phrasebook • Slovenia • Spain • Spanish phrasebook • St Petersburg • Switzerland •Trekking in Spain • Ukrainian phrasebook • Vienna • Walking in Britain • Walking in Italy • Walking in Switzerland • Western Europe on a shoestring • Western Europe phrasebook

Travel Literature: The Olive Grove: Travels in Greece • On the Shores of the Mediterranean • Round Ireland in Low Gear

NORTH AMERICA

Alaska • Backpacking in Alaska • Baja California • California & Nevada • Canada • Chicago • Deep South• Florida • Hawaii • Honolulu • Los Angeles • Mexico • Mexico City • Miami • New England • New Orleans • New York City • New York, New Jersey & Pennsylvania • Pacific Northwest USA • Rocky Mountain States • San Francisco • Seattle • Southwest USA • USA phrasebook • Washington, DC & the Capital Region

Travel Literature: Drive thru America

CENTRAL AMERICA & THE CARIBBEAN

•Bahamas and Turks & Caicos •Bermuda •Central America on a shoestring • Costa Rica • Cuba •Eastern Caribbean •Guatemala, Belize & Yucatán: La Ruta Maya • Jamaica

Travel Literature Green Dreams: Travels in Central America

SOUTH AMERICA

Argentina, Uruguay & Paraguay • Bolivia • Brazil • Brazilian phrasebook • Buenos Aires • Chile & Easter Island • Chile & Easter Island travel atlas • Colombia Ecuador & the Galápagos Islands • Latin American Spanish phrasebook • Peru • Quechua phrasebook • Rio de Janeiro • South America on a shoestring • Trekking in the Patagonian Andes • Venezuela

Travel Literature: Full Circle: A South American Journey

ISLANDS OF THE INDIAN OCEAN

Madagascar & Comoros • Maldives• Mauritius, Réunion & Seychelles

AFRICA

Africa - the South • Africa on a shoestring • Arabic (Moroccan) phrasebook • Cairo • Cape Town • Central Africa • East Africa • Egypt • Egypt travel atlas• Ethiopian (Amharic) phrasebook • Kenya • Kenya travel atlas • Malawi, Mozambique & Zambia • Morocco • North Africa • South Africa, Lesotho & Swaziland • South Africa, Lesotho & Swaziland travel atlas • Swahili phrasebook • Tunisia • Trekking in East Africa • West Africa • Zimbabwe, Botswana & Namibia • Zimbabwe, Botswana & Namibia travel atlas

Travel Literature: Mali Blues • The Rainbird: A Central African Journey • Songs to an African Sunset: A Zimbabwean Story

MAIL ORDER

Lonely Planet products are distributed worldwide. They are also available by mail order from Lonely Planet, so if you have difficulty finding a title please write to us. North American and South American residents should write to 150 Linden St, Oakland CA 94607, USA; European and African residents should write to 10a Spring Place, London NW5 3BH; and residents of other countries to PO Box 617, Hawthorn, Victoria 3122, Australia.

NORTH-EAST ASIA

Beijing • Cantonese phrasebook • China • Hong Kong • Hong Kong, Macau & Guangzhou • Japan • Japanese phrasebook • Japanese audio pack • Korea • Korean phrasebook • Kyoto • Mandarin phrasebook • Mongolia • Mongolian phrasebook • North-East Asia on a shoestring • Seoul • Taiwan • Tibet • Tibet phrasebook • Tokyo
Travel Literature: Lost Japan

MIDDLE EAST & CENTRAL ASIA

Arab Gulf States • Arabic (Egyptian) phrasebook • Central Asia • Central Asia phrasebook • Iran • Israel & the Palestinian Territories • Israel & the Palestinian Territories travel atlas • Istanbul • Jerusalem • Jordan & Syria • Jordan, Syria & Lebanon travel atlas • Lebanon • Middle East • Turkey • Turkish phrasebook • Turkey travel atlas • Yemen
Travel Literature: The Gates of Damascus • Kingdom of the Film Stars: Journey into Jordan

ALSO AVAILABLE:

Brief Encounters • Travel with Children • Traveller's Tales

INDIAN SUBCONTINENT

Bangladesh • Bengali phrasebook • Bhutan • Delhi • Goa • Hindi/Urdu phrasebook • India • India & Bangladesh travel atlas • Indian Himalaya • Karakoram Highway • Nepal • Nepali phrasebook • Pakistan • Rajasthan • Sri Lanka • Sri Lanka phrasebook • Trekking in the Indian Himalaya • Trekking in the Karakoram & Hindukush • Trekking in the Nepal Himalaya
Travel Literature: In Rajasthan • Shopping for Buddhas • A Season in Heaven • A Short Walk in the Hindu Kush • Slowly Down the Ganges

SOUTH-EAST ASIA

Bali & Lombok • Bangkok • Burmese phrasebook • Cambodia • Ho Chi Minh City • Indonesia • Indonesian phrasebook • Indonesian audio pack • Indonesia's Eastern Islands • Jakarta • Java • Laos • Lao phrasebook • Laos travel atlas • Malay phrasebook • Malaysia, Singapore & Brunei • Myanmar (Burma) • Philippines • Pilipino phrasebook • Singapore • South-East Asia on a shoestring • South-East Asia phrasebook • South-West China • Thailand • Thailand's Islands & Beaches • Thailand travel atlas • Thai phrasebook • Thai audio pack • Thai Hill Tribes phrasebook • Vietnam • Vietnamese phrasebook • Vietnam travel atlas

AUSTRALIA & THE PACIFIC

Australia • Australian phrasebook • Bushwalking in Australia • Bushwalking in Papua New Guinea • Fiji • Fijian phrasebook • Islands of Australia's Great Barrier Reef • Melbourne • Micronesia • New Caledonia • New South Wales • New Zealand • Northern Territory • Outback Australia • Papua New Guinea • Papua New Guinea phrasebook • Queensland • Rarotonga & the Cook Islands • Samoa • Solomon Islands • South Australia • Sydney • Tahiti & French Polynesia • Tasmania • Tonga • Tramping in New Zealand • Vanuatu • Victoria • Western Australia
Travel Literature: Islands in the Clouds • Sean & David's Long Drive

ANTARCTICA

Antarctica

THE LONELY PLANET STORY

Lonely Planet published its first book in 1973 in response to the numerous 'How did you do it?' questions Maureen and Tony Wheeler were asked after driving, busing, hitching, sailing and railing their way from England to Australia.

Written at a kitchen table and hand collated, trimmed and stapled, *Across Asia on the Cheap* became an instant local bestseller, inspiring thoughts of another book.

Eighteen months in South-East Asia resulted in their second guide, *South-East Asia on a shoestring*, which they put together in a backstreet Chinese hotel in Singapore in 1975. The 'yellow bible', as it quickly became known to backpackers around the world, soon became *the* guide to the region. It has sold well over half a million copies and is now in its 9th edition, still retaining its familiar yellow cover.

Today there are over 350 titles, including travel guides, walking guides, language kits & phrasebooks, travel atlases and travel literature. The company is the largest independent travel publisher in the world. Although Lonely Planet initially specialised in guides to Asia, today there are few corners of the globe that have not been covered.

The emphasis continues to be on travel for independent travellers. Tony and Maureen still travel for several months of each year and play an active part in the writing, updating and quality control of Lonely Planet's guides.

They have been joined by over 80 authors and 200 staff at our offices in Melbourne (Australia), Oakland (USA), London (UK) and Paris (France). Travellers themselves also make a valuable contribution to the guides through the feedback we receive in thousands of letters each year and on our web site.

The people at Lonely Planet strongly believe that travellers can make a positive contribution to the countries they visit, both through their appreciation of the countries' culture, wildlife and natural features, and through the money they spend. In addition, the company makes a direct contribution to the countries and regions it covers. Since 1986 a percentage of the income from each book has been donated to ventures such as famine relief in Africa; aid projects in India; agricultural projects in Central America; Greenpeace's efforts to halt French nuclear testing in the Pacific; and Amnesty International.

'I hope we send people out with the right attitude about travel. You realise when you travel that there are so many different perspectives about the world, so we hope these books will make people more interested in what they see. Guidebooks can't really guide people. All you can do is point them in the right direction.'

– Tony Wheeler

LONELY PLANET PUBLICATIONS

Australia
PO Box 617, Hawthorn 3122, Victoria
tel: (03) 9819 1877 fax: (03) 9819 6459
e-mail: talk2us@lonelyplanet.com.au

USA
150 Linden St
Oakland, CA 94607
tel: (510) 893 8555 TOLL FREE: 800 275-8555
fax: (510) 893 8572
e-mail: info@lonelyplanet.com

UK
10a Spring Place,
London NW5 3BH
tel: (0171) 428 4800 fax: (0171) 428 4828
e-mail: go@lonelyplanet.co.uk

France:
71 bis rue du Cardinal Lemoine, 75005 Paris
tel: 01 44 32 06 20 fax: 01 46 34 72 55
e-mail: bip@lonelyplanet.fr

**World Wide Web: http://www.lonelyplanet.com
or *AOL keyword: lp***

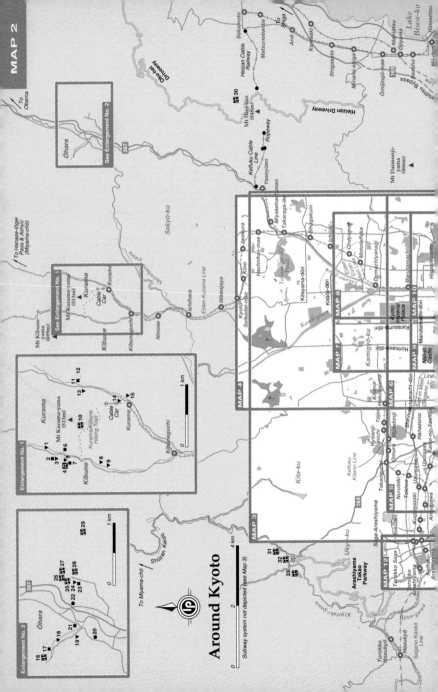

MAP 2

Around Kyoto

Subway system not depicted (see Map 3)

To Miyama-chō

Enlargement No. 2

Ōhara

16
17
18
21
19
20
22 24 23
25 26 27 28
29

0   1 km

Enlargement No. 1

Kurama
Mt Kurama-yama
(513m)

Kibune

1
2
3
4
5
6
7
8
9
10
Kurama–Kibune
Hiking Trail
11
12
13
14
15

Cable
Car

Kurama

Kibuneguchi

0   1 km

To Obama

To Hanase-tōge
Pass & Ashyū
(Miyama-chō)

Mt Kibune-
yama
(699m)

Oku-hiei
Driveway

Ōhara

See Enlargement No. 2

See Enlargement No. 1

Mt Kurama-
yama (513m)

Cable
Car

Kurama

Kibune

Kibuneguchi

Ninose

Ichihara

Nikenjaya

Eiden Kurama Line

Shizuhara-gawa

Sakyō-ku

Sakamoto
To Shiga
Matsunobaba
Heizan Cable Railway
Hieizan
Cable
Line
Yaseyūen
Ropeway
Mt Hieizan
(848m)
30

Lake
Biwa-ko

Hiei-zan

Hanaotsu
Nishihotsu
Ōtsu
Keage-zaki
Shigasato
Minami-shiga
Ōmijingū-mae
Shūto Bypass
Mii-dera

Hieizan Driveway

Mt Daimonji-
yama (466m)

Ichijōji
Iwakura
Miyakehachiman
Takaragaike
Shūgakuin
30

MAP 4

Kyōto
Seikadai-mae
Kino
Hachiman-mae
Tadasu-gawa-
chō
Kitayama-dōri
Kitaōji-dōri

Kamo-gawa

MAP 8
Tanaka-
miyaji-chō
Ecchūdera
Ōtakara
Mototanaka
Demachiyanagi
Ichijōji

MAP 10
Marutamachi
Higashiyama

Kyoto
Imperial
Palace
Karasuma-dōri

MAP 9
Marutamachi-dōri

Kyoto-gosho

MAP 7
Kamigyō-ku
Horikawa-dōri

Nijō-jō
Castle

MAP 6
Kitano-
Hakubaichō

MAP 5
Kita-ku
Kitano
Kitano Line
Keifuku
Takaoguchi
Narutaki
Tokiwa
Utsumasa
Uzumasa
Arisugawa

164

Shimmaruta machi-dōri
Shirumaruta machi-dōri
San'in Main
Line (Sagano
Line)

Kyōanji-
michi
Ryōanji
Myōshinji
Omuro
Hanazono

Ukyō-ku

MAP 3
Kita-ku

Arashiyama
Takao
Parkway

Toranoko Saga
MAP 12

Arashiyama
Randen-
Arashiyama

Kurama
Kitano Line
Keifuku

Saga-Arashiyama

164

31
32
33

Araki

Tokaido
Hozukyō

Torokko
Hozukyō

Sagano Kankō
Line

Kiyotaki-gawa

Hozu-gawa

To Miyama-chō

Shūzan Kaidō

31
32
33

4 km

0   2   4 km

MAP 2 KEY

PLACES TO STAY
2 Pension Sagano
ペンション嵯峨野
6 Hiroya Ryokan
京貴船ひろや
7 Kibune Fujiya
貴船ふじや
11 Kurama Onsen Hot Spring Resort
くらま温泉
17 Ōhara Sansō
大原山荘
21 Ryosō Chatani
旅荘茶谷
23 Seryō Ryokan
芹生旅館

PLACES TO EAT
1 Hirobun
ひろ文
3 Nakayoshi
仲よし
5 Torii-jaya
鳥居茶屋
8 Kibune Tochigiku
希船栃喜久
9 Beniya
べにや
13 Shōsai-an
匠斉庵
14 Yōshūji
雍州路

15 Aburaya-shokudō
油屋食堂
18 Kumoi-jaya
雲井茶屋
19 Tamba-jaya
たんば茶屋
24 Seryō-jaya
芹生茶屋
43 Renge-jaya
蓮華茶屋
44 Tsūen-jaya
通園茶屋

TEMPLES & SHRINES
4 Kibune-jinja Shrine
貴船神社
10 Kurama-dera Temple
鞍馬寺
25 Jikkō-in Temple
実光院
26 Hōsen-in Tempie
宝泉院
27 Shōrin-in Temple
勝林院
28 Sanzen-in Temple
三千院
29 Raigō-in Temple
来迎院
30 Enryaku-ji Temple
延暦寺
31 Kōzan-ji Temple
高山寺
32 Saimyō-ji Temple
西明寺

33 Jingo-ji Temple
神護寺
35 Zuishin-in Temple
随心院
36 Sampō-in Temple
三宝院
37 Daigo-ji Temple
醍醐寺
39 Hōkai-ji Temple
法界寺
40 Mampuku-ji Temple
万福寺
42 Ujigami-jinja Shrine
宇治上神社
46 Byōdō-in Temple
平等院

OTHER
12 Kurama Onsen
鞍馬温泉
16 Jakkō-in Convent
寂光院
20 Ōhara Kōbō
大原工房
22 Motoshiro Washi
手すき和紙もとしろ
34 Hashimoto Pediatric Clinic
橋本小児科
38 Hōju-in Treasure House
宝聚院
41 Organ Building
FOBアソシエーション
45 Taihō-an Teahouse
対鳳庵

MASON FLORENCE

Entrance gate to Kurama-dera Temple, just below the peak of Mt Kurama.

Kinkaku-ji, the famed Golden Temple, reflects brightly in Kyō-ko Pond below.

MAP 3

MASON FLORENCE

A walkway at Fushimi-Inari Taisha Shrine, which sprawls across the wooded slopes of Mt Inari.

Top: A traditional *kayabuki-yane* (thatched-roof) farmhouse in Miyama-chō.
Bottom: A fisherman on the Uji-gawa River, Uji.

MAP 4

Funa-gata
(boat)

Kyoto
Sangyō
University

Ko-the
Pond

2

1

Funaoka-higashi-dōri

Kamo Kaidō

19

▼20

Kita-Ku

3

4

5

Kitayama

31

Kitayama-
Ohashi

21

22

30

23

24

18

Kitayama-dōri

Honkawa-dōri

Kyoto
Botanical
Gardens

17

▼16

15

14

Kitaōji

Kitaōji-dōri

Hidari
Daimonji

13

MAP 7

Daiji-in
Subtemple

Otani
University

MAP 8

▼12

6

Funaokayama-
kōen Park

Senbon-dōri

Kuramaguchi-dōri

Kuramaguchi

Kamigyō-ku

Karasuma-dōri

Karasuma Line

Shōkoku-ji
Temple

11

Nishioji-dōri

7

10

8

9

Imadegawa-dōri

Imadegawa

Dōshisha
University

Kitano
Hakubaichō

Kyoto
Imperial

Map 4 Key

PLACES TO STAY
25 Ryokan Rakucho
旅館洛頂
28 Greenpeace Inn Kyoto
Guest House
グリーンピースイン
京都

PLACES TO EAT
12 Knuckles
ナックルス
16 Kazariya
かざりや
20 Azekura
愛染倉
30 Taiyō-ga-Ippai
太陽がいっぱい
36 Haruya Organic Restaurant
はるや
37 Mago's
マゴース
38 Speakeasy
スピークイージー
39 Papa Jon's (3)
パパジョンズ

TEMPLES & SHRINES
2 Shōden-ji Temple
正伝寺
3 Jōshō-ji Temple
常照寺
4 Genkō-an Temple
源光庵

5 Kōetsu-ji Temple
光悦寺
6 Kinkaku-ji Temple
金閣寺
7 Hirano-jinja Shrine
平野神社
8 Kitano Tenman-gū Shrine
北野天満宮
10 Senbon Shaka-dō Temple
千本釈迦堂
11 Injō-ji Temple
引接寺
14 Daitoku-ji Temple
大徳寺
15 Daisen-in Subtemple
大仙院
17 Imamiya-jinja Shrine
今宮神社
19 Kamigamo-jinja Shrine
上賀茂神社
32 Entsū-ji Temple
円通寺
41 Manshu-in Temple
曼殊院
42 Enkō-ji Temple
圓光寺
43 Shisen-dō Temple
詩仙堂
44 Tanuki-dani Fudō-in
Temple
狸谷不動院

OTHER
1 Mekhong
メコン

9 Kamishichiken Kaburen-jō
Theatre
上七軒歌舞練場
13 Bukkyō University
仏教大学
18 Teatro Marron
テアトロマロン
21 WEEK Building
ウィーク
22 B-Lock Building
ビーロック北山
23 Garden of Fine Art
京都府立陶板名画の庭
24 Kyoto Concert
Hall
京都コンサートホール
26 Ining '23 Building
イニング23
27 Kawabata-dōki
川端道喜
29 Syntax Building
シンタックス
31 Alfa Station
アルファステーション
33 Honky Tonk
ホンキートンク
34 Kyoto International
Conference Hall
京都国際会館
35 Takara-ga-ike Park
宝が池
40 Shūgaku-in Rikyū Imperial
Villa
修学院離宮

Map 5 Key

1 Pension Sagano
ペンション嵯峨野
2 Kōryū-ji Temple
広隆寺
3 Tōei Uzumasa Movie Village
東映太秦映画村
4 Taizō-in Temple
退蔵院
5 Myōshin-ji Temple
妙心寺
6 Kawahito Hands
川人ハンズ
7 Yūzen Cultural Hall
京都友禅文化会館
8 Katsura Rikyū Imperial Villa
桂離宮

MASON FLORENCE

A monk waits for a train at Osaka station.

MAP 5

Myōshinji

Ōmuro

Narutaki

1 ■

Tokiwa

Shizan-kaidō

5

4

6 ●

Shinmarutamachi-dōri

San-in Main Line (Sagano Line)

Hanazono

Uzumasa

Nakagyō-ku

Arisugawa

Katabira-no-Tsuji

3 ●

Tenjin-gawa

2 ■

Uzumasa

Kaiiku-no-Yashiro

Sanō-dōri

Yamanouchi

Keifuku Arashiyama Line

Ōmuro-gawa

Kyoto
University of
Foreign
Studies

Shijō-dōri

Shimogyō-ku

Ueno-
bashi

Nishi-
Ōhashi

Gojō-dōri

Nishikyōgoku
Comprehensive
Sports Park

7 ●

Nishikyōgoku

Hankyū Arashiyama Line

9

Hankyū Kyoto Line

Shichijō-dōri

Kamikatsura

Nishikyō-ku

8

Katsura-gawa

Hachijō-dōri

Katsura-
Ōhashi

0   250   500 m

Katsura

MAP 6 ▷

MAP 6

Kyoto Imperial Palace

Sentō Gosho Palace

Kamigyō-ku

MAP 7
MAP 9

Marutamachi-dōri

Marutamachi Ⓜ

Karasuma-dōri

Nishiōji-dōri

Nijō-jō Castle

Nijō
Nijō

Senbon-dōri

Nijōjō-mae Ⓜ

Karasuma-Oike Ⓜ
Karasuma-Oike

Oike-dōri

Nakagyō-ku

Sanjō-dōri

Sanjōguchi

Keifuku Arashiyama Line

Sai

Sai

Sanin Main Line

Omiya

Shijō-dōri

Karasuma

Kawaramachi

Shijō Omiya

Hankyū Kyoto Line

Shijō Ⓜ

Horikawa-dōri

Karasuma Line

Mibu-dera Temple

2

Gojō-dōri

Tanbaguchi

3

MAP 11

Gojō Ⓜ

Shimogyō-ku

Shōsei-en Garden

4

5

Nishi Hongan-ji Temple

Higashi Hongan-ji Temple

Shichijō-dōri

6

Omiya-dōri

Kyoto Ⓜ

Kyoto

Tōkaidō Main Line (Kyoto Line)

Hachijō-dōri

9

Tōkaidō Shinkansen Line

Kintetsu Kyoto Line

Minami-ku

Nishiōji

8

7 ●

Tōji

Kujō Ⓜ

Map 6 Key

PLACES TO STAY
5 Tani Guest House
谷ゲストハウス
9 Tōji-An Guest House
東寺庵ゲストハウス
10 Ryokan Seiki
旅館晴輝
13 Ryokan Mishima (Mishima Shrine)
旅館三島（三島神社）
20 Hiden-in Temple
悲田院

TEMPLES & SHRINES
8 Tō-ji Temple
東寺
12 Kiyomizu-dera Temple
清水寺

17 Chishaku-in Temple
智積院
18 Sanjūsangen-dō Temple
三十三間堂
19 Sokujō-in Temple
即成院
21 Imagumano Kannon-ji Temple
今熊野観音寺

OTHER
1 Kyoto Holiday Emergency Clinic
京都市休日急病診療所
2 Kyoto Research Park
京都リサーチパーク
3 Kyoto City Hospital
京都市立病院
4 Sumiya Pleasure House
角屋

6 Umekōji Steam Locomotive Museum
梅小路蒸気機関車館
7 Rent Pia Service Centre
レンタピアサービスセンター
11 Gojō-zaka
五条坂
14 Kawai Kanjirō Memorial Hall
河井寛治郎記念館
15 Nishimura Koken
窯元西村菰軒
16 Kyoto National Museum
京都国立博物館
22 Kiyomizu-danchi
清水団地
23 Kotobuki Tōshun
コトブキ陶春

Map 7 Key

PLACES TO STAY
2 Tani House
谷ハウス
9 Aoi-Sō Inn
アオイソウ
12 Myōren-ji Temple
妙蓮寺
13 Lady's Hotel Nishijin
レディースホテル西陣
25 Takaya
鷹屋ゲストハウス
27 YWCA Women's Accommodation

PLACES TO EAT
4 Izusen
泉仙
6 Daitoku-ji Ikkyū
大徳寺一休
18 Tsuruya Yoshinobu
鶴屋吉信
22 Fiasco
フィアスコ

23 Papa Jon's (3)
パパジョンズ
31 Mankamerō
萬亀楼

TEMPLES & SHRINES
1 Kōtō-in Subtemple
高桐院
3 Zuihō-in Subtemple
瑞峯院
5 Daiji-in Subtemple
大慈院
10 Kamigoryō-jinja Shrine
上御霊神社
19 Shiramine-jingū Shrine
白峯神宮

OTHER
7 Wakuden Restaurant
和久傳
8 Kyoto Holiday Emergency Dental Clinic
京都休日歯科診療所
11 Urasenke Chadō Reseach Center
裏千家センター

14 Funaoka Onsen
船岡温泉
15 Orinasu-kan
織成館
16 Aizen-Kōbō
愛染工房
17 Nishijin Textile Center
西陣織会館
20 Origin I, II and III Buildings
織陣
21 Kawamura Nō Stage
川能能舞台
24 Imperial Household Agency
宮内庁京都事務所
26 ALTI (Kyoto Fumin Hall)
京都府民ホール
アルティ
28 Aoibashi Family Clinic
あおいばし
ファミリークリニック
29 Adachi Kumihimo-kan
安達くみひも館
30 Kyoto St Agnes Episcopal Church
聖アグネス教会

MAP 7

MAP 8

- 1
- 2
- 3
- 5
- 4
- 6
- 7

Otani
University

Kitaōji-dōri

Horikawa-Kitaōji
Crossing

Kitaōji-dōri

- 8

Shimei-dōri

- 9

Kenkun-dōri

Kuramaguchi-dōri
14

Kuramaguchi

10

Funaokayama-
kōen Park

Kamigoryōmae

- 11

Teranouchi-dōri

13 ■ 12

15

20

21
22
23

Kamitachiuri-dōri

Kamigyō-ku

Dōshisha
University

18 19

Imadegawa

Horikawa-Imadegawa
Crossing
17

Nakasuji-dōri

16

Imadegawa-dōri
Karasuma-Imadegawa
Crossing

Motoseiganji-dōri

Sasayachō-dōri

Mushakōji-dōri

*Jōfuku-ji
Temple*

Yokoshinmei-dōri

Chieikōin-dōri

Ichijō-dōri

- 24

*Kyoto
Imperial
Palace*

Ōmiya-dōri

25 ■
26 ●

Nakatachiuri-dōri

0   126   251

Kamichōjamachi-dōri

Nakachōjamachi-dōri

Karasuma Line

Shimōchojamachi-dōri

Jōfukuji-dōri

Uramon-dōri

Inokuma-dōri

Horikawa-dōri

Shinmachi-dōri

Shinmei-dōri

31 ▼

27 ■
28
29

Demizu-dōri

Higurashi-dōri

Shimotachiuri-dōri

MAP 9

30

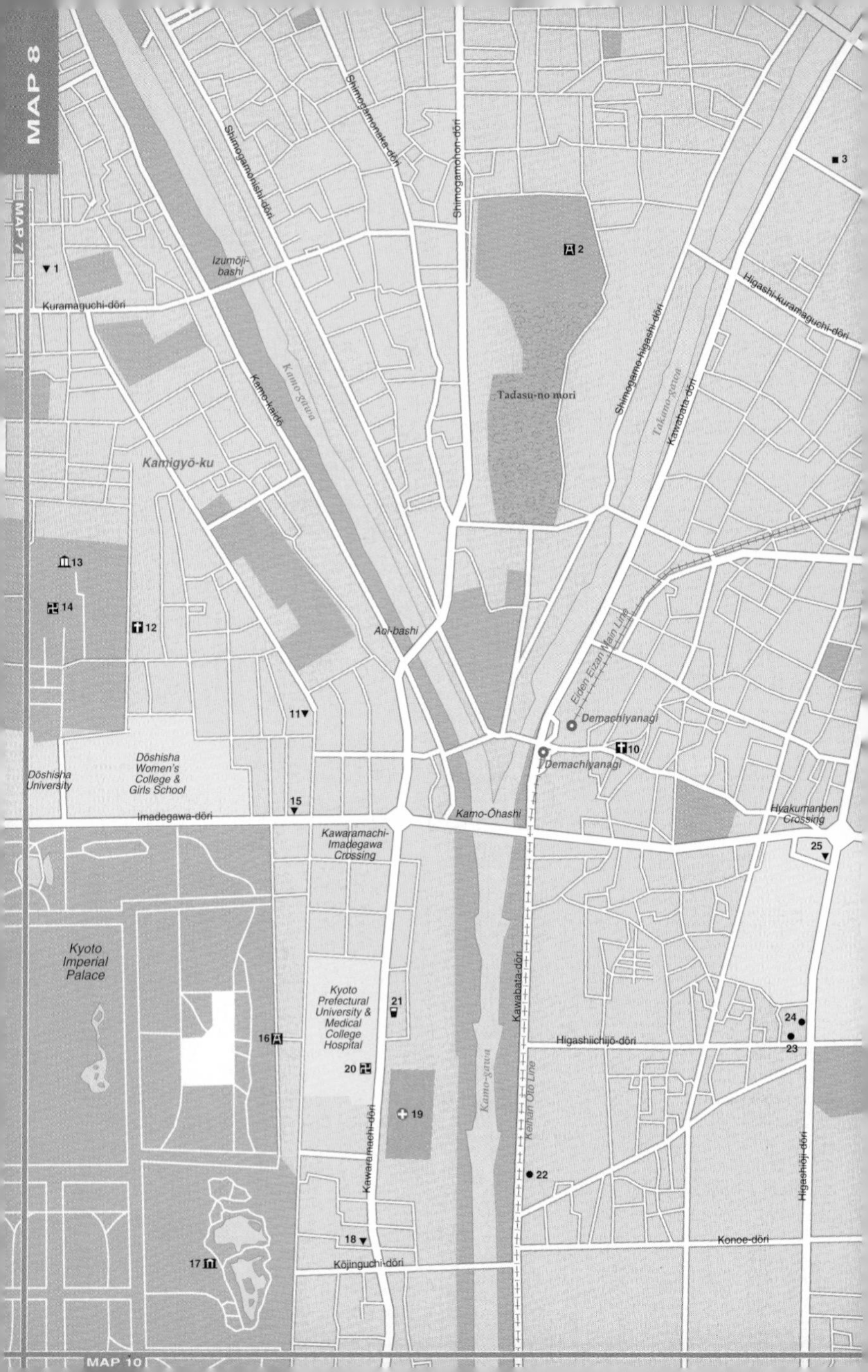

MAP 8

MAP 7

▼ 1

Kuramaguchi-dōri

Izumōji-
bashi

■ 3

☒ 2

Higashi-kuramaguchi-dōri

Kamigyō-ku

Tadasu-no mori

Kamo-gawa

Kamo-gawa

🏛 13

🏩 14

🏕 12

Aoi-bashi

11▼

Dōshisha
Women's
College &
Girls School

Dōshisha
University

Imadegawa-dōri

15
▼

Kawaramachi-
Imadegawa
Crossing

Kamo-Ōhashi

Kamo-gawa

Shimogamo-hongori-dōri

Takano-gawa

Eizan Electric Main Line

● Demachiyanagi
◉ Demachiyanagi
🏕 10

Hyakumanben
Crossing

25
▼

Kyoto
Imperial
Palace

16 🏯

Kyoto
Prefectural
University &
Medical
College Hospital

🏕 21

20 🏩

✚ 19

Kawaramachi-dōri

Keihan Ōtō Line

Higashiichijō-dōri

24 ●
23 ●

17 🏯

18 ▼

Kōjinguchi-dōri

● 22

Konoe-dōri

Higashiōji-dōri

MAP 10

Kitaōji-dōri

Takano
Crossing

Higashihōri-dōri

Chayama

▼7

Mototanaka

Tanaka-Satonomae
Crossing

Sakyō-ku

6
▼

Okage-dōri

9

Shirakawa-Kitaōji
Crossing

Shirakawa-dōri

5

Kitashirakawa-Betto
Crossing

Shirai-kyouai

Kyoto
University
Sports Ground

26

Imadegawa-dōri

Shirakawadōri-Imadegawa
Crossing

Kyoto
University

Shirakawa-dōri

Finish

27

28
▼

Yoshida-jinja
Shrine

29

31

30 ▼

Okazaki-dōri

Tour continued
from Map 10

0   125   250 m

Northen Higashiyama
Walking Tour

Map 8 Key

PLACES TO STAY
3 Holiday Inn Kyoto
ホリデーイン京都

PLACES TO EAT
1 Kanga-an
閑臥庵
6 Hiragana-kan
ひらがな館
7 Didi
ディディ
11 Kiyosu
きよす
15 Honyarado
ほんやら堂
18 Tengu
天狗
25 Kagiya Masaaki
かぎや政秋
28 Omen
おめん
30 Buttercups
バターカップス

TEMPLES & SHRINES
2 Shimogamo-jinja Shrine
下鴨神社
14 Shōkoku-ji Temple
相国寺
16 Nashinoki-jinja Shrine
梨木神社
20 Rozan-ji Temple
廬山寺
27 Ginkaku-ji Temple
銀閣寺
29 Hōnen-in Temple
法然院
31 Kōshō-ji Temple
迎称寺

OTHER
4 TAK Building
タック
5 Baptist Hospital
バプテスト病院
8 The Flying Keg
フライングケッグ
9 Post Coitus
ポストコイタス
10 Kyoto Lutheran Church
ルーサイン教会
12 Kyoto City Church
京都市教会
13 Jōtenkaku Museum
承天閣美術館
17 Sentō Gosho Palace
仙洞御所
19 Kyoto Prefectural University Hospital
京都府立医科大学
付属病院
21 Other Side
アザーサイド
22 Goethe Institute Kyoto
京都ドイツ文化
センター
23 Instituto Italiano di Cultura di Kansai
関西イタリア文化会館
24 Institut Franco-Japonais du Kansai
関西日仏学館京都
26 British Council
英国文化センター

MASON FLORENCE

Bamboo blinds with decorative tassels at Shimogamo-jinja Shrine.

Boarding a bus in Kyoto.

MAP 9

MAP 7

1

Sawaragichō-dōri

Kokusai

Horikawa-Marutamachi
Crossing

Karasuma-Marutamachi
Crossing

Marutamachi-dōri

Marutamachi

Takeyamachi-dōri

2
3

Koromonotana-dōri

Ryogaemachi-dōri

Karasuma-dōri

Karasuma Line

Ebisugawa-dōri

Nijo

Nijō-jō
Castle

Horikawa-dōri

Aburanokōji-dōri

Nijō-dōri

Muromachi-dōri

4

5

Ogawa-dōri

Ōshikōji-dōri

8

Tōzai Line

6

Nijōjō-mae

Horikawa-Oike
Crossing

Karasuma-Oike

Oike-dōri

Karasuma-Oike
Crossing

7

Aneyakōji-dōri

Karasuma-Oike

9

Kamaza-dōri

Sanjō-dōri

11

Rokkaku-dōri

12

Nakagyō-ku

Takoyakushi-dōri

14

15

16

Nishikikōji-dōri

18

17

26

Ōmiya

25

Shijō-Horikawa
Crossing

Shijō-dōri

Karasuma

Shijō-Ōmiya

Shijō-Ōmiya
Crossing

Hankyū Kyoto Line

24

20

19

Shijō

27

Mibu-dōri

Ōmiya-dōri

Kuromon-dōri

Horikawa-dōri

Nishinotōin-dōri

21

Bukkōji-dōri

22

23

Takech

Takatsuji-dōri

28

29

0   125   250 m

MAP 11

MAP 10

Map 9 Key

PLACES TO STAY
4 International Hotel Kyoto
京都国際ホテル
5 ANA Hotel
全日空ホテル
21 Karasuma Kyoto Hotel
からすま京都ホテル
29 Shōhō-in Temple
正法院

PLACES TO EAT
8 Obanzai
おばんざい
11 Biotei
びお亭
12 Toroku
とろく
14 Mukade-ya
百足屋
25 Cafe du Monde (2)
カフェデュモンド

OTHER
1 Juttoku
拾得
2 Create
クリエート
3 Kyoto Convention Bureau/Kyoto Chamber of Commerce
京都コンベンションビューロー／京都商工会議所
6 Shinsen-en Garden
神泉苑
7 Nijō Jinya
二条陣屋
9 Tomita Maternity Clinic
富田産婦人科病院
10 Nakagyō Post Office
中京郵便局
13 A'cross Travellers' Bureau
アクロストラベラーズ
15 Japan Foundation Kyoto Office
国際交流基金京都支部

16 Tokyo-Mitsubishi Bank
東京三菱銀行
17 Nippō Rent-a-Car
日邦レンタカー
18 Kongō-dō Nō Stage
金剛能楽堂
19 Tokyo-Mitsubishi Bank
東京三菱銀行
20 Sumitomo Bank
住友信託銀行
22 Nippon Rent-a-Car
日本レンタカー
23 Kyo-kimono Plaza
京きものプラザ
24 Shikunshi
四君子
26 Kyoto City Association for Disabled Persons
京都身体障害者福祉会館
27 Mibu-dera Temple
壬生寺
28 Kodai Yūzen-en Gallery
古代友禅苑

MASON FLORENCE

Services like firefighting are adapted to Japan's narrow urban confines – the only thing missing here is the remote-control dalmatian.

MAP 10

MAP 9

MAP 11

MAP 9

MAP 8

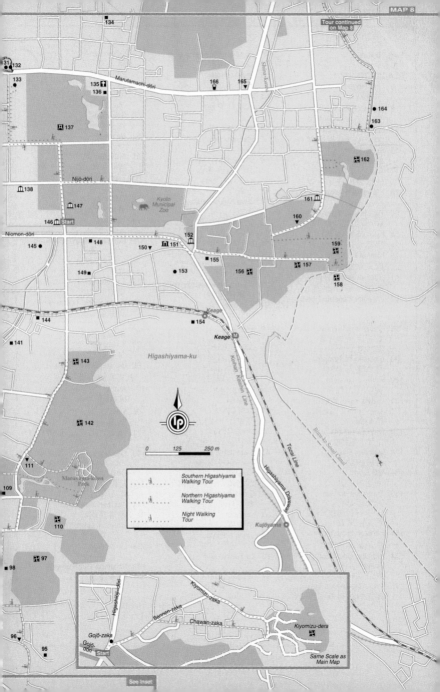

Tour continued on Map 8

■ 134

●131
■132

● 133

Marutamachi-dōri

135 ■
136 ■

● 166   ■ 165

● 164

163 ●

🅿 137

■ 162

Nijō-dōri

161 🏛

🏛 138

160 ▼

🏛 147

Kyoto Municipal Zoo

146 🏛 Start

159 ■

Niomon-dōri

152

155 ■

● 145   ■ 148

150 ▼

151 🏛

156 ■

157 ■

149 ■

● 153

158 ■

Keage

■ 144

■ 154

Keage Ⓜ

141 ■

Higashiyama-ku

143 ■

Biwa-ko Sosui Canal

Keihan Keishin Line

142 ■

Tōzai Line

Higashiyama Driveway

0   125   250 m

Southern Higashiyama Walking Tour

Northern Higashiyama Walking Tour

Night Walking Tour

▼ 111

Maruyama-kōen Park

109 ■

110 ■

Kujōyama ◎

97 ■

98 ■

Kiyomizu-zaka

Higashiōji-dōri

Sannen-zaka

Chawan-zaka

Kiyomizu-dera

96 ▼

95 ■

Gojō-zaka

Gojō-dōri   Start

Same Scale as Main Map

See Inset

Map 10 Key

PLACES TO STAY

3 Uno House
宇野ハウス

5 Hirota Guest House
広田ゲストハウス

11 Hotel Fujita Kyoto
ホテルフジタ京都

15 Kyoto Hotel
京都ホテル

17 Tawaraya Ryokan
俵屋旅館

18 Hiiragiya Ryokan
柊屋旅館

38 Tani House Annexe
谷ハウスアネックス

68 Kyoto Central Inn
京都セントラルイン

70 Kinmata Ryokan
近又旅館

81 Ryokan Hinomoto
旅館ひのもと

93 Amenity Capsule Hotel
アメニティ
カプセルホテル

95 Lady's Inn Sakata
レディースイン
さかた

98 Gesshin-in Temple
月真院

100 Ryokan Uemura
旅館うえむら

109 Lady's Hotel Chōraku-kan
レディースホテル
長楽館

112 Gion Fukuzumi
ギオン福住

119 Iwanami Ryokan
岩波旅館

134 ISE Dorm
イセドーム

136 Three Sisters Inn
(Rakutō-sō)
スリーシスターズ
イン洛東荘

141 Pension Higashiyama
ペンション東山

144 Higashiyama Youth
Hostel
東山ユースホステル

148 Kyoto Traveller's Inn
京都トラベラーズ
イン

149 Lady's Inn Higashiyama
レディースイン東山

154 Miyako Hotel
都ホテル

155 Yachiyo Ryokan
八千代旅館

PLACES TO EAT

7 Shin-shin-tei
新進亭

8 Okonomiyaki Mai
お好み焼き舞

10 Kyoto Al Dente
京都アルデンテ

12 Ōiwa Kushi-katsu
大岩

13 Ganko Zushi (2)
がんこ寿司

14 Merry Island Cafe
メリーアイランド

19 Yoshikawa Tempura
吉川

21 Misoka-an Kawamichi-ya
晦庵河道屋

27 Karyō-an
迦陵庵

28 Morita-ya
モリタ屋

29 Ganko Zushi (2)
がんこ寿司

31 Musashi Sushi
むさし寿司

33 Mishima-tei
三嶋亭

35 Cafe David
カフェデイビッド

36 Inoda Coffee
イノダコーヒー

40 Papa Jon's (3)
パパジョンズ

41 Kane-yo
かねよ

44 Capricciosa
カプリチョーザ

51 Karyō-an
迦陵庵

52 Uzuki Kaiseki
うずき

55 Zu Zu Izakaya
ずず

57 Kappa Zushi
かっぱ寿司

58 Fujino-ya
藤の家

59 Yamatomi
山とみ

60 A-Bar
アバー

62 Shiruko
志る幸

64 Sancho
サンチョ

65 Shizuka
静

67 Tomi-zushi
とみ寿司

73 Kinoshita Coffee
きのした

74 Tagoto
田ごと

75 Daniel's Italian Restaurant
ダニエルス

78 Doutor Coffee
ドトールコーヒー

82 Tachibana-ya
橘屋

85 Takasebune Tempura
高瀬船

87 Tōkasai-kan
東華菜館

96 Kasagi-ya
かさぎ屋

99 Bun-no-Suke-jaya
文の助茶屋

101 Aunbo
阿吽坊

106 Minokō
美濃幸

111 Imobō Hiranoya Honten
いもぼう平野屋本店

113 Gion Kaikan Theatre/CK
Cafe Nightclub/Ninniku-ya
Restaurant
祇園会館／CK Cafe／
にんにくや

116 Kagizen Yoshifusa
鍵善良房

120 Ichi-ban Yakitori
一番やきとり

123 Le Zephyr
レゼファ

125 Chabana Okonomiyaki
ちゃばな

107 Gion Hotel
祇園ホテル

114 Gion Freak Building
祇園フリーク
（丸東第１７ビル）

115 Kyoto Craft Center
京都クラフト
センター ~~to 7PM~~

117 Kikusui Beer Garden
菊水ビアガーデン

118 Nexus Building
ビル
（スーパーポテト）

121 Pig & Whistle
ピッグ＆ホイッスル

122 Rental Cycle Yasumoto
レンタサイクル
やすもと

124 Kitazawa Bicycle Shop
キタザワサイクル

126 Metro
メトロ

128 Kyoto Branch of the
Osaka Immigration
Bureau
大阪入国管理局
京都出張所

131 Kyoto Handicraft Center
京都ハンディ ~~9AM - 6PM~~
クラフトセンター

132 Amita-honten
アミタ本店

133 Budo Centre
京都市武道センター

135 St Mary's Episcopal
Church
聖マリア教会

138 Kyoto Museum of
Traditional Crafts
京都伝統産業
ふれあい館

145 Kanze Kaikan Nō Theatre
観世会館

146 National Museum of
Modern Art
京都国立近代美術館

147 Kyoto Municipal Museum
of Art
京都市美術館

151 Murin-an Villa
無鄰菴

152 Lake Biwa Aqueduct
Museum
琵琶湖疎水記念館

153 Kyoto International
Community House (KICH)
京都市国際交流会館

161 Nomura Museum
野村美術館

163 Nyakuōji Bridge
若王子橋

164 Kanō Shōju-an Teahouse
叶匠寿庵

166 Sunflower Hotel
サンフラワーホテル

Map 11 Key

PLACES TO STAY

3 Riverside Takase
リバーサイド高瀬

4 Ryokan Hiraiwa
旅館平岩

6 Yuhara Ryokan
ゆはら旅館

9 Ryokan Murakamiya
旅館村上屋

10 Ryokan Kyōka
旅館京花

11 Matsubaya Ryokan
松葉屋旅館

13 Pension Station Kyoto
ペンション
ステーション京都

16 Rihga Royal Hotel Kyoto
リーガロイヤル
ホテル京都

17 Kyoto Dai-San Tower Hotel
京都第三タワーホテル

20 Kyoto New Hankyū Hotel
京都新阪急ホテル

21 Hokke Club Kyoto
法華クラブ京都

25 Kyoto White Hotel
京都ホワイトホテル

29 Hotel Granvia Kyoto
ホテルグランビア京都

31 Kyōmai Inn
京舞イン

34 Kyoto Century Hotel
京都センチュリー
ホテル

36 Ryokan Ōtō
京乃宿鴨東

38 Kyoto Dai-Ichi Hotel
京都第一ホテル

PLACES TO EAT

26 Chūgoku Chūbō Yamucha-
no-mise Kyūraku
中国厨房Ｑ楽

32 Shinpuku Saikan Ramen
新福菜館

33 Dai Ichi Asahi Ramen
第一旭

35 Yamamoto Manbo
山本まんぼ

39 Red Pepper
レッドペパー

OTHER

1 Matsuda Rent-a-Car
マツダレンタカー

2 Yamani
山二

5 Shomen-yu
正面湯

7 Shōsei-en Garden
渉成園

8 Kyōsen-dō
京扇堂

12 Higashi Hongan-ji Temple
東本願寺

14 Period Costume Museum
風俗博物館

15 Nishi Hongan-ji Temple
西本願寺

18 Eki Rent-a-Car
駅レンタカー

19 Kyoto Central Post Office
京都中央郵便局

22 TIC/Kyoto Tower/Kyoto
Tower Hotel
旅行案内所／
京都タワー／
京都タワーホテル

23 Kintetsu Department Store
近鉄百貨店

24 Kyoto Minshuku
Reservation Center
京都民宿予約センター

27 Tōkai
トウカイ

28 Isetan Department Store
伊勢丹百貨店

30 Renaissance Hall
ルネッサンスホール

37 Tōkai/Avanti Shopping
Center
トウカイ／アバンティ

MAP 9 MAP 10
MAP 11

Gojō-Ōmiya
Crossing

Kyoto
Tokyū

Karasuma-Gojō
Crossing

Kawaramachi-
Gojō Crossing

Gojō

Gojō-dōri

Gojō-
Ōhashi

1

Yōbai-dōri

2

Gojō

Kagiyamachi-dōri

Matoba-dōri

Rokujō-dōri

Hanayachō-dōri

14

Higashinakasuji-dōri

Nishinotōin-dōri

Shōmen-dōri

Kitakōji-dōri

13

Shichijō-
Horikawa
Crossing

15

Shichijō-dōri

Horikawa-dōri

Kamijuzūyachō-dōri

11

8

9

10

Shimojuzūyachō-dōri

3

4

6

7

8

5

Higashinotōin-dōri

Higashinotōin-dōri

Kawaramachi-
Shichijō
Crossing

Shichijō-
Ōhashi

Shichijō

Kawabata-dōri

Toiyamachi-dōri

Sayamachi-dōri

Honmachi-dōri

Karasuma-dōri

Karasuma-
Shichijō
Crossing

24

Shichijō-
Ōhashi
Crossing

36

17

23

25

Muromachi-dōri

Shimogyō-ku

20

21

22

26

27

30

31

Shiokōji-
bashi

Shiokōji-dōri

18

19

28

Kyoto

29

35

32

33

34

Shichijō-Ōhashi
Crossing

16

Tōkaidō Main Line (Kyoto Line)

Tōkaidō Main Line (Biwako Line) & Kōsei Line

Kyoto

Tōkaidō Shinkansen Line

Tōkaidō Shinkansen Line

Kamogawa Main Line

Nara Line

Keihan Main Line

Hachijō-dōri

37

Kintetsu Kyoto Line

Tōji-dōri

Tōfukuji

Tōfukuji

Higashiyama-
bashi

Tōji

38

Kujō-dōri

Kujō

Kujō-
Kawaramachi
Crossing

39

Kujō-
Aburanokōji
Crossing

Aburanokōji-dōri

Takeda Kaidō

Kawaramachi-dōri

Kamo-gawa

0   125   250 m

Jūjō

Jūjō-dōri

Tōkabashi

Tōbakaidō

MAP 11

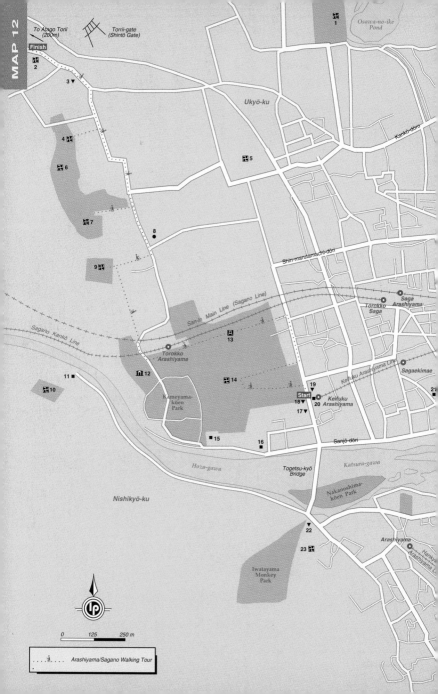

MAP 12

Osawa-no-ike Pond

1

To Atago Torii
(200m)

Torii-gate
(Shintō Gate)

Finish

2

Kankō-dōro

Ukyō-ku

3 ▼

4

6

Shin-marutamachi-dōri

5

7

8

9

San-In Main Line (Sagano Line)

Saga
Arashiyama

Torokko
Saga

Sagano Kankō Line

13

Torokko
Arashiyama

Keifuku Arashiyama Line

Sagaekimae

12

14

11

Start

19

21

10

Kameyama-
kōen
Park

18 ▼

20

Keifuku
Arashiyama

17 ▼

15

Sanjō-dōri

16

Hozu-gawa

Togetsu-kyō
Bridge

Katsura-gawa

Nishikyō-ku

Nakanoshima-
kōen Park

22

Arashiyama

23

Hankyu
Arashiyama L

Iwatayama
Monkey
Park

0   125   250 m

···🚶··· Arashiyama/Sagano Walking Tour

Map Legend

BOUNDARIES

.... International Boundary

.... Provincial Boundary

ROUTES

A26 ..... Freeway, with Route Number

.... Major Road

.... Minor Road

.... Minor Road - Unsealed

.... City Road

.... City Street

.... City Lane

.... JR Train Line, with Station

.... Shinkansen Train Line

.... Private Train Line, with Station

.... Subway Route, with Station

.... Cable Car or Chairlift

.... Ferry Route

.... Walking Tour

AREA FEATURES

.... Building

.... Cemetery

.... Hotel

.... Market

.... Park, Gardens

.... Pedestrian Mall

.... Urban Area

HYDROGRAPHIC FEATURES

.... Canal

.... Coastline

.... River

.... Creek

.... Lake

.... Intermittent Lake

.... Rapids, Waterfalls

.... Salt Lake

.... Swamp

SYMBOLS

○ **CAPITAL** .... National Capital

◉ **CAPITAL** .... Provincial Capital

● **CITY** .... City

● **Town** .... Town

● Village .... Village

■ .... Place to Stay

▼ .... Place to Eat

▮ .... Pub or Bar

✈ .... Airport

⊖ .... Bank

➚ .... Beach

♣ .... Castle

✠ ⊞ ...... Cathedral, Church

◔ .... Embassy

⊢ .... Gate

🏌 .... Golf

✛ .... Hospital

☀ .... Lookout

🏛 .... Monument

▲ .... Mountain

🏛 .... Museum

☂ .... National Park

★ .... Police Station

✉ .... Post Office

∴ .... Ruins

🗾 .... Shrine

❖ .... Shopping

○ .... Spring

🏛 .... Stately Home

☎ .... Telephone

🏯 .... Temple

❶ ..... Tourist Information

◒ .... Transport

🐘 .... Zoo

Note: not all symbols displayed above appear in this book

MASON FLORENCE

Taking a break along the banks of
the Kamo-gawa River.